eBusiness Legal Kit
For Dummies®

Putting Your Web Site in Order

What to Provide	The Specifics
Identifying information	Your company name, e-mail address, and, if you like or if the law requires for your type of site, your physical or mailing address.
Personalized information	Background about the company, such as the mission statement and background of the company's founders and executives.
Intellectual property notices	Copyright, trademark, and patent notices for all intellectual property on the site.
User Agreement (Terms of Use)	All terms and conditions that users of your Web site must agree to before using the site. Provide a link on the home page to this agreement.
Privacy Policy	The policy regarding the collection and use of information from users of the Web site stated in clear and understandable language. Provide links to this policy wherever information is collected from users on the site. If you collect information from children under the age of 13, provide a clear and conspicuous link different from other links.
Order information	If you accept orders for goods or services on your site, provide instructions on how to order, state your return or refund policy, and list all prices and charges for any taxes, shipping, and packaging.
Special offers	If you offer rebates, coupons, or affiliate programs, provide information about these offers. You may include your terms and conditions in your user agreement.
Contest information	If you're offering contests or sweepstakes, state all rules in clear and understandable language and make sure they comply with the law.
Auction information	If you run an auction site, state all rules in clear and understandable language and make sure they comply with the law.
Links	Make sure the links work and are used lawfully.
E-Mail	Make sure all links that enable users to send an e-mail to you work.
Technology	Make sure every aspect of your site works properly.
Content from others	Make sure your contracts are in place, such as licenses to use content created by others.
Your content	Protect your work legally and digitally with copyright and trademark registrations and technology such as digital watermarks or encryption.

D1709760

For Dummies™: Bestselling Book Series for Beginners

eBusiness Legal Kit
For Dummies®

Quick Reference Card

Putting Your Contract in Order

The Question	The Answer (Put It in Writing)
Who	State the parties' names, forms of business, and addresses. Also state the names and company titles for the people signing the contract.
What	Describe the services or products to be provided. Describe any property or rights being licensed (permission to use) or assigned (transfer of ownership).
When	State when the contract begins and ends and how long it lasts (the *term* of the agreement). State when the goods or services will be delivered by each party or when the rights will be transferred, such as when all parties have signed the agreement or when a party receives payment.
Where	State where delivery of any goods or property will be made. If applicable, include the territory (countries) covered by the contract.
How	Describe how products or technology will be tested, if applicable. State how delivery of goods will be made and who will pay for delivery.
How much	State what amount of money will be paid, when it will be paid, and by whom to whom. If sharing profits or paying a royalty (percentage of some price), explain how accountings will be provided and any recourse to verify those accounting records.
Restrictions	Include any restrictions or limits regarding use of confidential information, warranties, liability, termination of the agreement, indemnity, relationship between the parties, and rights under the contract that either party may assign to others.
Other information	Include any traditional miscellaneous provisions such as the written contract constituting the entire agreement, how changes to the agreement (amendments) may be made, the parties' choice of law and forum (place to sue), any agreement regarding arbitration of disputes to avoid lawsuits in court, and any right to recover attorney's fees in the event of a dispute.

For Dummies™: Bestselling Book Series for Beginners

Praise for eBusiness Legal Kit For Dummies

"If you're walking the high wire of e-business, this book is your safety net. Susan Butler achieves an inspiring balance of accessibility and authority, helping you make the right moves today while minimizing the potential for legal entanglements tomorrow. For building strategic insight, competitive advantage, and just plain peace of mind, this book is indispensable."

> — Jason Roberts, author and founding CEO of Learn2.com, Sausalito, California

"*eBusiness Legal Kit For Dummies* is a real must. If you are beginning in the fastest business world ever known, you will soon realize how your day-to-day actions must be reactive and efficient. This book gives you, in a clear and understandable language, the operational legal tools you will need to use."

> — Thierry Domas, Avocat à la Cour, Partner with Ciantar Darcet Domas & Associes (Law Firm), Paris, France

"We're small business owners. Susan's legal direction has made running our business safe, simple and affordable. They say God sends us helpers along the way. Susan is definitely one of his angels!"

> — Maxine Jones and Rose Hill, General Partners of M & R Trading Company, San Rafael, California

"I read this book with strong interest. All important issues around the e-commerce business are explained in a clear and understandable way, accompanied by various examples. Precious legal and business tips complete this work. Nobody working in the e-business should miss this book."

> — Tim Schott, partner with Detten Kugler Schott & Hermann, Rechtsanwälte & Steuerberater (attorneys at law and tax consultants), Munich, Germany

"Susan's book is a valuable tool for those who desire freedom of artistry within the framework of the machine."

> — Steve Vai, Grammy-nominated guitarist and record label owner, Favored Nations LLC, Sherman Oaks, California

"*eBusiness Legal Kit For Dummies* is a refreshing book about operating a business on the Web. The information presented is clear and concise and of tremendous benefit to a non-legal mind like mine. *eBusiness Legal Kit For Dummies* is a well-written book that is a must have for the small and medium-size business owners who dream of an e-commerce site."

> — Cecil Young, president, Scorpion Enterprises, Mississauga, Ontario, Canada

"An absolute necessity for both the seasoned veteran as well as newcomers to the industry. *eBusiness Legal Kit For Dummies* provides the reader with clear, easy-to-read, understandable, and concise information regarding all aspects of legal matters surrounding our discipline. I expect many will keep this book within reach even after its first reading."

> — David Romero, CEO, WebEasy, Inc., Santa Monica, California

"Susan Butler navigates murky legalese with incomparable flair and finesse. If you're looking for the straight scoop on legal issues, look no further — this is it."

> — Gina Smith, CEO, The New Internet Computer Company, San Francisco, California

"If you are creating or managing a web business, *eBusiness Legal Kit For Dummies* is essential reading. Susan Butler brings her legal acumen, web-savvy business insight, and fluid writing into a book that covers all the elements you need to jump-start your online business."

> — Dan Farber, VP/editor in chief, ZDNet, San Francisco, California

"If you are just beginning to open up business on the Internet or have a thriving business already, you absolutely should read this! Susan Butler has created an incredible book that can be used as a reference to doing business legally on the Internet anywhere in the world, as well as how to choose professionals to assist you if you run into problems. She draws on her vast knowledge of law and explains things in a straightforward and informative manner!"

> — David Boloker, Java chief technologist, IBM, Cambridge, Massachusetts

"Susan — even the table of contents is great reading! The chapter on trade secrets is worth twenty times the book price at least. And as the owner of a Web design and marketing firm, I can tell you that the chapter on marketing and advertising will help a LOT of people! Including me."

> — Marco Watkins, CEO, MediaGalaxy, Inc., South Lake Tahoe, California

 TM

References for the Rest of Us!™

BESTSELLING BOOK SERIES

Do you find that traditional reference books are overloaded with technical details and advice you'll never use? Do you postpone important life decisions because you just don't want to deal with them? Then our *...For Dummies*® business and general reference book series is for you.

...For Dummies business and general reference books are written for those frustrated and hard-working souls who know they aren't dumb, but find that the myriad of personal and business issues and the accompanying horror stories make them feel helpless. *...For Dummies* books use a lighthearted approach, a down-to-earth style, and even cartoons and humorous icons to dispel fears and build confidence. Lighthearted but not lightweight, these books are perfect survival guides to solve your everyday personal and business problems.

> *"More than a publishing phenomenon, 'Dummies' is a sign of the times."*
>
> — The New York Times

> *"A world of detailed and authoritative information is packed into them..."*
>
> — U.S. News and World Report

> *"...you won't go wrong buying them."*
>
> — Walter Mossberg, Wall Street Journal, on IDG Books' ...For Dummies books

Already, millions of satisfied readers agree. They have made *...For Dummies* the #1 introductory level computer book series and a best-selling business book series. They have written asking for more. So, if you're looking for the best and easiest way to learn about business and other general reference topics, look to *...For Dummies* to give you a helping hand.

® IDG BOOKS WORLDWIDE

1/99

eBusiness Legal Kit FOR DUMMIES®

by Susan P. Butler

IDG Books Worldwide, Inc.
An International Data Group Company

Foster City, CA ◆ Chicago, IL ◆ Indianapolis, IN ◆ New York, NY

eBusiness Legal Kit For Dummies®

Published by
IDG Books Worldwide, Inc.
An International Data Group Company
919 E. Hillsdale Blvd.
Suite 400
Foster City, CA 94404
www.idgbooks.com (IDG Books Worldwide Web site)
www.dummies.com (Dummies Press Web site)

Library of Congress Control Number.: 00-104215

ISBN: 0-7645-5265-1

Printed in the United States of America

10 9 8 7 6 5 4 3 2 1

1O/ST/QY/QQ/IN

Distributed in the United States by IDG Books Worldwide, Inc.

Distributed by CDG Books Canada Inc. for Canada; by Transworld Publishers Limited in the United Kingdom; by IDG Norge Books for Norway; by IDG Sweden Books for Sweden; by IDG Books Australia Publishing Corporation Pty. Ltd. for Australia and New Zealand; by TransQuest Publishers Pte Ltd. for Singapore, Malaysia, Thailand, Indonesia, and Hong Kong; by Gotop Information Inc. for Taiwan; by ICG Muse, Inc. for Japan; by Intersoft for South Africa; by Eyrolles for France; by International Thomson Publishing for Germany, Austria and Switzerland; by Distribuidora Cuspide for Argentina; by LR International for Brazil; by Galileo Libros for Chile; by Ediciones ZETA S.C.R. Ltda. for Peru; by WS Computer Publishing Corporation, Inc., for the Philippines; by Contemporanea de Ediciones for Venezuela; by Express Computer Distributors for the Caribbean and West Indies; by Micronesia Media Distributor, Inc. for Micronesia; by Chips Computadoras S.A. de C.V. for Mexico; by Editorial Norma de Panama S.A. for Panama; by American Bookshops for Finland.

For general information on IDG Books Worldwide's books in the U.S., please call our Consumer Customer Service department at 800-762-2974. For reseller information, including discounts and premium sales, please call our Reseller Customer Service department at 800-434-3422.

For information on where to purchase IDG Books Worldwide's books outside the U.S., please contact our International Sales department at 317-572-3993 or fax 317-572-4002.

For consumer information on foreign language translations, please contact our Customer Service department at 1-800-434-3422, fax 317-572-4002, or e-mail rights@idgbooks.com.

For information on licensing foreign or domestic rights, please phone +1-650-653-7098.

For sales inquiries and special prices for bulk quantities, please contact our Order Services department at 800-434-3422 or write to the address above.

For information on using IDG Books Worldwide's books in the classroom or for ordering examination copies, please contact our Educational Sales department at 800-434-2086 or fax 317-572-4005.

For press review copies, author interviews, or other publicity information, please contact our Public Relations department at 650-653-7000 or fax 650-653-7500.

For authorization to photocopy items for corporate, personal, or educational use, please contact Copyright Clearance Center, 222 Rosewood Drive, Danvers, MA 01923, or fax 978-750-4470.

About the Author

On a cold, rainy winter night in the 1970s, college student and part-time bartender Susan Butler drove her car over a water-filled pothole that was hidden by the streetlight's reflection. As a result, her car was disabled. Believing that the city should be checking for such dangerous craters, she filed a small claims lawsuit against the city of Omaha, Nebraska, for the damages to her car — the first lawsuit of its kind in that city. The litigation drew the interest of a newspaper reporter, who helped her discover evidence to support her case. She won. After a few others filed lawsuits as well, the city opened a telephone hotline for citizens to report dangerous potholes. A couple years later, Susan began studying law at Southwestern University School of Law in Los Angeles.

For nearly 20 years, Susan P. Butler has been working as a litigator and a transactional lawyer with individuals and companies to resolve their business problems and to set up their contractual relationships. Susan's work for her clients in the entertainment industry involves negotiating with people around the globe, including Japan, Taiwan, Canada, Brazil, the United Kingdom, Australia, the Netherlands, Germany, France, Italy, Spain, and the United States. The issues include publicity and privacy rights, defamation, copyrights, trademarks, and the creation, distribution, sale, and promotion of entertainment products. In 1991, she was elected to serve on the Board of Governors for the National Academy of Recording Arts and Sciences, Los Angeles Chapter (the Grammy Awards organization) and was elected by board members to serve as an officer for two terms.

In 1995, Susan moved to the San Francisco Bay area and expanded her practice into new media and the Internet. She wrote for national and international magazines such as *Computer Life Magazine* (a Ziff-Davis publication), *Screen Multimedia* (in Germany), and *Macworld*. Since 1998 she has been the monthly legal columnist for ZDNet on its Small Business Channel.

Currently, Susan divides her time between writing and representing her clients in the Internet and entertainment industries. You can visit her Web site at www.susanbutler.com.

ABOUT IDG BOOKS WORLDWIDE

Welcome to the world of IDG Books Worldwide.

IDG Books Worldwide, Inc., is a subsidiary of International Data Group, the world's largest publisher of computer-related information and the leading global provider of information services on information technology. IDG was founded more than 30 years ago by Patrick J. McGovern and now employs more than 9,000 people worldwide. IDG publishes more than 290 computer publications in over 75 countries. More than 90 million people read one or more IDG publications each month.

Launched in 1990, IDG Books Worldwide is today the #1 publisher of best-selling computer books in the United States. We are proud to have received eight awards from the Computer Press Association in recognition of editorial excellence and three from Computer Currents' First Annual Readers' Choice Awards. Our best-selling *...For Dummies®* series has more than 50 million copies in print with translations in 31 languages. IDG Books Worldwide, through a joint venture with IDG's Hi-Tech Beijing, became the first U.S. publisher to publish a computer book in the People's Republic of China. In record time, IDG Books Worldwide has become the first choice for millions of readers around the world who want to learn how to better manage their businesses.

Our mission is simple: Every one of our books is designed to bring extra value and skill-building instructions to the reader. Our books are written by experts who understand and care about our readers. The knowledge base of our editorial staff comes from years of experience in publishing, education, and journalism — experience we use to produce books to carry us into the new millennium. In short, we care about books, so we attract the best people. We devote special attention to details such as audience, interior design, use of icons, and illustrations. And because we use an efficient process of authoring, editing, and desktop publishing our books electronically, we can spend more time ensuring superior content and less time on the technicalities of making books.

You can count on our commitment to deliver high-quality books at competitive prices on topics you want to read about. At IDG Books Worldwide, we continue in the IDG tradition of delivering quality for more than 30 years. You'll find no better book on a subject than one from IDG Books Worldwide.

John J. Kilcullen
John Kilcullen
Chairman and CEO
IDG Books Worldwide, Inc.

*Eighth Annual
Computer Press
Awards ≥1992*

*Ninth Annual
Computer Press
Awards ≥1993*

*Tenth Annual
Computer Press
Awards ≥1994*

*Eleventh Annual
Computer Press
Awards ≥1995*

Dedication

This book is dedicated to every person around the world who works so hard to make his or her business succeed. I hope this information helps you make the right choices and provides you with some peace of mind. Also to my parents, Eldon and Helen, who taught me how to work hard, compete fairly, follow my instincts, and enjoy life.

Author's Acknowledgments

Very special thanks to Julian Milenbach, David Boloker, David Romero, Eldon and Helen Butler, DeAnne Ozaki, and my clients who were so patient and supportive during this writing process, especially David Rubinson, David Romero, and Steve Vai.

Very special thanks to the very special team of Andrea Burnett, Mark "No Relation" Butler, Keith Peterson, Pam Mourouzis, Tina Sims, Ben Nussbaum, Kathy Welton, John Hislop, John Malysiak, April Whitney, Robin Lockwood, and everyone at IDG Books Worldwide.

Thank you to those who encourage me to write: ZDNet editors Jim Montgomery and David Berlind, Dan Farber, Michael Penwarden, Rita Rapacon, Susan Antonelli, Linda and Mark Johnston, Karin and Phil Brown, Diane Whiteley, Kristine and Tom Lewis, Kyle and Katie Kimball, Jennifer and Robert Matthews, Brian Mills, Dolores Crites, Deborah Molinar, Ruby Yeh, Sylvia Paull and Fred Davis, Henry Schaeffer, Gina Smith, Ryuichi Sakamoto and Norika Sky-Sora, Evan Balmer, Randy Peskin, Tim Goodwin, Ritz Groszmann, and Jordan Barness.

Thanks to those who offered their support: Joanna Fessl and Amy Landers, Jeff Slott, and everyone who offered testimonials and contributions for this book.

Publisher's Acknowledgments

We're proud of this book; please register your comments through our IDG Books Worldwide Online Registration Form located at http://my2cents.dummies.com.

Some of the people who helped bring this book to market include the following:

Acquisitions, Editorial, and Media Development

Project Editor: Keith Peterson

Acquisitions Editor: Mark Butler

Copy Editor: Tina Sims

Acquisitions Coordinator: Jon Malysiak

Technical Editor: DeAnne Ozaki

Permissions Editor: Carmen Krikorian

Associate Media Development Specialist: Megan Decraene

Editorial Manager: Pamela Mourouzis

Media Development Manager: Heather Heath Dismore

Editorial Assistants: Carol Strickland, Melissa Bluhm

Production

Project Coordinator: Valery Bourke

Layout and Graphics: Brian Drumm, Barry Offringa, Tracy K. Oliver, Jill Piscitelli, Brent Savage

Proofreaders: Laura Albert, Vickie Broyles, John Greenough, Susan Moritz, Christine Pingleton, Charles Spencer

Indexer: Liz Cunningham

Special Help: Neil Johnson, Ben Nussbaum, Patricia Yuu Pan, Michael Seija, Regina Snyder

---

General and Administrative

IDG Books Worldwide, Inc.: John Kilcullen, CEO

IDG Books Technology Publishing Group: Richard Swadley, Senior Vice President and Publisher; Walter R. Bruce III, Vice President and Publisher; Joseph Wikert, Vice President and Publisher; Mary Bednarek, Vice President and Director, Product Development; Andy Cummings, Publishing Director, General User Group; Mary C. Corder, Editorial Director; Barry Pruett, Publishing Director

IDG Books Consumer Publishing Group: Roland Elgey, Senior Vice President and Publisher; Kathleen A. Welton, Vice President and Publisher; Kevin Thornton, Acquisitions Manager; Kristin A. Cocks, Editorial Director

IDG Books Internet Publishing Group: Brenda McLaughlin, Senior Vice President and Publisher; Sofia Marchant, Online Marketing Manager

IDG Books Production for Branded Press: Debbie Stailey, Director of Production; Cindy L. Phipps, Manager of Project Coordination, Production Proofreading, and Indexing; Tony Augsburger, Manager of Prepress, Reprints, and Systems; Shelley Lea, Supervisor of Graphics and Design; Debbie J. Gates, Production Systems Specialist; Steve Arany, Associate Automation Supervisor; Robert Springer, Supervisor of Proofreading; Trudy Coler, Page Layout Manager; Kathie Schutte, Senior Page Layout Supervisor; Janet Seib, Associate Page Layout Supervisor; Michael Sullivan, Production Supervisor

Packaging and Book Design: Patty Page, Manager, Promotions Marketing

◆

The publisher would like to give special thanks to Patrick J. McGovern, without whom this book would not have been possible.

◆

Contents at a Glance

Cartoons at a Glance

By Rich Tennant

page 9

page 115

page 171

page 53

page 341

page 205

Fax: 978-546-7747
E-mail: richtennant@the5thwave.com
World Wide Web: www.the5thwave.com

Table of Contents

Introduction

*T*ake a moment and bow your head. Give thanks for all those dot-com companies that failed, the ones the financial analysts and the media hyped and targeted and then bade farewell to. They were the frontline troops that moved in to conquer the new territory. Their rapid movement attracted the foot soldiers — those lawmakers, litigators, and citizens' rights organizations — that went in to secure the region. Now that the smoke is clearing, it's the perfect time for you to move in, build your communities, and reap the benefits from their hard work. It's not as complicated as the demised dot-coms would have you believe.

All any business entrepreneur needs to succeed is an idea, an opportunity, information, and hard work. The idea comes from you. Focus on your skills, talent, and interests. Create your niche. The opportunity is the Internet. It provides you with a storefront, a communication network, a distribution channel, and resources. The information begins in this book.

Whether you're thinking about starting an e-business, you just left a dot-com, or you're already running a successful e-business, this book contains something for you. The title is accurate — it's truly an e-business legal kit. It provides business information and tips, legal information from around the world, and a kit (CD) with sample contracts and explanations I prepared to help you understand e-business deals.

As an attorney for nearly two decades and an Internet legal writer and columnist since 1995, I have seen every subject in this book cross my desk at some point during my career. The information in this book comes from working with individuals and businesses to anticipate and solve their business problems, litigating matters that couldn't be resolved, negotiating and drafting contracts to create new relationships and deals, reporting on business and legal issues surrounding the Internet, and conducting extensive research to include some of the latest issues involving e-commerce. Small business entrepreneurs, executives, consultants, and freelancers are always in search of affordable information and guidance. Unfortunately, finding such information is not easy. I hope that this book provides you with information you need to run your successful e-business.

Going for the Global Market

Small business is defined in many ways. For some, small business means a company with fewer than 100 employees. For others, it means one or two people working out of a small office or a home office. Whatever the size of your business, the Internet changes this definition. *Small* no longer means *local*.

I am a lawyer, a legal columnist, and now an author. Most importantly, I am a small business. However, I am an *international* small business with clients who reside in San Francisco, Los Angeles, New York, Japan, France, and Germany. In the past I've represented clients who resided in Canada, the United Kingdom, and Australia. How can this be? Their businesses are international in nature — entertainment, new media, and technology — and they seek my advice on issues involving these industries.

My clients understand something very important: Business is an international language. For them, business comes first. The law then works within the business framework so that everyone benefits from truth and fair play. International lawmakers understand this meet-the-business-needs principle — they form international treaties to help the law work with changing business tides. These laws make it easier for companies to do business internationally.

The Web provides small businesses with the opportunity to meet potential customers and clients and form new alliances around the globe. The Internet allows small businesses to communicate with customers, clients, and businesses anywhere in the world easily and quickly. Time zones and delivery services become relatively unimportant; we can share messages and documents within seconds at any hour of the day or night. You can be a local, national, or international e-business. It's entirely your choice.

Competing Online

Once upon a time a small corner store couldn't compete with the big chain store down the block. Not so on the Internet. The small business no longer competes for customers within a small geographic area and no longer relies on its own resources to make a go of it. Small businesses can form alliances with other businesses that provide complementary goods and services anywhere in the world. You don't need to become a conglomerate; you just need to form relationships to share the work and the benefits.

The larger your alliance of e-businesses, the better chance you all have to reach a broad global market. You don't really need to be king or queen of the cyberhill to succeed, however. The Net has enough room for millions of e-businesses. All you really have to shoot for is enough customers and clients of your own to fulfill your needs and desires.

Watching Your Overhead

What can we learn from the demise of so many dot-coms? A lot. Most importantly, keep your overhead costs as low as possible so you have money when business is slow. *Overhead* is that money you must pay out every month, like rent, utilities, telephone service, employee salaries, and taxes.

Even if you raise millions of dollars to fund your e-business, you must keep your overhead down. Hiring too many employees took its toll on most of the early Internet companies. Finding the best people to work with you as you're starting out may mean hiring people who will take on a variety of tasks. If you have to hire two people because one specialist won't lend a helping hand in other areas of your business, you've hired one too many people. Start-ups (companies just starting out) need people who will pitch in whenever needed for the good of the company. You need a team, not a group of individuals, to help keep your overhead low.

Spending Money Wisely

Plan ahead and use your money wisely. Thousands of dot-com executives were driving around in sports cars and buying new houses, relying on the value of their stock in Internet companies. Some of them are in trouble now. Many companies were also giving up ownership equity in their companies all too easily. For instance, office space is in high demand in the San Francisco Bay area. Some office-building landlords are demanding an equity share (ownership interest) in the dot-coms before renting space to them — and the companies are agreeing to it! Think about your long-term needs and your alternatives before doling out your dollars or equity. And wait to buy the luxuries until you build a solid base for your e-business.

Persisting Patiently

Many of the now-defunct dot-coms also mistakenly believed that name recognition meant revenue, so they spent millions of dollars on advertising and promotion of their Web sites. They believed that spending this money would draw people to their sites, and in a relatively short time their domain names and trademarks would then be brand names. They didn't understand that name recognition and brand names are not the same thing.

People who recognize a name may visit a Web site, but they don't necessarily keep going back for more. Brand names, on the other hand, create an association within the minds of customers between certain goods or services and a level of quality and customer service. Brand names help to create customer loyalty.

Customer loyalty takes time. Many Internet company founders and executives in the late 1900s never planned on building a business and establishing long-term customer loyalty. They simply wanted to build their companies to a certain level very quickly so they could sell out and make millions. Kind of a get-rich-quick mentality. For a virtual handful of them it worked, but for most of them it wasn't that easy to do because they expected too much too soon. They spent millions to try to make it happen fast.

Those who became multi-millionaires attracted media attention. So did those who lost millions. But are these the only companies doing business on the Internet? No way! There are many companies whose businesses depend on the Internet, and they're making money. In some cases, lots of money. They simply prefer to stay out of the limelight and avoid media attention, so you don't hear about all those success stories. But they're around. They're doing business on the Internet for the long run because they understand it takes time, persistence, and patience to build a brand and customer loyalty.

How This Book Is Organized

This book does not divide legal topics into chapters, so you won't find a chapter on copyright, a chapter on trademarks, and so on. Business deals aren't so neatly categorized. I organized this book to reflect the business world and to show you how the law comes into play when you're running your e-business. I begin by taking you around the world, virtually. Part I gives you a feel for the international nature of the Internet. Part II helps you set up your place on the Net — your Web site. Part III provides guidelines and ideas for sharing your work with others. Part IV offers tips to attract potential customers, clients, and alliances to your home page. Part V explains issues involved with providing information or entertainment on your site. Part VI describes important points for you to consider when you sell goods, information, or services on your site. The Part of Tens offers tips to make sure your site is ready for showtime and your assets are covered. The appendix offers you addresses for cool Web sites so that you can make the information in this book work for you.

Part I: Around the World in 80 Nanoseconds

When you're searching for a new home or office space, you first visit the place and look around. You get a feel for the place. You won't discover some things initially, like the door that doesn't quite close or the lovely view of the sunset from the west window, until you move in and stay there for a while. Read Part I to taste the international flavor of the Internet and to learn some basics about contracts. You're not expected to grasp everything in this part all at once, so don't panic! The information will still be here to read again when questions arise while running your e-business.

Part II: Getting Ready to Launch Your Web Site

Putting your Web site together can be really fun. This part describes how to plan for your Web site and how to design and develop it (and the difference between the two terms). If you decide to hire someone to develop it, you'll read about points to make a part of your deal. It also offers guidelines for finding the right company to connect your site to the Internet. You'll discover how to register a domain name, wrestle with anyone who claims rights in your domain name, and protect your names and other marks under trademark laws around the world.

Part III: Sharing the Work

Working with others can be very rewarding for an e-business. This part describes different types of businesses on the Internet that work together and provides tips on how to form strategic alliances around the world. If you're hiring consultants, guidelines for preparing work-for-hire agreements help you sort out ownership rights to the work they create. Sharing information with others may involve trade secrets and confidential information, so you find out how to set up your contracts to protect your rights. For those employers who want to protect their computer networks and restrict employees from using company time for personal e-mail and Internet surfing, this part also provides guidelines for setting up company e-mail and Internet use policies.

Part IV: Attracting People to Your Site

We all hear about advertising, marketing, and public relations, but many people don't really understand how it all works. This part helps you discover how to target your market, the different options available to promote your e-business and your Web site, the difference between that awful spam and effective direct marketing, and how to run a sweepstakes or contest on your site.

Part V: Information and Entertainment Sites

You've probably heard news reports about entertainment companies suing Internet companies. This part helps you sort through business and legal issues if you want to offer entertainment on your site. In case you want your site to include work that other people create, you find out about their rights and how to follow a step-by-step process for obtaining permission to use their work. For those of you who provide information on your site, this part introduces you to the legal issues that surface when you communicate false information about others (libel and slander) and explains how to link your site to other sites without getting into trouble. If you're collecting information, you get the tips you need about the privacy rights of your visitors and how to write your Web site privacy policy.

Part VI: Making Money from Your Site

Making money. That's one goal of an e-business, right? This part discusses business and legal issues involved in selling goods or information throughout the world as well as offering warranties for goods. A special chapter is devoted to those professionals working in the healing arts, law, and public accounting who want to extend their services to the Net. With money comes taxes. This part includes information on the Internet tax debate. And to make sure you know about all the rules, this part offers some insight on how to work with a lawyer — and how to find the right one for you.

Part VII: The Part of Tens

Keep it simple, right? Well, to keep things simple for you, I've narrowed a couple checklists down to ten each. This part includes a list of ten things to check on your Web site when you're ready to open the gates and let the people see your show. To make sure that you make money from your site, this part also offers tips to protect your assets along your way to success.

Icons Used in This Book

To help point out some especially important information as you read this book, I use the following icons in the margins:

This icon flags important suggestions on making your e-business fly.

I use this icon to point out tips about laws in countries outside the United States.

This icon alerts you to information that may vary quite a bit from state to state.

This icon offers technical explanations for those who like to get technical.

When you see this icon, you'll know that the CD in the back of the book contains samples of these documents.

This icon flags particularly noteworthy information that you should keep in mind as you venture forward with your Internet endeavors.

This icon highlights areas that can cause you harm and possibly derail your e-business, your personal finances, or your peace of mind.

Hoisting Your Own Shingle

Many special projects have been very rewarding to me professionally, personally, and financially. Without the Internet, I would never have been a part of them because they required me to access international information. Before the Internet, only large international law firms had that access. I can now form my own alliances with other small businesses and attorneys around the world and access all sorts of information on the Web.

You can do it, too! You don't need expensive office space or financial support. You can start slow during your evenings and weekends at home and build from there. It feels so cool to be your own boss and to know that every dollar you receive is yours (or yours and your business partners'). You don't need hundreds of thousands of dollars to launch your e-business. You just need that idea, a connection to the Internet, the information, and some hard work. If you follow a few simple rules, odds are in your favor that you'll be operating legally: Be truthful, be fair, respect others' property and rights, and confirm your deals in writing. And when you're ready to launch your site, e-mail me so I can be one of the first to congratulate you!

Part I
Around the World in 80 Nanoseconds

The 5th Wave   By Rich Tennant

"Sometimes I feel behind the times. I asked my 13-year-old to build a Web site for my business, and he said he would, only after he finishes writing an IPO for his dot.com."

In this part . . .

*J*ump on board the e-train. It departs from your computer and arrives at destinations around the world. If you're new to the international business scene, ease back and enjoy the virtual ride. Chapter 1 introduces you to legal systems in countries where you'll probably do business over the Internet in the next few years.

Are you nervous that you may be sued in a court thousands of miles away? Chapter 2 provides insight on how to minimize your risk of traveling to courts in distant places. You'll also discover new types of liability insurance to cover the risk. When you're ready to make your e-business deals, Chapter 3 begins with the basics and ends with the digital signature. It's all about contracts, with information for everyone from the novice to the expert negotiator.

Chapter 1

Becoming an International e-Business

The Internet is a global playing field. You can cross national borders in a matter of seconds and welcome foreign visitors to your own home page. Because you're in the relative privacy of your office — whether it's in a high-rise or your home — you feel like you can do just about anything without a worry in the world.

Not so. Consider a young woman who merely provided a link on her Web site to another Web site. The German police arrived at her door, and a criminal prosecution soon followed! Read more about her link in Chapter 18. But don't be scared. And don't avoid operating an international e-business simply because it involves some risk. It's the Internet, after all. The virtual land of opportunity. Simply reduce your risk by getting to know the territory. Introduce yourself to some basics about international law.

Grappling with the Law

Ignorance of the law is no defense. In other words, everyone who is governed by laws after they go into effect must abide by those laws — whether or not the person knows about the laws — or suffer the consequences. The consequences could make or break your e-business. The problem is that it's not easy to know which laws affect you, which court decisions have no effect on your e-business, and which court cases could crash your site.

For instance, suppose that you live in Dallas. You have a Web site with links to other Web sites that provide news reports from around the world. You hear about a lawsuit in the New York Supreme Court filed by a dozen news publishers against someone for linking to their sites. Wow. A supreme court! Should you be looking for somewhere to hide? Not necessarily. First, anyone (individuals or companies) can *file* a lawsuit if he has reason to believe that someone violated his rights. Filing a lawsuit doesn't mean that the news publishers will win their lawsuit or that their rights really have been violated. Therefore, the mere fact that the publishers filed a lawsuit has no effect on your e-company as long as you're not doing business with any of the companies involved in the lawsuit and not linking to their sites.

Second, the *supreme court* in most states is the highest court with statewide authority, and *superior courts* are lower courts with less clout. New York, however, does some things differently. Its lower court is called the supreme court, and its highest court is called the superior court. So instead of saying "Wow" when you hear about the lawsuit, you could simply reply, "Oh, that's interesting," because a lower court decision affects only the actual parties to the lawsuit — it doesn't become legal precedent. What happens in the New York court probably won't have any effect on you in Texas. For more information, see the section "Court decisions," later in this chapter, and see Chapter 2.

Trying to figure out which laws govern your activities and which court cases affect your e-business can be complicated, but don't shy away from crossing the borders. An old lawyer passed on a tip to me that I'll pass on to you. Even if you can't know all the laws, try to learn some basic legal principles. Then simply use common sense and maintain a sense of fair play to stay within the boundaries of the law. After you get a handle on the difference between common law countries and civil law countries, you'll find it a little easier to know whether to panic or to smile when someone in uniform knocks on your door.

Exploring international law

Who decides which laws govern your international e-business activities? Ultimately, courts that have *jurisdiction* over a person (that is, the legal right or power to force the person to comply with the courts' rulings) decide which laws govern a person's business activities. A court makes this decision when there is a legal dispute that results in a lawsuit.

One basic legal principle is that laws in one country have no effect on your e-business located in another country *unless* you are doing business or have some other type of contact in that country. In that case, the laws of that country may then apply to you. For more information on doing business or having contacts in another country or state, see Chapter 2.

If you want to do business internationally and are trying to figure out which laws to learn about, you'll be pleased to know that laws in many countries around the world won't be completely foreign to you and your lawyer.

Thanks to a number of international treaties and similar business practices within the same industries, the laws are much more similar to each other than some of the languages! After you understand some legal basics, you can structure your business practices to comply with them.

Learning about international treaties

International treaties are agreements made between governments of various countries. The governments that adopt treaties enforce these laws within their countries. If a treaty is *self-executing,* it automatically becomes law in every country that signed it. If a treaty is not self-executing, each country's government must write and adopt legislation that complies with the treaty before it has any legal effect in that country.

Treaties help people who do business internationally. They attempt to protect rights and to ensure fair compensation to the people in a consistent or equal way. Some treaties that affect e-business involve intellectual property (copyrights, trademarks, and patents).

Understanding who makes laws

Most democratic countries are governed under a separation of powers. They have legislative, judicial, and executive branches of government. The legislative branch makes laws, changes laws, and repeals laws. After the Powers That Be in any country okay the legislature's bills, they become laws. These laws, which are usually called *statutes* or *codes*, regulate areas such as criminal activity (criminal law), government activity (public law), and personal and business dealings between private citizens (called private law in some countries and civil law in others). Commercial law is the name given to much of the private or civil law that applies to businesses.

The judiciary branch (courts and lawyers) involves itself with liabilities (deciding legal responsibility) under these laws. Judges are in charge of courts, so "court" refers to the judge or judges in any particular court. In order to resolve a legal dispute, a court interprets the laws and decides how they should govern the facts in each case filed with the court.

If you're wondering how a jury fits into this process, a jury decides what it believes to be the true facts in a case. After a conference between the judge and the lawyers, the judge tells ("instructs") the jury what law it must follow in the case. The jury considers the facts and the law and tries to decide whether a party is legally responsible ("liable" in a civil case or "guilty" in a criminal case) for what the party did or failed to do. In some cases, the judge in charge of the trial may change a jury's verdict, or judges in a higher court (an *appellate court*) may change the lower court's decision.

The executive branch is the police power, which makes sure that people comply with the law. It also helps enforce the courts' judgments. Most nations are either common law countries or civil law countries. This distinction describes how they make and enforce their laws.

Common Law Countries

In common law countries, pay special attention to certain court decisions that you hear about. When it sounds like the result of a case may affect your e-business, find out which court made the ruling. Then you can revisit this chapter to refresh your memory on how it may affect you. The legislative branch *and* the judicial branch make laws in common law countries. These countries include the United States (except Louisiana whose laws are based on French civil law), the United Kingdom, Canada (except Quebec whose laws are based on French civil law), Australia, Israel, and Singapore.

Court decisions

Common law, which began in England, is judge-made law. As more and more cases involving the same legal issues came before the courts over the centuries, the judges began following the decisions made in prior cases. Thus began the principle of "legal precedent" known as *stare decisis* ("let the decision stand"). In general, legal precedent means that a court decides how a principle of law applies to a certain set of facts, and then other courts must decide future cases the same way if the facts are substantially the same. By requiring courts to do this, the governments hope to bring predictability and stability to the law.

However, the only courts that must follow the prior decisions are courts of either the same level of authority or lesser authority within the same jurisdiction, such as the same state or the same federal circuit. If a court doesn't have jurisdiction over you because you don't live in, or perform certain types of activities within, that court's legal territory, then the court's decisions can have no legal effect on you. For more information on jurisdiction, see Chapter 2.

In the United States, there are state courts and federal courts. Rules determine which kinds of cases are filed in either state or federal court. Court decisions in the lower courts, where cases begin and trials are held, usually affect only the parties to the particular lawsuit. In the state judiciary, they include municipal and superior courts (in New York, the supreme court). In the federal judiciary, the lower courts are federal district courts. Usually only one judge presides over cases in a lower court.

When a party challenges a judgment in a lower court, the person files documents with a higher court (an appellate court) to review the decision, which is often reviewed by more than one judge. The person is "appealing" (saying please, please, please) to the other judges to reconsider what happened down below in the lower court. In some places, there is only one appellate level above the lower court. The losing party can't climb any higher on the court ladder to try to get a decision changed. In other places, there are two or more appellate levels between the lowest court and the highest court. In between the lowest and the highest are intermediate appellate courts or Courts of Appeal. If the losing party isn't satisfied at one level, she may often appeal to the next level until she reaches the highest court.

These appellate court decisions could become legal precedent if a majority of the judges agree on the point of law and the court publishes its written opinion in official legal books. Therefore, pay special attention to these published decisions by the courts of appeal and by the highest court in the state, territory, province, and country where you do business.

TIP

Circuitous circuitry

The U.S. (federal) "intermediate" appellate courts are called *circuit courts of appeal*. These circuits are geographical regions that include more than one state. Pay attention to these court decisions in any circuit that includes any state that may have jurisdiction over your activities. For instance, you may hear a report about a decision by the Second Circuit Court of Appeal. The decision may affect activities in the second circuit, that is, in Connecticut, New York, and Vermont. Courts of appeal in other circuits may follow the same legal reasoning in their circuit or they may refuse to follow that reasoning. Here are the circuit numbers and the states they cover:

✔ **D.C. Circuit:** District of Columbia

✔ **First Circuit:** Maine, Massachusetts, New Hampshire, Puerto Rico, Rhode Island

✔ **Second Circuit:** Connecticut, New York, Vermont

✔ **Third Circuit:** Delaware, New Jersey, Pennsylvania, Virgin Islands

✔ **Fourth Circuit:** Maryland, North Carolina, South Carolina, Virginia, West Virginia

✔ **Fifth Circuit:** District of the Canal Zone, Louisiana, Mississippi, Texas

✔ **Sixth Circuit:** Kentucky, Michigan, Ohio, Tennessee

✔ **Seventh Circuit:** Illinois, Indiana, Wisconsin

✔ **Eighth Circuit:** Arkansas, Iowa, Minnesota, Missouri, Nebraska, North Dakota, South Dakota

✔ **Ninth Circuit:** Alaska, Arizona, California, Idaho, Montana, Nevada, Oregon, Washington, Guam, Hawaii

✔ **Tenth Circuit:** Colorado, Kansas, New Mexico, Oklahoma, Utah, Wyoming

✔ **Eleventh Circuit:** Alabama, Florida, Georgia

Although courts should always follow legal precedent, exceptions do exist — this principle is not written in stone. Another court may decide that the precedent is an unreasonable principle of law or that changing conditions require the law to change. The court may refuse to follow the precedent. That's one reason litigation lawyers always try to find a new argument for each case even if legal precedent should govern a particular case.

Courts in one state don't have to follow decisions in other states. However, they often consider the opinions as guides to help them decide how they should rule in a similar case.

Louisiana and Quebec, although in common law countries, both follow civil law, which is described later in this chapter. These places must still follow the federal law in their countries. The law in common law countries doesn't come only from court decisions, however. Legislatures keep making laws (statutes and codes) that also govern your e-business.

Federal statutes

When your business involves activity across the borders of states, federal statutes often apply. Constitutional and federal laws are the *supreme law of the land*. Usually state courts must enforce federal laws. If a state law conflicts with a federal law, the state law must yield.

The final word

Perk up if you hear about a decision from one of these high courts in the land of your e-business. E-mail your lawyer to get a legal opinion if you think that one of their decisions involves the type of activities you're conducting in their country.

✔ **United States:** The U.S. Supreme Court, federal circuit courts of appeal, state courts of appeal, and state supreme courts (in New York, the superior court)

✔ **United Kingdom:** The House of Lords and the Court of Appeal

✔ **Canada:** The Supreme Court of Canada and other courts of appeal

✔ **Australia:** The High Court of Australia and state full supreme courts (or other courts of appeal)

✔ **Israel:** The Supreme Court

✔ **Singapore:** The Court of Appeal

Who's watching the kids?

Imagine the following scenario.

A Web site owner in California collects names, birth dates, and e-mail addresses from kids, monitors how long kids spend on different parts of its site, and then shares all that information with marketing companies. Suppose that a U.S. federal law requires Web site owners who collect *personal information* from kids to get permission from their parents before selling that information to marketing companies.

The people who run the Web site really can't afford to hire someone to e-mail all the parents, so they just post a notice on the site stating, "Kids, get permission from your parents before giving us this information." The site owners don't "sell" the information, but they "share" it with other companies. One kid doesn't get his parents' permission, so he starts getting tons of junk e-mail — some of it not so nice. His parents find out, and they figure the Web site in question was responsible for obtaining and sharing the kid's personal information. The parents and kid sue the Web site owner. The case goes to trial in a federal district court in California, and the Web site owner is held liable for violating the federal statute. The court decides that the law that prohibits "selling" information also prohibits "sharing" information. The court also decides that merely posting a notice to kids isn't sufficient to comply with the law. Because the owner didn't get parental consent to share the personal information, the company has to pay the parents and kid $500,000.

News of this case hits the Internet. You read about it and wonder, "Does this mean I'm in trouble, too, since I only e-mail notices to parents before sharing information about their kids who use my site?" Not yet. It's a *district court* (lower court) decision.

The lawyers for the Web site owner disagree with the decision, so they file an appeal. Nine months later, the federal Ninth Circuit Court of Appeal decides the case, writes an opinion agreed upon by all the judges involved, and publishes it in the official legal books. The court writes that its interpretation of the federal statute requires Web site owners to actually get permission from parents before they can sell *or share* personal information. This opinion becomes legal precedent in the Ninth Circuit Court.

If you're in Florida, does this ruling mean that you must also get parents' permission to share information and not just send an e-mail to them? Technically, no. Because you're in Florida, that particular federal court (the Ninth Circuit) doesn't govern your actions in the Eleventh Circuit.

However, other federal courts (including the one in your circuit) could decide to follow the decision so the laws across the country are consistent. Then you could be in trouble. By keeping an eye on what's happening in other circuits, you can detect trends in law. Just remember that your circuit court could decide not to follow the trend.

Agency regulations

Federal and state administrative agencies around the world often make regulations governing specific areas of our lives and businesses. For example, the U.S. Federal Trade Commission is an agency that is very involved with e-businesses. It can make regulations governing certain aspects of your e-business, including advertising, warranties, certain privacy notices, and sales practices. Agencies can enforce the regulations because statutes say they can.

State statutes

The laws of one state have no effect in another state. In fact, there is no requirement that any state legislature must harmonize its laws with those of another state. In some areas of law such as commercial sales transactions, state legislatures have adopted "uniform" laws for consistency throughout the country. Some of these uniform laws are described throughout other chapters. If you're doing business in another state, you may have to comply with its laws as well as your state's laws.

Putting it all together

All this legal stuff means that you must be especially alert in two areas if you're doing business in a common law country. First, before you start doing business, check to make sure that you're complying with any state statutes, federal statutes, common law, and administrative agency regulations that might regulate your e-business. To be safe, set up a consultation with an experienced e-business or Internet lawyer. Second, always keep your ears and eyes open for reports on court decisions that may affect your e-business. If any court opinion sounds like it could hurt you, get your lawyer's opinion. The appendix and CD include URLs for Web sites that provide news on some of the latest court decisions affecting e-commerce. Taking care of certain details could prevent downtime and major expense for your e-business down the road.

Civil Law Countries

In countries governed by civil law, court decisions generally affect only the parties to the lawsuit. Focus your attention on the statutes/codes and regulations. The laws of these countries are made by the legislative branch.

Civil law generally comes from Roman law, which is based on the principle that all rights belong to the sovereign (the government) rather than the people. The sovereign grants rights to the people. The law in civil law countries is based primarily on their statutes. Civil law countries include Brazil, Japan, Taiwan, and most of the European continent, including France, Germany, Spain, Italy, and so on. From Roman law came French/Roman law and Germanic/Roman law. There are, therefore, differences in the laws of countries that follow French Civil Law (such as France, Italy, and Spain) and of countries that follow Germanic Civil Law (such as Germany, Denmark, and Japan). Japanese law is also influenced by English/American legal principles. For more information on European countries, see the section on "The European Union," later in this chapter.

Like the common law countries, the courts in civil law countries apply the law to the facts in the cases they consider. They may also consider local customs to reach a fair outcome, especially in disputes involving business transactions. For instance, following customs in Germany may be more important than following written law in some cases. In France, however, acknowledging customs may be important, but customs will not usually be more important than the written law. Unlike common law countries, the courts don't need to follow decisions made in prior cases.

The European Union

The European Union is an example of a body formed by treaties. It's called the EU for short. Fifteen European countries (called member states) agree to be part of the EU, which makes and enforces laws in certain areas for all member states to follow. They are Austria, Belgium, Denmark, Finland, France, Germany, Greece, Ireland, Italy, Luxembourg, The Netherlands, Portugal, Spain, Sweden, and the United Kingdom.

The EU's purpose is, among other things, to promote the European economy and fair competition. The European Council, the European Commission, and the Parliament are the main EU institutions in the EU's legislative process. The Court of Justice ensures that the institutions observe the law. Regulations that the council or the commission issues are binding on member states and private parties within the member states without any further need for any country to enact additional laws regarding the regulations. Directives that the council, the commission, or the parliament issues must be adopted or implemented into law in the member states. Often the countries must adopt the law within a certain number of years. Reportedly, the EU will be issuing directives to encourage e-commerce across the European countries' borders.

If you do business in these countries, don't forget to take a look at the EU laws. Doing so is especially important if you're dealing in intellectual property (copyrights, trademarks, and patents).

Enforcing International Business Deals

Many contracts between people in different countries are not protected by treaties. However, courts around the world often enforce these contracts because of something called the comity of nations. It's a theory that many nations follow. Think of it as tit-for-tat or "what goes around comes around," depending upon your particular slant on things.

Comity of nations means that courts in one country may be nice and enforce laws of another country if the laws are in sync with what they see as their international duty. Enforcing these laws must also be in concert with the rights of their own citizens and others protected by their laws. So when contracts are made, certain rights are acquired, or obligations are incurred under the laws of one country, other countries may also enforce these laws within their countries. This helps businesses enforce their deals around the globe.

To become an effective, international e-business, make "legal" just as important as "business." When you put your business plan together, include a section for legal fees. Budget time and money to make sure that your deals and your Web site comply with international laws. Chapter 23 provides tips on working with lawyers. After you launch your site, keep your eyes and ears open to new business *and* legal developments. But don't panic every time you hear about a lawsuit or a big judgment. Just be proactive by reading the news and keeping in touch with your lawyer from time to time. With a little foresight, you'll have smooth sailing around the globe.

Chapter 2

You're Being Sued Where?

*F*or some people, traveling to a foreign country is scary — they're afraid of the unknown, they may not know the language, and they're worried about getting lost. Movies about people being tortured in foreign prisons certainly don't help diminish this anxiety.

However, after people learn some words of the language and a bit about their destination, they figure out how to get from the airport to the hotel. By reading a map of the area, they discover how to reach the tourist attractions and shops. Before they know it, they're buying tons of stuff and then telling everyone they know about all their worldly experiences!

Similarly, you need to become familiar with certain documents and topics, including jurisdiction, in order to get ready for your e-business venture across the borders. This knowledge won't eliminate all your business risk, but you'll at least be able to calculate the risk.

Understanding Jurisdiction

Jurisdiction means that a branch of a government has the ability to force you to comply with its laws. These laws are important because they ultimately affect how profitable your e-business becomes. You'll go out of business if judgments and fines are levied against you. You may even lose your personal assets.

As an e-business entrepreneur, you need to know the following:

✔ Which courts could haul you into their courtrooms and force you to defend yourself in a lawsuit

✔ Whose laws you should follow

The answers to these questions are being hotly debated by practicing lawyers, law professors, legal writers, and judges around the world. Court decisions have been inconsistent, and most experts wonder whether there will be any clear answers for many years to come. The lack of definite answers from lawyers, judges, and the legal systems frustrates so many businesspeople. "Just tell me what I should do!" they all too often say.

Unfortunately, lawyers don't like to be wrong or to be held accountable for wrong answers. So the advice ends up sounding like, "Well, either this could occur or that might happen, depending upon what you do. Be aware it could go either way. It's your decision to make." Often lawyers don't want to take the next step to say, "Even so, I think you should do this."

Well, I take that next step to discuss answers to these questions. I can't promise that judges will agree with me, but I can tell you what I would do based on my education and experience. First I explain some of the potential pitfalls so that you're aware of what could happen. Then I show you how I would protect myself.

Being courted

To answer the question of whose laws to follow, first figure out which courts could force you into their courtrooms. After all, courts ultimately decide legal responsibility. The courts will ask, "Do the laws of our state (or country) allow us to order you to appear in our courts? Can we insist that you abide by the laws of our state (or country)?" If the answers are "yes," then you should check out their laws and comply with them so that you won't be hauled into court.

Personal jurisdiction is the phrase that describes a court's power to order you to appear in its courtroom and comply with laws. When determining whether they have personal jurisdiction over someone in particular, U.S. courts first look at their state's statutes that describe the situations when they may exercise this power. In addition, they often consider whether someone has "sufficient minimum contacts" with that state or has "purposefully availed" himself of the laws of that state.

There is _contact_ with people in a state when someone is physically present there or when something occurs in the state. However, this contact may not be a sufficient minimum contact if your presence is very brief or your activity is indirect or extremely minimal; a court may not have power over you. On the other hand, you could still be _purposefully availing_ yourself of their laws when your activities imply that you expect the laws of that state to protect your rights just as they protect others' rights in that state.

For instance, an easy jurisdiction situation occurs when a California business breaches a contract with another California business regarding work to be performed in California. Everyone and everything are in California, and the companies would expect California law to protect their businesses. Therefore, the breach of contract lawsuit is filed in California, and California laws apply.

The real business world is rarely this simple, especially the e-business world. A company doing business over the Internet often enters into contracts with people in other states or countries without a face-to-face meeting. They make deals while people are sitting in different states, the parties to the contract perform work in a number of places around the globe, and one party may even breach the contract by its activities over the Internet. Where are the people, where are the activities taking place, and where is the harm from the breach of contract occurring? Maybe in ten states and three countries! Luckily, most countries don't allow more than one litigation about the same event or transaction to occur in more than one place within their countries, so one court decides legal responsibility. Which one could it be?

The first person to file a lawsuit (the *plaintiff*) chooses the court. However, the company being sued (the *defendant*) may object to that court's jurisdiction and try to get the lawsuit dismissed entirely or transferred to a court somewhere else. When the defendant objects to personal jurisdiction, the court will consider whether it has the power to decide the legal responsibility of the defendant. If it doesn't have jurisdiction, the court can't allow the lawsuit to proceed against that defendant in that court.

Don't ever, ever, ever ignore a summons and complaint you receive, no matter where in the world the lawsuit is filed. If you don't respond or object properly and promptly, you could end up with a judgment against you that could be even more expensive to get rid of — *if* you can get rid of it. *Always* contact a lawyer immediately. In some places, judgments can be collected from your earnings for the next 20 years!

Interacting on the Internet

Many articles are available on Web sites about personal jurisdiction and how courts might decide this question for Internet activities. Most of the lawyers writing the articles only describe the activities that might be sufficient minimum contacts or purposeful availment. For example, the lawyers try to help people figure out personal jurisdiction by focusing on whether the Web site owner or operator does the following:

- Advertises and sells goods or services on the Web site to people in other states or countries

- Interacts with users in other states or countries through the Web site

- Conducts continuous transactions, such as processing payments made by credit card, with people in other states or countries on the Web site

- Merely advertises on the Web site without selling to, interacting with, or processing transactions made by people who visit the site from other states or countries

Although the Internet activities are important, I disagree with the lawyers who consider only the Web site activities when advising their clients about which courts might exercise jurisdiction over them or which laws they should follow. I believe there's something more important to consider first: people and social priorities.

Focusing on social priorities

Laws of states and countries are supposed to protect the citizens of that place. New York laws protect New Yorkers, German laws protect Germans, and Canadian laws protect Canadians. Lawmakers also have certain priorities.

The highest priority of a democratic government is the health and safety of its citizens. For example, suppose that a business executive calls the police station reporting that an employee is, at that very moment, downloading customer lists (trade secrets) onto a disk and is about to steal them. On the other line at the police station, a caller is reporting that someone is being violently beaten in a parking lot. Which report do you think the police are going to respond to first? The beating, of course. Physical safety is more important than commercial secrets. In general, here's the list of priorities from highest to, well, least high (I don't want to imply that anything is unimportant):

✔ Physical well-being is a top priority.

✔ Personal rights usually come next.

✔ When it comes to business deals, including purchases and sales, consumers have the upper hand. Consumers rarely have bargaining power equal to a business, so lawmakers provide them with greater protection.

✔ Finally, companies are normally given equal protection in their business deals. Companies that want to do business together tend to have equal bargaining power. Courts often make them keep the agreements they make with each other — for better or for worse.

With this information in mind, it's understandable that lawmakers and courts might want to make it easier for

✔ Physically injured people to sue close to home.

✔ People whose personal rights were violated (involving such things as privacy, publicity, and defamation) to sue where they were harmed.

✔ Consumers to sue close to home.

✔ Businesses to sue where much of the performance under a contract was performed.

✔ Companies to agree among themselves in their contracts where to sue.

✔ Everyone else to sue where the person being sued (the defendant) resides (defendants do have some choices!).

Hundreds of court decisions over the years involving off-line events and business transactions around the world focus primarily on these priorities. The defendant's activities are often secondary in importance when deciding whether a court has jurisdiction over a particular defendant. Therefore, focus on social priorities and then your e-business activities to figure out where in the world you could be sued and whose laws you should follow.

Knowing where your assets are exposed

To figure out where you could be sued and whose laws you should follow, start compiling a list. Make two columns. Complete the left column as you read the section, "The leftists: Where you could be sued." Complete the right column as you read the section, "The rightists: Whose laws to follow." If your list starts getting long, don't worry. I offer some solutions later on in "Obtaining Liability Insurance: Don't Leave Your Home Page without It."

The leftists: where you could be sued

Use this list to help fill in the left column of your list:

✔ **Advertising on your Web site:** If you simply advertise on your Web site and someone sees it in a state or country where you conduct no other type of business and have no other physical contacts with that place (in

Litigious episodes

Everyone hopes that nothing will ever go wrong with her e-business, but stuff happens. When it does, an e-business could have to hire lawyers in different parts of the world. Here's how it could happen.

Suppose that a man in Germany buys an attic fan sold through a Web site. A Maryland company manufactured the fan. The man files a lawsuit in Munich, claiming that the fan should have a safety cover over the blades. Because it didn't, the fan cut off his finger when he was installing the fan. Another lawsuit is brought in California against the same Maryland manufacturer. This plaintiff is a company that claims the Maryland company breached its contract to pay for banner ads on a Web site hosted in California.

The Maryland company may have to defend itself in Germany since the man injured himself in Germany. He's a consumer who purchased a product and was physically injured by it. Laws often prefer to allow consumers to sue for physical injuries in the home region. On the other hand, the Maryland company may not have to defend itself in California. If the California Web site owner solicited the Maryland company's business in Maryland (the owner first approached the Maryland company) and the sales contract was completed in Maryland, the California company may be in the "everyone else" category described in the section "Focusing on social priorities" in this chapter.

other words, you don't rent a physical site there), you probably won't be subject to the jurisdiction in that state or country. There's no risk of physical injury or harm to consumers. It would be unreasonable to sue you there. So who might try to sue you in a state where you advertise? Someone may make a claim that you're infringing on intellectual property rights, like a trademark. Although these personal rights are important, most courts wouldn't let someone sue you in a state simply because someone can access your site and see advertisements. However, in at least one court case in the mid-1990s, an out-of-state Web site owner was pulled into court for allegedly infringing on an in-state company's trademark. You'll always find one of those apples in the bunch. You can probably leave your left column blank for this question if you only advertise on your site.

✔ **Advertising on your Web site *and* in other media:** After you take a more active role in advertising by placing ads in newspapers, on radio and television, or on taxi cabs and buses, you're *availing* yourself. You'll probably be subject to personal jurisdiction in those states and countries. List in your left column the countries and states where you're purchasing these ads. Generally courts shouldn't pull you into court in every state where your ads in national publications are distributed.

✔ **Collecting information from subscribers:** If your Web site has subscribers to your service, start listing the countries and states that they list as their addresses. The more you have from any country or state, the more likely you are to be subject to their jurisdiction, especially if your customers are consumers. List the locations of your subscribers.

✔ **Collecting information without subscription:** Merely collecting general information from anonymous users may not subject you to jurisdiction in their countries or states, especially if they don't list where they're connecting to the Internet. However, privacy is one of those high-priority rights. If you're collecting or selling users' personal information, you may be dragged into a court in their state or country. In your left column, list the addresses you're given.

✔ **Doing business with someone else in a state:** If you're doing business with companies in a state, others can usually sue you there, too. List 'em.

✔ **Promoting services:** Merely providing a description of services is informative. Most courts wouldn't consider this to be doing business, or soliciting business, in other countries or states. If you accept business from people in another state or country through your Web site and conduct business by e-mail, you may be subject to jurisdiction in their state or country. To be safe, list those places.

✔ **Selling goods:** If you deliver goods to consumers in a particular state or country, you will probably be subject to jurisdiction there unless you only have one sale or very few sales. Add those places to your list. If you're selling to other businesses, you may not be subject to jurisdiction in their states — only in your state — if you include that provision in your sales contract (see Chapter 3 and the CD for a "choice of law" provision for a contract). If you make sales by digital transmission or computer downloads, the jurisdiction rules are unclear. Add to your list the states where these types of purchases are made, just in case.

The rightists: Whose laws to follow

Courts don't apply the laws in their states or countries to every case. Sometimes a court must apply laws from other jurisdictions; it depends on certain choice-of-law or conflict-of-law rules (very complex laws that guide courts in deciding whose laws apply to certain types of cases). For instance, a California court could be the place where a contract dispute ends up, even though the contract provides that Canadian law applies to any contract dispute. The California court could decide to apply Canadian law to the lawsuit in California. Therefore, you should consider the laws that might apply to your activities, not only the laws of the places where you could be sued.

So move to the right column of the list to include the names of the states and countries whose laws might apply to your e-business. The questions now focus on *why* people might sue you rather than *what* you're doing and *who* you're doing it with. Think about all aspects of your e-business to answer the following questions.

- ✔ **Could the products you sell physically injure someone?** Health and safety are very important, so the law where the injured party lives may apply because the injured party's state wants to protect its residents. Other possible laws that may apply are those of the state or country where the product is purchased or acquired or the law of the place where the product manufacturer's principal place of business is located. If this category applies to you, list these countries and states in your right column. See the sidebar "Litigious episodes" for an example.

- ✔ **Could you harm personal rights by invading someone's privacy, violating someone's right to publicity, making fraudulent representations to people who do business with you (in business deals or by advertising), or defaming someone (libel or slander)?** Personal rights are important enough that states and countries want to protect them. Chapters 11, 14, 15, and 16 explain these rights. Some courts apply the law where the harm occurred, and they consider that to be where the plaintiff (the injured party) lives. If you cause harm by something you write, however, other courts may apply the law of the place where it's written. List all these places.

- ✔ **Could you be using someone else's intellectual property, such as copyrights, trademarks, or patents, without the necessary permission?** Chapters 7 (trademarks), 9 (trade secrets), 16 (copyrights, trademarks, and patents), and 17 (entertainment) cover intellectual property. Most countries apply the law of the place where the infringement occurs. For copyrights, that place could be the location where someone's intellectual property is copied, reproduced, performed to the public, displayed to the public, or distributed. On the Internet, it's difficult to always specify the location of these types of violations because they could be displayed on a Web site anywhere. For now, add those countries where you're allowing people to download things from your Web site, the state or country where you're located, the state or country where your files are uploaded, and the state or country where your Internet Service Provider is located.

✔ **Could you breach a contract with a consumer?** Laws protect consumers. Countries and states don't like it when other places don't protect them as well. Therefore, the law where the consumer lives applies. However, if a company does nothing to attract consumers in a particular location and the consumer takes an active role in searching out and finding the company, some courts follow the law where the company is located. Contracts with consumers that contain a clause stating that the law of a certain state governs the deal may be followed if that state's laws don't restrict the rights the consumers have in their own states or countries. In the European Union, this is an absolute requirement. A consumer cannot be given fewer rights in one country than in her EU home.

✔ **Could you breach a contract with another business?** You may find yourself using three types of contracts in your e-business: contracts for the sale of goods, contracts regarding rights (personal or intellectual property), and contracts for information. Chapters 3 and 19 include information on contracts. Normally the law of the place chosen by the parties, as stated in their written contract, applies. If their choice is not in the contract, usually the law of the seller's place of business (or the company that owns the rights or information — the licensor) applies. Occasionally, the law of the buyer's place governs the deal if the seller visits the buyer in person to try selling the goods to him. This makes sense because the seller sought out the buyer in his home territory. Sometimes the place where most of the activities involved with the contract occur is the place where the law applies. Add all these places to your right column.

Now your list has all the states and countries whose laws may apply to you and where you could be sued. Make the places in your right column — the laws that may apply to you — your priority. Check out their laws and make every effort to comply with them. Do the same with the places in the left column. You should then be in really good shape to operate your e-business across borders.

You don't have to hire a lawyer in every single state and country. Choose your main lawyer and make sure that she looks up those laws, checks them out, and then verifies them with other lawyers in those jurisdictions who practice the same type of law. This approach should keep your legal bills manageable.

Obtaining Liability Insurance: Don't Leave Your Home Page without It

Keeping up with all the laws as they change is difficult for anyone, especially when it involves the Internet and e-businesses. Even the best lawyers can make mistakes or overlook something.

You won't find hundreds of insurance companies offering liability insurance for doing business over the Internet yet because the risks are relatively unknown. But several insurance companies around the world do offer this insurance, and some are large and very reputable insurers.

Finding out about liability insurance

Insurance companies offer contracts, called *insurance policies,* to people whom they will insure (the insureds) for certain types of losses under certain circumstances. In this contract (policy), the company promises to assume a specific and defined amount of risk for an insured in exchange for payment of a premium. The company determines the premium amount based on the insured's risk of loss that the company figures out from data that analyzes loss histories for millions of policyholders over many years. In this way, the company can estimate the number of claims that will be made and the cost to the company during the term of the policy. Because the Internet and e-businesses haven't been around very long, you can see why insurance companies don't have much data on which to base their pricing.

Various kinds of liability policies are available for different kinds of situations, such as damage to property, breach of contract, employer/employee litigation, and so on. With liability insurance, insurance companies may agree to pay for any judgment against you, to pay attorney's fees to defend you in a lawsuit, or both.

Look for a liability policy that states the insurance company will *defend* and *indemnify* you. This means the insurance company hires lawyers at its expense and pays related court costs like filing fees and jury fees (to defend you) and pays any settlement or judgment (indemnifies you). The only things you might pay for are the premiums, your deductible amount, and any judgment that exceeds your policy limit. The policy doesn't normally pay for your expenses to travel to court or for the loss of time from work for you or your witnesses. Also, you won't usually have any right to select the lawyers or to reject a settlement. The insurance company decides these matters.

The cool thing is that a U.S. policy should cover you *in every state!* If you're in California and you're sued in a Virginia court, your insurance company hires Virginia lawyers for you. Some insurance companies are reportedly issuing

Internet liability policies that will cover you for losses up to $1 million for as low as $1,600 per year!

Getting the insurance policy

Locating an insurance broker who sells policies from a variety of companies is your best bet. Some brokers sell only certain kinds of policies, however. Therefore, they may not be able to offer you exactly what you really need. Also, some brokers may not understand the difference between e-commerce and Internet publishing. So it's important to ask the following questions to find a reputable broker:

- ✔ Is the broker large enough to offer all kinds of policies?
- ✔ Does the broker have experience working with Internet companies in your state, or at least have a lot of business experience?
- ✔ Will the broker spend the time with you to go over policies to make sure that you get the ones you need?
- ✔ Can the broker get you foreign insurance if you're going to do business overseas?

 You can usually locate some of these brokers in your state by searching for insurance broker directories on the Internet or by using keywords. Phrases like "media liability," "e-business insurance," "e-commerce insurance," and "Internet insurance" should bring up some information in a search.

Knowing what to look for

Insurance companies pay only for certain types of losses that are stated in the written policy. There are always exclusions and conditions. An important part of every policy is the kind of loss it covers.

Some policies are called *All Risk* or *Special Form* policies. If you have one of these policies, the insurance company pays for losses from all perils *except* those perils that are specifically listed under the exclusions section. Be sure to read all the definitions, including the definition of "perils." The policy describes exactly what types of events will trigger a possible obligation to pay.

Insurance companies also offer *Named Perils* policies, meaning that the insurance company pays only for losses caused by perils that are specifically listed in the policy. If the policy doesn't specifically mention a type of loss that you incur, the company usually won't defend you in that kind of lawsuit, either.

Spend time with your insurance broker and explain exactly what types of risks you're concerned about. Discuss your risk of being sued for any of the following reasons:

- ✔ The content of advertisements that appear on your Web site (false advertising by others) and your own advertising that might be false

- ✔ Collecting information from people, or selling that information, in violation of privacy and other laws and regulations

- ✔ Breach of contract with your Web site subscribers

- ✔ Breach of contract with your independent contractors and with other companies

- ✔ Breach of contract with purchasers of your goods or services

- ✔ Violating a confidentiality agreement

- ✔ Product liability for the goods you manufacture or sell

- ✔ Violating someone's rights through what's written, published, or said (by you or by someone else) on your Web site

- ✔ Violating someone's intellectual property rights (copyright, trademark, or patent)

A Comprehensive General Liability policy usually doesn't cover intellectual property claims. Sometimes insureds try to have the *advertising liability* clause cover claims for trademark infringement. This approach rarely works, but many brokers don't realize it. If your broker says that this kind of policy covers all trademark claims under the advertising liability clause, find another broker.

A new form of media liability insurance for Internet liabilities might cover claims like invasion of privacy, defamation (libel and slander), and infringement of intellectual property rights. Product liability insurance covers injuries caused by products. Employment Practices Liability policies help you if your employees sue you. Web site developers can get a type of property insurance (not liability insurance) that covers Electronic Media and Records. If you create intellectual property (such as copyright and patents), maintain it for your customers on your computers and then lose it in some way that's defined in the policy (one of their perils), the policy covers your expense to re-create or restore the records or intellectual property for your customer! That type of policy could certainly help you avoid liability to your client.

I bet you're now asking, "If I can get insurance, why should I take the time to make sure that I comply with all the laws?" Good question. And I have an even better answer. If for some reason your insurance doesn't cover some claim, you could spend a hundred times more money defending yourself than you would spend to check out the laws up front. Also, no insurance company wants to insure you if you get sued a lot. Then you'll really be out in the cold. Liability insurance is a safety net, but it doesn't totally ensure a safe landing. Be diligent and be prepared.

Chapter 3

Contracts in a Digital World

Do you keep all your promises? Honestly? Everyone breaks a promise now and then. Most of the time a broken promise only becomes a hassle or hurts someone's feelings. Other times it causes harm to a company's financial position or business reputation. When this happens, the law often steps in to resolve the problem.

Contracts are promises. A contract and an ordinary promise are different, however. Often no one forces a person to keep an ordinary promise. Contracts are promises agreed upon between two or more people or companies, called *parties* to the contract, that the law forces them to keep. Breaking any of these promises is called *breaching* the contract.

Doing business over the Internet presents special concerns when it comes to enforcing the terms of a contract against someone who breached the contract. Many companies are making promises in e-mails or attaching contracts as document files to e-mails, which raises questions about whether the e-mailed promises are legal contracts and whether contracts received were altered en route over the Internet. If they were altered, can the person receiving the altered agreement enforce it against the other party? Providing goods and services on Web sites to customers who agree to certain terms posted on the sites also raises questions about whether the customers are bound by the terms on the sites.

To answer these questions, it's important to understand some basics about contracts and contract law. With this knowledge, the issues involving contracts transmitted digitally and contracts posted on sites will be easier to comprehend.

Understanding Contract Basics

What happens if someone breaches a contract? There are a few options. The other party may choose to do nothing about it and just consider the deal a bad one. The parties may try to resolve the problem with each other out of court. The party who did not breach the contract may, on the other hand, decide to sue the breaching party in court.

A court may force any party who breaches a contract to do the following:

- Do what he promised to do, that is, to specifically perform the promise (called *specific performance*)

- Stop doing something (called *enjoining* the party's actions or *issuing an injunction against the party* to stop doing something)

- Pay money (called *damages*) to the other party

People usually don't breach a contract without a reason. Often a party breaches a contract because circumstances change and she can no longer keep all her promises. Maybe she promised to pay money for someone's services, but she ran out of money when the IRS audited her.

Other times a miscommunication causes a party to breach a contract. Perhaps the parties weren't clear about a completion or delivery date. One party didn't think he was supposed to complete the job within six months and deliver the finished goods; he thought he had ten months to complete it and deliver them. The delay may harm the other party financially.

Sometimes one party doesn't understand what he promises to do in the agreement because he doesn't read the written contract carefully. This often happens when a person uses a form or boilerplate contract that includes certain obligations that the person didn't realize he was supposed to keep. It also occurs when a person's lawyer doesn't explain the contract to him. Regardless of the reason, a breach of contract has still occurred in these situations that the parties must resolve — either out of court or in court. Avoid a breach by understanding your contracts.

Understanding some terms

Here are some words used in contracts that may need some explanation:

The word *terms* is used in two ways. The phrase *contract terms* refers to the points, or the basis for the deal, that make up the contract, such as how much money the party will pay to the other party, what each party will do for each other, and so on.

Contracts quiz

Why don't you take a test to see whether you understand some basics about contracts? Try answering the following true-or-false questions.

✔ "I didn't sign anything, so there's no contract." False. Contracts don't always need to be in writing or to be signed. Some contracts are oral (spoken), and occasionally someone's actions bind her to an agreement without signing anything.

✔ "I don't have to do anything that's not spelled out in the written contract." False. Often things you *do* (your actions) may become part of the agreement. In addition, the law implies certain obligations in contracts even if they aren't written or discussed.

✔ "I agree with everything in their written contract, so it's okay to sign it." Sometimes false. You probably should *add* some provisions to the contract. Often it's what someone doesn't put in a contract that can hurt him.

✔ "If we agree to something in a contract, the law must enforce what we agree to." False. You may include something in a contract that the courts will not enforce. The law does not permit parties to agree to things that violate the law or make the contract, or any part of it, *unconscionable* (explained in the section "Posting Contracts on Your Site: Just Point and Click Here").

The *term of the contract* means the duration of the agreement — how long it will last.

Provisions are the things actually stated in a written contract. You might refer to a provision for the payment of money by saying, "The contract *provides* (states) that you will pay $5,000."

Covenants are promises in the written contract.

Conditions are provisions in the contract that require something else to happen. For instance, "The company will deliver the product *after* receipt of payment." The condition is that payment must be made before the company will deliver the product.

Creating a contract

Contracts come into existence when there is bargaining between the parties. Often contracts between businesses, called *commercial contracts,* result after the parties negotiate their deal. Contracts between a business and consumers normally result when consumers accept what a business offers; it's often a take-it-or-leave-it deal. These are normally called *consumer contracts.*

Commercial contracts normally involve negotiable terms. For example, an e-business may negotiate with a Web site designer to design a site. The parties try to reach an agreement by negotiating such terms as what the designer will create, what the designer will have other people create for the site, when the designer will complete the project, who will own the rights to the things that the designer creates, how much the owner will pay the designer, when the owner will pay the designer, and so on. These negotiations result in terms that they both agree to, and that become part of the contract.

Consumer contracts rarely involve negotiations. For instance, a business may offer goods for sale at a certain price, and the business promises to deliver them to the consumer after receiving payment for them. Either the consumer buys the goods for the price and agrees to the delivery date, or the consumer doesn't buy them. Even though there is no negotiation, there is still bargaining. The consumer has the choice to buy the goods or not to buy them on those terms (price and delivery date).

To become a full-fledged contract that a court will enforce, the following things must occur:

- ✔ The parties must agree on the promises they exchange with one another. This is called *mutual assent* to the agreement. It's as if the parties both (mutually) nod their heads in agreement to the terms.

- ✔ The essential terms of the agreement must be definite enough so that the parties and a court can determine the nature and extent of each party's obligations.

- ✔ There must be legal *consideration* for the agreement.

- ✔ The parties to the agreement must be able to enter into a contract under the law. This is called having the *capacity* to enter a contract.

International contracts

Every day, millions of contracts are being negotiated across international borders. Contract principles are very similar throughout the world, but you should always check with a local attorney (or have your attorney check with a local attorney). Because of differences in language and customs, some words used in contracts may have slightly different meanings. For commercial contracts, the custom in the particular industry often guides the interpretation of these agreements. When negotiating with people in other parts of the world, ask them to explain any words you don't understand or that you believe that they may interpret differently. Remember that people form contracts because they want to work together. Don't be afraid or embarrassed to let them know you want to know how they interpret a contract provision. Hopefully such honesty will lead the way to open communication throughout your business relationship.

Nodding mutual assent

Exchanging promises normally involves one party offering a deal and another party accepting the offer. In other words, two activities occur: an offer and an acceptance. The party properly accepting a valid, legal offer may enforce the deal described in the offer.

To be valid and legal, the offer must describe the deal with reasonable certainty. For example, a marketing company may send an e-mail to a potential client describing the services it's offering to promote the e-business over a period of time for a certain price. This is a written offer to perform those services during that time for that price. The company could also make the offer verbally during a face-to-face meeting or over the telephone. If the e-business properly accepts this offer, it may hold the company to that price if it later tries to charge a higher fee.

Merely stating hopes, intentions, desires, or opinions is not usually an offer. An offer must indicate a clear intention to enter an agreement based on definite terms rather than wishes. For instance, a Web site operator's *hope* that 5 million people will see your banner ad on its site during one week is not a definite offer; it won't become one of the terms of your deal to advertise on the site. On the other hand, a promise that your banner ad will stay on a Web page until there have been 5 million impressions (people accessing that page) is more than an opinion and will be part of the deal.

The acceptance must also meet certain requirements to create a contract. For instance, an offer may restrict how someone may accept the offer, such as requiring acceptance within a certain number of days or in writing. If the acceptance does not comply with these restrictions, the person making the offer may withdraw it. Therefore, the other party may not be able to force the party to comply with the offer or make the terms in the offer part of the contract.

In addition, a party accepting an offer must communicate the acceptance to the other party. The communication doesn't always have to be written or spoken, however. Sometimes conduct, such as beginning to perform the agreement, can be acceptance.

If the accepting party changes the terms in the offer, then it's usually not a valid acceptance; it's a counteroffer. The other party (the one who made the original offer) may then either accept or reject the deal with these new terms.

Business-to-business deals are often treated differently than business-to-consumer deals. When a company's response to an offer made by another business includes additional terms or conditions that don't make major changes to the offer, the response may be a legal acceptance; the offer and the additional terms become part of the contract. There are a couple ways to avoid any changes in your offers. The offer could restrict the other party from changing any terms in the offer by stating that "the offer may only be accepted on the specific terms in the offer without any changes." You may also notify the other party that the additional terms are unacceptable. This notice must be sent promptly after receipt of the response containing the additional terms.

Accentuating the essential terms

To become a contract, the essential terms of the agreement must be definite. The parties and a court must be able to determine the essential terms — the basic promises and obligations — of each party. What are the essential terms? That often depends upon the subject matter of your contract and laws that govern that subject matter.

State and federal laws regulating sales to consumers may require certain terms to be in every sales contract or may restrict certain types of contract provisions. State and federal consumer protection laws may also require or restrict certain contract terms. Intellectual property law has certain requirements when a contract deals with copyrights, trademarks, or patents. Unfair competition law prohibits some contract terms. All of these laws affect contracts. How can anyone know them all? No one does, which is why lawyers tend to work with specific types of businesses or legal matters.

At the very least, the contract should do the following:

- Identify each party to the contract. Is the agreement between individual people, corporations, partnerships, or some other legal entity? What is each party's address?

- Define each party's role in the deal. What will each party do?

- State how and when any payment will be made.

- State when the agreement begins and how long it will last (the *term* of the agreement).

- Include signatures of both parties or at least the signature of the party who may breach the contract.

Signatures on a contract are important only when someone is trying to enforce it. However, because you don't know when forming a contract whether the other party will breach it in the future, always include signatures from all parties to the contract.

When a person claims she did not enter into a particular contract, she is *repudiating* the contract. One of the reasons people prefer to have contracts in writing is to prevent someone from repudiating her agreement. Although oral contracts are enforceable, proving the terms of such a deal or proving that someone agreed to the terms of such a deal is often more difficult. Signatures are the way that courts determine whether the contract is authentic, that is, if the person really agreed to the terms in that particular contract. It's called *authenticating* the contract.

A signature doesn't always have to be a handwritten name, and it doesn't always have to be in any particular part of the agreement. Depending upon the law that applies, a signature may be any symbol that a party adopts to show his intent to agree to the terms of the contract. Sometimes initials, thumbprints, typewritten names, or stamped names are sufficient signatures as long as the party providing the initials, print, or stamped name intends that symbol to be his signature.

Keep in mind that people don't always tell the truth, especially if they want to get out of a contract. If they claim that they didn't intend their initials, type-written name, or stamped name to be a signature, the other party has to find some way of proving that to be a lie. Doing so isn't always easy. Authenticating a contract becomes especially important in digital contracts, as explained in the section, "Digital signatures." It's also a good idea to have signatures at the end of the agreement to ensure that no one added more terms after it was signed. Be careful about having signatures appearing alone on a single page, however. They could become attached to anything! I prefer to have some part of the actual contract on the page that includes the signatures.

Considering consideration

Contracts must include legal consideration to be valid. *Consideration* means that each person receives a benefit and incurs some detriment as part of the bargain. Think tit for tat or *quid pro quo*. Benefits and detriments.

In an exchange of promises — the bargain — most parties each get something and give up something. For example, consideration for a Web site design agreement may be that a Web designer spends time and uses skill to design a Web site (a detriment — giving up something) for the payment of money (a benefit — getting something). The Web site owner pays money (detriment) and receives the Web site design (benefit).

Another example is an agreement between two people who want to form a partnership. What's the consideration in a partnership agreement? Here's a typical scenario. Partner A may contribute his experience and time to run the partnership business (detriment) and receive Partner B's promise to provide part of the profits to Partner A (benefit). Partner B may contribute money to fund the business (detriment) and receive Partner A's promise to provide part of the profits to Partner B (benefit).

In some civil law countries such as France, a contract does not involve consideration. There must, however, be proper cause to enforce the promise. To determine whether there is proper cause, the court may consider common business practices and moral issues. If these customs and moral issues indicate that a promise should be enforced, it probably will be enforced according to the agreement and in compliance with the specific laws.

Special promises that break the rules

In some common law countries such as the United States, courts may enforce certain promises even though the parties don't form a legal contract. One of these situations is called *promissory estoppel*. The court stops someone who made a promise from reneging on the promise under certain circumstances. For instance, Mr. Someone makes a promise to Ms. Person to do something. If Ms. Person believes the promise, relies on the promise, and changes her position because of the promise, courts may force Mr. Someone to keep the promise. Changing her position could involve many types of activities, such as spending money (changing her financial position) or entering into other contractual obligations (changing her position regarding legal obligations).

Courts may also enforce promises when someone unjustly receives a benefit from someone else. Sometimes the law says that the person who received the benefit should pay for that benefit even if the parties don't have a formal contract. This is called an *implied-in-law contract* or a *quasi-contract*. The person receiving the benefit is "unjustly enriched" at the expense of the other party.

For example, a company finds a story that it wants to display on its Web site. It takes the story from a book. The company licenses the right to use a copyrighted story with the same title from a publisher and pays $2,000. Before posting the story, the company realizes that it licensed the wrong story (same title but wrong story) and promptly asks for its money back. The publisher refuses. A court would probably force the publisher to return the money; otherwise, the publisher would be unjustly enriched. It received money for something the company never intended to license or to use.

Having capacity

Under the law, some people will not be forced to keep their promises. These people don't have the legal *capacity* to enter the agreement. The law considers them incapable of understanding the consequences of their contractual obligations or acting without proper authority. They include minors, unauthorized representatives of companies (such as a mail room clerk attempting to sign a contract obligating his employer to pay for Internet service), and, in certain states, suspended corporations.

In some states, a minor is anyone under the age of 18 years. In other states, a minor is anyone under the age of 19. Depending on individual state laws, minors may get out of most of their contracts. The contracts are voidable at the option of the minor or the minor's guardian until he reaches legal age or for a reasonable time after reaching the age of majority. Some special contracts cannot be voided; often courts must approve these contracts when they are being formed. For example, California law requires a court to approve certain children's entertainment agreements. If the court approves the terms of the entertainment contract, the minor may not get out of the contract just because she's a minor.

In addition, individuals agreeing to a contract on behalf of a legal entity, such as a partnership, corporation, or limited liability company, must be authorized by the company to enter into the contract. Under certain circumstances, the company may ignore the contract if the person doesn't have authority to enter into contracts for the company. If the company takes action under the contract as if it were in effect, however, the company may have to comply with it; the company's actions may indicate that it *adopted* the terms and has implied it will comply with them.

When an agreement is signed by an authorized representative of a corporation for the corporation (not as an individual), normally the corporation is the only one obligated under the agreement; the individual signing the contract is not responsible for any obligations. However, anyone who signs an agreement before the corporation is actually formed may be personally responsible under the contract.

In some states, corporations that don't file all their documents with the state agency or pay their taxes may be suspended from doing business. Laws may prohibit suspended corporations from entering contracts. This law, however, often harms the corporation more than the other party to the contract. The other party may usually enforce the agreement; however, the corporation may not be able to defend itself in court because the state no longer recognizes its existence.

Embellishing a contract

Nearly every written contract includes many more provisions than the bare necessities required to create a legally enforceable contract. These additional provisions may fill 5 pages or 700 pages! How lengthy a contract becomes depends upon the subject matter of the deal, what the parties want, and what the parties' attorneys want.

Providing specifics

Regardless of the length of the entire contract, some provisions are basic to all contracts. Therefore, your contracts should include the following provisions.

- **Payment:** State when and how each party will be paid.
- **Personal property rights:** Describe the rights to any personal property that a party is creating, transferring, or using.
- **Intellectual property rights:** Describe the rights to any intellectual property that a party is creating, transferring, or using.
- **Delivery or testing:** Describe how and when a party will deliver any work performed under the contract and, if applicable, how the work will be tested, accepted, or rejected.

✔ **Performance warranties:** State all warranties regarding the performance of any work under the contract.

✔ **Other warranties:** State all warranties regarding ownership or rights to use any property for the contract.

✔ **Confidential information:** Define confidential information, explain when the parties may share confidential information, describe how the parties may use it, and describe how they will return it to the owner, if applicable.

✔ **Territory:** State the territory for the contract, if important.

✔ **Choice of law and forum:** State the parties' choice of law to govern the contract and choice of legal forum (the court and state or country) to bring any legal dispute.

✔ **Notices:** Describe how formal notices to each party may be provided in the event that a problem arises or a party claims that the other party is in breach of contract.

✔ **Arbitration and attorney's fees:** State any agreement regarding out-of-court dispute resolutions, such as arbitration, and whether a losing party will pay the winning party's legal fees if a dispute arises.

✔ **Amendments:** Describe how a party may amend or add to the agreement.

The preceding list describes only some provisions. Don't forget to include all the provisions necessary to create a legally enforceable contract and any other provisions that may be important to the particular deal. Check with your lawyer, too.

Some of the sample agreements on the CD include comments. Take a look at the agreements to get an idea of how these provisions fit into a contract.

Putting it in writing

Many people believe that the only reason to put a contract in writing is to protect them in court if something goes wrong. Rather than focusing on the negative, try considering the positive reasons to put it in writing. Business relationships are important. You want to encourage clear communication and discourage misunderstanding. Preparing a concise written agreement describing the deal and what will happen under certain circumstances can help reach this goal.

Also, your written agreement will be available to review if a disagreement ever occurs. Memories aren't perfect, so a written contract helps you both remember the specifics of your agreement. The more carefully you write your contract, the stronger the possibility that you will resolve any problems *without* going to court.

Good faith and good business

The law implies in every contract a promise by the parties to act in good faith. It's called the Covenant of Good Faith and Fair Dealing. If a party deals with the other party unfairly, doing so may be cause for a lawsuit. Don't wait for someone to sue you to force you to act in good faith. When you treat all your contractual parties in good faith and deal with them fairly, your e-business will thrive for a very long time. And knowing that you can keep your promises feels good, doesn't it?

Some laws require certain contracts to be in writing. If they aren't, courts won't enforce them. For example, a law called the Statute of Frauds requires any contract that the parties cannot perform completely within one year from its making to be in writing. The Uniform Commercial Code requires most contracts for the sale of goods that amount to more than $500 to be in writing. U.S. copyright law requires copyright assignments (the sale of rights) and independent contractors' work-for-hire agreements to be in writing (see Chapter 8 regarding work-for-hire agreements).

Other laws also require contracts involving certain subject matter to be in writing. As you can see, always putting your contract in writing is probably a good idea. If you want to enforce an oral contract or you want to get out of one, check with your lawyer about any laws that require contracts to be in writing.

The CD includes a Checklist of Contract Provisions.

Doing the Digital Deal

Contracts that parties form by e-mail or over the Internet must still comply with contract law and other applicable laws. However, digital transmission raises some special questions about contracts. For instance, how can you be sure that the document attached to an e-mail is authentic, that is, it's the exact document that someone sent? Can you be sure of the identity of the person signing an agreement?

Naturally, problems usually arise only when someone doesn't keep his promises. If you want to enforce a contract, being able to verify the signature and authenticate the contract (show that it's the real thing) is important. Luckily, lawyers and lawmakers are moving fairly quickly in this area of Internet law so they don't hold back e-commerce. The prominent methods to verify and authenticate messages and files that are entering the digital arena are digital signatures, certification authorities, and cybernotaries.

Digital signatures

Each person has his or her own writing style. Therefore, a handwritten signature identifies a person. Because you can't sign an e-mail or other digital document in your own handwriting, how can you sign a digital document? How can you make sure that a digital document is authentic? With a digital signature, of course!

Remember, digits are numbers; therefore, your signature is transformed from handwritten letters into mathematical equations and algorithms. Please don't expect me to explain algorithms; it's been way too long since I studied mathematics.

Anyway, you create a digital signature with technology that allows you to encrypt and decrypt a message. Scramble it and unscramble it. Encryption transforms plain text messages into unreadable (encrypted) text; decryption transforms cipher text into plain text messages. Cryptography is a type of encryption.

Although there are different kinds of encryption techniques, digital signatures usually involve cryptographic software and a pair of complementary keys — keys that only work together. These keys are not like car keys. They're merely parts of the software that lock and unlock the encrypted messages. Think of them as secret decoder rings built into computer software.

Here's how it works. You complete a contract and save it in a computer file. You then begin creating a digital signature by typing in your name, address, and any other information you like. You run these through your cryptographic software, which creates a message digest in digits. The software then uses your private key to encrypt the message digest so that it becomes your digital signature, which is unique to the message (your contract) and to the private key you use. You may then send the digital signature along with the contract by e-mail.

Creating a digital signature does not encrypt the contract. You can combine the two if you like so that they're both encrypted.

When the other person receives the contract with the digital signature, he runs it through the cryptographic software. It generates a new message digest of the document as received. But the recipient and the sender may have questions: Is it the same document that was sent? Did anyone mess with it en route over the Internet or in the recipient's computer when he wasn't around?

Using the public key that you gave to him, the recipient decrypts your digital signature to get the original message digest that you encrypted. The software then compares the new message digest from the document he received with the message digest contained in your digital signature. If they match, then it's the real thing from you!

A digital signature is one kind of an electronic signature. *Electronic signatures* is a broader term that includes any electronic symbol that a party uses to authenticate a digital document.

At least 40 states have laws authorizing the use of digital or electronic signatures, and bills are pending in the remaining states. Some of them apply only to documents people file with the government, such as tax returns. Many professionals are encouraging all state legislatures to adopt the Uniform Electronic Transactions Act, which covers the use of digital signatures. Also, the federal government passed a digital signature bill that supports digital signatures. See the sidebar "Signs of the times" for more information.

The U.S. government restricts exporting cryptography to other countries as a matter of national security. Check with a lawyer familiar with these laws before you send cryptographic software out of the country! The appendix includes Web site addresses for some companies that offer encryption software.

Signs of the times

Many laws require certain records and contracts to be in writing, which means on paper. Many laws also require certain records and contracts to be signed (see the section "Putting it in writing," earlier in this chapter).

To promote electronic transactions and remove paper-based obstacles, the federal Electronic Signatures in Global and National Commerce Act is in effect October 1, 2000, in the United States. This law applies to transactions that involve interstate or foreign commerce — transactions "entered into, provided in, or affecting interstate or foreign commerce." The act uses the terms *electronic record* and *electronic signature*.

Specifically, the law concerns contracts, agreements, and records (including government and health records) and those laws that require certain contracts or other records to be in writing and signed. In essence, an electronic contract, agreement, or record will be as legally valid as a paper contract, agreement, or record. If a signature is required, an electronic signature is legally valid.

The act states that parties to a contract have the right to decide whether they want to use or accept electronic records and electronic signatures. They may establish their own procedures or requirements for them. The parties also can decide the type or method of electronic record and electronic signature they want to use.

In fact, no one is *required* to use or accept electronic records or electronic signatures. However, the act requires the Secretary of Commerce to promote the acceptance and use of electronic signatures on an international basis. The secretary must report back to Congress about any barriers or constraints imposed by foreign nations.

There is a special section regarding consumers. When any law requires someone to give a record in writing to a consumer, or to make a record available in writing to a consumer (like making a written warranty available for the consumer to review at some location), the written record may be an electronic record only if the following conditions are met:

(continued)

(continued)

- ✔ The consumer must affirmatively consent (actually do something to show consent) that the written record may be an electronic record, and must not have withdrawn that consent (this last part acknowledges the right of the consumer to withdraw consent later).

- ✔ The consent, when made part of a notice or a contract, must be conspicuous and visually separate from other terms in the notice or agreement.

- ✔ Prior to consenting, the consumer must be provided with a statement describing the hardware and software required for the consumer to access and keep the electronic record.

- ✔ At the time of the consumer's consent, the electronic record must be capable of review, retention (keeping), and printing by the consumer if accessed by using the hardware and software described in the statement (in other words, the hardware and software described in the statement must really do the job).

- ✔ The consumer must affirmatively acknowledge (actually do something) that the consumer understands and agrees to the following requirements: (1) The consumer must notify the provider of electronic records of any change in the consumer's electronic mail address or other location to which the electronic records may be provided. (2) If the consumer withdraws consent, the consumer must notify the provider of electronic records of the electronic mail address or other location to which the records may be provided.

- ✔ The acknowledgment, when placed in a notice or a contract, must be conspicuous and visually separate from other terms of the notice or contract.

This law does not affect a person's right to contest the validity of his signature. A person may claim that the signature is a forgery, the person's signature was used without authority, or the signature is invalid for reasons that would invalidate the effect of a written signature. In other words, if any applicable law gives a person the right to contest the validity of a written signature, that right also applies to a person regarding an electronic signature.

Don't assume that this federal law will govern all your e-business activities. Generally, federal law takes precedence over state laws that may come into conflict with federal law. However, this law permits state legislatures to pass laws regarding electronic records and electronic signatures that may govern the same subject matter under certain conditions. For example, a state may enact the Uniform Electronic Transactions Act (see the section "Digital signatures," in this chapter).

States may also enact laws that specify alternative procedures or requirements for using and accepting electronic records or electronic signatures as long as the state laws meet several conditions so that the requirements are specific, as opposed to general, and do not discriminate for or against any specific technology or any specific type or size of entity (company) engaged in the business of facilitating the use of electronic records or electronic signatures.

In addition, this act applies to transactions involving the sale of goods even though the Uniform Commercial Code under state law governs these types of transactions (see Chapter 19).

Certification authorities and cybernotaries

Just in case the digital signature isn't enough, companies called certification authorities help parties validate digital documents. The authorities act like an independent and trusted third party to verify the documents.

When a company subscribes to the service, the authorities review the digital documents sent back and forth. They certify the link between a pair of keys. If the document is really from its subscriber, then the company attaches its own digital certificate authenticating the document.

Some organizations are working toward creating a category of professionals called *cybernotaries*. Like traditional notaries, they would be licensed to attest to statements and electronically certify facts and actions taken in their presence.

Posting Contracts on Your Site: Just Point and Click Here

You may want to post (display) three types of contracts on your e-site for all your customers or visitors to read and agree to. One is a contract for the sale of products you ship to customers (see Chapter 19). Another contract is for services that you provide to customers, clients, or Web site visitors through your site. A third type of contract permits people to download software, games, entertainment, or news from your site. The latter two types may be part of the Terms of Use or User Agreement (see "User agreements," later in this chapter).

Embracing the mass market

If you're doing business with a small number of individuals or companies, you may want to negotiate the terms of each contract with them individually. Therefore, you wouldn't post the contract on your site for everyone to agree to. However, quick deals with large numbers of people often require standardized contracts outlining your terms. In other words, they're mass-market contracts.

Potential customers or visitors must accept a mass-market agreement "as is" if they want to do business with you. For example, software products that people buy in packages include standardized contract licenses regulating the way the buyer may use the software. They are called *shrink-wrap* agreements. Once the buyer tears open the shrink-wrap packaging and uses the product, the buyer is accepting the terms of the license agreement.

A license is a special kind of contract. Generally, it's a contract that gives someone permission to use property instead of transferring any ownership rights to the person. Software developers are only giving permission to the buyers to use the copyrighted computer software; they're not selling the intellectual property rights (such as the right to make mass copies of it and sell it to others) of the software.

The Web's version of shrink-wrap agreements are called Web-wrap agreements or point-and-click agreements. The buyer or user must do something — tear open the package (shrink-wrap), go into the Web site and use the site (Web-wrap), or point the computer mouse and click on a button (point-and-click) — to indicate that she agrees to the terms of the contract. Are these mass-market contracts enforceable? They can be under certain conditions.

Here are a few guidelines for contracts posted on your Web site.

- ✔ Bring to the person's attention the fact that the purchase, download, or use of the information or use of the Web site is subject to the terms of the contract. Make it clear that by purchasing, downloading, or using your stuff, the person agrees to everything in your contract.

- ✔ Make sure that the notice about the contract terms is in a place where you can be assured that the person sees it *before* the purchase, download, or use. Make the notice conspicuous.

- ✔ Provide the complete contract on the site so that the person has the opportunity to read it. Use language that makes it understandable.

- ✔ Do not include any *unconscionable* terms in the contract. These are terms that are illegal, depending upon the law that applies to the subject matter of your contract. For example, a contract provision that makes a consumer agree that you are not responsible if your product physically injures the consumer will normally not be enforced. Sometimes contracts involving excessive prices are unconscionable, too.

- ✔ Include all provisions to create and embellish your contract that you and your lawyer believe are important.

- ✔ Require the person to do something — to take some action — to show that she agrees to the terms of the contract. In other words, make the person point and click on a button that says, "I Agree." Also give the person the opportunity to reject the terms of the contract. You must be able to show mutual assent. Simply having a contract on your site without requiring the visitors or customers to do something to "sign" the agreement, like pointing and clicking, may not be enforceable in some places under certain circumstances. Although some courts have enforced Terms of Use agreements posted on Web sites against Web site users when they violated the terms of that agreement, it's always a good idea to have the user *do* something to make sure you can prove the user knew about your terms.

Wrapping up your Web site guests

Anyone from anywhere could be visiting (using) your site. Most e-businesses and Web site operators want to control the way people use their site and to reduce the risk of being sued by anyone who uses their site. Therefore, they put together certain terms and conditions to post as a contract on their site. Often these contracts include *disclaimers*, which are provisions that limit the Web site operators' liability or obligations in some way (explained later in this chapter). The contract may be called *Terms of Use*, *Terms of Service*, or *User Agreement*. I prefer calling this kind of contract a User Agreement because it's an agreement for the Web site user to agree to.

User agreements

Your visitors must be able to read your agreement *before* they purchase anything. Even if they're simply using your site and not purchasing any goods, it's a good idea to make sure that they know where your agreement is so they can read it. Many Web sites provide links at the bottom of the home page to this agreement.

The User Agreement generally states that the site (its owner and operator) is providing the visitor (user) the services or products on the site on the condition that the user agrees to the terms. Some agreements are very long, while others are somewhat short and basic.

Depending upon your particular needs and the law that applies to your e-business, you may want to cover the following in your User Agreement:

- ✔ Your complete, legal business name and address. This information is necessary in order to make a valid contract in most places.

- ✔ An introductory paragraph that legally binds the user to the terms of the agreement, such as, "We provide the services to you subject to the following terms, which may be updated by us from time to time without prior notice to you and without requiring acceptance by you."

- ✔ A description of the services you're providing on your site and what users must do to use your site, such as pay any fees or complete a registration form. If you want them to provide only accurate and truthful information to you, put that in your agreement.

- ✔ Any additional rules for using your site. These may include extra safety precautions if you provide e-mail for your users. For instance, you might restrict users from allowing third parties to use their Internet account, disclosing their passwords to others, and asking others for their passwords, which could result in people impersonating the identity of others for unlawful purposes.

- ✔ If you're selling goods, any specific conditions you have regarding the sales, such as return policies and how users may make a claim under a warranty. (For more on sales and warranties, see Chapters 19 and 20.)

✔ A description of any user conduct that will not be tolerated on your site. For example, sites that provide chat rooms, interactive areas, or e-mail may prohibit anyone from transmitting any messages or content that is unlawful, threatening, abusive, defamatory, vulgar, obscene, libelous, slanderous, an invasion of another's privacy, hateful, racially objectionable, and so on. You may want to prohibit or limit use of the services for spam. (For more on spam, see Chapter 12.)

✔ Any restriction on others providing links on their sites to your material. (For more on linking, see Chapter 18.)

✔ An acknowledgement by the user of your proprietary (ownership) rights to things such as your intellectual property, and an acknowledgement that they will not use your property without your permission. (For intellectual property notices for Web sites, see Chapter 24.)

✔ Any disclaimers of warranties or limitations of liability as explained in the section "Disclaimers and limitations of liability," later in this chapter.

✔ A reference to your privacy policy or a link in the User Agreement to your privacy policy page. See Chapter 15 for tips on preparing a privacy policy.

✔ All other contract provisions that may be necessary for your particular site.

You can read various agreements on Web sites to get some ideas for your agreement. However, check with your lawyer. Don't start throwing anything on your site until you figure out whether it really applies to your e-business and complies with the law.

A sample Web Site User Agreement with explanations and a copy of it without explanations are on the CD in the back of this book.

Disclaimers and limitations of liability

When your contract, whether it's a User Agreement or any other type of agreement, includes a disclaimer, you're attempting to deny all responsibility for certain things. A contract including a limitation of liability means that you're attempting to limit some of your legal responsibility in the event that certain events occur.

Not all disclaimers or limitations of liability are enforceable. Generally, courts enforce them more often when they appear in commercial contracts than when they appear in consumer contracts.

Some, but not all, disclaimers are enforceable in consumer contracts, but only under certain conditions. The words in the disclaimer or limitation of liability must be very clear and to-the-point. The words must comply with all legal requirements pertaining to that type of contract and be very noticeable in the agreement. They may not be in tiny writing buried in a lengthy agreement. Often disclaimers and limitations are typed in capital letters to draw the party's attention to that point.

A disclaimer often involves warranties that one party to the contract does not want to provide. It may state: "SELLER MAKES NO WARRANTY, EXPRESS OR IMPLIED, EXCEPT AS STATED IN THIS AGREEMENT, AND SELLER DIS-CLAIMS ANY WARRANTY OF ANY OTHER KIND, INCLUDING ANY WARRANTY OF MERCHANTABILITY OR FITNESS FOR A PARTICULAR PURPOSE."

As explained in Chapter 20, some states don't permit businesses to disclaim the implied warranty of merchantability or the implied warranty of fitness for a particular purpose. Other states require that the disclaimer of these war-ranties include certain specific words to be effective.

Many companies want to limit their liability in a contract. They want to make sure that they're not taking on a project or providing a service that involves too much risk. Therefore, the parties may agree to limit liability for certain types of damages, such as the amount of money that one party may receive in a lawsuit.

Contract provisions limiting liability often refer to special damages, conse-quential damages, and exemplary (punitive) damages. The party is trying to limit the types of damages the other party may receive in court (or in some other legal proceeding) if he breaches the contract. This limitation does not prevent the other party from receiving general damages; it only limits the party's right to receive certain *additional* types of damages. This contract provision is a way to limit the party's risk if something goes wrong.

General damages for breach of contract are those monetary losses that result from the breach and that the breaching party, when the contract was made, could anticipate to occur if there were a breach. *Special* and *consequential damages* in contract law are the same; some courts or laws just give them dif-ferent names. These damages occur from special circumstances involved in the particular situation. A party may only obtain these damages if they were foreseeable to the breaching party when the contract was made.

For example, assume that you agree to create gift baskets for an e-site to sell. You agree to deliver 5,000 of them by November 30 for $25,000. You get sick, you stress, you blow it. You can't deliver. In a mad rush, the e-business obtains baskets from someone else. However, it costs him $35,000 plus an extra $5,000 to hire extra employees to get baskets shipped for holiday orders he received. What are his damages for your breach of contract?

His general damages would be $10,000, the extra amount he paid to get what you promised to do. It's reasonable for someone (you) to expect that he may have to pay more to get the same product that you promised. The extra $5,000 he paid to employees is probably special damages.

If you didn't realize that he had specific orders he had to fill, you probably wouldn't have to pay that amount. If you knew about these orders, you may have to pay these special damages, too. If your contract limited your liability for any special damages, however, you wouldn't have to pay them.

Special damages and exemplary damages apply to *torts* — unlawful acts that harm others. Torts include acts that cause injury to others, such as defamation (libel and slander), invasion of privacy, and product liability (physical injury resulting from the use of products). General damages for torts usually include emotional distress or pain and suffering. Special damages often include things like medical expenses and loss of earnings. *Exemplary damages* are awarded only when there are willful, fraudulent, or really awful acts; they are damages meant to punish (also called *punitive damages*) a defendant for really awful acts and bad intentions. Depending on the circumstances, some courts won't enforce disclaimers for torts to consumers.

A contract that tries to exclude liability for personal injury or death won't usually fly. Most courts throughout the world consider this an unconscionable clause. Courts don't enforce unconscionable contracts.

The Uniform Commercial Code (governing contracts for the sale of goods) also restricts unconscionable terms in a contract. A consumer sales contract that limits someone's liability for special damages for injury to a person is unconscionable. Sometimes, depending on the circumstances, excessive price terms may also be unconscionable.

In most European countries, contract terms that exclude or restrict liability for most things in a commercial contract are enforceable if they're fair and reasonable under the circumstances. However, contract law in Israel severely restricts disclaimers.

The CD in this book includes samples of Limitation of Liability Provisions with explanations and Warranty Disclaimer Provisions with explanations.

Part II
Getting Ready
to Launch Your
Web Site

The 5th Wave   By Rich Tennant

"Just how accurately should my Web site reflect
my place of business?"

In this part . . .

You're moving into the development and production stages. It's time to build your entrance to the Internet: your e-business Web site. It all starts with the intricate details of Web site development agreements. You must, of course, give your site a name. This part leads you through the process of selecting and registering a domain name. What if someone already staked a claim to your domain? You'll learn how to wrestle over domain names with anyone in the world without going to court. Rights in trademarks and service marks are recognized around the world, but there are some important technicalities you'll learn about here.

Chapter 4

Building Your Web Site

Close your eyes and imagine that you're a film producer standing in front of Mann's Chinese Theatre in Hollywood. After a year of hard work, your movie is about to premiere. Searchlights span the sky. The red carpet rolls out to greet crowds lining up along Hollywood Boulevard. Everyone wants to see your production! Anticipation and excitement rush through your body. Come on, let your imagination run. Can you feel the adrenaline pumping?

Now pretend you're that producer just starting out. Do you know where it all began? It's really quite simple. It all began with an idea and a vision.

Building your e-business Web site is where your production begins. All you need to do is plan your site, develop your presentation, cast cool people to work with you, make the right deals, and keep your production up and running. It's not that difficult. And the best part is: You don't have to be a Hollywood producer to feel the thrill!

Planning Your Site

Whether you develop your own Web site or hire another professional to do the work, advance planning is the key to success. You'll keep your costs down and be better equipped to make the right choices when it's time to connect to the Internet if you plot a course. Planning your site begins with thinking about your market, your image, and the product or service you want to offer your visitors. Answering the questions posed in the following sections may start your mind rolling.

Who do you want to visit the site?

In marketing terms, who is your target market? You must learn about the people you want to attract to the site. Think about the type of people who want what you're offering. Consider their age group, gender, educational level, lifestyle, likes, and dislikes. Search the Internet for information on your audience and check out some of the Web sites listed in the marketing section of the appendix. After you're clear on whom you want to reach, think about your image.

What do you want the visitors to see?

Your Web site projects an image. What image do you want to portray on the site? Be yourself, but portray your business image. After all, you're building an e-business site, not a home scrapbook. Some types of businesses succeed by bringing in a personal touch, while others don't. It all depends upon the nature of your business and your audience.

Are you having a hard time imagining how to portray your image? If so, browse other sites and decide what you like in colors, backgrounds, graphics, typeset, buttons, bars, and sounds. Whether it's a squirming e-mail envelope with sexy, blinking eyes or a big, brown square block with E-MAIL written on it, each part of your Web site projects an image. Make sure that you know what best fits you, and then keep these things in mind during the design process.

What will visitors do on the site?

With your image in mind, think about your target audience again. What will they enjoy doing on your site? If your market is 10-year-olds who spend most of their time playing video games, you'll want your site to include lots of flash and fast-moving stuff for them to play with. If your market is the intellectual, over-50 type, a vast supply of in-depth information could be good. The MTV generation probably falls somewhere in between the flash and the heady stuff, so they may want to hear music, watch videos, and see alternative sports activities.

The point of the Internet is to draw people to your site and keep them there. The longer they stay, the more apt they are to buy what you're selling. Visit your competitors' sites to see what they're doing. Try out other sites to find out how well they work.

When you decide what you want to offer your audience, consider the technology that may be necessary to run the site. Will you offer e-mail, interactive chat rooms, or digital files containing music or software to download? Will you process private information such as purchase orders or credit card numbers? How will you keep this information secure and private? These are things to keep in mind when exploring your options to build your own site or to hire an outside individual or company to do it for you.

In my opinion, one of the biggest mistakes made by all those failed dot-coms involves Web site technology. When developing your site, you must consider whether you can use software that's already available, whether you must hire someone to develop custom technology to operate your site, or whether you will hire someone to use a combination of both to develop the site. Never, ever forget that technology is fallible — there is no such thing as software or technology that works with everything perfectly all the time. Therefore, you will need to deal with technology problems even after your site is up and running.

Some dot-coms spent hundreds of thousands of dollars to have custom technology built for their sites. But they learned too late that they couldn't find any employees who were qualified to keep it running or couldn't afford to hire those experts anyway! In fact, many companies began offering BMWs and other sports cars to any qualified programmer who would work for them! Use technology that works well, that you can maintain affordably, and that will accommodate a larger audience in the future so you won't need to create new technology when your audience grows from a thousand to a million per week.

Developing Your Site

A Web site has two basic parts: the front end and the back end. The front end is the design and other visuals the visitor sees on the site, such as graphics, colors, text, and order forms. The back end is the technology that runs the site, such as computer code and software applications. Web site designers generally design the front end of a site. Web site developers usually develop the technology. Sometimes companies design *and* develop sites.

Software is available to help you build your own Web site. My first Web site was simple to design because it provided only information, a few graphics and photographs, links, and a way to e-mail me. I built my Web site in less than one week in my off time. I used Sausage Software's HotDog Professional software that I purchased and downloaded from its Web site (`www.sausage.com`) and followed a book explaining how to build a Web site. One helpful book is *Creating Web Pages For Dummies* (I'm not saying that just because it's a *For Dummies* book; I really do think it's an excellent book), by Bud Smith and Arthur Bebak (IDG Books Worldwide, Inc.). Whether you *should* design your own site depends upon the type of site you need and the amount of time you have. A word of caution: Web site designing is addictive. My friends and I had so much fun designing our sites that we had a hard time stopping — we worked into the wee hours of the morning!

Even if you decide to design your own Web site, reading the following sections will be helpful. They alert you to possible problems you can avoid if you're aware of them before you begin your work. The business and legal tips may also help you in other types of deals you make to run your e-business.

Preparing a Request for Proposal

If you decide to hire an outside company to design or develop your site, you need to get some proposals or estimates from at least a few companies so that you can select the right one for your e-business. Developers can't really give you an accurate estimate to create a Web site unless they know what you want. That's why you should prepare a *Request for Proposal*, simply called an RFP. An RFP is a letter with the words "Request for Proposal" at the top. It describes your business and poses questions for the Web site developer to answer.

Address the letter to the Web site developer and state that it is a Request for Proposal to create an e-business site for you. Divide the letter into sections that provide the developer with information about your company's background and goals, your ideas (or specifications) for your site, and your desire to receive a proposal from the developer.

In the section about your company's background and goals, you may want to describe your business, your target market, and the image you want to portray.

In the section about your ideas for your site, you may do the following:

- ✔ Briefly list some features you'd like on your site.
- ✔ Describe whether you want lots of flash or mostly simple graphics.
- ✔ List some URLs of sites you like and jot down a few words on why you like the sites.
- ✔ List some URLs of sites you don't like with a few words about why you don't like them.

In the last section, ask prospective Web site developers to do the following:

- ✔ Describe their experience in Web design (artistic) and Web development (programming).
- ✔ List some URLs for sites they've designed.
- ✔ Describe the services they offer.
- ✔ State any warranty they provide for their work to ensure that the site is working properly.
- ✔ List their pricing structure for the type of site described in the RFP.
- ✔ State when they could begin work and when they would complete the site.
- ✔ Send a written response by a specific date.

A sample RFP with my comments and the RFP without my comments are on the CD. The sample does not include every item discussed above; you may wish to include more information in your RFP than is in the sample.

Your RFP should be short, simple, and precise. If you're ready to spend $60,000, you can make it long and be somewhat demanding in your expectations. Otherwise, keep it to one or two pages in length. Everyone is busy, and companies don't have time to read long dissertations during the estimate process — especially if they may not get the job.

Finding the firm

When you're satisfied with your RFP, start searching for developers to send it to. Look for Web site developers' credit lines on sites that have a look similar to the one you want to convey. Explore companies all around the world — but make sure that you speak each other's language so the text won't be all messed up! The Internet is full of sites listing Web site developers and professional Web site developers' organizations. Some Web site URLs are in the appendix to help your search.

When you find at least a half-dozen developers that you like, e-mail them. Explain that you want a site developed, and ask them their price ranges so that you will know whether to submit an RFP to them. If they're in your price range, ask them whether they will sign a simple confidentiality agreement (also called a Nondisclosure Agreement, or NDA for short) to keep your RFP confidential.

The CD in this book contains sample Nondisclosure Agreements with my comments explaining some provisions and the same agreements without my comments.

Wait for the developer to sign the NDA before you send your RFP. If the developer won't sign one, then you have to decide how important confidentiality is to you. If you won't be providing anything of a confidential nature to the company at this point, then you may send the RFP to the developer without a signed NDA. If you need to share confidential information to get a good estimate, ask yourself whether you want to do business with a developer who won't keep your RFP or confidential information confidential (as long as your nondisclosure agreement is a reasonable one). When you're ready, e-mail your RFP to the developers.

Talking things over

Your e-business site will be effective only if it works well. How well it works depends upon how well the designer or developer builds it. Specifically, the site's effectiveness involves how it looks, how it performs, and how portable it is (see the discussion on portability later in this section).

Visitors to your site will be using different computer *platforms*, which are the underlying hardware and software for a system of components. Put more simply, you must anticipate that visitors will be using Macs, PCs, and UNIX-based systems, as well as different versions of Web browsers, slow and fast modems, and various sizes of monitors. They all affect what visitors see on your site and how well the site responds to them. The developer needs to anticipate these things.

By analogy, suppose that you want to perform a dive into the water for different audiences around the world. You want everyone to see the same type of dive. In Los Angeles, you'll dive off a spring diving board into a swimming pool. In Geneva, you'll dive off a wooden dock into a lake. In Acapulco, you'll dive off a cliff into the ocean. You'll be diving off three different platforms — a diving board, a dock, and a cliff. They can all affect how your dive looks.

If your dive is going to be two somersaults with three twists, it may look good off a cliff. You might complete a twist or two off the diving board. But you'll splat off the dock. So your dive won't look good from some of the platforms. But if you decide to do a swan dive, it will look pretty much the same from all three platforms.

The Web site developer you select must know how to deal with these variables. The visitors' hardware and software affect color, graphics, text, page size, and download times. The site may also require certain programming for plug-ins that allow people to enjoy music and videos on your site. The programming for these plug-ins may be affected by the types of computer servers you use — meaning that you may have problems with your site if you change Web site hosting services. This affects the *portability* of your site — how easily you can move it from server to server without problems. Therefore, you need to talk a few things over with the potential developers:

- How do they ensure that your site will appear and perform the same on the various platforms and browsers?
- Which browsers will they use to test your site?
- Which browsers will work with your site?
- Will you be limited to using only certain computer servers used by certain Web site hosts?
- Will you be able to change Web site hosts without having problems with your site?
- Will they upgrade the site?
- Will they maintain the site?
- Will they give you the source code (the copyrightable portion of the technology) to all the technology they create for your site? (See the discussion on ownership rights in the section "Deciphering the deal points," later in this chapter.)

Know your audience

Always remember your target audience. If you're after an audience who can't afford the latest computer, they'll have slow download times and they may not have all the plug-ins needed to view your site (especially if you use *flash* on your site, which is a special kind of graphic animation). You may want two or more versions of your Web pages for visitors to use, such as a graphics version, a flash version, and a text-only version. If your market is high-tech professionals, you can be assured that they'll have the latest computer equipment, browsers, and plug-ins.

Are you confused about some computer or Internet words? A quick way to find the definition is by logging on the Internet and going to www. zdwebopedia.com. Enter the term, click on "define it," and the definition appears!

If you're satisfied with the way the developers answer your questions about the variables, discuss ideas about the look and feel of your site with them. Get to know the people a little bit to decide whether you like them well enough to work with them. Trust your initial instincts.

If you're spending several thousand dollars for your site, most developers will share with you their ideas for your site in order to get the job. Others may want you to pay them an hourly consultation fee in return for some ideas for your site. Still others may not share any of their ideas with you unless you hire them for the entire job. Don't hire anyone unless you can discuss ideas first — even if you have to pay an hourly consultation fee. You'll save more money in the long run.

Also, be a bit cautious if the developer wants you to promise never to use any of the developer's ideas if you don't hire that company. The ideas may not be original, and agreeing to this could really restrict your ability to build a good site. Sometimes developers and designers try to bully others into believing titles or ideas are their copyrighted property — titles and ideas can't be copyrighted. Bone up on copyright in Chapter 16. Also make sure that you're working with a reputable company that won't be stealing work from other companies' Web sites. Learn how to check out who companies are in Chapter 25.

After you hear some ideas that you like, narrow the list of potential companies down to about three. Ask them the following questions:

✔ Who will own the work that the developer and the designer (more than one person or company may be involved) create for the Web site? (See the "Ownership rights" section, later in this chapter.)

✔ When will the work begin and when will it be completed? Now that you have definite plans for your site, the developer or designer can be more specific than in the initial proposal. (See the section "Development phases," later in this chapter.)

✔ How does the company want to be paid? (For more information, check out the "Payment milestones" section, later in this chapter.)

✔ How will the company let you test the site? (See the section "Testing procedures," later in this chapter.)

✔ What warranties is the company offering you? (The "Warranties" section, later in this chapter, can help you in this area.)

✔ Most importantly, is the company willing to negotiate the terms of the contract or is its contract a "take it or leave it" deal? Your Web site is an essential part of your e-business. Insist on your right to negotiate!

These preceding questions cover the *basic deal points* in Web site development deals (explained in "Deciphering the deal points"). You and the developer should discuss the deal points before you make a final decision on whom to hire. Do not agree to any of the points without consulting with an experienced lawyer; simply discuss the points with the company. Clearly communicate to the company that you're only discussing — not agreeing to — the points.

If you believe that you've found the coolest and most qualified people to design and develop your site within your budget and you're happy with the way they answer your questions, cast them! Book 'em for the show! Do the deal!

Doing the Web Site Development Deal

Always have a written contract with anyone who designs and develops your e-business Web site. (Chapter 3 provides tips about contracts.) Another smart move is to invest your money in the services of an experienced attorney to help you with your Web site development contract. Whether your attorney works with you in selecting a developer or merely handles the legal issues is up to you. (See Chapter 8 for some hints about negotiating with companies in other countries.) The following information helps you understand some of the legalese you will encounter when you do the deal.

Avoiding the form fatale

Web site developers usually have their own contract forms because they use them over and over again. Web Site Development Agreements often include an addendum or an exhibit. The standard part of this contract contains terms that generally apply to most of their deals, and the addendum or exhibit is specific to a particular job. Every contract is negotiable; don't let the line "this is the form we always use" persuade you to sign without first negotiating.

Don't fall for the "we like to keep our contracts short" bit that might lull you into signing a short contract without adding important points. Short contracts aren't always better than long ones. Often it's a paragraph that's *not* in the contract — rather than what's *in* the contract — that will hurt you.

If a developer doesn't want to pay the legal expense to have the main part of the contract changed, then have an amendment prepared. The *amendment* is a short agreement that changes some terms in the contract. It says something like, "Notwithstanding anything to the contrary stated in the master agreement . . ." and includes the terms of your deal. It may change any part of the contract, such as ownership rights, testing procedures, or other rights under the contract. Be sure that everyone dates and signs the amendment.

If you don't like what the developer's contract says and the developer refuses to change it, go somewhere else. In my experience, businesses that aren't flexible really don't want your business. If you ever run into a problem with them, you can expect to end up in court instead of resolving it out of court.

The CD in the back of the book contains a sample Web Site Development Agreement (one copy with explanations of the contract provisions and another copy without explanations), a Web Site Design Agreement (with and without explanations), and an Amendment to a Contract (with and without explanations).

Deciphering the deal points

Most business deals involve several critical points to raise and to discuss. The *basic deal points* involve important points that are very specific to one person's situation or deal. The *standard* or boilerplate provisions apply in contracts for all kinds of similar deals.

For example, suppose that you want to buy a three-bedroom house in Cincinnati near a good school for your kids. In this real estate deal, the basic deal points are that the house must have three bedrooms, it must be in Cincinnati, it must be near a school, and the school must be good for your kids. The standard provisions in the contract are things that are typical in real estate deals, like termite inspection reports, loan approval, and move-in date.

In Web site development deals, the basic deal points cover ownership rights, development phases, payment milestones, testing procedures, and warranties.

The standard provisions may include many elements, depending on the particular lawyer's preference. However, they normally cover these topics:

- ✔ Parties involved
- ✔ Definitions
- ✔ Term of the agreement
- ✔ Contract administrators
- ✔ Delays in the project
- ✔ Delivery of the work
- ✔ Services provided
- ✔ Expenses
- ✔ Specifications for the design and development of the site

- ✔ Payment of money
- ✔ Confidential information
- ✔ Indemnification
- ✔ Warranties and representations
- ✔ Limitation of liability
- ✔ Termination of the agreement
- ✔ The law that will govern the agreement

Ownership rights

Your site may contain certain copyrighted and trademarked material, that is, certain intellectual property (often called IP for short). For real estate or personal property, the one who pays for it normally owns it. Not so with intellectual property. Unless you're creating it for your employer, the one who *creates* IP owns it regardless of who pays for it — unless a written contract says differently. Therefore, you must have a written contract for any Web site that involves any transfer of ownership rights in intellectual property.

IP includes original text in some situations, logos, photographs, certain graphics, computer programs, and so on (see Chapter 16). The developer may do any of the following for your site:

- ✔ Create intellectual property, which may include technology, specifically for your site.
- ✔ Use technology or work the developer created in the past for itself or for other Web sites.
- ✔ Use material that belongs to you.
- ✔ With the proper permission, use property that belongs to a third party.

Many developers try to keep ownership of everything they create for you even though you're paying them to create it. For your own protection, insist that a developer assign to you (give you ownership of) all ownership rights in anything the developer creates specifically for you.

If the developer insists on keeping ownership in the work created for you, it usually means the developer wants to use it again. Beware! These components could become part of your competitor's Web site. Some developers may even approach your competitors and show them what a great job they did on your site!

Developers may also reuse certain technology that they created in the past for themselves or for other sites. Doing so often helps them keep their prices down. It's customary for them to keep ownership of work they created previously — before they ever began working with you. You need to have the unlimited right to copy it, to continue using it in your Web site forever ("in perpetuity"), and to make any future changes necessary for your site even if you don't hire the developers again. You won't own the work, but you will have the right to use, copy, and change the work for your site if you obtain a license from the developer/owner. A *license* is a contract giving you permission to do certain things with the technology. (For more on this topic, turn to Chapter 16.)

When the developer uses anything that belongs to a third party, that party must give you permission to use the work. If the developer obtains that material for your site, the developer normally obtains permission from the owner for the material to be part of your site. If you obtain the material for the developer to add to your site, it's customary for you to obtain permission from the owner. (See Chapter 16 for information on using stuff that belongs to someone else.)

Development phases

Examining and testing the site in progress are important steps. If you come across something that you don't want, you can stop it before the developer spends a lot of time and before you spend money on something you don't like. Set up distinct points or phases during the development process to approve the plan, approve the design materials, approve part of the site, and approve the final site.

The Web Site Development Agreement on the CD in this book includes a sample Addendum that shows how the parties to the contract divided development into phases.

Payment milestones

Developers shouldn't wait until the work is complete to be paid. It's too risky. Likewise, you shouldn't pay the entire amount up front before you see their work. Establish a schedule of partial payments due upon your approval of each development phase.

The Web Site Development Agreement on the CD in this book includes a sample Addendum that shows how the parties to the contract set up payment milestones.

Testing procedures

So many problems arise when companies don't describe specific testing procedures in their contracts. Be very specific in your agreement about how this process will proceed. Be sure that you'll be allowed to test the Web pages during development. Your contract may provide for a testing procedure like the following.

Your contract may specify that you have ten business days to test the site while it's under construction (*business* days don't include weekends and holidays; *calendar* days include every day). The number of days you provide in your contract depends upon your production deadlines; you may want fewer or more testing days. When you test, try the pages on different computers with different modem speeds and on different browsers to make sure that everything looks right and works properly. For instance, test your Web pages by using a PC with Netscape Communicator and Internet Explorer (in various versions). Then test them using another PC or notebook with all the various browsers and plug-ins. Test them again by using old and new Macs with various browsers and plug-ins, and so on.

The contract may state that if everything is okay, you must let the developer know so he can proceed to the next development phase. The agreement should include whether you let the developer know by e-mail, by fax, or by telephone (mail takes too long!). If something is wrong, the contract may state that you must give the developer written notice that explains what you did when the problem occurred. Then the developer checks the site, too.

Development agreements often state that the developer must fix the problem within a certain number of days. Again, the number of days depends upon your production schedule. If the developer can't duplicate the problem you found, then the two of you need to work together so that you can demonstrate how the problem happened. If the developer has the same problem, he tries to fix it. If he fixes it, you may have another ten days to test it, depending upon how many days you and the developer negotiate to include in your contract. You keep going through this process until all the problems are solved and all the bugs are exterminated!

However, sometimes a developer can't correct a problem after two or three tries (or whatever number of times you negotiate). For this reason, make sure that your contract gives you the right to either let the developer keep trying to fix it or to end the contract (terminate the agreement) and work with someone else.

Pay attention to any *implied approval* in the contract. Developers' contracts often state that if you don't notify them of problems within a certain time, it is implied that you approved the work and accepted it. You may then be stuck with the bug or have to pay the developer more money to fix it.

Warranties

Ask for some type of warranty, such as a warranty that the site will be error-free for six months after being completed or the developer will fix it at his expense. Of course, this applies only if the problem is due to the developer's work rather than the Internet service provider, the Web site host, or the maintenance people.

The CD with this book includes sample Express Warranty Provisions for Deliverables (one copy with explanations and another copy without explanations) that are often included as part of a Web site contract. For developers who don't provide warranties, the CD includes sample Warranty Disclaimer Provisions with explanations that may be part of a contract.

Parties

Identify all parties by their full legal names, their complete addresses, the type of organization if the party is a business, and where the companies were legally organized or formed. For example, the agreement may state that Lumexia Co. is a California general partnership at 555 Fifth Avenue, Los Angeles, California 55555. The other party to a contract may be a Florida sole proprietorship, a German GmbH, a Delaware corporation, and so on. You may need to find the other company some day, and this information will be important.

Definitions

If certain words in the contract may have different meanings depending upon who is reading them, define them in the contract. For instance, if the developer may use technology created by others as background technology for the site and the contract includes provisions regarding the right to use background technology, define *background technology* in the agreement. Define *deliverables* — the exact work the developer will be expected to deliver to you when the site is completed. Also, you may want to define which browsers must work properly with the site.

The sample Web Site Development Agreement on the CD in this book includes definitions that may be helpful to review. The version of the agreement with comments includes explanations of these definitions.

Term

The *terms* of an agreement refer to the deal points in the agreement, such as "terms and conditions of this agreement." But *term* of the agreement (*term* is often capitalized in a contract in this usage) means how long the contract lasts. Because contracts must have a beginning and an end, state precisely the date the contract begins and how long it lasts. Don't assume that it simply begins on the date signed and continues for a certain period of years, because the parties often sign the contract on different dates.

Contract administrators

Set up a contract administrator — a contact person — for each party to the agreement if you and the developer have several people working with you. Identify the contract administrators by name and include their direct telephone numbers and e-mail addresses. Require that these people act as coordinators to set up meetings between the parties, receive invoices or notices of delays in the project, and schedule all activities between the parties.

Everyone avoids a lot of headaches if you have one point person for each party who keeps things organized and running efficiently.

Changes

Require that any requested changes in the work or the project that may affect the fee, expenses, or completion date of the site be in writing and signed by both parties. Make sure that a written change order is required to state the amount of any increase in fees, expenses, and time.

Delays

Make sure that the contract requires the developer to let you know promptly as soon as the developer discovers that there will be a delay in the production. Agreements often require developers to notify people of delays in writing (by e-mail) and to explain the reason for the delay.

Specifications for design and development

Be clear in the specifications (the design and development plans) about what is going to be developed and designed for the site, and make your approval a condition before design or development begins for the next phase.

Delivery

Be specific about what will be delivered from the developer and when it must be delivered. Most development agreements require the developer to deliver the *deliverables* as defined in the agreement. Now *that's* computer legalese! Often deliverables are the computer code, the documentation that explains how the code works, and any other material created by the developer or necessary for the Web site owner to have in order to operate the Web site.

Services

Be specific about what the developer will do for the stated fee. Often the main part of the agreement simply states that the developer will provide those services that are described in the Addendum, which describes specific services for the specific project. These specific services may include providing advice regarding the concept for the Web site, creating a design for the site, and drafting, developing, and writing computer code for the Web site.

Expenses

Be clear about any expenses that the developer may incur, and that you may be required to pay, in addition to the development fee. You can require that no one incur any expenses over a certain amount that the other party will be responsible for unless it's approved in advance and in writing.

Payment

Be very, very specific about the payment due date. For example, the Addendum might state that payment is due at each milestone, but the main body of the contract might also state that payment is due 30 days after each due date. Watch out for inconsistencies and clear them up right away in writing.

Confidentiality

Make sure that the definition of confidential information is very clear so that everyone understands it. Many agreements include a confidential information provision in the contract. Under certain circumstances, agreements also include separate contracts, or confidentiality agreements, often called nondisclosure agreements (or NDAs for short). In a Web Site Development Agreement, confidentiality provisions are part of the agreement. This agreement may also require the developer's employees and independent contractors who work on the project to sign separate NDAs that require these people to keep confidential information confidential.

The CD in this book includes sample confidentiality provisions for contracts and sample Nondisclosure Agreements.

Indemnification

This is the "*They* screwed up, make *them* pay" clause. *Indemnity* is basically a type of security — to secure someone from being hurt or losing money. Indemnification is critical to cover your assets just in case the other party to the contract makes mistakes. For Web development deals, indemnification becomes an issue when the developer or the Web site owner (or both) is sued (or a legal claim is made) by someone else (a third party) because the developer or the owner didn't get permission to use some of the third party's material. This oversight leads to the developer, the Web site owner, or both being sued for copyright infringement or trademark infringement or something like that. The indemnity clause usually states that the one who failed to get the necessary permission has to pay all the attorney's fees and any judgment resulting from a lawsuit. (The contract doesn't state it exactly that way, but it usually means the same thing.)

When a lawyer writes a contract for his client, he may write an indemnity provision that requires the other party to indemnify his client but it doesn't require his client to indemnify the other party. With very few exceptions, this isn't fair. Always, always, always negotiate this clause so that the parties to the contract agree to defend and indemnify each other. For instance, the provision may state: "The parties agree to defend, indemnify and hold each other harmless from and against any and all claims, losses, damages, liabilities, costs and expenses (including reasonable attorney's fees) which arise out of, are connected with or directly relate to any breach or alleged breach of any representation or warranty by the other party hereunder."

Many sample contracts on the CD in this book, including the Web Site Development Agreement, include indemnification provisions with explanations.

Warranties and representations

These are promises, similar to vows, made to each other. They include promises that the work the parties to the agreement create is original, their work doesn't infringe on anyone else's rights, and their work won't invade anyone's right to privacy or publicity. When one of these promises is broken and some third party sues, the indemnification clause comes into play.

Beware if you see a section called "Disclaimers" or "Warranties" that includes something like this: "Developer does not warrant or guarantee that the Web pages will meet the Client's expectations and/or requirements, or that the operation of the Web pages will be without error or function uninterrupted, timely, secure, or error free. The entire risk as to the quality and performance of the Web pages resides with the Client." Although the first sentence means that there may be some bugs, that's probably okay. That's the nature of computer programming. But the second sentence means that it's *your* risk if the quality or performance isn't up to par. If your Web site isn't working, that's just too bad. You still have to pay them. My question is, "If they don't stand behind their work, why are you working with them!?" Sometimes developers don't even realize that their lawyers threw in this last sentence in their contracts. Take it out if you want developers to stand behind their work.

The CD includes a sample Warranty Disclaimer Provisions with explanations that may be part of a contract.

Limitation of liability

Developers often want to make sure that they will not be responsible for any lost profits that the Web site owner may suffer if the Web site isn't completed by a certain date. Web site owners may want to ensure that they're not responsible for extraordinary expenses or money unexpectedly paid by the developers to outside contractors if the owners breach the contract. Therefore, many companies agree to a contract provision that limits both parties' liability to a certain extent.

For instance, if either party breaches the contract, the other party may sue for *general* damages. Normally these damages may include the price one has to pay another to complete the work promised under the contract. The limitation of liability provision often restricts either party from being responsible for anything more than general damages, such as special or consequential damages (such as those lost profits from potential deals had the site gone up in time).

The CD includes sample Limitation of Liability Provisions with explanations, as well as agreements that include a limitation of liability provision, such as the Web Site Development Agreement.

Termination

You can choose from a number of ways to end a contract without a lawsuit. For instance, you may want to agree that either party may end the contract if you both agree to end it. However, be cautious about who keeps what money and who owns what deliverables in that event.

A developer may want to terminate the contract if your business becomes insolvent (runs out of money) before the project is complete (and before your final payment is due). You may hope to get the Web site complete even though you're out of money, but the developer won't want to put in the time and work just to risk not getting paid at the end of the production. You may want to terminate the agreement if the developer can't fix certain problems or bugs with the site after trying to fix them two or three times.

The CD in this book includes many sample agreements with various termination provisions, including the Web Site Development Agreement.

Governing law

Governing law is a particularly important issue when the e-business owner and the Web developer are in different parts of the country or different parts of the world. Particular laws may affect how certain contract provisions may be enforced if there is ever a dispute between the parties. Local attorneys may provide this information. Web site owners should always try to have the law in their state apply and should specifically say in the contract that the laws of their state will guide interpretation of the contract. If you can't get your way, however, don't let it blow the deal. It isn't always essential that the laws of your state rule the world, and developers often insist that the laws in their states or countries guide interpretation of the agreement. In addition, developers often require that any legal dispute regarding the contract be filed in a court near the developer's home base.

With the development deal complete, think about how you're going to maintain your site. You must keep it up and running smoothly to stay in business.

Maintaining Your Site

Web sites are living creatures. At least they are to those of us who spend hundreds of hours gazing at our monitors. Because they're supposed to grow and develop as the things around them change, they need attention and maintenance.

Maintaining the site includes the following jobs:

- ✓ Modifying various features of the site
- ✓ Checking links to other sites to ensure those sites are current
- ✓ Changing text as requested

 ✔ Updating other parts of the site upon request

 ✔ Fixing any bugs that crawl into your site (computer bugs are nasty creatures that make your site do funky things you don't want it to do)

Many Web site developers also provide maintenance services. Often they include a maintenance deal as part of their development agreement. You may, however, prefer to hire someone else to maintain your site. In either case, a maintenance deal is a fairly easy deal to do. Simply make sure that your agreement does the following, which are often the same provisions included in the development deal:

 ✔ Identifies the parties

 ✔ States a term for how long the services will be provided

 ✔ Describes the services

 ✔ Clearly indicates what fees are charged for which services

 ✔ States when payment is due

 ✔ Designates a contact person for each company

 ✔ Ensures that the maintenance company will maintain confidentiality

 ✔ Includes the date of the agreement

 ✔ Is signed by both parties

Maintenance contracts don't need to be long-term deals. Each party should have the right to terminate the agreement for any reason with advance notice, such as 14 days notice or 30 days notice.

If the Web site developer or Web site host will provide maintenance services for your site, your agreement could be as simple as slipping a paragraph into the Web site development contract or the Web site hosting agreement. It might state something like this: "Company will provide maintenance services up to an average of one (1) hour per month per Web page for a 6-month period. This service includes minor changes or updates to links, text, and graphics to existing Web pages. Any design or development of new Web pages, extensive changes, or services provided in excess of the stated hours will be billed to Client at the hourly rate of $___. Either party may terminate this Maintenance Agreement thirty (30) days after providing written notice of termination to the other party."

A sample Web Site Maintenance Agreement (a copy with explanations and a copy without explanations) is on the CD with this book.

Chapter 5

Finding a Launch Pad

● ●

In This Chapter

▶ Selecting a Web site host

▶ Pricing the services

▶ Putting together your hosting agreement

● ●

Back in the prehistoric times of the 1950s, the fastest flying machines were ballistic missiles that could soar to foreign countries. Shortly after Russia's launch of Sputnik, an American team of rocket experts began planning a super-rocket that would shoot into space. Someday it would land men on the moon.

Planning this mission meant figuring out things like the necessary orbital speed to reach space, the size and type of hardware to use for the rocket, and ways to track and communicate with the rocket in orbit. Experienced engineers emphasized the importance of the launching facility: They could not reach their goals unless, in the design stage, they could make the rocket and the launching pad compatible mates. Ultimately each be useless without the other.

Such is the connection between your Web site and the place that will host your Web site. Unless you select the right launching pad to thrust your e-business into the digital domain, your site will be a dud.

Finding the Right Web Site Host

You can choose from a few ways to get onto the Net. A dial-up connection with an Internet Service Provider (ISP for short) may get *you* to the Internet, but it will leave your Web site behind. It merely connects you, as a user, to the Internet.

For your Web site to be on the Internet for other people to see, the files that make up the pages of your Web site must be stored on a *server* (a special kind of computer) that connects to the Internet through an ISP. This is where a Web host comes into play. Unless you're really tech savvy and plan to buy your own servers to keep at your own pad, you need a Web host.

Exploring your options

A *Web site host* is a computer server that stores your Web site files and connects them to the Internet. A company that offers Web site owners the opportunity to have their Web sites on the host computer is said to provide Web site hosting services. The company is often called a Web site host or Web site hosting service.

These companies may offer a variety of services. Depending upon the company, you might do one of the following:

- ✔ Use the host's servers to store your Web site and connect you to the Internet (very basic hosting services).

- ✔ Use the host's servers to store your Web site and connect you to the Internet as well as hire the company to perform other Web site services for you (special hosting services).

- ✔ Make a deal with another company to have your Web pages part of its Web site that uses a third party to host the site (called *co-branding*).

- ✔ Buy your own servers to keep at the host's facility, where the host connects them to the Internet (called *co-location services*).

Many Web portals, which are Web sites that offer a variety of information, community chat rooms, and links to other sites, offer co-branding opportunities for people who want to have their Web sites on the portals' Web sites. These companies often attract millions of visitors from around the world, and include America Online, MSN, and Yahoo!. Some portals are also known as online services.

Which host you should select depends upon the type of e-business you run and the amount of traffic (visitors) you anticipate at your Web site. If you're brand spanking new to this Internet thing, read some e-business newspapers or online magazines, hit some parties, schmooze, network, and eavesdrop on conversations to find out all you can about Internet technology. The appendix includes a list of some sources for industry information. You need to determine, either on your own or with the help of an Internet consultant, your special requirements.

Getting in touch with your needs

Planning an e-business can be quite different from planning a traditional storefront business (also called a brick-and-mortar business). Planning an interactive Web site requires you to think about the logical steps necessary to make these kinds of transactions work well. Different e-businesses have different needs. Companies selling goods for online purchasing have special technical requirements to enable visitors to shop, compare, order, and pay for the items online in an easy-to-use and secure environment.

Someone who provides advice by e-mail may be using his Web site merely to advertise those services. His site needs only a reliable e-mail service. A person promoting services that she performs only in person has very few technical requirements for her Web site because it's only used to describe the services. However, it may be important to her that all information about the customers she solicits from her Web site be kept confidential.

The owners of a media Web site providing news and information must have constant access to the site to update the information from day to day. Someone who entertains online may need special speed and download capabilities for his Web site to offer videos and music to visitors.

Some types of e-businesses need a site that allows visitors (also called users) to be very interactive. Other businesses may require nothing more than a connection to the Internet and e-mail. As for anticipated traffic at your site, the number of visitors to expect depends upon your particular target market, whether it's local or international, and how much money you plan on spending for advertising and marketing to let people know about your site.

Because you may not know your Web site's technical requirements until you develop your site, it may be too early to decide on a Web site host before you build your site. As you work on the design for your Web site, you'll better understand your needs and your expectations. At that point, it's a good time to start looking for your launch pad.

Hosts in foreign lands

Some Web sites are hosted in countries far away from the home of the Web site owner. Some e-companies attempt to avoid laws in certain states that may restrict their business activities or tax their sales by using hosting services in other states or countries. See Chapter 2 for more information on personal jurisdiction. Many gambling sites try to avoid laws that prohibit their activities by using a hosting service on an island or a Native American reservation where gambling may be legal. Using hosts in other lands sometimes meets the Web site owners' business and legal needs, and other times it doesn't. The law is still unsettled in this area.

Finding a company

Personal referrals to companies are often the best way to find a company to suit your needs. Ask other e-businesses who hosts their sites. If you don't gather enough names, searching the Internet can help you locate a Web host.

Asking the right questions

Once you decide what you're going to offer to your Web site visitors, how many users you're expecting, and how you're going to design your site, you'll be ready to compare Web host companies. You'll want to know whether their services can meet your site's technical requirements, your business concerns, and your service needs. Think of lots of "what if" questions to ask, such as, "What if your servers go down? What happens to my data?"

The CD in this book includes a Checklist of Questions to Ask Web Site Hosting Services so you can print it out and hold it in your hand when asking questions.

Technical questions

In this section, you get to learn some technical words. You'll probably hear them from Web hosts. It's your first step toward becoming a full-fledged techie. Or at least sounding like you know one.

It's probably difficult to find an affordable Internet consultant who has a technical background to help you with this part of the process. Therefore, ask any techie you know for some advice and spend some time reading up on these topics (books or the Net) so you'll get a better idea of what may work for you. The appendix lists some Web sites that may be useful. Depending upon the type of e-business you're setting up, the following issues may be important to you. Ask the Web hosts about these technical issues.

Being aware of hardware and software

Your Web site is designed to work with various types of servers (hardware) and software that connect you to the Internet. Make sure that the Web host uses hardware and software that are compatible with your Web site's format.

Connecting to the Internet

Many Web hosts and ISPs put too many Web sites and users on the same, small Internet connection. Doing so causes traffic jams that slow down your site, making your visitors feel like it will take another millennium to get your site to respond to them. They won't stick around that long, and you'll lose potential customers.

Web hosts offer shared lines to the Internet, dedicated lines that devote themselves entirely to your Web site (very expensive), and various types of lines that affect speed (T-1 lines are very fast). Ask the Web hosts what they offer and what percentage of their lines are filled at their peak time. The lower the percentage, the better. If your Web site shares a line with zillions of people because the service is free, you might get trapped in rush-hour grid-lock. However, I often find that the salespeople can't answer these questions. Testing other sites hosted by the same service may be your best bet. Ask the company for a list of addresses for Web sites that it hosts.

Securing your site

Web hosts may or may not have complete control over access to your Web site on their servers. You and those to whom you give special access may be responsible for maintaining the site. Anyone else should not be able to change the content on your site or to access any information from your site that you don't provide to the public. Therefore, you should ask about the following:

✔ The type of security the Web hosts have at their facilities to prevent people from breaking into their buildings and getting information from the servers

✔ The host's process for preventing security breaches or security holes that allow unauthorized users (those infamous hackers) to access your Web site to change your content or gain information about your customers

✔ How the host detects intruders (hackers)

✔ How the host might prevent search engines from automatically indexing and linking those pages on your Web site that only allow users with passwords to use them

✔ How, and how quickly, the host notifies you when a security problem may affect your Web site

✔ What procedures the host has in place to resolve any security problems

The term *firewall* refers to a system designed to prevent unauthorized users from accessing a network of computers. This system can be implemented in hardware, in software, or in a combination of both. As messages pass through the firewall, the system examines them to determine whether they're okay to pass through. If the messages don't meet certain security criteria, the system blocks them. Ask the hosts about their firewalls.

Server response time and throughput capacity

Server response time is the amount of time the server takes to respond to a click on your Web site. *Throughput capacity* is the amount of data that the server can pump through the lines. When a visitor clicks on various parts of your site, you want your site to respond quickly. If it doesn't, the visitor may leave.

Although this response time is also affected by the user's Internet connection, you want to make sure your end is as fast as it can be. With the help of your Web site developer, you can determine whether the host's capabilities in this regard are sufficient for your site. Server response time of one-half of one second is a good time to request.

Ask the Web hosts for URLs (the Web site addresses) for some of the sites they host. Visit those sites during really busy times to see whether the response times are good enough for you. Keep in mind that the individual Web site content, such as lots of graphics or animation, also affects the speed of the response time.

Server uptime

When a server is down, it means something isn't working properly and people won't see your Web site on the Internet. You want to minimize down-time and maximize uptime. Therefore, you want the host to assure you that the server uptime will be *24/7,* meaning 24 hours per day, 7 days per week, except for a certain amount of time for the host to do maintenance work on the server (like one hour per day in the early morning hours).

Unexpected occurrences cause servers to go down. Ask the host how such problems are handled.

Server and system redundancy

Earthquakes, floods, fires, power outages, and telecommunication glitches occur from time to time, causing computer systems to crash. Some e-businesses and many Internet companies want a Web host to provide system redundancy — a duplicate so the entire system won't fail.

The host may provide this service by offering to *mirror* the servers. This term means that another server at a different building acts just like the server at the main location. If something goes wrong with one, the other will be working.

The host may also connect the servers to more than one Internet Service Provider that connects them to the Internet just in case one of the ISPs goes down (stops working). Some Web hosts have personnel on their premises 24 hours per day to make sure that everything is working properly. Other companies have systems that page key personnel if a problem arises — kinda like a computer doctor on call.

Asking the right business questions

In addition to the technical requirements, you need to consider several important business points concerning your content and customer information. Discuss the following subjects with the Web hosts.

Backing up

If something goes wrong with the Web host's servers, make sure that you have a current backup copy of your entire Web site. Doing so is especially important if your employees or independent contractors upload information from their computers directly to your Web site from time to time, changing the site.

Ask the Web hosts how often they make complete backup copies of the Web sites on their servers. Also ask them whether they deliver copies to site owners. They shouldn't charge you extra for delivering copies to you.

Customer information

The host you select will have access to your Web site. Making sure the host keeps your customer information confidential is important for a number of reasons:

- ✔ The information is valuable and useful data that you may use for future business strategies.

- ✔ You may not want your customers' personal information, such as e-mail addresses, ending up on junk e-mailers' lists simply because customers visit your site.

- ✔ You don't want your customer information in the hands of your competitors (see Chapter 9).

- ✔ You must ensure that you're complying with privacy laws and your own privacy policy (see Chapter 15).

When you and the Web site hosts discuss your reasons for wanting to keep your information confidential, they should have no problem agreeing to it. However, if you're co-branding on another company's Web site, these issues may become negotiating points with that company. Part of the reason they're co-branding your site may be to access your customer information. For more information on joint marketing, see Chapter 11.

Servicing your needs and desires

Many Web hosts offer a myriad of additional services for e-businesses. They may offer the following extras.

Domain name registration

Hosts may offer to register your domain name, a topic that I discuss in more detail in Chapter 6. This service makes things easier for you because you don't have to provide all the technical details to the registrar.

When registering a domain name, you must provide an administrative contact person's name (for things like billing) and a technical contact person's name (for technical stuff). The Web host often lists one of its employees as the technical contact person and lists you or your employee as the administrative contact person. However, in the past some hosts listed their employees as both contacts. Therefore, only the host could make any changes in the registration. This situation could be a major hassle if you decide to switch hosts or to change your mailing address. Some unscrupulous companies out there may even list themselves as the owner of the domain name rather than you! Require the host to list you as the owner of the domain name, you or one of your employees as the administrative contact, and your company as the only one that may authorize changes.

Search engine submission

Hosts often submit your Web site URL to Internet search engines. Search engines allow people to find your Web site when they enter keywords with those engines. This is easy to do on your own because most search engines' Web sites provide instructions on how to submit your site to their search engine. Many people prefer to save the money and invest their own time to submit their sites. It's a good idea to search for your site on those search engines' sites the month following your submission to make sure that your site comes up. You can gather the names of search engines from online directories and by searching for search engines on search engines!

Promotion

Some hosts offer advertising, marketing, and publicity services to customers. In general, advertising involves creating or placing specific advertisements in various media. Marketing focuses on sales efforts. Publicity targets media coverage of your e-business and Web site.

If you're not looking for business from the masses, be sure to target your promotional campaigns to the areas where you'll most likely reach your potential customer base.

If you're going to spend money on those services, make sure that the people are very experienced. Even experienced professionals have a hard time getting their e-business clients noticed. You'll definitely be wasting your money working with amateurs. For more information on promotion, see Chapter 11.

User support

People who visit your site may have questions about your company, your goods, or your services. They may also have problems navigating through your site. Some hosts offer to respond to company inquiries, technical questions, or both. If they do, ask the hosts who answers the inquiries; how quickly they will respond, and what they will do if they can't answer the question or resolve the problem.

When you have people who do not work for you providing support and interacting with your potential customers, be very cautious. Your business policies, image, and reputation are at stake. If people whom you don't know or can't control treat your customers in a manner that's contrary to your way of doing business, it could really hurt your e-business. Unfortunately, you may never know whether they're treating your customers badly. Customer service is crucial to the success of your e-business, so limit any strangers' contact with your customers to indirect responses and offer your customers an alternative way to contact you directly, such as a special e-mail address link on your site.

Customer information and server logs

Most Web hosts provide basic data concerning visitors to your Web site and other similar information. It's often raw data that you have to put together and figure out. This information can be invaluable in making your future business plans.

Some hosts analyze this data and prepare a report for you so you can learn more about the people who visit your Web site and how they use your site. Even if you receive an analyzed report, however, make sure you get copies of the raw data, too. You may decide to have someone else help you analyze the information as well, such as a marketing consultant.

Modifications

Some Web hosts offer to maintain or make some modifications to your Web site for you. They may check the links on your site periodically to ensure they still connect to active sites. If you opt for this service, make sure that the host doesn't make any modifications without your approval and that you review the changes before they go live on your site. That's *live* with a long *i* as in alive. Going live means making the Web content available to the world on your site when your site is online as opposed to working on a file privately in your computer.

Budgeting the Cost

How much will hiring a Web site host cost? It starts at "free." Some online companies that want to co-brand with you may include hosting as part of their subscription fee that you're already paying to use their service.

Basic hosting services with a Web host begin as low as $19 per month. The average price for a small, basic site is $25 per month. If you need a dedicated line that connects only you to the Internet, the monthly fees can run you thousands of dollars per month. Fees for special services will either be part of a package price or priced separately. Make sure that the Web host goes over all the prices with you.

Suiting Up for Takeoff

After you have your technical, business, and service questions answered, it's time to see whether the topics you discussed are in the actual Web hosting services agreement.

The Web host normally prepares the contract for Web hosting. Because the company is in that business, it usually uses the same basic contract form for most of its customers. The company may negotiate changes with individual customers. However, some companies do not enter formal contracts for small Web sites. They simply list their services and other information on their Web site. If you sign up with one of these companies, save a copy in a file on your hard drive and as a print-out. If the company makes additional promises or representations to you by e-mail, save these, too. Take notes during any telephone conversations and save them as further documentation.

If the host isn't charging you a fee or is charging you only a basic, low-rate monthly fee, don't expect to negotiate your contract. It may be a "take it or leave it" deal. Negotiating for a relatively small hosting fee isn't worth the time and expense to them. Ditto if you're dealing with a huge company and you're a mini, itsy-bitsy, tiny, little e-business site with only a handful of customers. On the other hand, smaller Web host companies may be willing to accommodate you.

If you're paying a good chunk of money and the host hedges in making changes to the contract by saying, "it's a standard form we use," don't accept that as a final answer. You and the host can always prepare an amendment or an addendum to the basic contract to change some terms or add special requirements and promises that relate specifically to your Web site. Remember, if you're paying big money to a Web site host, include legal fees in your budget to pay an attorney to go over the agreement for you.

Covering the technical requirements

Make sure that the Web host promises to provide at least the minimum technical requirements that you need. These promises should cover hardware, software, Internet connection, security, server response time and throughput capacity, server uptime, and system redundancy. For server response time, you could set a guaranteed maximum time limit.

Agreeing on the services

List all the services the Web host promises to provide. Be specific. The services may include any of the following:

- Making backups of your Web site and delivering copies to you at certain times
- Registering or transferring your domain name and submitting your Web site URL with search engines
- Providing promotional services

✔ Providing you with technical support and user support

✔ Maintaining server logs with information about your users and providing you with that information

✔ Maintaining and making modifications to your Web site

✔ Processing the changeover of your Web site to a different host when the agreement ends or if the host goes out of business

Handing off the site

At some point you'll probably leave your Web host. Anticipate this parting and include arrangements for it in your contract. The agreement should require the host to transfer files and your domain name registrations upon your request within a certain period of time. You might consider requesting the host to keep your site up for an additional 30, 60, or 90 days so that you'll have time to make sure your site at the new location is free of bugs. In this way, you can avoid downtime.

If you're in a co-branding situation or dependent upon any of the host's services, such as e-mail, make sure that you state in the contract whether you may use these services at your new location.

If you change domain names, it's especially important to have the right to leave a pointer at your old address that provides your new Web site address (URL), name, and a link to the new site. Be sure to include a statement in the contract about how long you can leave the pointer on the previous host's site.

Reacting to problems

Response time to notify you of security or other problems is extremely important. You may want to describe the procedures that the host promises to follow if there's a security problem or if the servers go down and no one can access your Web site. When servers go down, you can lose valuable data, such as customer orders. State the time periods during which these problems should be resolved.

Also specify how soon the host must notify you about security problems and how long the host has to transfer your domain name and files to another Web host at the end of your agreement. Specify the number of days within which the host must perform these actions.

Protecting confidential information

Maintaining the confidentiality of your information, including any data about your customers and other users of your site, is extremely important. No one should be able to use this information without your permission. Often Web site hosting services are connecting your Web site through another company, an Internet Service Provider. Make sure that the hosting service can guarantee that the ISP will also keep all your information confidential.

The contract should include the Web host's agreement not to disclose any of your confidential information. Be sure to state that the names and raw data may not be used for any purpose without your permission. In addition, the contract should prohibit the host from altering, copying, or disclosing the content of your Web site or any of your other information without your consent. You may also want to prohibit the host from commercially exploiting (promoting or selling) the content of your site for any reason without your permission.

Managing the money

The contract must list the fee you are to pay and any additional charges. If possible, lock in your prices so you won't have to worry about price hikes. Watch out for catchall phrases like "and any other charges." A huge and unexpected invoice could end up on your desk one day for those other charges.

Maintain control of how much money the host is charging you. Make sure that any expenditures or additional services are subject to your *prior* approval. This means the host must get your approval *before* spending money or performing the services.

Chapter 6

Staking a Claim to a Domain Name

In This Chapter

▶ Selecting a domain name

▶ Registering your domain name

▶ Resolving domain name disputes

SCENE ONE: 1922. A woman wants to locate a dress shop. She walks down a mud-filled street looking in store windows. Eventually she finds one store at the other end of town.

SCENE TWO: 1993. A man needs to find a plumber as water from a broken pipe leaks toward his antique record collection. His fingers do the walking through local telephone directories, but he only has the white pages and he doesn't know the names of any plumbers. He cries as he tries to save his collection.

SCENE THREE: Today. A teenager wants to buy toys for her newborn niece, but she doesn't know the name of any toy stores. Where should she shop? She sits at her computer and types www.toys.com.

Would a Domain by Any Other Name Be as Sweet?

Today you can find a business anywhere in the world without leaving your desk, even if you don't know the company's name. You can search by subject matter or keywords in online directories, search engines, or navigation software like RealNames. Or simply type a name as a URL (Uniform Resource Locator) — a domain name.

Domain names identify specific Web site locations. The Latin alphabet uses the letters a through z and the numbers 0 through 9. Technically, domain names represent the Latin equivalent of an address in the form of xxx.xxx.xxx.xxx. Letters and numbers take the place of the x's. When you type the domain name, your Web browser looks through the Internet for the address represented by those numbers. Your computer and the computer at that address talk and agree to make that Web site appear on your monitor. Some companies are exploring ways to use non-Latin alphabets so that Chinese and other symbols may be a part of domain names.

The first way many people try to locate an e-business is by typing the name as a domain name. For instance, if I want to find information about the *For Dummies* book series, I might simply type www.dummies.com. You don't need psychic powers to find a business's Web site — just intuitive reasoning. Or dumb luck.

Good domain names not only help people find a Web site, but, if they're catchy or simple, also make the Web site easy to remember. Staking a claim to a domain requires more than pulling a name out of a hat, however. It requires selecting the right name and registering it as a domain. When you try to register a name, you may find yourself wrestling with those *cybersquatters,* who register domain names using famous trademarks and then try to sell them back to the trademark owners or to their competitors. They must not realize that there's a law against that in the United States.

Selecting a name

Selecting the right name for your domain is a three-step process. First, come up with a great name and the right generic Top Level Domain to use (explained in the section "What's in a name (and a gTLD)?"). Second, make sure that someone else isn't using the domain name. Third, determine whether your name is a trademark that legally belongs to someone else.

What's in a name (and a gTLD)?

Founders of a company usually name their business and products. Because not everyone has this talent, however, some companies hire consultants in the name game. Yes, there are companies — often called *branding consultants* or *branding firms* — that specialize only in naming companies and products.

When e-businesses want to come up with a domain name, they want an easy-to-remember name or a clever, creative name. An easy-to-remember name is often a generic word like *business* or *travel* or *toys*. The companies hope that people will try typing a common term like these when searching for certain goods or services on the Internet.

Clever or creative names are words that an e-business wants to brand. In marketing terms, some words have *name recognition*, and some words become *brands*. Name recognition simply means that people know who you are. Familiarity draws customers.

Branding is much more than name recognition. It means that the name is associated with the goods or services as well as a certain level of quality. A brand has some kind of special meaning to customers. They want to buy it or use it because it's important to them in some way. For instance, many types of cola are on the market. However, Coca-Cola and Pepsi-Cola are distinctive brands of cola. Most cola drinkers prefer one over the other for some reason other than the name alone. A strong brand may even extend to a company's other products, making customers believe that an entire line of products meets the same quality standards.

Using certain generic Top Level Domains is also important to many businesses. Called gTLD for short, they're the letters at the end of a domain address that designate certain things: .com for commercial enterprises and individuals, .org for nonprofit organizations, and .net for Internet networks. There are also country-code domains, such as jp for Japan, fr for France, de for Germany (Deutschland), and il for Israel.

There's no strict requirement on how gTLDs are used, however. Don't assume that a .net is actually an Internet network, an .org is a non-profit venture, or a .jp is truly someone in Japan. Although some countries are beginning to restrict use of their country-code domains and the government restricts use of .gov, people use just about any gTLD that they want to use.

People searching for a business often try typing the name followed by .com before using a search engine or directory. For this reason, a domain with a .com address is coveted by businesses. The .com address is also developing into something very special because the media, investors, and others now refer to Internet businesses as "dot-coms." Dot-com is taking on a life of its own! If available, go with a .com for your e-business, but don't select a hard-to-remember name simply because you want to use a .com but greatname. com isn't available; go with greatname.org or greatname.net if they're available and make sense.

Name availability

When you come up with a list of possible names, go to the Web site of a domain name registrar to determine whether the domain name is available. The section "Registering your domain name," later in this chapter, describes how to find domain name registrars.

If you really want a .com domain name and it's unavailable, you may offer to buy the name from the registered owner. The names and contact addresses for the owners of domain names are available to the public through most registrars' sites or at www.whois.com.

Brand-building basics

Any e-business should consider building a brand name from the very start. Here are some tips about creating an effective brand:

- Make building your brand part of your overall business plan.

- A brand is more than a name. It's part of a business. Make the time to understand what your customers want, and provide those things to them in connection with the name.

- When trying on some names for the right fit, share them with close friends or associates. If they remember them ten days later, it's a good sign.

- Use a name that allows you to expand into other products or services and doesn't limit you to just one thing. For example, you may be selling food now. In the future, you may sell CDs and videos. Don't use a name that makes people think only of food.

- The name should fit the business, the image, and the people who run the company.

- People who work for you affect your brand — your company image. Often the CEO of a company has a major impact on branding when speaking on behalf of the company. Select the right CEO.

- Branding requires that you have quality to back up the name.

- Branding isn't about marketing to everyone. It's about marketing to a target audience. If your market is consumers, focus on specific types of consumers. If you're a business-to-business (B2B) company, do something to really set your services and products apart from competing businesses because establishing a brand with other businesses is often more difficult than establishing a brand with consumers.

- Don't expect results in a few months. It may take years to establish a brand. The "Kodak Moment" didn't happen overnight.

Some people register domain names to use in connection with their business or personal Web sites. Other people are in the business of simply registering domain names, but they have no intention of ever using these names for businesses they own. They buy up dozens or hundreds or thousands of common names and then try to sell them to people for a profit. They sell them either through direct solicitation or by auctioning them off on the Internet.

Registering domain names just to sell them to others for a profit creates a stumbling block for small business that can't afford the inflated prices. Trademark laws require the owner of a trademark to use it or lose the right to prevent others from using it. Hopefully, someday people must use their domain names. If they don't, they should give them up so others can use them.

If you're going to buy a domain name from someone else, you may get lucky and meet someone who is willing to sell it for a fair and affordable price. Unfortunately, some companies are paying millions of dollars for domain names. They've created such a frenzy that it's hard to find someone who doesn't want to become a millionaire for a name. You may have to put that thinking cap back on and come up with another name.

Things are changing all the time in the world of the Internet. In the future, more gTLDs may become available to describe certain goods and services more specifically than .com. Keep checking press releases on the sites of domain name registrars and other organizations involved with domain names to get your new gTLD as soon as it comes out. Web sites listing directories of registrars around the world are in the appendix.

Legal rights

Is the name you want to use actually a trademark that belongs to someone else? A trademark can be a name, a phrase, or a symbol, such as a logo. They're collectively called *marks*. Not all marks are trademarks that the law protects, however. (See Chapter 7 for more on trademarks).

If you use someone's registered trademark as your domain name, you could end up as a defendant in a lawsuit. One guy reportedly spent over $250,000 in legal fees defending his right to use a domain name. He lost in the trial court to a big corporation, but he won on appeal. Then the corporation promised to appeal to the U.S. Supreme Court! That ain't cheap.

You can do some checking on registered trademarks in the U.S. on your own by using the U.S. Patent and Trademark Web site database for new and pending registrations. (See the appendix for more information.) Other countries don't currently have their trademark databases available on the Internet, but you can hire a company to conduct a search.

Just because you *can* search on your own doesn't mean you *should* search on your own. Trademark law prohibits use of similar trademarks as well as identical trademarks. However, the law prohibits use only for the goods or services that are the same *or* substantially similar to those used by someone else with that trademark. An experienced trademark attorney's opinion is often very important.

In common law countries (see Chapter 1), someone may have trademark rights even though the trademark isn't registered. Therefore, it's really best to hire an experienced trademark search firm to do the search. A partial list of firms is in the appendix. Hiring an attorney to review the search firm's report and render an opinion on your use of the name is also important.

Although no one can absolutely guarantee that you'll never get sued, receiving legal advice *not* to use a name may keep you out of hot water. Some people skip the legal step of searching trademarks when they select a domain name. Doing so is up to the individual. However, budgeting money for preventive measures like checking legal rights is important. You could lose your house and your business by making the wrong legal move.

Registering your domain name

Your domain name is an address that allows one computer to communicate with other computers. Just like a social security number or other unique identifier, no two domain names can be exactly the same. Therefore, certain organizations are authorized to distribute these names to ensure that they comply with Internet Protocol.

The registrars

Until the late 1990s, the U.S. government was in charge of Internet addresses, and only one company could register .com, .net, and .org domain names. In late 1998, an international nonprofit organization run by private enterprises (rather than a government) took over this function. It's called the Internet Corporation for Assigned Names and Numbers (ICANN for short). Registering domain names is now under ICANN's guidance. Figure 6-1 shows the ICANN home page.

ICANN accredits many companies around the world to register domain names ending in .com, .net, and .org for you. The companies are called *accredited registrars.* You can find out who they are on the ICANN Web site listed in the appendix. Various entities, called country-code domain registrars, have authority to register domain names ending in country codes. In some countries, the government is the registrar. In other countries a university, a for-profit company, or some other organization is the registrar.

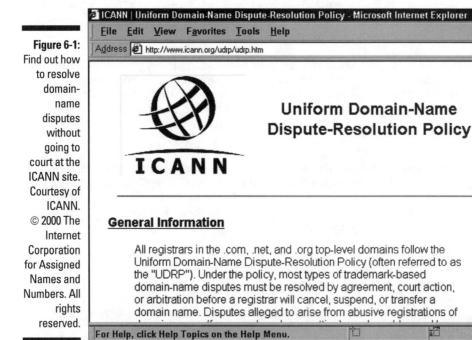

Figure 6-1: Find out how to resolve domain-name disputes without going to court at the ICANN site. Courtesy of ICANN. © 2000 The Internet Corporation for Assigned Names and Numbers. All rights reserved.

Just because a company offers to register your domain name doesn't mean that it is the accredited or authorized registrar. Many companies are in the business of doing it for you, that is, acting as your agent to register your domain name. Using such a company means that you're probably paying more to register the name. Register with a company on the ICANN list if you're using .com, .net, or .org. For country-code domain names, ask the registrar whether it's going through any other registrar to obtain the name for you. The appendix lists a Web site directory for country-code domain registrars.

The registration process

The registration process is simple. You can either register the name for immediate use or reserve the name for later use. Instructions and Frequently Asked Questions (FAQs) with answers are on the registrars' Web sites. If one registrar's instructions confuse you, try looking at another registrar's site.

To register, you must provide information like your address, telephone number, and fax number. You must also provide names of the people acting as a technical contact to deal with computer questions, an administrative contact to handle business questions, and a billing contact to receive invoices and pay the fees.

You must also sign a Registration Agreement that may include the following information:

- ✔ The owner of the rights to the domain name. Normally the administrative contact is considered the owner, so make sure that your name, not someone who registers the name for you, is the administrative contact.

- ✔ Notice of the registrar's right to suspend, cancel, transfer, and modify the domain name or other information under certain circumstances.

- ✔ How the registrar uses your information. Some registrars may sell it to marketing companies, so make sure that you're aware of this and compare the policy with the policy of other registrars.

- ✔ Your agreement to abide by the Dispute Resolution Policy adopted by ICANN or some other policy described in the agreement.

- ✔ A limitation of liability so that no one will haul the registrar into court for something you do.

- ✔ Your representations and warranties (promises) that you will use the domain name in a lawful manner and that the information you provide in the registration is accurate.

- ✔ An explanation of which state's or country's laws govern the contract terms and the court in which you agree to appear if a dispute arises.

Be aware of the jurisdiction paragraph, and refer to Chapter 2 for more information on jurisdiction. This paragraph normally requires you to agree that if you end up in a lawsuit over your domain name, you may have to go to court where the registrar is located. In fact, if you're having one registrar register your domain name with another registrar, you may have to appear even farther away. For example, you may have a New York registrar handle registration of an Israeli country-code domain for you. The terms for using that domain may require you to appear in a court in Israel if there's a dispute. If you live in Israel, that's cool. But if you don't live there and aren't into traveling a lot, watch out for this clause. You may want to use a registrar closer to home.

After signing up, you pay the fee and you're the proud owner of the domain name. It really does feel kinda cool when you get your first one!

Wrestling over Domains

Organizations all over the world are trying to figure out ways to resolve domain name disputes out of court and in more cost-effective ways. For example, the World Intellectual Property Organization (WIPO) is talking to registrars to develop a Dispute Avoidance and Resolution System (called DARS). By the time you read this, some systems may be in place. You can check for updates on the WIPO Web site listed in the appendix.

In the meantime, governments and organizations are taking on cybersquatters and other people who register domain names in bad faith. These are people who try to make money by registering and selling domain names that include famous or not-so-famous trademarks.

ICANN came up with one way of dealing with these people. In late 1999, it approved a Uniform Domain-Name Dispute-Resolution Policy with procedures to help enforce the policy. The policy is supposed to help resolve disputes between the registered owner of a domain name and any other person or company that claims that the domain name violates its rights. This policy applies only to domain names ending in .com, .net, and .org. However, anyone may use the policy in a registration agreement, so it may apply to other domain names as well.

All registrars for the .com, .net, and .org gTLDs must include this policy in their registration agreements. A mandatory administrative proceeding is part of the policy. It's an informal resolution process handled by approved organizations around the world called Administrative-Dispute-Resolution Service Providers (providers for short). (You can locate the providers and obtain more information at the Web sites listed in the appendix.) By signing the registration agreement containing this policy, the domain name registrant agrees to go through this proceeding for certain kinds of disputes, as described in the sidebar "The name in the domain falls mainly in the claim."

The party who has a problem with a domain name files a complaint with, and pays a fee to, one of the approved providers. The fee can be $1,000 or more (far less than the cost of a lawsuit). The provider notifies the domain name registrant, who must then respond in writing. The parties don't appear in person for the proceeding; they submit papers with their arguments to the approved provider.

The provider has a panel of experts review the papers. One or more of these panelists makes a final decision. The provider can then order the domain name to be canceled or transferred to the other party. The whole process should take only a couple months to complete. This time period may seem long, but it's much shorter than the year or more that it takes to resolve a lawsuit.

Although domain name registrants must agree to go through the proceeding for certain types of disputes, either party may still file a lawsuit in court. However, the proceeding does offer a more cost-effective and expedient solution for certain problems.

You don't have to hire an attorney to represent you in this proceeding. Doing so may be more helpful, however, because you may need someone who can argue trademark or other legal issues. Rules for the proceedings, including how to file complaints and responses, are on the providers' Web sites. Keep in mind that the outcome is based on the written papers submitted, so make sure that you hire a lawyer who communicates effectively in writing. Litigation lawyers, as opposed to those who handle contracts, may be more effective in writing persuasive arguments.

Registration agreements aren't the only tool that people are using against bad-faith registrations. The United States now has a law prohibiting *cybersquatting*, which is registering domain names that use famous trademarks and then trying to sell them back to the trademark owners or to their competitors (see Chapter 7 for more on trademarks).

I hope that you never have to wrestle over a domain name. Conduct some research before you claim a name. Do your best to protect your name: Stake your claim, and then stand your ground. It's still pretty wild territory out there. But with the right name and the right plan, you may become one of those e-businesses yelling "Yahoo!"

The name in the domain falls mainly in the claim

The Uniform Domain-Name Dispute-Resolution Policy requires that you, as the person registering a domain name, must agree to allow a person appointed by an organization (called a provider) to try to resolve claims made about your domain name. The process begins when a person or company (the complainant) makes a claim contesting someone's right to a domain name to the provider. The claim must conform

(continued)

(continued)

to the provider's rules. The claim must assert the following:

- The domain name is identical or confusingly similar to a trademark or service mark in which the complainant has rights; *and*

- The other person has no rights or legitimate interest in the domain name; *and*

- The domain name has been registered and is being used by the person in bad faith.

The *ands* are in italics because the person complaining must claim that *all* of these things are true, including the part about bad faith. The policy also defines bad faith, which means *any one* of the following:

- Circumstances indicate that the person registered or acquired the domain name primarily for the purpose of selling, renting, or otherwise transferring the domain name registration to the complainant (who is the owner of the trademark or service mark) or to the complainant's competitor. The person did this for valuable consideration (to make money or receive other property) in excess of documented out-of-pocket costs directly related to the domain name. In other words, you tried to make a profit off the complainant's name.

- The person registered the domain name in order to prevent the owner of the trademark or service mark from using the mark in a corresponding domain name. This guideline applies only if you've been engaging in a pattern of this type of conduct (you've done it more than once).

- The person registered the domain name primarily for the purpose of disrupting the business of a competitor.

- By using the domain name, you intentionally attempted to attract, for commercial gain, Internet users to her Web site or online location. She did this by creating a likelihood of confusion with the complainant's mark (using a name that's the same or substantially similar to the mark). The confusion means that people may believe the complainant is the source or sponsor of the person's site or of any goods or services on the site, the complainant is affiliated with the site (or goods or services on the site), or endorses the site (or goods or services on the site).

If someone believes that the domain name registration breaches the good faith requirements and fits one of these categories, then complainant files a complaint with one of the providers. The complainant must follow specific rules in preparing the complaint. Both ICANN and the provider have procedures, so the complaining party must follow both sets of rules.

The complainant selects which provider to use and pays a fee. The provider notifies the domain name registrant of the complaint. The registered owner of the domain name must then respond in writing within a matter of days, usually 20 days. The panel of experts will then decide the case. This policy does not limit the right to file a lawsuit in a court.

The only thing that can happen to the domain name owner during this process is that the domain name is canceled or transferred to someone else. The complainant can't be awarded money or a judgment of any kind.

The policy may change from time to time. Changes are posted on the Web sites of the registrars, ICANN, and the providers, some of which you can find in the appendix.

Chapter 7

Protecting Your Name

*H*ave you come up with a really great name and logo for your e-business? How about names, logos, and slogans to identify and describe your products or services? And don't forget that domain name!

Names or symbols identify everything from models of cars to medical associations. Names, logos, and slogans are collectively referred to as *marks*. Names and other types of marks can do much more than identify people or things, however. As someone continues to use the same name or other mark over time, a distinct association in people's minds begins to develop between the name, the person or thing, and a level of quality. At that point, the mark can impact an individual's behavior when he decides which product to purchase or which company he wants to do business with.

Companies spend time and money to build this distinct association in the minds of the general public or a specific group of people. Therefore, a company using a specific name or other mark doesn't want other companies to use the same, or a substantially similar, mark. Doing so could confuse the company's market (customers, potential customers, and other business alliances) regarding the source of the goods or services associated with the mark, divert sales or profits from the company, and benefit the other companies unfairly.

To prevent this confusion and unfair use of another's mark, the law provides people with the right to prevent others from using names and other marks that qualify as trade names or trademarks. *Trade names* are names that identify a company or business. *Trademarks* and service marks (often referred to collectively as trademarks) are words, phrases, or designs (like logos) used to identify the source of goods (trademarks) and services (service marks) and to distinguish them from the goods and services of others. Some trade names that identify a company *and* identify and distinguish certain goods or services may also be trademarks. The law, however, affords greater protection to owners of trademarks than to owners of trade names, as you will see in this chapter.

To protect company assets, e-business entrepreneurs must be aware of the rights in names and other marks. They must protect their rights in the names and other marks that they use in connection with their businesses, goods, and services. The entrepreneurs must also avoid the risk of legal liability for unlawfully using a name or other mark that belongs to someone else. Most importantly, e-business entrepreneurs must learn to defend their rights in names and other marks when big bullies that are using similar marks try to scare the new entrepreneurs into giving up their names.

Understanding Why Trademarks Need Special Attention

As early as medieval times, people who produced various goods for sale affixed *marks* — names or logos — onto their goods. These "marks of trade" identified the origin of the goods. Purchasers could then determine who made them and whether they wanted to buy them from that particular tradesman. Once a tradesman's mark began to be associated with a certain level of quality, he ran the risk of competitors using the same mark to benefit from his reputation. Therefore, the law began to protect a right in certain types of marks.

Not every mark is protected by trademark law. Only those marks that meet certain legal requirements are protected by trademark law, as discussed in the section "Getting trademark rights," later in this chapter. Therefore, I use *name* or *mark* in this chapter to refer to a name, phrase (like a slogan), or design (such as a logo) and *trademark* to refer to a name or other mark that may be protected by trademark law.

Weaving a web of trademark laws

In the United States, the earliest laws protecting marks were made by state courts (common law) and state legislatures (state statutes). These laws granted rights to the owners of certain types of marks in order to prevent other tradesmen from deceiving or confusing purchasers as to the true origin of a product. Trademarks also became a way to establish goodwill for a company's goods and services.

Eventually federal law began to protect rights in trademarks when the U.S. Congress enacted the Lanham Act. This law governs the rights in marks used to identify and distinguish goods and services sold in interstate and foreign commerce (across state lines or from the United States into another country).

Today, a single trademark dispute involving an e-business may involve rights under common law, state law, federal law, and foreign law that require an experienced trademark (or intellectual property) attorney to sort out. However, the basic definition of a trademark and the rights of trademark owners are essentially the same throughout the United States and the world.

Sorting out trademark rights

Does it really matter much whether a word or a logo is a trademark? Well, if you're using it, then yes. If you're using a word or phrase or logo in connection with your goods or services, then you're spending time, energy, and money on it. If it can be a trademark, then certain rights go along with that distinction. Those rights in a trademark may be your rights that need protecting, or they may be another person's rights that you're violating (infringing). Therefore, it's important to understand the rights that belong to a trademark owner.

Generally, owners of trademarks can prevent others from using the following:

- The *same* mark on goods/services that are the *same* as the owner's goods/services. For instance, you may not sell candy lawfully in the United States under the name See's Candies because that mark already belongs to someone else who sells candy in the United States.

- The *same* mark on goods/services that are *substantially similar* to the owner's goods/services. If you want to develop and sell software that helps people using personal computers share digital files, you can't lawfully call it Acrobat Reader. A product called Acrobat Reader is already on the market. Although the product may not be exactly the same as your software, it's still a software product to be used with personal computers.

- A mark that's *substantially similar* to the owner's mark on goods/services that are the *same* as the owner's goods/services. You may not lawfully sell chocolate candy under the name Sea's Candy since Sea's is a mark that's substantially similar to the mark See's that is used for the same goods — candy.

- A mark that's *substantially similar* to the owner's mark on goods/services that are *substantially similar* to the owner's goods/services. You may not lawfully sell your software that shares digital files under the name Acrobatic Readers. The mark and the product are substantially similar to the mark Acrobat Reader that identifies certain software.

Getting Trademark Rights

Selecting a name, registering a domain name, writing a slogan, or designing a logo doesn't mean you have trademark rights in those marks. The law protects only certain types of marks. In addition, you must do more than simply select, register, write, or design a mark. In most countries, you must use the mark in commerce or register the mark with a governmental authority.

When more than one person is using the same mark or substantially similar marks, determining who owns rights to the mark is rarely a simple process. Usually an experienced trademark attorney must analyze a complex combination of laws with the particular facts. The most important factors to consider are the following:

- ✔ Whether the mark is the kind of mark protected by trademark law
- ✔ How the mark is being used by the person who claims to be the trademark owner
- ✔ Whether the mark is a registered trademark
- ✔ When the trademark was registered

Selecting the right kind of mark

Trademark law does not protect all types of marks. It protects only names or other marks that *distinguish* the goods and services from the goods and services of others. That is, the mark must be *distinctive*.

Usually marks are categorized as one of the following:

- ✔ Generic (not distinctive)
- ✔ Descriptive (usually not distinctive)
- ✔ Suggestive (usually distinctive)
- ✔ Arbitrary or fanciful (always distinctive)

Generic names basically define a product or service. Trademark laws don't protect these names because other people have to use them to identify those particular goods or services. Therefore, generic names cannot be trademarks. For instance, *e-business* defines a type of business. *Computer* defines a certain type of product. Therefore, any company that uses "e-business" for its e-business services may not trademark *e-business* or prevent others from using it. Any company that uses *computer* for any computer products or services may not trademark that name or prevent others from using it. Generic names also include .com, .org, .net and other generic Top Level Domains (gTLDs). No one may trademark a gTLD or prevent others from using it.

Descriptive names are words that describe the goods or services. Trademark laws don't protect these types of marks, either. Descriptive names and other marks (such as logos) are more specific than generic ones, but they still don't distinguish goods or services from those of another. For instance, the name San Francisco Computer Museum doesn't distinguish it from any other computer museum in San Francisco. A name like The Coffee Shop doesn't distinguish it from other coffee shops — the word *the* isn't enough to distinguish it.

On the other hand, sometimes people use descriptive marks for things other than what they describe. For example, *pink carnations* describes a color and type of flower and apples *describes* a fruit. However, you may want to use the name Pink Carnations or a logo depicting pink carnations for a tuxedo rental business. Or a computer company sells Apples and uses a logo of the fruit, but the goods aren't fruit — they're computers. These names and logos are no longer descriptive because they don't describe the thing normally associated with the word or picture. These marks become suggestive, arbitrary, or fanciful, which trademark laws protect.

Suggestive marks may be trademarks. These names are normally somewhat descriptive, but they have more, well, oomph. They suggest, rather than describe, the nature of the goods or services. An example might be iRead for a service providing library directories over the Internet. It suggests something to do with reading over the Internet.

Arbitrary and fanciful marks are definitely trademarks. They usually convey nothing about the nature of the product at all. These marks uniquely identify the products or services. Examples are Kodak for photographic prints and Starbucks for ready-to-drink coffee.

Generic and descriptive marks may be *part* of a trademark that includes suggestive, arbitrary, or fanciful marks protected by trademark law. For instance, Amazon.com may prevent others from using amazon or amazon.com for certain goods or services, but Amazon.com may not prevent anyone from using .com.

Although suggestive, arbitrary, and fanciful marks can be trademarks, there are a few exceptions:

- The law usually doesn't recognize geographic, immoral, or offensive words or logos as trademarks. However, geographic words may be part of a trademark as long as they don't confuse or deceive anyone regarding the source of the goods or services. For instance, the name of a famous wine-growing region can't be used on a wine that has no relation to that region.

- Names or logos that deceive the purchaser — deceptive marks — can't be trademarks, either. For instance, "Fresh" as a name for a canned food product may be deceptive.

- Usually surnames are trademarks only when used with other words, such as Ford Trucks or Flamingo Hilton.

Using the mark

The purpose of trademark law is to identify the source of goods and services and to distinguish them from the goods and services of others. Logically, if there are no goods or services sold in commerce, there is no need to identify their source. Therefore, the law requires the mark to be used in connection with the sale of goods or services in commerce (in commercial trade) before a mark becomes a trademark that others may be prevented from using.

In some countries, trademark rights do not begin until the mark is registered with a governmental authority. In other countries, such as the United States, certain rights begin as soon as the person uses the mark in commerce. Upon registration, the trademark owner has additional rights. The distinction between trademark rights in civil law countries and common law countries is important for international e-businesses to understand.

Using the mark in civil law countries

In civil law countries, you must register the mark with them before trademark laws will protect it in those countries. Civil law countries include Japan, France, Germany, and Brazil.

The first to register the mark has the right to use the mark in connection with the goods and services. Anyone who tries to register the same or a similar mark for the same or similar goods/services is out of luck. There are various ways to register the mark for civil law countries, as set out in the section "Registering trademarks around the world," later in this chapter.

Although civil law countries may not require you to be using a mark in commerce when you apply for registration, they normally require you to actually use the mark in commerce in their country within a certain number of years after registration or you may lose your trademark rights in that country.

Using the mark in common law countries

Common law countries include the United States, Canada, England, Australia, and Israel. Generally in common law countries, the first party to actually use a mark in commerce — in connection with the sale of goods or the rendering of services — is the one who owns trademark rights for that mark. However, there are some technicalities, explained in the sections "Using the mark first" and "Defending Trademark Rights," later in this chapter. It's not as simple as it sounds, of course.

A mark is used on goods when it's placed on the goods that are sold or transported in commerce. A mark is used for services when it's used or displayed in the sale or advertising of services, the services are rendered in more than one state, and the person rendering the services is engaged in commerce in connection with the services.

In general, using the mark means using it in a public manner so that it creates an association in the minds of the public or your potential customers between the mark and its owner. For example, a U.S. court of appeals held that using a mark in limited e-mail correspondence with lawyers and a few customers was not actual use of the mark in commerce. On the other hand, including the mark in a press release announcing the imminent launch of a Web site may be actual use if the release is widely distributed to the public.

So what is *not* use in commerce? Here are some examples:

- Selecting a name to use
- Printing letterhead with the mark
- Posting the mark on a bulletin board (the traditional kind)
- Merely registering or using the mark as a domain name
- Filing a trademark application or obtaining registration for the mark
- Displaying the mark on a prototype or demo for a potential buyer
- Depending upon the individual circumstances, merely advertising without making any sales

When you own rights in a trademark, your rights exist as long as you continue to use your mark in commerce or until someone else successfully challenges your rights and establishes that their rights are superior to your rights. See the sections "The senior user" and "Abandoning rights," later in this chapter.

You can get some early protection for your mark before you begin using it by filing an Intent to Use application for registration. I explain this more in the section "Registering trademarks around the world," later in this chapter.

Using the mark first

In civil law countries, the first one to register a mark gets the rights. In common law countries, the first one to use the mark in commerce gets the rights. Except what if more than one person is using the mark and they don't know about each other? Then one person files for trademark registration, but the other one is using it in *tons* of markets already. Who gets what?

As long as a mark is not a famous mark like Kodak or Disney, two or more people can be using the same marks, or substantially similar marks, at the same time as long as they're using them for different goods or services. Famous marks get special treatment, which I discuss in the section "Diluting a famous trademark," later in this chapter. When people are using similar marks for similar goods or services, figuring out each party's trademark rights gets very tricky.

The senior user

When more than one person is using the same (or a substantially similar) mark for the same (or substantially similar) goods or services, ownership rights generally belong to the first user. This person is called the *senior user*. The person who begins using it later is the *junior user*.

If no one registers a particular mark with the federal trademark office, the senior user has the rights to the mark *in the geographical location where she's using it in connection with the goods or services*. The junior user has rights in his geographic location on two conditions. First, the location must be somewhat distant from the senior user's location. Second, he must have begun using the mark in good faith, which means without knowledge that someone else was using it first.

For instance, someone uses a mark in New York. Later, another person uses the same mark in Texas without knowing about the New York person. They both have rights to use the marks in their geographic locations.

The important point about junior use is good faith. This is where federal registration plays an important role. If a mark is registered with the federal trademark office, the law presumes that everyone nationwide has notice that someone owns, and is using, that mark. It's called *constructive notice*. It makes no difference whether or not the junior user actually knows about the registration or researches the Internet and finds nothing. If a mark is registered, other users are said to have knowledge of it. Therefore, the junior user can't be using a mark in good faith if the mark was registered before he began using it.

Tacking on time

What happens if you have a name you've been using for a long time, but you're changing it a bit? What if you're selling different things now, but you still want to use that mark? Can you claim seniority because you're using a mark you've had for a long time? Not necessarily.

Courts in some jurisdictions allow a trademark owner to claim seniority in a new mark based upon the date it first used a similar, but technically distinct, mark. The trademark holder is asking the court to "tack" his first-use date in the earlier mark onto the subsequent mark to give it an earlier date of first use. Therefore, tacking gives his new mark seniority over marks of other users.

Courts allow tacking because they don't want to discourage trademark owners from altering their marks in response to changing consumer preferences, evolving aesthetic developments, or new advertising and marketing styles. However, tacking is allowed only in exceptionally narrow instances.

For movie buffs

Here's how one court ruled in a tacking situation. One company registered The Movie Buff's Movie Store, another person registered MovieBuff, and then the original company began using moviebuff.com. The owner of the registered mark MovieBuff filed a lawsuit to stop moviebuff.com. The court wouldn't allow the owner of moviebuff.com to acquire the seniority of its older mark, The Movie Buff's Movie Store. The court stated that there would have to be evidence that consumers considered The Movie Buff's Movie Store and moviebuff.com to be the same service or evidence that the two services were indistinguishable before there could be any tacking.

To be able to tack the seniority onto the new mark, the two marks must be so similar that consumers generally regard them as essentially the same. When a court must decide whether tacking applies to a situation, the court considers whether the two marks would be viewed as the legal equivalent of (or indistinguishable from) one another such that consumers consider both as the same mark.

Registering trademarks around the world

If you're using your trademark in interstate or international commerce (across state lines or between the United States and another country), it's important to register your trademark with the U.S. Patent and Trademark Office (referred to as the U.S. PTO or the federal trademark office; the Web site address is provided in the appendix). Once a trademark becomes a federally registered trademark, anyone else using the same or a substantially similar mark for the same or substantially similar goods or services can't use the trademark in additional areas of the country. The use of the mark that's not registered is basically frozen to the territories where it was used up to the time the other trademark holder filed the application to register the mark. The person who registers the mark may use the mark in every territory throughout the country where the other person is not using the mark.

Federal registration also provides many legal benefits if the registered owner ever has to sue anyone for trademark infringement. These benefits are fairly technical. Basically having a federal trademark registration is like having Goliath added to the trademark owner's team of lawyers.

If you're expanding your business into an e-business, double-check the status of your trademarks! Any changes you made to older trademarks may not be protected. Don't assume that the original trademark will cover the new e-business.

Do you need to hire a lawyer to register a trademark? According to the various government Web sites, no. However, I've heard lots of stories about people messing things up so badly on the applications that they have to start all over again and lose their filing fees — as well as their rights connected to the earlier filing date of the application.

In the United States, for instance, someone could file an application for the same name between the time your application gets kicked out of the system and the time you file it again. The federal trademark office doesn't check who used a mark first, only who filed the application first. If you've been using the mark longer than the other applicant, you need to start special proceedings to get the other application denied. Otherwise, *your* registration could be denied!

So, again, are you required to hire a lawyer to file your trademark application? No. Should you hire a lawyer or a "trademark agent" (a person outside the U.S. who's an important trademark expert but not a lawyer)? Probably. Just make sure that the person is experienced in handling trademark registrations. See Chapter 23 for tips on finding a lawyer.

If you want to continue receiving the benefits of registration, you may have to file certain documents with the appropriate trademark office to confirm that you're still using the trademark after a certain number of years (like 10 years). Check the trademark filing requirements with an attorney in that country or on that country's trademark office Web site. Some of their Web site addresses are in the appendix.

Searching for available trademarks

The government offices where you file your application will not normally return your filing fee if they find that someone else registered the same or similar mark before you. Using an Internet search engine to determine whether someone else is using the mark you want to use doesn't necessarily lead you to registered trademarks. Whether or not someone is using the name on the Internet or as a domain name is important, but a Web search doesn't provide complete trademark information.

The place to search for registered trademarks in civil law countries is through their official registrars. If you don't live there or know how to conduct a search, it's best to hire an experienced search firm.

For common law countries, searching is more challenging. Because rights arise from first use rather than registration, the search must be more extensive. Professional search firms often check databases for fictitious business name filings in states and counties, state trademark registrations, and other possible databases, in addition to the official registrar.

At the time of this writing, the trademark offices in the U.S., Australia, and Canada offer databases of registered trademarks on their Web sites. Anyone may search the databases for free. However, make sure that you understand how to search it properly before you rely on your own results. The Web site addresses are www.uspto.gov/web/menu/tm.html, www.ipaustralia. gov.au, strategis.ic.gc.ca/sc_mrksv/cipo/welcome/welcom-e.html. You can also find these addresses in Appendix A and on the CD.

If a search firm's report shows any similar names, be sure to seek the advice of a lawyer on using the mark. Don't assume that you can't use it, but don't use it without seeking experienced advice.

Many companies on the Internet offer trademark search services. Not all of them sufficiently train their employees or thoroughly search important databases for you. The appendix lists some search firms. I can't guarantee they'll be perfect or that there aren't other good services out there, but these are names that various governments provided to me or that lawyers use for their clients.

Filing an application

Depending upon how much you can afford, you'll probably want to register your marks in every country in which you plan to do business using your mark. In the United States, state registration really protects you only within that state. Registration with the U.S. Patent and Trademark Office protects you nationwide. Their Web site address is www.uspto.gov as shown in Figure 7-1.

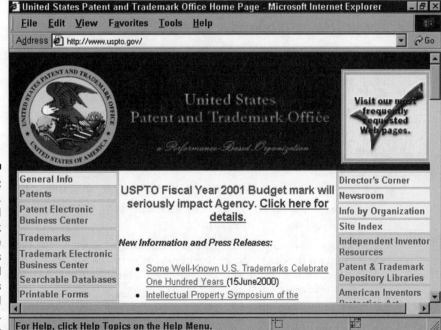

Figure 7-1: The U.S. Patent and Trademark Office registers federal trademarks in the United States.

If you actually use the mark in interstate commerce (across state lines or from the U.S. to a foreign country), you can file an application based on your actual use of the mark. If you truly intend to use the mark relatively soon, you can file an application based upon your intent to use the mark.

 The CD with this book includes copies of the U.S. PTO's Trademark and Service Mark Application, the Trademark and Service Mark Statement of Use, and the Trademark and Service Mark Request for Extension to File a Statement of Use. Additional information for these forms may be found at the U.S. PTO's Web site. The Web site address is provided in the appendix.

 Many countries are parties to treaties regarding trademarks. The Trademark Law Treaty requires the countries that signed this treaty to provide basic *maximum* requirements for filing applications. In other words, these countries can't make it too burdensome or difficult. Australia, Japan, the United Kingdom, and the United States are among the countries that signed this treaty.

The government offices normally charge a filing fee for your application or registration. The filing fee is based upon the number of classes of goods or services in which you're using your mark.

 Most countries follow the same classification for goods and services in the treaty called the Nice Agreement. Therefore, the classes are the same for Australia, France, Germany, Israel, Japan, the United Kingdom, and the United States, among others.

Depending upon the country, applications are normally mailed or transmitted electronically to the appropriate office. Basically the application requires the owner of the mark to provide the following:

- ✔ Name, address, and form of business (such as individual, partnership, corporation, and so on)

- ✔ The mark (in words or design or both)

- ✔ A declaration of intent to use the mark in commerce or of actual use, signed by the applicant (or certain other specified people)

- ✔ A statement indicating that the applicant seeks registration of the mark (the word, logo design, or both)

- ✔ A reproduction of the mark (a typed or drawn example of it)

- ✔ A list of the goods or services with which the mark is used (to specify which class they fall into)

- ✔ Copies of the mark as it's used in commerce, such as the actual label used on products, advertisements for services, or print-outs of Web pages (not all countries require proof of use before registration — the United States and Canada do)

- ✔ The filing fee

Calculating class

Here's an example of how filing fees are figured. Suppose that you're using your mark for computer software and for providing computer consulting services. The mark would then be in two classes — one for the software (goods) and one for the consulting (services). Perhaps you create advertising banners for others and produce a radio show. These services fall into two different classes: advertising services and entertainment services. If the filing fee is $325 per class, your filing fee for two classes would be $650 (not including legal fees).

When filing an application, some people also include a self-addressed and stamped postcard listing the name of the mark and the names of the documents enclosed in the package (application, declaration, check, samples or specimens of the mark). Usually the federal trademark office returns the postcard stamped with the date the documents are received. This way you'll know it actually got there. It's also a good idea to send the application envelope by certified mail or use a service that allows you to track it if it's lost or if you need to contact the trademark office's mail room for some reason.

Many countries have excellent Web sites explaining the application process, trademark rights, and other information. Some of them are listed in the appendix.

Registering your trademark in more than one country

As you know by now, it's important to be the first to register your mark. If your e-business reaches into other countries, international protection is important. An important treaty, which includes provisions concerning trademarks, is the Paris Convention. A basic principle of this treaty is that citizens of the member countries (the countries who signed the treaty) may seek protection of their marks under the trademark laws of any other member country. Paris Convention member countries include Australia, Brazil, Canada, France, Germany, Israel, Japan, Singapore, the United Kingdom, and the United States.

One advantage of this treaty involves filing dates. If you file an application for trademark registration in any Paris Convention member country, and then you file applications in other Paris Convention member countries within six months, you are given the filing date of the *first* application for the other applications. In other words, your application is given priority over any other applications that were filed after that date in the other countries. This treaty provision can be important when you're planning to launch a new product or service.

Other international treaties also help make registering the mark in more than one country a bit easier. If you're only going to do business and use your mark in a couple countries, you probably only need to register the mark in those countries. However, if you plan on using the mark in at least a few European countries, there's another way to register your mark that may be beneficial for you. It's called the Community Trade Mark.

The Community Trade Mark covers rights for all the countries that are part of the European Union, even if you use it in only one of the countries. And you don't have to be a citizen of one of those countries to register the mark and receive Community Trade Mark rights and protections for all of the EU countries.

You can file the application for this type of registration with the Office for Harmonization of the Internal Market (OHIM) in Alicante, Spain. Once filed, the office checks the registries for all of the countries in addition to the Community Trade Mark registries. The application can be filed in any of the official languages, which are English, French, German, Italian, and Spanish. The Web site address for the OHIM is in the appendix.

Deciding the best and most effective way to register your mark around the globe is up to you and your advisor, including your financial guru.

Although registration provides certain benefits to trademark owners, trademark rights can be challenged under certain circumstances. In other words, the mere fact that someone obtained a federal registration for a trademark doesn't mean that the owner actually used the mark as stated in the application. Often a company's registered trademark is challenged by others through an administrative proceeding or in a lawsuit. Registration may add Goliath to the team, but Goliath can be challenged.

Defending Trademark Rights

When someone uses another's mark in connection with their goods or services, that person may be violating someone's trademark rights. It's called *trademark infringement*. The infringer can be sued, required to pay money, or forced to stop using the mark immediately. For certain types of trademark infringement, courts may impose criminal penalties such as imprisonment and huge fines.

All too often with the Internet, however, the *big guys* try to squash the *little guys* by claiming to have very broad trademark rights. These big and powerful companies may not have the rights they claim to have. Therefore, don't give up your name before you check out everyone's rights.

Assume that you receive one of those nasty cease-and-desist letters that are flying into e-businesses all over the world. It goes something like this:

"Dear Person We Are About to Sue:

We are the legal representatives for OURGREATCLIENT, who is the registered trademark owner of the mark THISISAGREATNAME. We have learned that you are blah blah blahing and using this mark. Our client owns exclusive rights to this mark. You shall immediately cease and desist from any further use of this mark. You shall deliver to us all of your products upon which the mark is affixed and shall provide an accounting to us for all profits derived from use of this mark. If you do not comply with this demand within 10 days, we will [they explain how they're going to get nasty, file a lawsuit, seek an injunction to take all your products, and so on].

Yours Very Sincerely,

Mr. Angry Lawyer"

A Cease-and-Desist Letter with explanations and a copy without explanation are on the CD with this book.

What should you do if you get a cease-and-desist letter? First, call your trademark lawyer. Next, you can think about some of the following information in this section so you don't go completely crazy while you're waiting for your lawyer to call you back.

Designating the registered goods and services

Even if a mark is registered, it is registered only in connection with very specific goods or services within a designated class. There could be 20 different trademarks for the name Aria — from macaroni to clothing to earplugs to body lotion — all owned and registered by different people.

Before assuming that someone else owns rights to a name you want to use or have been using, check some things out. If it's a U.S. trademark, you can check the following information on the trademark database with the U.S. Patent and Trademark Office on its Web site (the address is in the appendix):

- ✔ Under which classification is their trademark registered?
- ✔ How is their product/service described in the registration?
- ✔ When was it first used?
- ✔ When was it first registered?

From this information you can get some idea about whether you're in a lot of trouble or just a big hassle.

Abandoning rights

The next question that often comes up from trademark owners who receive cease-and-desist letters is, "But are they still using the trademark?" A person can obtain rights in another's mark if it's been abandoned. However, a mark is abandoned only if the owner's actions indicate that it's abandoned and if the owner actually intends to abandon it. Not using the mark for a while doesn't mean it's abandoned.

On the other hand, if the mark hasn't been used for a very long time (a number of years), a court may decide that it's abandoned if the owner doesn't prove an intent to resume using it. Proving abandonment can be an expensive and time-consuming process if the owner disputes the claim of abandonment.

Infringing rights

When a trademark owner claims someone is infringing upon his trademark rights and threatens a lawsuit, the owner usually seeks an *injunction,* a court order forcing the other person to stop using the mark. The owner may also seek payment of money damages by the infringer.

Obviously, one of the most important questions to be answered is, "Who has senior rights to the mark?" After this question is answered, the next question is whether the senior owner's rights were infringed.

The senior mark and the junior mark do not need to be identical to prove infringement. Using a substantially similar mark in commerce is an illegal infringement if it meets the following conditions:

- ✔ It's used in connection with goods or services.

- ✔ It's presented in a manner that is likely to mislead other people as to (a) the source, (b) the origin, or (c) sponsorship of the goods/services. This is called "likelihood of confusion." The question is not whether the two marks would be confused for each other. The question is whether use of the similar mark is likely to cause consumers or purchasers to confuse the source of the goods or services as being that of the senior mark owner.

Whether there is a likelihood of confusion is not determined easily. It requires an analysis of various factors described in numerous court opinions. To make this determination, you need to consult an experienced trademark lawyer. Find a lawyer who keeps up with the various court opinions and interpretations and then, using that knowledge and experience, analyzes your unique set of facts based on those legal decisions to give you an opinion on how a court may decide your issues. Chapter 23 provides tips on finding a lawyer.

Arbitrary and fanciful marks, due to their distinctiveness, tend to receive more protection by the courts than suggestive marks. Here are some other factors that a court typically considers when answering the question of whether there's a likelihood of confusion between the marks:

- ✔ The similarity and uniqueness of the marks and how they're used
- ✔ The similarity of the products or services and their markets
- ✔ The sophistication of the target consumers/purchasers to distinguish the two marks
- ✔ Any actual confusion in the market for the two marks
- ✔ Any intent of the alleged infringer to pass off the products as those of the other

If, in balancing the answers to these and other questions, a court believes that use by the alleged infringer is likely to cause confusion, an infringement will be found.

Courts may find an infringement when someone uses a domain name with a trademark that belongs to someone else, if the Web site is used to sell a product aimed at the same target audience — even if the product is somewhat different. Conditions of the marketplace are often a guide. The more common it would be for the product to come from the same company, the more likely consumers might be confused.

Cybersquatting

A cybersquatter is someone who registers a domain name of a well-known trademark that belongs to someone else and then tries to sell the domain name back to the trademark owner or someone else at a much higher rate. For instance, one cybersquatter registered panavision.com and tried to sell it to the owner of the trademark panavision for a profit. In effect, the cybersquatter is holding the domain name in ransom — the trademark owner won't be able to use the domain name unless he pays the cybersquatter money to buy the domain name at a higher price.

In 1999, the federal Anticybersquatting Consumer Protection Act became law. It makes cybersquatting unlawful if the following two conditions are met:

- ✔ The person registers, uses, or traffics in a domain name that is a trademark, or confusingly similar to a trademark, that belongs to someone else. *Traffics in* essentially means that the person is in the business of buying and selling these domain names.
- ✔ The person has a bad faith intent to profit from that trademark.

Although the law doesn't define *bad faith*, it lists some factors to consider to determine whether someone is acting in bad faith. All of these factors aren't included here since some of them need quite a bit of legal explanation. However, the answers to the following questions can help determine whether someone is acting in bad faith:

- ✔ Does the person who claims to own the trademark truly own the trademark rights?

- ✔ Is the alleged cybersquatter trying to divert consumers from the trademark owner by creating a likelihood of confusion? Is he doing this in such a way that could harm the goodwill represented by the trademark? Is he doing this for profit or to tarnish or disparage the trademark?

- ✔ Is the alleged cybersquatter trying to sell the domain name to the trademark owner or to someone else for a financial gain? Does he have no intention to use the domain name to offer goods or services? Has he never used the domain name to offer goods or services?

- ✔ Did the alleged cybersquatter provide any false information when applying for registration of the domain name?

- ✔ Did the alleged cybersquatter register a number of domain names that he knows are identical or confusingly similar to the trademarks of others?

- ✔ Does the domain name not include any legal names that belong to the alleged cybersquatter?

- ✔ Does the alleged cybersquatter not have any legal right to use the mark under any legal principles such as fair use (see the section "Fair use," later in this chapter)?

If any or all of these questions are answered with a *yes*, then the person who registered or used the domain name could be a cybersquatter. The decision depends upon the individual circumstances of the case. A court must consider all relevant evidence presented regarding any bad faith intent of the alleged cybersquatter before the person can be held liable for cybersquatting.

If the person is liable for violating this law, then he will have to give up the domain name and pay the trademark owner either profits lost by the trademark owner or damages that can range from $1,000 up to $100,000 *per domain name*.

Fair use

Sometimes a person can use someone else's trademark without permission. This use is very limited, however.

Fair use means that someone may use the mark if it's only incidental to fair comment. For instance, a mark may be used to compare two similar products in advertising. It must truly be fair. The courts won't tolerate untrue claims.

Newspapers and other reporting agencies may also incidentally include trademarks in their reports. Such is the case in this book. The trademarks are examples used for educational purposes rather than for trade.

Diluting a famous trademark

Famous trademarks receive greater protection than other trademarks. After the trademark is famous, the owner may prevent others from using the mark on completely different goods and services.

Owners of famous marks may prevent others from using them when the use may tarnish the name by linking it to poor quality or unwholesome products or when it might blur the value or selling power of the famous mark. For instance, a court stopped the operator of an adult entertainment Web site from using the domain name candyland.com. It tarnished the Candy Land trademark for the children's board game.

Protecting Trade Names

Trade names identify corporate and other businesses. They're protected under the same general *principle* as trademarks, but not necessarily to the same extent. They may, however, also qualify as a trademark or service mark.

Trade names, like trademarks, must be distinctive in order to prevent others from using it. The senior owner of the trade name may normally prevent others from later using the same or a substantially similar name in the same state or other geographic location. However, there should be circumstances showing that people may become confused about the companies.

Trade names cannot be registered with the U.S. trademark office. The federal trademark law does, however, protect owners of trade names. State laws, both common law and statutes, also protect trade names. Filing documents with your state's Secretary of State Office or similar state government agency to incorporate or to form other legal business entities often protects trade names. In addition, a document called a Fictitious Business Name Statement should be filed with your county to establish senior use of a trade name. For more information on setting up businesses and protecting trade names, see *Small Business Kit For Dummies*, by Richard D. Harroch (IDG Books Worldwide).

Protecting your assets includes protecting your names. After you spend so much time selecting a name, it would be sad to lose out just because you didn't spend the time to get the proper registrations. Hang on to what you've got by registering your names and then watching to make sure that other people aren't trying to take them away from you!

Part III
Sharing the Work

The 5th Wave   By Rich Tennant

Well, there's your Web page, Crypto. Designed like you asked. But personally, I think it has too many spinning spirals and blinking lights. It makes...hard reading. Make...tired...look...at...lose...all...con...cen...tra...tion...

Perfect!

CRYPTO THE HYPNOTIST

In this part . . .

Alliances, affiliates, associates, consultants, employees, independent contractors, partners. They all
have one thing in common: they can help your e-business
succeed. There's strength in numbers, but you don't have
to hire dozens of employees. This part shows you how to
form strategic alliances and work with others around the
globe to transform your small e-business into an international power site. When you share information with others,
you could be losing something that gives you a competitive edge. This part shows you how to protect what's
rightfully yours. Having employees who use e-mail and the
Internet raises special issues for employers. What if they
send e-mail to harass other employees or surf the Internet
all afternoon instead of working? This part has the answer.

Chapter 8

Strategic Alliances and Consultants

*T*he *Art of War* by Sun Tzu is a story about military strategy from 2,000 years ago. The author's discussion of strategy, conflict, and leadership principles adapts well to business strategies of today. In fact, entrepreneurs around the world praise the book as an unparalleled guide to running a successful company. For me, the story supports the premise that you can accomplish anything when you form alliances and work together.

Strategic alliances and consultants play an important role in successful e-strategies. You form a strategic alliance with another company when you agree to work together to reach a common goal. It's like forming some sort of partnership with the company and sharing the financial rewards. Consultants are individuals or companies you hire to assist your e-business temporarily. They may provide information, advice, insight, personal services, or products for you.

Strategic alliances may take a variety of legal forms. For instance, two companies may decide to form a *general partnership* to continue doing business together for many projects. On the other hand, they may prefer to form a *joint venture*, which is very similar to a general partnership except that it is formed for a particular purpose or project. The companies may decide to form a separate *limited partnership* or *limited liability company* if the laws make it more advantageous for them to form this type of entity. When hiring a consultant, you may decide to retain the person as a full-time employee, a part-time employee, or an independent contractor.

A sample Joint Venture Agreement with explanations and a copy of the agreement without explanations are on the CD with this book.

The most important points to remember about forming alliances and retaining consultants are to form the relationship *after* you know some things about the company, set up the terms of the relationship thoughtfully (that is, give it some thought), and don't unlawfully interfere in the relationships of others.

Now get into formation as we plan to take the next cyberhill. Amazon, you handle intelligence. eBay, can you take on the bargaining? Webvan, spread out already!

Forming Business Relationships

Strategic alliances and consultants can help you build and expand your e-business smoothly and effectively. You may discover many reasons to work with others. For example, you may want someone else to perform the following services:

- ✔ Provide content for your Web site
- ✔ Develop technology for your e-business
- ✔ Manufacture or distribute products for you
- ✔ Provide special services for you or your customers
- ✔ Help your e-business expand your customer base into new markets or into other parts of the world

Maybe you're setting up a cooking site. You could provide everything for the site, or you could form alliances. For instance, you may want your visitors to be able to download recipes, get advice from nutritionists, buy cookware, and take online cooking lessons. Other e-companies that provide these products or services may want to join forces with you.

Perhaps you build the technology that makes Web sites work. Your clients are dot-coms that need e-sites. Maybe you want to become a one-stop shop for your clients. Instead of keeping full-time specialists on your payroll, you set up alliances with several companies and consultants. For example, you make a deal with a company of computer programmers to work with your people so that you don't have to employ so many programmers full-time. You work out a deal with a graphic arts company to create the interface that users see on the Web sites. You align yourself with a company to train clients to use your technology. Another e-business will provide technical support to keep your clients' Web sites working every day. Now you're a force to reckon with!

The companies that form the alliance should fit into each other's strategy to reach the goal. The Internet offers a variety of possibilities.

Net alliances

The Internet has spawned all kinds of alliances. You may want to join forces with incubators, application service providers (ASPs), B2B digital market-places, and e-businesses' affiliate (or associate) programs.

Incubators

When an e-company forms, it often seeks money to support itself in the early years. Funding for start-up e-companies may come from its owners, venture capitalists called VCs (who often invest the most money), angel investors (who invest less money than VCs), or incubators.

Incubators are companies that help small e-companies grow. When they learn about a new company (often simply referred to as a *start-up*) that they believe has great potential but little money, they offer money as well as other things to get the company off the ground quickly. For example, the incubator may offer the start-up free office space, accounting services, executive recruiting to build up management, technical support with computer programmers and other professionals, and access to support services like receptionists, secretaries, and others. In return, the incubator takes a big ownership piece of the company.

Incubators often contribute far less money than other types of investors; however, they want a far greater ownership share of the start-up company. Sometimes they want as much as 50 percent of your company. VCs often contribute substantially more money for a smaller ownership share than incubators want.

So why do e-companies join forces with incubators? Some e-businesses need all that additional support. Often e-businesses can be up and running in a very short time because they don't have to find all the executives, support staff, technical support, and professional advice. Sometimes having a powerful incubator behind them also helps their credibility.

Many professionals believe that incubated start-ups fail when they join an incubator that does not have other incubated companies that are *complementary* to each other. In other words, the companies who work together really don't offer much to each other to help the group as a whole. If you want to align your e-company with an incubator, make sure that your e-business and the other e-companies will be able to truly help each other grow.

Demos and business plans: "I just want funding!"

The Internet industry is becoming more like the music industry every day. For years, musicians have been convinced that a great demo of their music is the most important thing to get a record deal — without it, their hopes to secure that sought-after contract with a major record company are shattered. Instead of performing shows, becoming better musicians, and building a following of fans so record companies will want to jump on their bandwagon, the musicians focus on raising money to record a demo to play for record company executives.

They often hire producers and engineers to record a few songs of the band at expensive recording studios. In addition to spending thousands of dollars for this demo, the musicians often promise the producer a percentage of the band's future earnings to keep the initial cost down. And guess what happens? If a record executive agrees to listen to the demo, he will probably listen to only a few seconds of each song. If the demo is great, the exec goes to a club to hear the band perform live for ten minutes (they rarely stay for the whole show). More often than not, the band's live performance sounds atrocious. And the record exec leaves. The band doesn't sound like its demo.

E-business entrepreneurs seem to believe that their chances to get funding from an investor depend heavily on professionally written business plans. The going rate charged by business-plan writers around San Francisco seems to be around $10,000, and some of them want ownership interest in the company whose plan they write. Just like record execs tell musicians, venture capitalists (VCs) will tell you that you're wasting your money hiring someone else to write your business plan *if* you can't personally back it up. In other words, people want to invest in your excitement, passion, knowledge, ideas, and understanding of your business and potential market, not a writer's research.

Most VCs seem to agree that you, the e-business entrepreneur, are the best person to write your plan. However, many people don't have the time or the skills to get one together. You may need someone to help you conduct some market research, project sales revenue, analyze your competitors, and put it all together in a presentable form. If you do, hire someone who knows your industry, has the experience and skill to perform the research, and charges a fee within your budget. Don't start giving up equity in your company already!

Most importantly, remember that *you* must be able to sell your company to the public. Investors don't want your document or your pitch — they want your performance. After you know you can perform, then pull in the help you need to polish up your act.

Keep in mind that it's important for an e-company to keep a large portion of its ownership for itself. This ownership percentage attracts high-level executives later on down the road when their experience and business contacts might be crucial to grow to the next level; these powerful people often expect to receive a piece of the company to come on board. The question for the e-business entrepreneur becomes whether the rent, support staff, and smaller amount of investment money offered by the incubator are worth the lost ownership shares. In fact, incubators may end up controlling the company. Therefore, whether to team up with an incubator is a decision to consider very carefully.

Application service providers (ASPs)

Application service providers (ASPs) are very helpful for small e-businesses. Essentially, they're companies that own all the costly software applications that you may need to get your e-company off and running. Instead of buying all this software yourself and hiring employees to handle all the transactions involved in your e-site (and other computer-related work), you can contract with these companies to do it for you for a fee.

ASPs often set up, host, and manage software applications and data over the Internet for you. Normally an e-company subscribes to the service instead of paying a large up-front fee for all the software. Some ASPs are small e-business specialists, others offer a large range of services, while others specialize in a single area, such as human resources, sales force automation, expense tracking, or office services. The appendix lists a selection of ASPs.

Content partners

Perhaps you want a content partner — someone who provides content for your Web site. Maybe you want your site to include news, stock updates, specific industry reports, or other information you believe is of value to your visitors. If so, you may want to hook up with a content partner.

Often these arrangements involve sharing revenue — money that you hope comes in from your visitors or advertisers. Naturally, large corporate content providers won't agree to a revenue split for sites that don't draw much traffic. Your best chance of finding a content partner of equal stature to your e-business is through networking — schmoozing. Get online, join Internet organizations, and get out to meet people. Just make sure that the content someone else provides to your site fits your needs and benefits your e-business. Quality lasts much longer.

A sample Content Provider Agreement with comments and a copy without comments are on the CD.

B2Bs

What is a B2B? It's a company that does business with other businesses rather than with consumers. It's a business-to-business company. B2B e-commerce includes companies involved in buy-side e-commerce, sell-side e-commerce, and digital marketplaces.

Buy-side e-commerce involves many companies selling to one buyer through a computer network. For example, one automaker may buy various car parts from a number of different suppliers by ordering them over a computer network.

Sell-side e-commerce means that one company sells its products on its Web site to many businesses. It's like an online wholesale or retail store, except its customers are other businesses.

A *digital marketplace* is a Web site that brings buyers and sellers together. It's normally related to a single industry, and the only ones that use the site are other businesses in that industry. There are three main types of B2B digital marketplaces: e-distributors, e-communities, and exchanges.

B2B e-distributors choose a specific industry, such as automobiles. They become a one-stop source for goods and services produced in that industry. They offer businesses a catalog from a number of suppliers of various parts. Buyers may then find any product or service they need from that one site.

This approach helps those buyers and sellers who are in different geographic locations. It also saves buyers time because they don't have to look for suppliers, and it helps suppliers find buyers. The goods or services may be purchased through the site, and the e-distributor normally receives a transaction fee from the seller. The fee is often a percentage of the price.

B2B e-communities are just what they sound like — Web site communities where people from the same industry visit to share information and obtain the latest news and industry updates from the site. The site may provide digital publications, business referrals, and other useful services or content. It's a place to network with others in your industry. E-communities normally stay afloat through advertising, sponsorships, referral fees, and transaction fees for anything sold on the site or through any of its partner sites (such as a partner e-distributor site).

B2B exchanges are also sites where buyers and sellers come to buy and sell things in a particular industry. Exchanges come in two forms: auction exchanges and commodity exchanges. They're much the same except for the types of things they sell. Auction exchanges often sell used or excess inventory. Commodity exchanges normally sell things like telecommunications capacity and electricity. Buyers and sellers find each other through these exchanges and bid for what they need.

The appendix lists some B2B sites so you can see what they're all about.

Affiliate programs

Affiliate programs are essentially business referral arrangements. If you put a logo or name of an e-site with a link to that site on your site, someone uses that link on your site, and that person purchases something from the affiliate, you receive some small dollar amount or percentage of the price. Simple, right?

It sure is. Reportedly thousands of sites have affiliate (also called associate) programs. In fact, some Web sites have nothing but links to their affiliates. The owners try to earn money just from those alliances! However, a site without anything but links doesn't draw many visitors for long.

The Amazon.com wrinkle

There's a wrinkle in the e-business affiliate program that hadn't been resolved at the time this book went to press. Amazon.com announced that it obtained a patent on its associate program. This means that the technology used to link and track users coming to its site from its associates is exclusively Amazon.com's. If Amazon.com wants, it could prevent others from using the technology or require others to pay a royalty for using it. Time will tell how Amazon.com is going to enforce this right and whether it will impact the affiliate programs of other e-sites. The possibility always exists that some company may sue Amazon.com to try to invalidate the patent, claiming that the U.S. Patent Office never should have granted a patent for this to Amazon.com in the first place.

For merchants, an affiliate program is a very simple and inexpensive marketing tool. According to one report, an average of 13 percent of online retail revenues come from affiliate programs, and that number is expected to grow. Commissions vary from around 5 percent to 20 percent of the sales price, sometimes up to a certain maximum dollar amount. Some sites offer bonus dollars for extra sales. Some online merchants find that their affiliate programs are so active that they need to hire companies to run their affiliate programs for them.

The CD includes a sample Online Affiliate Program Agreement with explanations and a copy of the agreement without explanations.

The appendix includes addresses for Web sites that offer directories to find e-sites that have affiliate programs.

Knowing your friends and enemies

Sometimes the opportunity to form an alliance with others is so exciting to a new e-business that everyone forgets to really think about the people they're dealing with. Spend time to find out things about your potential alliances and consultants. The morning after can be a harsh awakening unless you know whom you're getting into bed with, as the saying goes

Don't enter into a business relationship wearing a blindfold. You're not doing business with a company; you're doing business with *people* who make up the company. Some people can hurt you. Your allies should support you rather than harm you. Therefore, you should know something about the people.

Staying alert for hazards

Do you know anyone who is divorced and is paying off a huge debt that the spouse ran up? This unfortunate situation happens in business as well. General partners are each personally responsible for debts of the partnership if the company can't pay up. In a joint venture, each company (joint venturer) is like a general partner. If one company runs up debt for the joint venture and the venture never makes enough money to pay it off, each company/owner could be responsible to pay off that debt. If one owner doesn't have the money, the other owner may have to pay the entire debt. You don't want to form an alliance with someone who runs up debt without your knowledge and then disappears on you.

Will your ally or consultant have contact with the public or potential customers? Will he be talking to the press? Some people just love to stretch the truth. Doing so can hurt your business reputation or goodwill. Sometimes that stretch becomes a false representation — known as fraud. Work only with people you can trust.

Is the other company going to sign contracts or handle paperwork for your alliance? Some types of business entities, like corporations, must remain *in good standing* in a state in order to conduct business. If, for example, a business doesn't file the necessary paperwork with a state agency every year or pay its taxes, it may become a corporation that is *not in good standing*. Some state laws prohibit a corporation that is not in good standing from entering into contracts or from defending itself in court.

As you can see, hazards are possible when you form an alliance with someone you know little about. On the positive side, alliances can transform you from a neighborhood store into an international contender. Alliances can work for dot-coms that want to earn $100 million per year as well as e-businesses whose owners want to earn a modest living and have some fun. Just be sure you know some background information about everyone who becomes part of your alliance.

Checking out your potential ally or consultant is important. However, keeping things in balance is even more important. Treating the company like a potential employee isn't a good idea. Therefore, calling a company's clients, customers, or other business partners for a reference without their permission can harm that company's relationships. A company may not want these people to know about its business with you. You could also appear to be interfering with a company's private business matters that don't concern you directly. Even running a credit check on a company can be a real turn-off and blow your deal.

How can you find out information about a company without going too far? Here are some suggestions.

Checking on good standing

The word *limited* in limited partnership and limited liability company (LLC) means that some or all of the owners' personal responsibility — their legal liability for the company's obligations — is limited. Corporations are also in this category. If the company can't meets its obligations, the people to whom the company owes money may be out of luck. They can't recover money directly from the owners' personal funds unless some legal technicality exists.

All corporations and limited liability companies must file certain documents with a state agency to become a legal business. All businesses are formed in a particular state. Therefore, it's perfectly legitimate to ask your potential business ally the form of his company and where it was organized. You're entitled to know these things about the business. For example, is it a Delaware corporation (formed under the laws of Delaware)? A California limited liability company? A Texas limited partnership?

If the company doesn't file the proper paperwork with the state agency or pay its taxes, it is not in good standing. In some states, this means that the company can't enter binding contracts — the other party to the contract can avoid its obligations under the deal. In addition, the company may not be able to be represented in court, which could lead to a nasty judgment against the company if sued by someone. This is one of those technicalities where an owner may end up paying the bill.

You can determine whether a corporation or a limited liability company is in good standing by contacting the Secretary of State's office in the state where the company was formed. Usually the corporate division or limited liability company division of that office can give you that information. Figure 8-1 shows the home page for the California Secretary of State's office Web site. Ask for corporate (or LLC) status information. In other words, you want to know the status of the company — is it in good standing or not? If the company is not in good standing, the agency will normally tell you why.

Sometimes a corporation lets some paperwork slip through the cracks. If you like the company, give it a chance to fix the problem and then follow up with the state agency to make sure the company took care of it. Often I prefer letting the corporation's attorney (or executive) know that the company is not in good standing and suggesting that it get the paperwork in order before proceeding with the deal. Mistakes do happen. On the other hand, the company may have money problems (and didn't pay its taxes) or has really sloppy recordkeeping. These things may influence your decision to form an alliance with them.

Using names, backgrounds, and credits

Ask your potential ally for the names and backgrounds of the people who own and run their company. Also ask the company for this information regarding anyone you will be working with or who will be acting on behalf of the alliance. You may want to know their qualifications.

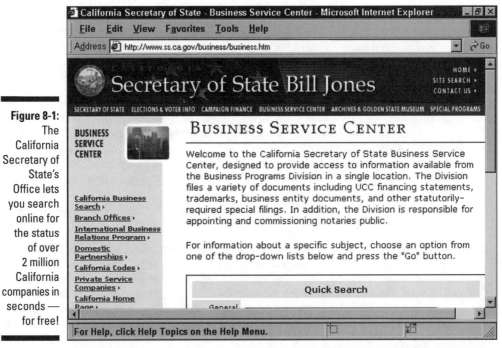

Figure 8-1:
The
California
Secretary of
State's
Office lets
you search
online for
the status
of over
2 million
California
companies in
seconds —
for free!

Courtesy of the California Secretary of State © 2000 California Secretary of State

To promote their businesses, many companies provide a list of well-known clients (or customers) and high-profile projects that they worked on. Do you believe everything that you read on a resume? Customer lists and credits can be a bit misleading at times, too. It's important to ask them about the individual projects that impress you.

For example, many companies work with the software giant Oracle at some point. A company may list Oracle on a project list. However, maybe the company only assisted another company that worked on one project for Oracle and was never rehired to do another job. Or perhaps a Web site designer lists NBC as a former employer, but he worked in the mailroom and never touched the NBC Web sites.

Ask. Ask. Ask about the type of work your potential ally or consultant performed for any well-known company. Ask about their contribution to any high-profile project. Don't let credits overly impress you until you learn more about their involvement. Also, ask how a person got that job — as long as you do it in a casual and professional way. The person may tell you the CEO's wife works for that famous company. This may, or may not, affect how impressed you are about the company's ability to land deals.

Meeting and greeting

Meet the people who run the company and spend some time with those who will be working for your alliance. When you're dealing with a huge corporation, it's okay if you don't meet the CEO and president of the company as long as you know the people who make decisions for your alliance. If you're dealing with a smaller company, know the people running the company.

Aligning yourself with people whose ethics and business styles are complementary to yours is important. You must be able to trust your allies and consultants. When you spend time with people, you can observe how they interact and communicate with you and others. For instance, if an executive walks you around to meet her company's employees, how do they respond to the executive? Personality conflicts could affect a person's response. However, negative or cold responses by most of the employees may be a sign that employees may bail on the company at any time and leave the alliance in a lurch.

These brief observations may provide you with some gut reactions, which may not be entirely accurate. Simply observe, process your observations based upon the amount of time you spend with a company's leaders, and make your hunch *one* of the factors in deciding whether the company is a good fit for your e-business.

Building International Alliances

Don't be afraid or hesitant to form alliances with companies in all parts of the world. You don't have to be a multinational corporation to form international alliances. The Internet is bringing us together.

I've been lucky enough to negotiate, on behalf of my clients, directly with business executives or lawyers in Japan, Taiwan, Australia, France, Spain, Italy, Germany, the United Kingdom, the Netherlands, and Canada. There is a common language among us: business. Take some time to learn a bit about their culture, a few words of their language, and their way of doing business. Then plan how you will present your proposal to them.

I asked executives and professionals around the world to provide Americans with some tips for negotiating with companies in their countries. Here's what they have to say about doing business in certain countries:

Germany: "German business executives, rather than lawyers, normally negotiate the big points in business deals (like money, what each company will do for each other, and so on). They let the lawyers finalize and structure the rest of the deal (the small points and the paper work). Many American executives begin talking about the deal, but their lawyers often step in early in the negotiations to handle many of the big points. For Germans who don't deal with Americans very often, they misinterpret this as a sign that the American company doesn't trust them. Lawyers are also more inflexible on business points, so there's a risk of blowing the deal with a lawyer who takes a strong approach. German businesses tend to be prompt and prefer to conclude a deal quickly. If the American company delays or takes too long to make the deal, it may vanish." Werner Schwarzer, General Manager of Mainhattan Marketing und Vertriebs, GmbH, Offenbach, Germany

Japan: "Americans negotiating with companies in Japan should understand that it is very important to be polite. Often Americans misinterpret our politeness as indifference. Relationships are very important to us. Like German companies, we also negotiate most of the deals with other business executives. Some Japanese companies do not expect the American lawyer to enter the scene until the contract is needed. While some Americans may 'go over someone's head' to deal with a more senior person during a negotiation, this should not be done with a Japanese company. It's a serious insult to everyone in the company. Business etiquette involves a complex mix of respect involving the title, age, and gender of each person. For example, an American female CEO negotiating with an older, Japanese man in middle management should treat the manager with the utmost respect if she wants to make the deal. One with a higher title deserves more respect, but older people deserve more respect than younger persons, and men are given more deference than women. It's a delicate blend that's very important in our business culture." Norika Sora-sky, Tokyo, Japan; President of KAB America, Inc., New York.

France: "You can achieve any deal in France over a good bottle of French wine. Do not expect quick responses or prompt results for deals in France. While Americans often go into 'urgent' mode as soon as they begin a project, the French rarely consider anything an emergency until two weeks after the due date — as long as they've also been harassed at least two or three times to complete the task. In comparison to America, there are relatively few female executives in France. In my experience, American businessmen expect a woman negotiating with them to be as smart as (but not smarter than) they are. In France, it's wise for a woman negotiator to need the help and guidance of the French businessman. It's probably a good idea for an American businessman to need the Frenchman's guidance as well." Florence Daumon, Président Directeur Général of Argos Films, Paris, France.

Joining international business organizations, such as the International Chamber of Commerce, or attending events sponsored or hosted by international organizations provides e-businesses with the opportunity to meet other business entrepreneurs around the world. The appendix lists Web site addresses for some of these organizations. Figure 8-2 shows the About ICC page of the International Chamber of Commerce's Web site.

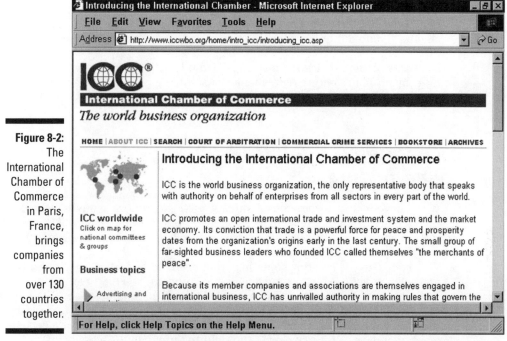

Figure 8-2:
The
International
Chamber of
Commerce
in Paris,
France,
brings
companies
from
over 130
countries
together.

Preparing for the Deal

Before you contact a potential ally, be clear in your mind about the possibilities. Be prepared. Don't approach anyone without some good ideas and a plan. Before you hire consultants, know exactly what you need from them. Preparation shows that you're professional, serious about your interest in doing business with them, and a worthy ally for them.

One way to be prepared is to review the points in the following sections, consider how you would like to see the relationship work regarding these issues, and discuss them with your potential business ally or consultant. Then put any of the provisions that are relevant to your deal in your contract.

A Checklist for Strategic Alliances is on the CD with this book.

Defining the roles — services or products

Define the role of each party. Whether you're forming an alliance or hiring a consultant, know who will provide what services or which products for the deal. Being extremely specific may limit everyone too much, but being too general could cause confusion down the road. Think about it. Talk about it. Then put it in writing so everyone remembers it later.

When you're hiring a consultant, defining the role can be extremely important. See the section "Interfering in someone else's relationship," later in this chapter to find out how a consultant could get sued for providing advice.

Examples of this provision are on the CD in the Web Site Development Agreement, Joint Venture Agreement, Consulting Agreement (Assignment), and Consulting Agreement (Work for Hire).

Describing property rights and testing

Will you, your ally, or your consultant be creating a product or anything someone can own, such as intellectual property? Who will own it? Who will have the right to use it? Describe the rights each party will have in this new property.

When one party is creating something that needs to be tested, spell out how you will handle that testing and acceptance process. You may want to include a certain number of days to test, a specific way to communicate acceptance or rejection based upon the test results (such as by e-mail or fax), and what happens if the product is not acceptable (such as giving the creator a certain number of days to fix it or having the right to terminate the agreement).

Your deal may also include sharing or using someone's real estate (office space), personal property (computers, inventory, or telephone systems), or intellectual property (copyrights, trademarks, service marks, patents, or trade secrets). Describe the rights each person will have in this existing property.

Examples of this provision are on the CD in the Web Site Development Agreement, Consulting Agreement (Assignment), and Consulting Agreement (Work for Hire).

Defining the relationship

Be specific about the type of legal relationship you're forming. Make sure that you understand the different obligations that accompany these relationships. Obligations to each other, to customers, and to other companies vary among merging companies, general partnerships, joint ventures, limited partnerships, limited liability companies, limited liability partnerships, and various forms of corporations. When you're hiring consultants, make it clear whether they're employees, independent contractors, or business partners (part owners) for the project. Confer with an attorney and a tax expert to ensure that you're forming an entity that's most advantageous for you, especially if you're dealing with international laws and taxes.

Examples of this provision are in the Joint Venture Agreement, Consulting Agreement (Assignment), and Consulting Agreement (Work for Hire) on the CD.

Remembering the money

Cover the financial contributions each party will make for an alliance. Discuss any fees, expenses, profits (gross and net), and other financial dealings between you. Specify how and when each party will be receiving or paying money.

For international deals, sending money by bank wire transfer is often the easiest method. It's time-consuming and difficult to obtain checks payable in a different currency that can be cashed in another country. Don't forget to include the bank's wire transfer fees when you discuss expenses.

Contracts should specify how any shared profits or payments based on sales will be accounted to the other company. Will one company send an accounting to the other person quarterly or semi-annually? If you're the one receiving money and then paying someone else, give yourself time to figure out how much you owe the person first.

An example of this provision is in the Joint Venture Agreement on the CD.

Also make sure that everyone who shares profits has the right to check the accounting books from time to time — but not so often that it becomes a hassle.

Setting up communication

When forming an alliance, talk about how you're going to communicate with each other. You could appoint a contact person at each company who handles all or most of the communications. If you're working internationally, discuss whether you'll be communicating by e-mail, fax, telephone, or mail.

International communications are much better by e-mail and fax, with occasional telephone calls. Deliveries through more expensive private carriers are often safer for shipments. Mail service in some countries is slower than a snail and often unreliable. I once received a box of 50 original slides from a French photographer that were sent through normal mail. Some type of acid spilled on the package en route, ate through the wrapper and box, and then burned or cracked most of the slides.

An example of this type of provision is in the sample Web Site Development Agreement on the CD with this book.

Accounting for payment periods

Here's an example of how to figure out payment dates for your commercial alliance. If you're selling through a distributor, maybe the distributor pays you within 60 days after the end of each quarterly period. You can't pay any portion to your allies within 60 days after the end of the quarter because you'll just be receiving the money from the distributor; you won't even have time to count the money to figure out their portion! Therefore, your contract should state that you would pay 90 days after the end of each quarterly period. This gives you 30 days to receive the money, figure out your allies' portion, and cut their check.

Considering confidentiality and noncompete clauses

If there's even the smallest chance that you'll be sharing confidential information, make sure that your agreement covers this point. Chapter 9 explains trade secrets and confidential information.

Restricting someone from competing with you falls into a tricky legal area. Some states prohibit this restriction, while others allow certain types of restrictions. Check with an *experienced* lawyer in this area.

When a national company based on the East Coast insisted that its current employees sign a new noncompete agreement, the company fired a California employee who refused to sign it. She sued in a California court and won a judgment against the company. Even though the restriction was legal where the company was based, it wasn't legal in California.

The CD includes sample Confidentiality Provisions (one copy with explanations and another copy without explanations) and Noncompete Provisions (with explanations).

Including warranties

There are a couple types of warranties. One type of warranty ensures the product will continue to work. Products like cars and computers have this kind of warranty.

Other warranties state that certain things are true. For example, a contract may state that a party *warrants and represents* that she is the owner of property and has the right to let you use it. A warranty could include a statement that the persons who sign (execute) the contract have their companies' authority to sign it. A contract may include several warranties, depending upon the specific business deal.

Examples of these provisions are in the sample Express Limited Warranty Provisions for Products, Content Provider Agreement, Assignment of Master Sound Recording, and other samples.

Including indemnity

What happens if a company sues you because of something your ally or consultant did to the company? You'll want *indemnity* — the promise from your ally or consultant that he will pay for a lawyer to defend you and pay any settlement or judgment as long as you're not at fault. Although an indemnity clause is good, it doesn't mean that your ally or consultant will actually have the money to pay for those legal fees or judgments, which means you may still be left financially responsible. Keep this in mind when selecting your allies and consultants. Work with reputable people who do their best to avoid infringing on any other company's rights so you won't need to worry about being sued.

Speaking of lawsuits, it's probably a good time for you to check out the part in Chapter 2 about liability insurance if you haven't read it yet.

Check out the CD for examples of indemnity provisions in the Web Site Development Agreement and many other samples.

Anticipating termination

Do you want a way out of the deal? If so, include a description of how you may terminate your relationship. Perhaps you could give the other party written notice of termination a certain number of days before ending the relationship.

Some companies want to be able to terminate a contract for any reason. Others will allow termination only when they can no longer perform the deal due to a *force majeure* event — an unexpected catastrophe, like a war, or an act of God, like an earthquake or flood. *Force majeure* is a French term used in contracts around the world; it means an act of God. Most companies want the right to terminate a contract if the other company files for bankruptcy or becomes insolvent.

Depending upon the deal, you may want to specify whether any rights will continue after termination. Sometimes companies want to keep certain information confidential forever. If so, put it in the agreement.

Examples of termination provisions are in the Web Site Development Agreement and other sample agreements on the CD.

Stating the term and territory

In most states, a contract must have a definite term — beginning and ending — to be valid. How long is the deal going to last? It's helpful for everyone to be very specific about the beginning and ending of the agreement. If you read the contract and can't figure out exactly when it will end, rewrite it.

When forming an alliance, include the territory where the parties will be doing business. Does it involve only the United States, the United States and Europe, Japan and Singapore, or the universe?

An example of this provision is in the Content Provider Agreement on the CD.

Don't forget the miscellaneous provisions

Contracts contain a lot of miscellaneous stuff, usually at the end. Miscellaneous provisions include such things as which state's law the parties want to govern the contract, where the parties want any lawsuit to be filed, and what they want to happen if a court finds part of the contract invalid.

An example of these provisions is in the Web Site Development Agreement as well as other sample agreements on the CD.

Working for Hire: Who Owns the Copyright?

Practically every time the subject of copyright comes up, someone asks, "Who owns the copyright to something an independent contractor creates? The company who hired the contractor or the contractor? What about something an employee creates at home, like a new software application? Does her employer own any rights in the software?" The answer to these questions lie in the U.S. Copyright Act's work-made-for-hire provisions.

Copyright protects "original works of authorship." To keep it simple, I refer to them as *work* or *works*. Copyrightable works include stories, portions of software code (such as the source code) or certain graphics that meet copyright requirements, pictures, and other works. See Chapter 16 for more details.

With only a few exceptions, copyright owners of a work are the only ones who may copy it, distribute (sell, rent, or give away) copies of it, display or perform it to the public (rather than in private), and make adaptations from it (derivative works). Therefore, it's crucial that you understand who owns the copyright when an employee or an independent consultant creates something for you or for your ally.

The creator of a work that qualifies for copyright protection is called the "author" and is the copyright owner of the work. In some countries, including the United States, however, the person or company that hires the creator is the author under certain circumstances. These are called "works made for hire." Some countries do not recognize this concept in their copyright laws.

There are two types of work-for-hire authors. One type is the employer of an employee who creates the *original* work *of authorship* while working within the scope of employment. The other type is the person or company that specially orders, or commissions, someone (an independent contractor) to create an *original work of authorship* that falls into one of nine categories of works listed in the U.S. Copyright Act. Sounds fairly simple, right? Not!

What if you ask your salesman, whom you employ, to write a part of your Web site content that has nothing to do with his sales duties? Who owns the copyright to that content? What if the full-time marketing representative for your B2B e-business develops a consumer video game at your office using the office computer while you're out of town? Who owns it? It depends.

Owning an employee's copyrightable work

When an employee creates something for her employer within the scope of her employment, the employer is the author (and therefore the owner) of the work. Who is an "employee," and when does someone create a work "within the scope of employment"? I'm glad you asked this question.

There's no absolute test to figure out the answer. You knew that was coming, didn't you? A court considers dozens of different things before deciding this question. Neither a single answer nor a majority of "yes" or "no" answers in any situation determines the outcome. It's one of those balancing tests that you really should talk to an *experienced* copyright lawyer about.

Who is an employee?

Several factors tend to make a person that you hire appear to be an employee rather than an independent contractor. If you, as an employer, do the following, the person you hire may be an employee:

- ✔ Deduct income taxes from her paycheck
- ✔ Pay workers' compensation and unemployment insurance for her
- ✔ Provide some type of fringe benefits to her
- ✔ Have a certain amount of control over her work

So many factors may affect a court's decision whether a person is truly an employee or is an independent contractor when it comes to copyright ownership of work. For instance, some U.S. courts will hold that someone working in Singapore for a U.S. company is governed by U.S. copyright law and, therefore, the work belongs to the U.S. company. It is crucial for you to check with an *experienced* copyright attorney who can discuss all of the particular details of your situation with you.

What work is within the scope of employment?

The work is probably within the scope of employment if the employer's business creates the same general type of work, the person creates it during working hours, and she creates it with materials that her employer provides.

An employer doesn't have to have a written employment contract for the employer to own the employee's copyrightable work that she creates within the scope of employment. If you think that a person at some point won't clearly be an employee or will create something that's not distinctly within the scope of her employment, however, put an employment contract together. Normally you can obtain certain rights by contract.

Some state laws prohibit employers from claiming rights to employees' creations under certain circumstances. Check the laws in your state.

Owning an independent contractor's copyrightable work

Many companies hire independent contractors, such as consultants, freelance writers, graphic artists, and computer programmers. These companies often assume that they own everything the contractors create or prepare for them because the companies pay for the work. If the work is copyrightable work, however, the companies are making a false assumption!

A person or company that specially orders, or commissions, someone to create a copyrightable work is the author (owner) of the work if the following conditions are met:

✔ The independent contractor creates the work in response to the special order or commission (in other words, it's not already made).

✔ The creator and the person or company that orders the work sign a written document that indicates the work is a *work for hire* or one *made for hire*.

✔ The work falls within one of the nine categories for this kind of work-for-hire ownership:

  • Contributions to a collective work. A collective work is a collection of copyrightable works. It could be a Web site, a magazine, or other collections. The contribution may be a story, artwork, certain graphics, or other works. Remember, only contributions *specially ordered* to be part of the collection may be a work-for-hire.

- Compilations. These are works that a person compiles in an original and creative way. Music CDs are compilations of a number of songs that play in a certain order; original directories may be compilations.

- Part of an audiovisual work or a motion picture. This category includes screenplays, music, animation, and some artistic designs specially ordered to become part of the work.

- Supplementary works, such as a foreword to a book.

- Translations.

- Instructional texts.

- Tests.

- Answers to tests.

- Atlases.

If, and only if, the work ordered falls into one of these categories can the work of an independent contractor be a work-for-hire and belong to the hiring company. See Chapter 16 for an explanation of copyrightable work.

Remember, the independent contractor must also agree *in writing* that the work is one made for hire, and both parties must sign the document. The kind of document that's acceptable may vary from state to state, however. In one state, a court held that a check with a work-for-hire notation, signed by the hiring party, and endorsed and cashed by the hired party was a proper written document signed by both parties. In some states, a written contract must be signed before creating the work. In other states, a written document signed after creation may be okay if the document states that the parties agreed before the work was created that the work is a work-for-hire.

Often contracts state that the parties agree the work is a work-for-hire. However, people really can't "agree" that something qualifies as a work-for-hire under the law if it really doesn't qualify. Therefore, many lawyers add an "assignment" to the agreement. Essentially, the assignment states that in the event the work is not a work-for-hire, the creator assigns (sells) all ownership and copyright to the work. It's a backup to make sure that copyright ownership actually transfers to the company.

The CD in this book includes a Consulting Agreement (Work-for-Hire) with explanations and a copy without explanations. You can also find a Consulting Agreement (Assignment), for those occasions when the work does not qualify as a work-for-hire, with explanations, and a copy without explanations.

Interfering in Someone Else's Relationship

When someone decides to form a business relationship with another person or company, he may be competing with someone else who also wants to form a relationship with that company. Perhaps you need to replace someone so that you can step into place. It's all part of competition, right? May you do just about anything to make a deal happen and nudge your competitor out of the way? No.

There's a *tort* — a certain kind of law — that prohibits anyone from intentionally interfering in someone else's contractual relationship. In some states, the law even prohibits interfering with a *potential economic relationship* between companies whether or not a contract is in place.

You know those fine lines? As in "don't cross that fine line"? Well, a fine line separates competition and intentional interference in a deal in bad faith.

Generally, you may be legally responsible for interfering in the relationship between other companies when all of the following occur:

- ✔ You know about the contractual relationship between two parties or the economic relationship between them with the probability of future economic benefit to at least one of them.

- ✔ You intentionally or negligently do something designed to disrupt the relationship.

- ✔ The relationship is disrupted.

- ✔ This disruption causes economic harm (business losses) to the company that's suing you.

It's the act — what you do — that distinguishes fair competition from unlawful interference. If the act itself is unlawful (such as slander or libel), it's anticompetitive behavior prohibited by law, or it's lawful but motivated by malice, then you could be in trouble.

For example, consultants provide advice. Even if the advice is wrong and it hurts a contractual relationship, it shouldn't be unlawful unless the advice is outside the scope of the consultant's job or it's given in bad faith.

In Illinois, one company (that I call the software supplier) signed a contract with another company to supply computer software and support. The latter company hired a consultant for some business advice. Although he wasn't a software expert and wasn't hired to critique the software supplier's contract, he advised the company to stop using the software and stop paying the software supplier.

Did this act go beyond the scope of his employment? Was it given in bad faith? The court held that the advice was within the scope of his job duties because the company wanted the consultant to approve all computer-related purchases. However, on appeal the court affirmed the jury award against the consultant for $2.3 million. The consultant provided bad advice for a bad reason — he did it to land a lucrative job with the company's parent company as director of information services.

The court explained that greed is not unlawful as long as the consultant makes his money by offering honest advice within the scope of his employment. However, when a consultant decides to make money by giving dishonest advice (or going outside the terms of his engagement), he's not protected against lawsuits.

In this situation, it's important to clearly define a consultant's job duties. If it covers many areas, then the consultant is safe in areas that may be beyond his/her expertise. Such an arrangement may not be good for your e-business; you may be receiving advice from inexperienced people. If you're a consultant, you may want the duties to be very broad so you won't be giving advice beyond the scope of your job.

Spend some time with the people you'll be working with. If you encounter major conflicts in the beginning regarding business philosophy, business goals, or how to make things happen, they'll only get worse once you get moving. Resolve things up front and trust your gut instincts. If something doesn't feel right, find another opportunity. If it feels right and you've done your research, march on e-soldier.

Chapter 9

Sharing Trade Secrets and Confidential Information

ou want to make money in your e-business, right? Well, there's value in the secrets you keep — at least in certain kinds of secrets. They're called *trade secrets*, and they're a type of intellectual property. Much like personal property such as a car, you can buy, sell, and lease intellectual property.

Maybe you've put together a formula over the last several months to give you an edge over your competitors. Or perhaps you've compiled enough information to put together a very special marketing plan to reach consumers online. These could be trade secrets.

To put that plan into effect, you may have to tell it to another company. You also may need to hire employees to work on your project, and some of them need to know your trade secret as well. But one key to a trade secret is that it must remain a secret.

As long as only a few people know the secret and they don't share it with anyone else, it's still your property. If too many people know about your formula or plan, it really isn't secret anymore. You no longer own a trade *secret*.

Think of a trade secret like an ice cube. As long as you keep it frozen and within a protected area, you have something to hold on to. If you start showing it to everyone under the sun, it will melt away and you're left empty-handed. You must take precautions in your e-business to keep your trade secrets confidential.

Here are some good ways to hold on to your trade secrets:

✔ Know what is and is not a trade secret.

✔ Know your rights in trade secrets.

✔ Keep your employees quiet.

✔ Tell other companies only in confidence.

✔ Put your confidentiality and noncompete agreements in writing.

Knowing a Trade Secret When You See It

It's not always easy to tell whether something is a trade secret. When you look at a car, you can tell that it's a car. Unfortunately, there is no single definition for a trade secret. Laws provide different definitions for trade secrets, so you must ask yourself a series of questions to determine whether you have a trade secret. Some of these questions may sound confusing at first, but read on for an explanation.

✔ Is your secret a compilation of information, a formula, a pattern, or a device?

✔ Does your secret give you the opportunity to obtain an economic advantage over competitors who don't know about your secret or don't use it?

✔ Is it really secret, or is it a matter of public knowledge or of general knowledge in your industry?

✔ Do you take reasonable measures to maintain its secrecy?

In the United States, each state's laws govern trade secrets. Unlike other intellectual property that federal laws define for everyone in the country (copyright, trademark, and patent), each state's trade secret law differs in minor ways. However, the basic principles are the same.

Figuring out if it fits the mold

Is what you want to keep secret a compilation of information, a formula, a pattern, or a device? If it is, you're on your way to owning a trade secret.

The compilation of information, the formula, the pattern, or the device (which I just call *information* to keep it simple) could be business or technical information. Certain marketing information and special customer lists are types of business information. Some computer programs and manufacturing know-how are types of technical information. In short, they're the result of an individual's labor and invention.

A mere idea or a simple accumulation of information is usually not a trade secret. Under most laws, you must expend a certain amount of money or effort to gather and compile the information, to develop the formula, to create the pattern, or to invent the device. Examples include your list of customers with their unique buying preferences and other demographic information, your marketing methods that will give you an edge over competitors, or your special business arrangements with other e-businesses that refer customers to you.

It's always a good idea to document (make a note of) the effort it takes to put your information together just in case you ever have to prove it's a trade secret. Just be sure to keep your notes confidential!

Maybe you're absolutely brilliant, and developing special information really doesn't take you much time or money. You could still have a trade secret if it's the type of information that a competitor would have to spend time or money to create. In other words, you could spend an evening or two writing a business plan that will make you the leader in your field. Even though you didn't spend six months writing it, the plan may still be a trade secret.

Under some laws, the information must also be continuously used in a business before it becomes a trade secret.

Giving you that competitive edge

Will your information give you an *economic advantage* over competitors? If it does, you're getting closer. However, don't ignore the word *trade* in *trade secrets*. The information must be about *trade*, as in commerce, doing business, making money from goods or services, or gaining business value. It's not a trade secret if it's about anything you may create for your own personal use; the information must involve something you want to use in your business.

To be a trade secret, the information must give you an *economic* advantage over competitors, either now or potentially. In this sense, value and secrecy go hand-in-hand. Secrecy is often what gives you that competitive advantage — the fact that the information isn't common knowledge in your industry.

For instance, an e-company may create Web site technology that allows visitors to purchase merchandise with a single mouse click. With this technology, the e-company may have an economic advantage over a competitor's technology for a site where buyers must click three times to purchase merchandise. It's likely that buyers will prefer shopping at a one-click site rather than a three-click site for similar merchandise. That technology could be a trade secret.

Some laws require that the information must not be *readily ascertainable* by others. Information that can be discovered by someone else fairly easily is

---

Public record?

Suppose that some people get together to form an e-business that sends demo files of music to record companies to try to get record deals for bands. To do this, they need to find out the names and addresses of all the A&R representatives at all the record companies — the Artist & Repertoire record company executives who listen to new bands and decide whether to offer a recording contract to musicians.

The e-business employees have to spend a lot of time calling record companies and going over directories to get this list together. They also spend money in long-distance telephone calls, buying music business directories, and paying assistants to help with this work. If they have complete, updated lists, they have a competitive advantage over others who have outdated lists. Is this list of A&R representatives a trade secret? No. It's readily ascertainable by other people in the music business. Many of these lists are generally known by people in the industry. Nearly anyone can put this list together by calling record companies and going through published directories. It's not a secret list.

---

readily ascertainable. If your information is simple for others to create, then it wouldn't be valuable enough for someone to want to buy it or to take it from you. Therefore, it wouldn't be a trade secret.

If others would want your information because it would give them a competitive advantage, then it has value. On the other hand, information that could benefit only you wouldn't have to be kept secret. No one else wants it, so it has no value. It wouldn't be a trade secret.

Creating a secret

Is your information secret? A trade secret must be a secret, but it doesn't have to be known only by you. You can own a trade secret even if you're not the first — or the only one — to come up with the information.

The test to decide whether the information is secret is whether it's *generally known*. What does this mean? Information is not secret if it's widely known either by the public or by people in your industry. This isn't always easy to figure out. Sometimes you may think your plan is pretty unusual, and then you hear that other companies in your line of business have known about it for years! It's usually after-the-fact that you learn your secret really isn't secret. Always assume it is secret — and treat it that way — until you learn differently.

The whole compilation of information or the entire formula can be a trade secret even if the individual parts are not secret. For instance, cinnamon is a common spice. Everyone knows about it. However, if I sell spaghetti sauce that includes cinnamon, my recipe may be secret because of the special way I mix things together — even if it includes cinnamon.

Keeping the secret secret

In order for information to qualify as a trade secret, the information must be secret, and you must take *reasonable precautions* to ensure that it stays secret. In other words, you must disclose the information only to those people who need the information in order to complete their work. You also should let these people know that they have confidential information that they are not to use or to share with anyone else.

If you're dealing in a one-on-one business relationship with your strategic alliance, consultant, or individual customer, maintaining secrecy is a bit easier. Stamping "confidential" on pages with secret information, requiring everyone to sign confidentiality agreements (see the section "Confidentiality agreements" later in this chapter), keeping documents in locked files, requiring passwords to access confidential information on computers, and taking similar measures to ensure limited access to the information are probably sufficient. If you're selling to the masses, however, you may lose your secret.

Once information is no longer secret, it's not a trade secret. This means that the general public knows about it or that it becomes general knowledge within your industry. It doesn't mean that just a couple other people know about it, as long as they are also keeping it secret.

Generally, the key to deciding whether other people can use the same trade secret is to ask *how* they learned your secret. They can use it without your permission if they learn about it *independently* and *lawfully*.

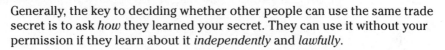

Computer programs

If you're developing a computer program for a specific market, and the type of program is complex and requires you to make a series of design decisions, the entire program could be a trade secret. Even combining elements of a program that are not secret could create a whole program that becomes a trade secret. The overall scheme and organization of the various parts must be new or innovative so that it gives you a competitive advantage. On the other hand, merely integrating commonly known business methods into a program probably won't be creative enough to become a trade secret. The entire one-click Web site technology described earlier in this chapter could be a trade secret. A simple word-processing program that you use to write letters may include secret elements, but the overall program probably won't be a trade secret because word-processing programs are commonly known in the industry.

For instance, if people can buy your product on the open market without restriction, they may take your product apart (reverse-engineer it) to discover your trade secret. They may then use your trade secret, too. If the software is copyrighted, however, reverse engineering may violate your copyright (by making an unauthorized copy). But it won't violate your trade secret rights.

Here's how others can find out about your secret independently and lawfully:

- They didn't need you to come up with the information.
- They didn't take the information from you.
- They didn't find out about the information from you in confidence and then use it without your permission.

Sometimes trade secrets are part of something that can also be patented or copyrighted. If you're applying for patent or copyright registration, be careful. After your trade secret becomes public, as listed in your application for a patent, once it's registered, or in your copy of the source code submitted for software copyright registration, the information is no longer secret. In most states, you then lose your trade secret rights.

If you don't have to include certain trade secrets in the patent application, then don't include them. If you're submitting a paper print-out copy of the source code for your software copyright application as often requested by the U.S. Copyright Office, black out any trade secrets so that others can't see them. Crossing out the secret portion with a black magic marker works well. However, Louisiana courts may make an exception for trade secrets in a patent registration and still protect your trade secret rights.

Customer lists

Contrary to popular belief, not all customer lists are trade secrets. If a customer list similar to yours can be compiled fairly easily by other people in your industry, then it probably isn't a trade secret. In other words, a list of people who live in your neighborhood won't be secret.

Some customer lists are trade secrets, however, if they provide a substantial business advantage. Often these lists contain specific information about customers — not just lists of possible or readily available clients.

For instance, in one case a court found that a computerized customer database enabled competitors to direct their sales efforts toward potential customers already using a compatible computer system. It was a trade secret. Another customer list was found to be a trade secret because its use enabled a former employee to solicit, both more selectively and more effectively, the customers who had already shown a willingness to use a particular service or product as opposed to people who simply might be interested.

Anticipating employee theft of trade secrets

One of the biggest problems facing companies as we begin the 21st century is trade secret theft by employees who leave their jobs. Sometimes they share the secrets with new employers. They believe it will help them move up the corporate ladder more quickly. Other times they use the secrets to start their own companies to compete with their former employers. They're even secretly selling the secrets to their former employers' competitors! Lawsuits involving companies suing former employees (and sometimes their new employers) over trade secrets are reportedly the fastest growing area of litigation in the United States.

In one such case, employees of a software company disclosed the company's trade secrets at a conference sponsored by their employer. They left the company, and then they tried using the trade secrets. The former employees claimed that the disclosure must have been okay because their employer sponsored the conference. They also maintained that the information became public so it was no longer a trade secret. The court, however, reviewed the employer's good procedures for maintaining secrecy and discovered that the employer did not authorize disclosure at the conference. Therefore, the ex-employees could not use their former employer's trade secrets because the public disclosure was improper.

When you begin doing business with companies in other nations, it's important to be aware of how *they* define and enforce trade secret rights. More than 130 countries, including those listed in the sidebar "Keeping secrets around the world," signed Trade-Related Aspects of Intellectual Property Rights (TRIPS), part of a treaty called the General Agreement on Tariffs and Trade (GATT). TRIPS requires the countries that sign the treaty to protect "undisclosed information." The definition of undisclosed information includes trade secrets.

Knowing Your Rights in Trade Secrets

Your trade secret is confidential information. Once you know what your rights are as a trade secret owner, you can see how you can protect these rights. One way is by going to court; another way is by taking safety precautions to prevent people from stealing your secrets.

What right through yonder Windows breaks?

Trade secret rights are property rights. Just like other property owners, you can file a lawsuit in court to prevent other people from messing with your property or to force them to pay you money. However, you can enforce these rights only against people who know (or should know because of the circumstances) that the information you're telling them is confidential.

Here's what you have the right to do:

- ✔ Prevent people who know your secret from telling other people your secret.
- ✔ Prevent people who know your secret from using your secret without your permission.
- ✔ Prevent people who know your secret from taking your secret by improper means or from selling it to others.

Keeping a secret is hard for some people. But that's one of your rights — to stop someone from disclosing the information. You can also stop people from using your information. This means more than just stopping them from directly competing with you. You can prohibit them from using the trade secrets in any way that could affect the value or secrecy of your information.

Even using part of the information and then modifying it is wrong. As long as someone is using a substantial part of your information, you may stop them. If someone isn't using a "substantial" amount of your information, then it's probably okay. In this situation, the person is not really using the trade secret because he's not using most of the information.

Taking a trade secret by improper means is unlawful. Someone who takes a trade secret by improper means takes it without permission or through some deceptive or criminal act (like hacking into a computer). In some states, even memorizing a trade secret may lead to a lawsuit. A trade secret "thief" doesn't necessarily have to take a computer disk, paper, or anything else that's tangible. Of course, no one will know that someone memorized a trade secret unless the person tells someone about it, uses the information, or tries to sell the secret to another company.

What if the person who broke your confidence tells someone else about your trade secret? Can you stop that third party from telling more people or from using it? There's no one rule on this issue. Sometimes yes, sometimes no. The answer depends on which state's or country's law you're trying to use and on the following factors:

- ✔ How the trade secret is disclosed. Did the person you tell accidentally disclose it, intentionally disclose it, or maliciously disclose the secret?
- ✔ What the third person knows. For example, does the person know that someone owns the trade secret? Does the person know whether something should make her question ownership of the trade secret? Or is the person flat-out stupid by not knowing that someone else owns it and, therefore, grossly negligent?

Keeping secrets around the world

Trade secret law throughout the world has very similar characteristics. Some countries protect more things as trade secrets than other countries, but there is much consistency among nations. What follows is a brief discussion of some countries' basic trade secret principles. Unless otherwise stated, their definitions for trade secrets are generally consistent with the discussion in "Knowing a Trade Secret When You See It" earlier in this chapter.

North America

Canada, Mexico, and the United States signed a treaty called the North American Free Trade Agreement (NAFTA). Part of this treaty involves trade secrets. It requires each country to protect trade secret rights.

NAFTA defines trade secrets in much the same way as United States laws do. Therefore, something that is a trade secret under U.S. laws most likely is a trade secret under Mexican and Canadian laws. Mexico has a national trade secrets law. Canada enforces its trade secret rights according to the law in each of its provinces.

The province of Quebec may not consider business information (like marketing plans, customer lists, and so on) to be a trade secret. Although you may be able to keep business information confidential, it may not be protected as intellectual property, which gives you more rights as a property owner. In the other nine provinces, trade secrets are customarily product secrets, technological secrets, strategic business information, or specialized compilations of information.

Asia

All the laws of the Asian countries discussed in this section define trade secrets by using a definition similar to the one that the United States uses. There are some slight differences in the type of specific information they may protect.

Singapore follows common law (judge-made law in court cases based on English law) for trade secrets. Therefore, a company's trade secret rights depend upon prior Singapore court decisions. If there are no such cases, the court might consider cases decided in England to guide it in deciding a case.

Japan has a statute for trade secrets called the Unfair Competition Prevention Law. Trade secret include technical and business information.

Korea also has a statute for trade secrets that's part of the Unfair Competition Preventions Act. Trade secrets are information of a technical or managerial nature that can be used in business activities, production, and marketing methods.

Hong Kong law appears to be unsettled. The Basic Law of the Hong Kong Special Administrative Region of the People's Republic of China is in effect. This law guides the transition of Hong Kong until the year 2049. According to this Basic Law, it appears that the common law (judge-made law in court cases based on English law) will still govern trade secrets. If so, the definition is similar to the United States' definition.

China's law protects "business secrets." This term refers to technical or business "operational" information (about the operation of a business) that is not publicly known, provides economic benefits to the owner, has practical application, and for which measures have been taken to preserve confidentiality.

Taiwan's Fair Trade Law protects trade secrets concerning production or sales information.

Europe

The United Kingdom protects trade secrets under its common law (judge-made law in court cases). The definition is similar to that of the United States. However, trade secrets may not

(continued)

(continued)

include business information unless it's particularly creative or special.

France protects trade secrets through its statutes for intellectual property and contracts. Trade secrets are either manufacturing secrets *(secrets de fabrique)*, confidential business information, or know-how *(savoir-faire)*. Business information may include such things as confidential commercial contracts and commercial arrangements, sales forecasts, and other similar information.

In Germany, the Statute of Unfair Competition involves industrial secrets *(Betriebsgeheimnis)* and commercial secrets *(Geschaftsgeheimnis)*. In addition to the basic requirements of secrecy and economic advantage, the information must be connected with a specific business. Commercial secrets include such things as

surveys, supplier lists, calculations of prices, and contracts that are under negotiation.

Israel

Israeli intellectual property law is based on English intellectual property law. Protection of trade secrets is primarily judge-made law, which often relies upon theories in English cases. Therefore, the definition is consistent with the United States definition.

Brazil

Brazilian law covers trade secret protection in the rules associated with the statute for unfair competition. Although there is no specific definition of a trade secret, the general reference appears to be consistent with the United States' definition. It most likely includes business information and technology.

Struttin' on down to court

If someone discloses, uses, or takes your trade secret by improper means, you have the right to stop the person by getting a special court order called an *injunction*. In many states and countries, you can also sue the person for *damages*. Damages means money, as in the amount the loser must pay to the one who wins a court judgment.

Stealing trade secrets — taking them by unlawful means — is also a crime under state law in almost half of the U.S. states, under U.S. federal law, and in France. Sometimes states and countries also use their criminal laws for fraud or theft to punish the wrongful taking of trade secrets. Punishment includes fines and jail time. Private citizens do not decide whether to prosecute someone under these laws. Prosecutors in each country make this decision. Private citizens merely report the crime to the police authority.

Pounds of prevention

I bet you're wondering how you can stop people from infringing on your rights without having to sue them, right? I'm glad you asked! You can follow these steps:

Frankly, my dear, I don't give a damage

When you sue someone for disclosing, using, or selling your trade secrets without your permission, you may ask a court for various things. You will want to stop the person from doing it anymore, you may want him to do something to fix the mess he caused, and you will want money damages.

Damages can include the profits you lost or the profits someone made from your secret.

Sometimes you may also sue for punitive damages, which may double, triple, or quadruple the amount someone must pay you. Punitive damages are often huge amounts of money meant to punish someone; the wealthier the company, the more money it usually must pay. Some laws also require the loser to pay the winner's attorney's fees.

✔ Prepare a policy for your employees to follow regarding confidential information.

✔ Prepare nondisclosure agreements (NDAs) for your employees and independent contractors to sign (see the section "Confidentiality agreements," later in this chapter).

✔ Most importantly, meet with your employees periodically to discuss the policy and to remind them of the importance of confidentiality.

✔ Include confidentiality paragraphs in your contracts with other companies (see "Confidentiality agreements").

In other words, keep your employees quiet and be careful when you share confidential information with other companies.

A sample Company Confidentiality Policy with explanations and a copy without explanations are on the CD in the back of this book. Cool, huh?

Keeping Your Employees Quiet

It's important to make sure your information stays secret. Before you insist that the employees keep quiet, however, make sure you know what secrets are yours.

Knowing who owns what

Employees may compile information or create work that you might believe is a trade secret, such as the following:

- **Knowledge, skills, and experience employees gain at work.** An employer cannot claim as a trade secret the general knowledge, skills, and experience the employee gains at work. However, when employees use personal knowledge in their assigned duties and create valuable information, the employer normally owns that information.

- **Trade secrets employees create at work.** People often take for granted that an employer who pays an employee to do something owns the fruit of the labor, although I've never figured out why it's called *fruit*. Under most laws around the world, everything that employees create at work or acquire by virtue of their employment (except compensation) belongs to the employer. Sometimes the work of independent contractors also belongs to the hiring company. However, don't assume this to be true in every situation. See Chapter 8 for more information. Often, independent contractors must sign agreements before the hiring party owns what they create.

- **Trade secrets employees create outside of work**. At times, an employer may not own the information or other work that could be a trade secret. For instance, an employee who isn't hired to invent may still devise something valuable while using the employer's property and other employees' services. In this case, the employer may not own the information. The employer may, however, have something called a *shop right* in the information or device.

Companies starting an employee suggestion program should be careful. If the announcement states that the company may offer some payment for suggestions, the company may have to pay for ideas even though it otherwise would have the right to own or use them without payment. Don't offer to pay extra money unless you plan on doing just that.

An employer usually has no right to the work that employees develop on their own time under certain conditions, including the following:

- Employees must be working on their own time.

- Employees must not be using the employer's equipment, supplies, work space, or trade secrets.

- The work cannot relate to the employer's business or to the employer's actual or anticipated research or development.

Chapter 8 explains more about these situations.

Shop rights

A shop right means that the employer may use the information forever without paying any money for it. Although the employer doesn't own the information, the employer can still use it.

Whether an employer owns the information or simply has a shop right in it depends upon how, when, where, and by whom the trade secret is created.

Making ownership clear in employment contracts

Employment contracts often state that an employer owns all the employee's inventions and discoveries conceived during employment. Most courts around the world enforce these contracts. Some contracts even state that the employer owns inventions or trade secrets that the employee develops *after* termination, in other words, after the job ends! Although some courts are reluctant to enforce these contracts, others will. Courts usually make sure that the agreement applies only to things created for a reasonable time after termination and for things relating to the subject matter the employee worked on, or had knowledge of, during the period of employment.

Sometimes employment contracts state that the employee *assigns* (sells), or promises to offer, to the employer all inventions the employee creates, including those that the employee creates outside of work. Some state laws forbid this provision and will not enforce it. California, Illinois, Minnesota, North Carolina, and Washington forbid such provisions.

Creating confidentiality

You don't usually need a written contract to create a confidential relationship with an employee. Most laws around the world *imply* (it's an unspoken requirement) that an employee will hold sacred any trade secrets or other confidential information acquired during the course of employment. (Occasionally, judges like to use heavy-duty words like *sacred* to get a point across, so I'll do it, too.) In any event, employees can't use trade secrets for their own benefit, or for a competitor's benefit, to the detriment of their former employers.

Even with this unspoken requirement, many companies also insist that their employees sign written confidentiality agreements (see the section "Primping your contracts," later in this chapter). In fact, many contracts between companies that will be working together require certain employees of both companies to sign confidentiality agreements. This requirement is a good idea, if only to remind the employees that they must keep certain information confidential.

In at least one state (Indiana), a court decided to follow the terms of the employment contract rather than the state's trade secret law when an employee violated trade secret rights. Such a court ruling may not be a good thing if your state law allows you to recover attorney's fees and punitive damages. If a court enforces a breach of contract claim (rather than a trade secret violation claim), then you may win a smaller amount as damages (no attorney fees or punitive damages). Because most laws don't allow someone to win attorney's fees or punitive damages for a breach of contract, whether a court enforces trade secret law or contract law can drastically change how much a lawsuit could cost you. Ask your lawyer whether your state law requires you to choose between the contract and the statute if a trade secret dispute ever arises.

When working with employees, disclose your trade secrets to only those employees who really need to know the information to get the job done. If you disclose secrets to employees at lower levels when they don't absolutely need to know the information, you may risk losing your trade secrets under the law; you may not be taking sufficient measures to protect their secrecy.

In some states, even though a customer list is a trade secret, it may still be okay for an employee who leaves to send announcements to customers about a new job position. It may even be okay to accept business from those customers as long as the ex-employee is not actually soliciting them or not trying to interfere with the ex-employer's business relationship with those customers (see Chapter 8 for an explanation about interference). In these states, courts recognize a person's individual right to engage in *fair* competition, assuming the person didn't sign an agreement restricting any competitive activities (see the section "Noncompete agreements," later in this chapter).

The CD includes sample Confidentiality Provisions for contracts (one copy with explanations and a copy without explanations), and an Employee Confidential Information and Proprietary Rights Agreement (copies with and without explanations).

Telling Other Companies — Carefully

You and the person with whom you are communicating must come to an understanding that the information being discussed is supposed to stay secret. However, this understanding doesn't need to be in writing. This fact always surprises those people who think that an agreement can be enforced only if they sign something. "I never signed anything" won't work as an excuse in this case. The understanding may be simply part of a conversation — even during negotiations that don't result in a business deal — or a court may infer the understanding of secrecy by considering the actions taken by the people. Putting an agreement in writing, however, is always a good business practice.

Some companies have a policy against signing nondisclosure agreements (NDAs), especially if they don't know you (see the section "Confidentiality agreements," later in this chapter). Other times, signing one just doesn't make sense. For example, suppose you're asking a company to fund your e-business or to help you raise money for your e-business. That company will have a hard time raising money for you if it can't disclose some facts about your company. Many companies that work with new Internet companies (start-ups) won't sign a nondisclosure agreement because they've probably heard the same or very similar ideas, business plans, and marketing strategies before anyway. You're not telling them anything new (secret).

Normally it's worth trying to get these agreements signed, but be cautious. When you're trying to raise money from a venture capital firm that funds Internet start-ups, they often consider any start-up that asks them to sign an NDA too amateurish a company to even consider working with.

Primping Your Contracts

To keep your information secret in a business relationship, whether with employees or with other companies, you can choose from two ways of going about it. First, you may require others to keep the information confidential by using contracts or paragraphs within contracts called *confidentiality agreements* or *nondisclosure agreements* (NDAs). Second, you may try to get others to agree not to compete with you for a certain amount of time. These contracts are called *noncompete agreements* or *restrictive covenants*.

When you're entering a contract involving trade secrets, hire a lawyer experienced in this area. It's especially crucial to do so if you're entering a contract with a foreign company. Many nations have laws that require government approval (by one of their agencies) of certain contracts involving technology or know-how. The points in the following sections are things you should keep in mind and talk over with your lawyer.

Confidentiality agreements (Nondisclosure agreements or NDAs)

Most countries enforce contracts involving trade secrets. However, trade secrets aren't the only information you can keep secret in a contract. You can agree to keep many things — within reason — confidential. Just make sure that the contract is very specific when it comes to the following:

- Defining confidential information
- Maintaining secrecy

Sharpening your clause

One contract definition states: "'Confidential Information' means the confidential information of the parties, including without limitation, financial information, business plans, identities of customers, clients or licensors, and technical data."

I don't like this definition because it includes too much. Take a close look. It's not just financial information, business plans, identities, and technical work. This definition *includes* these things but isn't limited to this information. This definition, therefore, means one person may think that other, undefined information is confidential while the other person has no idea that it's confidential!

I would change that paragraph to state: "'Confidential Information' means financial information, business plans, identities of customers, clients or licensors, technical data or other material that is either marked or otherwise designated as confidential by the disclosing party prior to providing such information to the receiving party."

This wording means that anything confidential must be marked (or communicated in some way) that it's confidential before it's given to the other person. If it's not somehow labeled confidential, it's not confidential.

If you're sharing the information with a *potential* business associate, that is, before you have a formal business deal together, the agreement is often a nondisclosure agreement. If such an agreement is part of your formal business contract for the whole deal, it will be the paragraphs regarding confidential information.

Sample Nondisclosure Agreement (Independent Contractors) and Nondisclosure Agreement (Third Party), both with explanations and copies without explanations, are on the CD with this book. The independent contractor version is for consultants and other people hired to do a job, and the third-party agreement relates to a company or person that you may be doing business with (rather than hiring to do a job).

Defining confidential information

The contract should define *confidential information*. This definition should be specific enough so that everyone understands what is confidential and what is not confidential. One way to do this is to state that any information that is confidential must be marked "confidential" by its owner. Then just make sure that you actually do what the contract says — mark all your confidential material during the project.

Sometimes contracts also define confidential information by stating what will not be confidential information. For example, it may state that it will not include the following:

✔ Information known by the recipient prior to disclosure (translated to mean stuff that the recipient already knew about)

✔ Information that becomes generally known other than as a result of the recipient's wrongful disclosure (other people find out about the information even though the recipient didn't blab)

✔ Information made available to the recipient by any third party who was under no legal duty not to disclose it (the recipient heard the information through the grapevine, but not from anyone who was supposed to keep it confidential)

✔ Developments made by the recipient subsequent to the disclosure but independent of the disclosing party (the recipient also created the information, but without using any information he got from you)

The CD in this book contains sample Confidentiality Provisions (with and without explanations). These provisions are normally one section of a contract for a business deal.

Maintaining secrecy

A contract should include three things if you want to keep it secret:

✔ A statement that the information must be kept secret

✔ A statement describing how long the information must be kept confidential

✔ A description of some requirements for keeping the information secret

Finally, include certain steps to keep the information secret. If you're going to share your valuable trade secrets with a number of people working on the project, at a minimum your contract should require the company that receives confidential information to do the following:

✔ Disclose the information only to people who need to know it to work on the project.

✔ Require all of the company's employees and independent contractors who need to know the information, or who may have access to the information, to sign confidentiality agreements.

✔ Take reasonable measures to preserve and protect the confidentiality of the information.

✔ Take reasonable measures to avoid wrongful disclosure by the company's employees and independent contractors.

✔ Return all confidential information when the project is complete or the contract ends.

Until we're old and gray

Most laws require a person to keep something confidential only until it becomes public knowledge. However, the trade secret could last over a hundred years if it stays secret! Be precise in the contract. You may want it to say: "Upon expiration of this agreement, the parties shall continue to maintain all Confidential Information in strict confidence." If you run into a contract that includes a *residuals* provision referring to a person's residual memory of trade secrets that belong to someone else, be sure to contact a laywer before signing it. These contracts are very tricky from a legal standpoint — they try to restrict someone from using or sharing information stored in her mind.

Keep in mind that putting precautionary measures to work often requires time and money, especially if the company needs to have several employees sign confidentiality agreements. Make sure that you have all your safety precautions in place before you make deals with others, so that you won't have to be running around getting people to sign your NDAs, creating computer passwords, and finding locks for your files at the last minute.

Requiring someone to keep information confidential is different from limiting *use* of the information. A contract that restricts someone from using the trade secret is a *restrictive covenant*.

A *covenant* is a promise or a pact. So a restrictive covenant is a paragraph in a contract that is a promise to restrict some kind of activity, such as competitive activity.

Noncompete agreements

Contracts that limit the right to compete in the marketplace, called *noncompete agreements,* are a way to ensure that your trade secret isn't used to your detriment. You try to limit any chance that someone else will use your stuff. These restrictions are found in all types of contracts, including trade secret licenses, employment contracts, and independent contractor agreements.

Be careful about trying too hard to limit someone's rights in a contract. Unfair competition laws around the world could make the whole contract void if it's too restrictive. The contract will disappear as quickly as the judge's gavel hits his bench.

Noncompete parts of a contract sometimes limit the right of a party to work in a competing field or business for awhile after the contract ends. Occasionally, contracts restrict one of the parties from acquiring any ownership interest in a competitor of the other party. Some contracts even prohibit doing business with the other party's competitors.

The laws in most nations permit these noncompete agreements in business-to-business contracts as long as they're reasonable. This means that the restriction must be

- For only a limited period of time
- Within a reasonable geographic location
- Within a specific competing industry

Employment and independent contractor agreements are much trickier, especially if you try to have current employees sign one after they've been working for you for a while. Laws on these agreements vary among the U.S. states:

- Some states allow you to restrict employees from working for a competitor for a while, but they don't allow you to restrict independent contractors.
- Some states don't allow any restrictions in certain professions, such as medicine.
- Some states prohibit any restrictions on employees after their jobs end.
- One state statute (California) prohibits restrictions that prevent employees from working for a competitor, but at least one court interprets the statute to allow restrictions if they restrict only a part of their job duties rather than their entire job. There are special rules, however, for an employee who owns shares of stock in her employer's corporation. When she leaves her job and sells her shares, there may be a way to prevent her from competing with her former employer. Check with a California attorney for more information on this exception.

Many contracts include a paragraph indicating that the parties agree to have the laws of a certain state or country govern the terms of the contract. If the parties have a dispute that goes to court, the judge normally follows the law of the state or country that's agreed upon in the contract if the contract is reasonable. The contract must have some reason for the laws of that place to apply, like one of the companies involved in the dispute is based in that state. But don't rely entirely on that general rule. If a state court believes that its laws are more important to protect its citizens, it definitely applies its own law.

One company ended the millennium with a bang. It got hit with a million-dollar judgment plus lost wages in California. Although the company is based in another state that allows noncompete agreements, it insisted that its current employees in other states sign the agreement. When a woman in California refused to sign it, the company fired her. Because the agreement was an unlawful contract in California, she sued the company for wrongful termination. The woman won big time. If you want to have the right to rehire an employee if a competitor offers her a job or to restrict someone from working with a competitor or from becoming your competitor for a while, talk to a lawyer in your particular state or country.

The CD in the back of the book contains sample Noncompete Provisions with explanations. Be sure to check with a lawyer because they may not be valid in some places.

Chapter 10

Employer E-Mail and Internet Use Policies

*W*hen you were a kid, did your parents or teachers ever read something of yours that you didn't want them to read? Did they ever keep an eye on what you were doing when you didn't know it? They had their reasons, of course. And you couldn't wait until you grew up so no one could spy on you anymore.

Guess what? Someone is still watching. Only the names and situations change. As a teenager, you worried about someone snooping in your diaries or peeking in the back seats of cars with fogged-up windows. Now you're an employer, and it's your employees who wonder whether you're monitoring their e-mail and Internet usage at work.

Many employers around the world monitor their employees' e-mail and Internet use. Other employers are thinking about it. Just like parents, employers have good reasons for monitoring what employees use their computers for. And just like kids, employees have good reasons for not wanting to be monitored. But it looks like monitoring is the way of the future. So perhaps the most important thing is *how* it's done.

Put the horse before the cart when you're dealing with the e-mail issue. Instead of checking e-mail without letting anyone know, put together a clear policy and communicate that policy to your employees. Then, when you enforce that policy by monitoring e-mail and Internet use, your employees won't be caught off guard. Having a policy leads to better employee relations.

Justifying the Monitor

In most situations, an employer may legally monitor an employee's e-mail and Internet use while on the job or at the company workplace. Why would you want to read, or at least monitor, your employees' e-mail? Why would you restrict their Internet use? Here are some of the reasons:

- The risk of being legally responsible for an employee's actions that harm others
- The necessity to maintain and protect your computer network
- The risk of reduced productivity in the workplace
- The need to protect your company's reputation and assets

Reducing the risk of legal liability

When can an employer become liable for employees' e-mail and Internet use? An employer can get into trouble when an employee discloses trade secrets or confidential information, violates security laws, or creates an abusive working environment for others.

Protecting confidential information

When an employee discloses trade secrets or confidential information that belongs to a customer, you're at risk. Companies often sign agreements to keep trade secrets and other information confidential (see Chapter 9). Employees who work with this information may share the information with someone through their e-mail, putting you in breach of contract and harming your customer. The employee may not even realize he's doing it.

For example, Jake could be sending a quick e-mail to his friend, Meredith, because he's excited that he just discovered how to solve a problem on a project. Although waiting until he sees her might give him a chance to think about whether he should say anything, e-mail access, right on his desktop, makes it so easy for him to leap before he looks. So Jake shoots off an e-mail: "Hey! Meet me for a drink around 7 tonight. I just finally figured out how to turn DotCom's $21 million bottom line into $32 million by next quarter — simply change Rubeck's job duties to take over Kripton's duties! I'm gonna get a promotion on this one." Is the financial information, executive strategy, or customer name confidential? Does Meredith or anyone she knows work for one of DotCom's competitors? Oops.

By discovering this e-mail, you can caution Jake and try to stop more harm from occurring. If necessary, you could limit Jake's access to confidential information or replace him with someone who can keep things secret. Otherwise, Jake's next e-mail could be even worse.

Mastering the employer-employee relationship

Current laws holding employers legally responsible for employee activities are based on very old laws developed when there were masters and servants. When servants hurt someone or messed with another person's property, the injured parties could sue the masters because they should have been able to control their servants' behavior.

Modern employer/employee relationships are governed in a similar way. Employers have a certain amount of control over employees' activities while they are performing work for their employers. Therefore, an employer should be responsible for how her employees act while performing their work. An employer is often liable when an employee harms others while the employee is performing his duties or while at work.

Avoiding violations

Employees can also get their corporate employers in trouble with security regulators (*security* as in corporate stock). People are investing in stock like never before because the Internet makes it so easy to do and some publicly traded companies create so much wealth. It's exciting! People are talking and sharing information about stocks. Even employees of corporations that are about to go public — to sell their stock on a stock exchange — are talking to friends and family.

Corporations preparing for an Initial Public Offering (IPO) of their stock to the public need to be especially careful. No matter how confidential you think your company meetings are, leaks occur in the most secure places. Word can get out to employees about company plans, potential contracts, financial losses, and other business matters. These factors can all affect stock prices.

Keeping corporate news quiet is often difficult for employees. Often an employee feels it's cool to know this kind of a secret, and some people can't resist showing people what they know. Some can't resist the temptation to jump onto an Internet Bulletin Board Service to strut their stuff. And maybe even unwittingly attract security regulators and disgruntled stockholders. This type of employee behavior could endanger your corporation.

Searching the Internet periodically to see where your company name shows up is a good idea. When information on the Net about your company might hurt you, try tracking down the source. The first place to look is on your own computer network. It's often surprising to learn which employee isn't too happy.

Attacking attitudes

The most common problem with employee e-mail is the effect that inappropriate e-mail has on the workplace. Certain types of e-mail could create an unlawful, discriminatory atmosphere. Racial or sexual jokes may be sent to people who don't want to see them. Even if an employee doesn't receive them, he may hear about them constantly. The e-mail could result in ongoing coffee room conversations: "Did you read the one about . . . ?" If the jokes are racially or sexually explicit and become so much a part of the workplace that an employee is extremely offended and can't complete her work, watch out. In this situation, employers risk being sued by employees.

Employers may not permit discrimination or harassment of their employees. In fact, an employer in the United States may be violating the federal Civil Rights Act if the workplace is "permeated with discriminatory intimidation, ridicule, and insult" that is so severe or pervasive that it creates an abusive working environment for an employee. I like that word *permeated*. It means to diffuse throughout a place, like filling a room with smoke.

E-mail is also a way for supervisors and workers to vent anger or frustration in writing when they would never say such things in person. These types of e-mail messages not only create an unprofessional atmosphere but also could set up a hostile environment if the e-mail is particularly severe. In the words of a lawyer (like me), an angry e-mail is a lawsuit waiting to happen.

A claim for harassment against an employer is often denied, however, if the employer acts reasonably in handling the situation. Once you receive a complaint or become aware of a problem, you must take prompt action to address *and* remedy the situation. Having an e-mail policy that you enforce can help.

When you're thinking about ways to resolve a problem in the workplace, keep in mind a proper balance so that your office doesn't resemble a hospital isolation ward. Look for alternative ways to provide employees opportunities to laugh and vent frustration. Some Internet companies let their employees take breaks to play foosball in their back room. It releases the pressure, especially if their boss lets them win once in a while.

Maintaining and protecting the computer network

Another reason for monitoring e-mail and Internet use is to maintain and protect your company's computer network. Networks ain't cheap. They're expensive to run, expensive to maintain, and expensive to keep working efficiently every day. A down day can be truly depressing. And expensive.

Think of each computer in your business as a freeway with four lanes in each direction. The business information you're trying to send or receive is a tiny moped moving through this freeway. Put these computers together in a network (computers hooked up to work with each other), and you have the potential for major traffic jams and accidents. Now add computers connecting to the Internet, and the flow of data could increase to the point of causing a major pileup that shuts down the system.

A computer network is a busy place. Employers have good reason to be concerned about the damage or inconvenience that could result when employees use e-mail improperly and browse certain Web sites. For example, consider these scenarios:

✔ An employee downloads an e-mail attachment or file from a Web site that contains a virus, which could infect your entire network, destroying files, data, and e-mail, and even disabling the computer network itself.

✔ Your computer system slows down when someone uses the network for personal stuff or to download Web pages with extensive graphics that aren't business related.

✔ A breach occurs in network security allowing others to eavesdrop and steal data from the company.

When company employees use their e-mail and the Internet exclusively for business purposes, these risks are somewhat reduced. Many businesses take precautions to ensure that they don't send viruses or create a dangerous Internet environment where technology on Web sites could crash a user's computer. The places most people surf for fun or excitement, however, may not be all that safe.

So you might restrict personal use of e-mail and the Internet to help protect the computer network. Losing data or connectivity between the computers or the Internet could result in a major business expense. Even receiving that stupid (but pretty) Happy New Year attachment to an e-mail is a hassle. When you open it up, you see an animated picture of fireworks exploding. Then the attachment periodically attaches itself to some e-mail you send (without your knowledge) to your clients and then attaches itself to the e-mail that your clients send, and so on.

Losing productivity

Productivity is always a concern for employers. Face it — there is no such thing as a company with employees who never gossip. Chatting and spreading gossip are much easier when employees use e-mail instead of standing in the coffee room or in someone's office where other people can see them. Typing on the computer makes it look like they're actually working! Productivity can really suffer if personal e-mail and Internet use aren't limited.

Productivity also drops after your employees surf the Net from work and leave a trail of their business e-mail addresses. The addresses will eventually land on a list for *spam* (tons of unwanted e-mails), chain letters, or long petitions. Spam can be a big drain of company time when employees have to sort through and delete the e-mails during business hours.

True confessions

Monitoring e-mail helped one U.S. company protect its trade secrets. A woman began stealing her employer's trade secrets that she accidentally found just before leaving the company. She e-mailed a friend, telling him what she did. Then she realized that her supervisor may have read that e-mail. She panicked and sent another e-mail telling her friend how afraid she was of being caught. The employer found out, and she was prosecuted for theft of trade secrets.

Protecting your reputation and assets

Protecting your business reputation is very important because your reputation creates the goodwill associated with a business. A company's goodwill has value. Employees have a major impact on this aspect of a business.

Some employers monitor e-mail to ensure their reputation stays intact. Imagine the effect on your business if an employee vents her frustration in an e-mail and you get sued! For example, say you own a consulting firm, and one of your employees is advising an e-business about the type of technology the e-business needs to upgrade its Web site. The e-business works with a number of companies that provide technology. Your employee/consultant learns that someone at one of the technology companies is trying to convince the e-business to buy a product your consultant doesn't think will work. Your employee decides that the technology company's employee is a complete idiot.

When your employee hears that the e-business is about to license the product against your employee's advice, she reacts instantly by sending an e-mail to the tech company's employee: "Where did you learn about technology? From the back of a cereal box!? Are you an idiot? You're going to screw that e-business! I'm going to tell them and everyone else I consult with not to do business with you or your company again." The e-business doesn't license the product from the tech company, and the tech company sues you.

An employer may be liable when an employee unlawfully interferes in the business relationship between other companies (see Chapter 8). E-mail makes it very easy for employees to vent their anger. Because it's in writing, the words can be retrieved and shown to others. This means that your employee's e-mail can be used as evidence that can hurt you.

A clear e-mail policy that also explains the type of e-mail that your employees should *not* send can help prevent e-mail that could detrimentally affect the relationships you have with employees, customers, and your customer's alliances.

Protecting your company's assets is also important. Employees must understand that your *intellectual property,* such as copyrights and trade secrets, is a valuable asset. Employees should not share this work or information with others.

Require employees to take precautions when sending intellectual property by e-mail or when uploading it to the Internet. Without caution, you risk illegal copying of the work or disclosure of the secret that could mess up your plans for the future.

Balancing Legal Rights

Do employees have any rights? What about privacy and freedom of speech? In most instances, an employer's right to monitor e-mail and Internet use on the company's computer systems is a stronger right than any right the individual may have regarding e-mail or Internet use.

Employers have fired employees because of the content of the employees' e-mail. In some instances, the employees then sued the employers. But the employers have been winning the lawsuits. Courts are balancing the interests of both parties to decide whose interest is more important in the particular situation. In other words, the court considers why the employer monitored e-mail or Internet use, how it was done, and whether the employee's rights are more important.

Before privacy laws protect a person's activities, the person must convince a court that she had a "reasonable expectation of privacy." For instance, suppose that you're using a public telephone booth and five people are waiting in line. They all can hear your half of the conversation. Would it be reasonable for you to expect that what you say is private, that is, that no one else will hear it? No.

U.S. courts have ruled that it isn't reasonable for an employee to expect the messages he sends or receives over the employer's computer network to be private. The company owns or pays for the network and controls it. Therefore, the employer may monitor what goes through it as long as the company has a legitimate business reason to do so. Often, the legitimate business reason includes some or all of the issues discussed in the section "Justifying the Monitor," earlier in this chapter.

The First Amendment stops here

Employees claiming freedom of speech in their e-mails usually aren't successful in court. Freedom of expression is not an absolute right. The law won't normally protect speech that harms someone or creates a hostile workplace. The rights of the employer and co-employees to an atmosphere free of harassment and discrimination is usually held to be more important.

Using Tracking Technology

How do employers keep track of their employees' activities? They do it with computer software.

When you send an e-mail to someone, it's stored on the recipient's mail server, a computer often on the premises of the employer or its Internet Service Provider (ISP), until the recipient reads it. Likewise, when an e-mail is sent to you, it's stored on your mail server (on your premises or your ISP's premises) until you read it.

Because e-mail goes through a mail server rather than going directly from the sender to the recipient, employers can monitor the e-mail on their servers in different ways. By using filtering software, they can enter certain keywords that are confidential, offensive, or sexually explicit. As the e-mail moves through the software in your system, the e-mail is *filtered* (screened) for those keywords. The program sounds an alert when those words appear in an e-mail.

In addition, you can manipulate e-mail programs you provide to your employees so that duplicates are made of every e-mail received. You can direct one copy of the e-mail to the employee/recipient and another copy to a supervisor.

One corporate employer did a lot of investigation when it suspected that its computers were being misused, but it still couldn't identify the employees who violated its Internet use policy. This corporation was headquartered in Wisconsin but had a plant in New York with around 1,000 employees. The employees used computers extensively in their business, but they were forbidden from using the Internet for personal purposes. In fact, the New York plant's computers couldn't access outside telephone lines.

However, the New York plant's computer operators could access the Wisconsin headquarters' main computer to make long-distance telephone calls. When long-distance telephone charges seemed high, a close look by corporate managers revealed calls to a New York library. The library offered its library cardholders free Internet access for up to 30 minutes. They just needed a special password I.D. number to use it.

An e-loophole

Tech-savvy employees who can use a TELNET connection (a special connection to Web sites and other databases) can try to get around an employer's filtering software by keeping a separate e-mail account with someone like Hotmail, Mindspring, Excite, or Yahoo! In this way, e-mail isn't on the employer's mail servers. As long as the other person or employee is also on a mail server that's not part of their employer's network, they may be able to e-mail each other without their employers monitoring them.

I'll see your loophole and raise you one

Tech-savvy *employers* can get around the employee loophole in a couple ways if they *really* want to. First, many mail programs on Web sites require the sender to write the e-mail on a form. When they use this form, the words are automatically changed to HTML, a computer program code used on the Internet. When this form is used and sent (submitted), some filtering software picks up these "forms." Second, some software can *capture* every stroke that's made on a keyboard connected to the computer network. It doesn't distinguish whether the typing is for correspondence, documents, or e-mail, but it can track and record every keyboard letter or symbol typed.

Over about 20 months, the corporation incurred an additional expense of about $23,000 for long-distance charges to the library. The company figured it also lost 1,770 man-hours of time for that personal use. The corporation deciphered about nine distinct 13-digit library I.D. numbers used on its computer network. But when company officials tried to get a court order forcing the library to disclose the identities of those nine people, the court protected their names.

A New York State law makes the names of library cardholders private. The court held that if it made an exception for the corporation, then parents would start wanting it to make exceptions so they could see what their kids were doing on the Internet. That would be too much to ask.

Employees who are not tech-savvy probably surf the Net from their employer's network. To monitor this use, tracking software is available. It follows employees on the Internet and tracks which Web sites they visit and how long they stay there.

Any type of monitoring can cause a general feeling of distrust in the workplace. Employees also may view monitoring as a degrading act that creates a *them* and *us* divide. Such an attitude is not good for morale or productivity. Therefore, if you decide that restricting and monitoring e-mail or Internet use are important, do it with a clear and written e-mail and Internet use policy.

Promoting Workplace Diplomacy: Preparing a Policy

You can implement an Internet/e-mail policy in the workplace with an old Management 101 principle — communicate with employees. Clear communication helps create a good working environment and increases productivity. As my old teachers used to say, it makes us happy campers.

Rules and guidelines are effective only if they're reasonable and explained to the employees. When it comes to e-mail and the Internet, you'll be surprised how many employees who use them all the time really don't understand how e-mail or Internet use could possibly harm their employers. So explain it to them.

When you're ready to put an e-mail and Internet use policy together, consider the following:

- ✔ Think about your policy carefully before you prepare it.
- ✔ Consult an attorney experienced in employment law in your state or territory.
- ✔ Put it in writing.
- ✔ Give it to your employees.
- ✔ Explain it to your employees.
- ✔ Don't put it into effect until the employees know about it.

Your e-mail and Internet use policy should do the following:

- ✔ Clearly describe the permissible uses of e-mail and the Internet.
- ✔ Emphasize any impermissible content for e-mail.
- ✔ State the type of Web sites that your employees should not surf.
- ✔ Inform your employees that you intend to enforce the policy by monitoring their e-mail and Internet use.
- ✔ State the consequences if employees don't follow the policy.
- ✔ Be clear if different standards apply to different classes of employees/managers.
- ✔ Remind employees of the confidential nature of your projects.

Samples of a Company E-Mail and Internet Use Policy (Mid-Sized Business) and a Company E-Mail and Internet Use Policy (Small Business), each with a version including explanations and a version without explanations, are on the CD in the back of this book.

Make your policy known to everyone. Don't bury it in the middle of a company policy book unless you make it stand out in some way, such as printing it on bright pink paper. Some companies also post their policy in a general employee area, such as the coffee room. You also could put it up in your new foosball room.

Finally, remind your employees about the policy from time to time and have occasional meetings to talk about it. Then, most importantly, enforce the policy consistently and fairly.

Part IV
Attracting People to Your Site

The 5th Wave   By Rich Tennant

"You can become a 'corporation' or a 'sole proprietor,' Mr. Holk. But there's simply no legal way of filing yourself as a 'formidable presence.'"

In this part . . .

*I*t's time to get your e-site into millions of offices and homes around the world. You do this by promoting your Web site and your e-business. Marketing, publicity, and advertising are three types of promotional activities. The Web is an extraordinary place to market directly to individuals, but spam is giving direct marketing a bad name. This part explains the difference between junk e-mail and direct marketing techniques. It also shows you how companies process the information they collect on the Web to create effective, targeted marketing campaigns, and what the government and companies are doing to battle spam. If you can't wow enough customers with your other promotional campaigns, win their attention with prizes! In this part, figure out how to avoid crossing the line between offering a legal contest and running an illegal gambling site.

Chapter 11

Letting People Know That You're Out There

Are you building your *Field of Dreams* on the Web? Are you hearing a voice whisper, "If you build it, they will come"? I've got news for you — ghosts will be your only visitors unless you promote your site. In the Web world, e-business success depends upon advertising, publicizing, and marketing your site to potential customers.

Promoting your e-site is like dating. People won't know about you when you're hidden in a dark corner of the Internet. They have to know you're here and available. And you really don't want to attract, well, just *anyone,* do you? You'll waste time and money unless you understand who you want to attract. You need to draw the right people who will give you what you want and will keep coming back for more. In online marketing lingo, you need a sticky site.

That's right. Stickiness. You want people to find your site, stick around your site long enough to do business with you or your advertisers, and stick with you for a long time to come. That's the right match. And on the Web, the more matches the merrier!

So what is your right match? Who are the people you need to attract to your e-business site? How will they know about you? Will you be able to keep them at your site? What kind of deals can you make with people to help you fill the virtual bleacher seats and make your dream come true?

Just step up to the plate, my friend. Warm up for the game, focus on your goal, and get ready to hear the crowd roar as you run around the Web and bring them on back to your home page.

Targeting Your Market

Who wants what you have to offer? How can you get those people to buy or use what you're offering? These are the billion-dollar questions that businesses, advertising agencies, and marketing firms are trying to figure out. Will college professors buy wine online or will teenagers download Bach? Maybe 35-year-old wine connoisseurs prefer alternative healing methods, like to snowboard, and decorate the feng shui way. Perhaps hockey fans who eat licorice and drive Harleys spend lots of money for dentists.

These demographics are the types of things advertising and marketing people want to know. Matching up likes, dislikes, and purchases with gender, age, income, location, and other things is the challenge. If you can make this match, the next trick is to get the right messages to the right people at the right times so they will respond promptly in positive ways.

To promotion companies and businesses, a perfect world is full of advertisements and incentives that are so individualized that only people who will actually buy the goods or services will see them. So they're searching the Net for this information to compile and analyze. Some call this process market research; others call it an invasion of privacy. Regardless of the label, it could help businesses figure out the right market for their goods and services.

Gathering information about your market

How do companies gather information about target audiences or markets? They collect data both offline (off the Internet) and online.

Finding information offline

You can collect information on your own. Books and magazine articles that detail current habits and trends are available at your local public library or nearby college library. Look for books on your particular trade or business. Read trade magazines. Begin with the current issue and then continue back for a year or so. The appendix includes Web site addresses for some Internet industry publications; search libraries, bookstores, newsstands, and the Net for additional resources for your particular type of e-business.

Read the advertisements and identify your competitors. Are there articles about them? What are they doing right or wrong? Also keep an eye out for organizations or associations in your industry that may have publications or information for sale. Sometimes you can only buy them directly from those associations.

You can also buy marketing research. Many companies collect information by tracking what people are doing in the offline world. They gather data from credit card purchases, mail orders, and marketing questionnaires (like those questions on new product warranty cards). Some companies keep this information extremely confidential. If they share it, they share it only for a price and as long as it's not legally restricted (such as certain credit card information).

Whether the research you buy is accurate, up-to-date, or understandable to you depends upon what you buy, who you buy it from, and how much you know. Prices range from a couple thousand dollars to hundreds of thousands of dollars; extremely thorough and specific research gathered and analyzed over a number of years costs a lot. But don't despair, small dot-coms. Read the next section to find out how to get some help.

The appendix includes Web site addresses of marketing associations around the world, as well as addresses of companies that sell market research.

Collecting information online

The other way to collect information is online. Reading articles on the Web sites of individuals, associations, and online publishers may provide you with valuable insight. This is the do-it-yourself way.

Some e-businesses collect information straight from the Web sites people visit and then exchange or sell the information. They use various types of software applications and other technology (see the section "Browser companions," later in this chapter). Much of this technology gathers information by using cookies and Web site registration forms.

The good, the bad, and the cookie

Cookies are special kinds of files. You're already familiar with files if you use a word processing program (like Word or WordPerfect) or surf the Net. Whenever you save a document, an e-mail, or a favorite Web address, you're saving the stuff in a file. If you send someone an e-mail and attach a document or a photograph, you're sending a file.

Some Web sites with special technology send their own files — via cookies — to everyone who visits their sites. Web browsers, like Internet Explorer and Netscape, greet the cookies when the visitor arrives at the Web site. If the browser accepts them, the cookies write themselves onto the hard drive on the person's computer.

The cookies then begin collecting information about where the person goes on the Internet, as well as other stuff, such as the type of Web browser she's using and her Internet service connection. The cookie sends this information back to the Web site.

The cookie collects anonymous information, and it may have a unique identifier, like a special filename the Web site keeps. Generally, the cookie doesn't identify the person by name or e-mail address unless the person's browser is set up to do so or the user completes a registration form on a Web site (see the section "Completing the registration form," later in this chapter).

Some people don't mind companies knowing where they go online, so they accept all cookies. Others reject them, but some sites won't let people use the site unless the person accepts a cookie. Still other people accept all cookies and then delete them when they log off the Internet. To learn more about your browser and cookie preferences, click Help on your browser and search for *cookies*. To delete them, Internet Explorer saves cookies at C:\Windows\ Cookies. Netscape normally saves them at C:\Program Files\Netscape\Users. If you're deleting, be sure to empty your trash bin, too.

Cookies, like most things in life, are neither all bad nor all good. Those who promote using cookies usually say that they want to cater to people's needs and desires. Those who diss cookies often say they don't want anyone knowing that much about them. Both are valid points. The balance is probably giving visitors a clear and easy choice to accept or reject cookies, to see what kind of information companies are collecting about them, and to have the opportunity to correct or delete that information easily.

Completing the registration form

Cookies collect anonymous information. In other words, they don't initially have a visitor's name, e-mail address, and so on. However, people often provide personal information by filling out forms on Web sites. Some of this is *personal identifying information*. It uniquely identifies the person with information such as a name, address, telephone number, fax number, e-mail address, and birth date. If you purchase something on the Web, this information includes a credit card number and expiration date.

Cookies on your computer detail your log-in information for a specific Web site. Different Web sites have different cookies. Some of the cookies may contain confidential information that you provided on that site, such as your password and log-in name for that site, credit card number, social security number, and telephone number. In most cases, cookies are safe, but there have been occurrences where users' credit card numbers have been stolen because the data was stored in a cookie. Beware of the Cookie Monster.

Some sites ask for social security numbers and suggest using a mother's maiden name as a password (obviously, the company sees this information on its computer, even though users may not see it). When the cookies connect information with the forms, *voilà*. The user becomes an individual. Social security numbers, complete birth dates, driver's license numbers, and mothers' maiden names all have special privacy implications. Some of this information accesses the individual's private financial, banking, and medical information. If you want to keep your customers happy and instill their trust in your e-site, avoid asking them for this information. To read about privacy, see Chapter 15.

Wouldn't it be great to know information about your competitors' sites? Who is visiting and buying stuff at their sites? How are the visitors finding your competitors' sites? Guess what? Your competitors won't share that information with you because it's confidential — it could be a trade secret! Make sure that you keep your information confidential as well. Check out Chapter 9 on trade secrets and confidential information.

Analyzing the data to find your match

The point of gathering information is to discover a great match between your e-business and the people who want to buy your products or services. By learning about the likes, dislikes, and certain habits of people who buy your kind of product or service, you can better understand the kind of people your site may or may not attract.

Many people don't provide accurate information about themselves when filling out registration forms — unless they're purchasing something. Even then, they may provide accurate billing and shipping information and inaccurate additional information. For example, I never provide my real birth date or range of income. Sometimes I don't even reveal what I do for a living. If I have to provide information to use a site, I put just about anything on the form to get at the site because I don't want unsolicited stuff. And I promise you, I'm not the only one doing that.

After you gather your data, you may target your promotional efforts to the people who will buy what you have to offer. Unfortunately, doing so is not all that easy (see Chapter 12). Often, people don't have a clue how to use the information they collect. What does the data tell you? How can you use it to attract more customers, keep current customers satisfied, and benefit your e-business? Even when you begin collecting information from your own site about who is, and who isn't, buying your stuff, you still may not know why, why not, or what to do about it!

If you can figure out how to use the information on your own, that's great. If you have no idea how to put this information to good use, you probably need a matchmaker — a consultant. Don't be shy. Millions of people do it. Think about it: You could be spending your time hiring someone and getting other aspects of your e-business ready for launch instead of trying to figure out how to analyze all your information on your own. You don't have to hire the people who charge $50,000 per month. Promotion companies come in all shapes and sizes to fit your needs.

Attracting the Right People

How can you attract the right people to your e-site? First you analyze that data to figure out who you want to attract, and then you get yourself out there! There are a few ways to let everyone know you're here. You can advertise, market, or publicize your site and your e-business.

Promoting to the world: Who does it?

Advertising, marketing, and public relations (PR) are different fields of business. The following very basic generalizations can help you distinguish them.

- **Advertising** involves preparing a message and communicating it to the public or to a target market through the media, such as Web sites, television, radio, and print (newspapers and magazines). Advertisements also appear on billboards, buses, taxis, subway trains, flyers, and so on. Generally, "advertisements" are in print and "commercials" are broadcast (radio and television). Many businesses rely on advertising agencies to create their ads for them. Media buyers, who may be independent companies or part of an ad agency, buy advertising space to sell to agencies or advertisers.

- **Marketing** focuses on sales incentives and promotional activities to get people to know about goods and services. Marketing firms may research specific markets (for example, those who travel abroad or people who send greeting cards on the Web), provide advice to e-companies, create incentive and promotional ideas for clients, or help implement or carry out the promotional activities. Again, some companies do it all while others specialize in one or more areas.

- **Public relations** companies generally try to get media attention for their clients. They want people to learn about their clients in magazines, newspapers, television news and interview programs, online magazines, and radio programs. The individuals working at these PR companies are usually called publicists or press agents. Sometimes corporations employ their own PR representatives rather than hire an independent firm. These employees may have various titles (such as vice president, director, or representative) with a reference to such things as media relations or communications (for example, vice president of corporate media relations).

I may refer to all three of these areas simply as *promotion*. When there's a distinction, I'll refer to the specific activity.

You may decide to hire someone who works in one of these fields, or you may choose to perform your own promotion. If you choose to hire a firm, make sure that the person assigned to your e-business has enough time for you. Businesses often spend thousands of dollars to retain a firm that really doesn't give them much attention, essentially wasting their money. Often, the people assigned to work with small e-businesses aren't very experienced. Although experienced specialists offer useful strategic planning advice, they may not have the time to carry out the plan. If you can't afford full service or you can't get the right attention, hiring the specialist to develop a plan and then hiring a part-time person to work only for you to carry out that plan may be more cost-effective. This way, you're assured that someone is devoting her complete time and attention during those hours to your e-business.

A sample Online Marketing Consulting Agreement with explanations, and a copy without explanations, are on the CD in this book.

Promoting the Super Bowl way

You're probably already familiar with ways to promote a company offline. Many e-companies are learning that promoting themselves offline is especially important because that's where people spend most of their time! However, you don't need to advertise during the Super Bowl to get people to your site. Less expensive forms of offline promotion exist.

Offline advertising includes radio commercials, television commercials, print advertisements in magazines and newspapers, and signs on billboards, taxis, buses, commuter trains, and underground trains. Which route you take depends on your target market. You've heard that already? Well, it's true. If you want to attract teenagers to your site, they might not read about you in the *Wall Street Journal*. What do your potential customers read, listen to, and watch? Target that media for your ads. Marketing options include coupons, rebates, giveaways, sweepstakes and contests, direct mail, and telemarketing.

Offline and online publicity is pretty much the same. You or a publicist pitches ideas to the media to write about your e-business or your site. PR also involves setting up public appearances at conventions or trade shows. The media that may want to write a story about your e-business or your site includes magazines, newspapers, television news and interview programs, and radio news or interview programs.

Promoting the cyber way

People working in the Internet industry often refer to the popularity of a site by referring to the site's *traffic*. In other words, how many people visit the site? There's no way to count the exact number of individuals who visit a site; however, there are ways to estimate the number. Web site technology can usually pick up the number of unique visits to a site by using *cookies,* which identify Internet service information for each visitor on her unique account.

You may hear someone boasting about his site because the site gets millions of *hits.* One million hits doesn't mean that one million people actually visited the site. A hit occurs whenever an item is retrieved from a Web server, whether it's a Web page or a graphic on that page. If a user visits one Web page that includes six graphics, that's seven hits to the site (one for the page and one for each of the six graphics). There aren't seven people hitting the site!

Online versions of advertising and marketing techniques are similar to their offline counterparts. There are a few new twists online, however. As time goes by, more will surely pop up.

Opting for an e-mail option

Most e-commerce Web sites automatically include every registered visitor who provides an e-mail address in a group of people to receive future promotions by e-mail. The site may have a place where visitors may *opt out* (get out of the group) by clicking a box somewhere on the Web site.

A few Web sites do not automatically include registered visitors in the group to receive promotions by e-mail; they allow visitors to request future promotions. A visitor must *opt in,* or choose to be included in the group of people who will receive future advertisements or other promotions. If your e-site will be sending promotional material directly to your visitors, be sure to read about positive direct marketing and spam (negative direct marketing by e-mail) in Chapter 12.

Advertising online

Banner ads are the traditional Web way to advertise. They look like little digital billboards on a Web site that often shake, rattle, and roll. The difference online is that the user can point to one, click the mouse, and instantly travel to the advertiser's Web site for more information and a sale. When the user does this, it's called a *click-through*. He's clicking the banner ad and going through to the site. Companies can follow this movement with tracking technology.

Advertisements may also suddenly pop up on a computer screen as if from nowhere. They're called *pop-up ads*. What else would they be called? They try to divert the viewers' attention to the ad.

Companies also e-mail advertisements directly to potential customers. Sometimes a visitor registers on a Web site and provides her e-mail address. While registering, she either requests that future ads be sent or she doesn't refuse to receive them.

Advertising dollars continue to pour into the Web, although money for banner ads is reportedly decreasing. Many people question the effectiveness of such ads. Are people reading them? Are they buying? It's unclear at this point. One thing is clear, however: Many e-companies will spend money for ads to appear only on sites that attract millions of unique visitors every week or every month. After all, people need to *see* the ads!

Because people may not read the ads on the Net, some companies are paying visitors to look at advertisements. (To see how some of them are doing it, see the section "Browser companions," later in this chapter.) Web surfers can make money (but not really that much) to look at advertisements. Some sites register visitors and pay them to watch ads. Whether this approach actually induces anyone to buy the product or service depends on how targeted the ad is to the individual's needs or desires — and only if the person can afford to buy it!

Online marketing

Online marketing is becoming very creative and competitive. You can handle some basics yourself. Beyond the basics, you may want to explore the option of hiring an Internet marketing consultant.

One basic marketing tool is a listing with Internet search engines. You must list your Web site address (URL) with Internet search engines so that people can find your site. When a person types in keywords at a search engine's Web site, its technology locates Web sites with that keyword. Search engine Web sites normally provide registration instruction on their sites. It's pretty simple to do.

There are firms that will register your site for you if you don't have the time to do it yourself. Listing your site doesn't involve that much work, so don't over-pay anyone to do it for you if you don't have the time. Compare prices and make sure that the company follows up to verify your listing. Make sure that the company agrees to provide you with a list of the search engines once the work is complete so you can check it on your own to verify that you're listed. If a company claims that its list is confidential and won't provide it to you, then you won't have any way to verify the company's work. Promise not to share the list with other people. If the company still won't tell you, find another company.

It takes time for search engines to list sites. They're pretty backed up. Some search engine sites don't list every site, either. They pick and choose which ones to list. Be sure to visit the search engine's site the following month and type in a keyword to search for your site. If it doesn't come up, you may need to register again.

Another marketing strategy is to sponsor (pay for) or offer contests, sweep-stakes, and free giveaways on a Web site. See Chapter 13 for information on contests and sweepstakes. Giveaways on the Net have included the following:

- ✔ Free e-mail, software, and home pages to stick people to a site

- ✔ Free personal computers for those who sign up with an Internet service provider for a number of years (sometimes costing people more than the value of the PC)

- ✔ Free Internet service for a certain number of months if the person agrees to read lots of advertisements

As you can see, there are different ways to attract people to your site. Just make sure you're attracting the *right* people; otherwise, you're giving things away for very little or no benefit to your e-business. Target your effort toward people who will stick to your site and buy your stuff.

Never metatag I didn't like

Hiding *metatags* in the computer code for Web sites is becoming popular with some Web site owners and developers. *Metatags* are hidden keywords that you can't see, but the search engine's robots can find them and lead people doing a Web search to the site. Some sites are using famous names, their competitors' names, or their competitors' product names in secret metatags to divert people to their sites. For example, one site wanted to attract millions of visitors, so it used the metatag *Playboy*. Whenever people searched for the magazine on a search engine, the other Web site came up in the list of sites. The search also attracted the magazine publisher, who sued the person for trademark infringement and won!

When metatags are words that are someone else's trademark, U.S. courts are holding the Web site owners liable for trademark infringement, dilution, or unfair competition. One federal court called it "initial interest confusion." It's like a company putting up a road sign using another company's famous name or trademark to try and lure travelers to its store. Not cool. If you're doing the metatag diversion routine, don't be surprised when you get slapped with a lawsuit.

Sticking 'Em to Your Site

Once people come to your site, you must have something to keep them there. More importantly, you want them to buy your products or services or your advertisers' goods and services and keep coming back for more. Whether it's information, entertainment, products, or services on your site, your content must be something your customers want.

When you provide links to other sites, try offering links to unique or different sites that are helpful and interesting to your specific customers. Offering tons of common links can take away from the character of a site. Plus, the more links you offer, the more often people will leave your site. (See Chapter 11.)

If you can get customers to stay at your site and spend money because you offer really cool stuff, you then have two choices. Your site can stick to them like dirty gum on their shoe or like new Velcro holding up their pants. In other words, your customer service can either frustrate them or help them.

Branding

Here's where branding comes into play. Branding is really important for Web sites — it increases your value. As discussed in Chapter 7 on trademarks, branding is not the same thing as name recognition. Branding means that there is a *strong* connection between the name and the quality or need the customer associates with that name.

Establishing a brand takes time because people need time to see that you provide consistent quality. People won't believe you have great customer service or high-quality goods until they become repeat buyers. You need to offer quality products and great customer service for quite a while before you can rise far above your competitors.

Incentives

Will people keep coming back to your site so you can prove your quality to them? Marketing incentives may help accomplish this for you.

Online incentives include cash rebates, discount coupons, and points to redeem for products, services, or frequent flyer miles. The difference between online and offline incentives is the way companies offer them on Web sites with new technology.

Browser companions

Some companies are developing *browser companions,* which work with the users' Web browsers while they surf the Net. The user provides information, and then the companion uses this information to fill out order forms quickly for the shopper who visits Web sites to place orders. Companions may also track the user's movements on the Internet, offer incentives to the users, and compile this information for marketing purposes. This book's appendix includes Web site addresses where you can find a number of these browser companions.

One type of browser companion is a digital wallet service, also called a smart shopping companion or credit cards 2.0. It tracks Internet browsing, helps the user fill out online forms to purchase things, offers alternative incentives, and asks users to look at advertisements.

Outsourcing your e-marketing

Letting someone else run a marketing incentive program is really worthwhile for many e-company executives. The e-companies don't have the time to process coupons and pay rebates. The businesses that run these programs for e-companies vary in price. Some charge flat fees, while others work on commission.

Viewbars

Some businesses use a tracking device called a *viewbar* — a bar that appears on the top of users' screens when they open their Web browser. People can download this viewbar from a company's Web site. When they begin surfing the Net, the product records visits to sites and sends the information back to the viewbar company. That company compares data with its merchant partners. If a shopper visits a competing site, the company sends its partner's discount offer as a rebate. If a user leaves the site and purchases through the merchant partner's product or service, the user gets a cash rebate in the mail or she may donate it to a charity.

An online shopper can download another companion from the company's Web site in return for the shopper's permission to let the company track his moves on the Internet. The shopper provides the personal information necessary to complete forms to make purchases at shopping sites. The information may include his name, billing address, credit card number, delivery address for his purchases, and preferred method of delivery (mail, Federal Express, and so on).

Some browser companions store this information on the shopper's computer, while others store it on their company computer servers. While the person shops, the company tracks (monitors) his movements. When he goes to certain sites, he will be alerted about a competitor's price — a company that advertises with the browser companion company (a *merchant partner*). The alert may appear as a pop-up window at that moment or in an e-mail sent by the browser companion company.

In addition, the shopper usually receives advertisements targeted toward that person's likes and dislikes. This information comes from tracking the shopper on the Internet while using the companion.

Advertising Fairly and Truthfully

You must follow rules of fair play when you advertise your goods and services to others. The rules come from laws, government agency regulations, and voluntary e-business guidelines. Here are a few of them:

- ✔ Your advertising must be truthful. Don't post information that's not true just to get attention. That's considered illegal false advertising.

- ✔ Your advertising must not be deceptive. In other words, the advertising may not mislead the *average person* who reads it and affect an average person's behavior or decision about the product or service. Although some individuals may misinterpret it, an ad is deceptive only if an average person under the circumstances would be deceived by it.

✔ It's not just what the advertisement states that determines whether it's truthful and nondeceptive. Advertisements are judged by what they state, what they *don't* state, and what they *imply.*

✔ You must be able to back up any claims you make in your ads. You must be able to substantiate them *before* you run the ads.

✔ Your ads cannot be unfair. Will the ads hurt consumers?

✔ You may compare your products or services with those of your competitors as long as the ads are truthful, nondeceptive, and fair.

✔ You may not use fine print to contradict statements in your ad or to clarify something that the reader may misinterpret. When you need to make a condition or disclaimer for a statement, it needs to be "clear and prominent" so that reasonable people can see it and understand it.

✔ When a "free" offer is tied to the purchase of another product or service, the price cannot be increased from its regular price.

✔ If you promise to make refunds to dissatisfied customers, you *must* make them.

Special advertising regulations apply to various types of products and services, ranging from jewelry to warranties and auctions to free giveaways. Special regulations also apply to companies that accept telephone orders for goods, sign up subscribers to buy merchandise (like books or music), and use endorsements to promote their products or services. The Federal Trade Commission's Web site provides very useful, informational guides to help you comply with advertising regulations. Check out the appendix for the Web site address.

The International Chamber of Commerce adopted Guidelines on Advertising and Marketing on the Internet. These voluntary guidelines recommend that businesses do the following:

✔ Disclose the identity of advertisers and marketers who post commercial messages on the Internet.

✔ Inform users of costs and responsibilities associated with electronic sales and marketing, such as higher than basic telecommunications rates, before the user accesses the message or service.

✔ Respect the rules of other groups when you're advertising, such as the rules and standards of bulletin boards or newsgroups.

✔ Disclose information to users of the site concerning collection and use of personal information, the privacy standards for the site, and how the information collected will be used.

- Do not send unsolicited commercial messages online to users who indicated they do not wish to receive them.

- Abide by special advertising rules when the ads are directed to children.

- Be respectful to the global audience by being sensitive to the different effects a message may have to someone living in another part of the world.

The appendix lists the Web site address for the International Chamber of Commerce, where you can find the complete guide and other valuable international information.

Federal and state laws regulate advertising and other promotional activity. In the United States, the Federal Trade Commission (FTC) is the watchdog agency. The states enforce their laws through the offices of their attorneys general. In some situations, individuals may sue companies for damages for deceptive advertising or may lodge complaints with the FTC. The FTC primarily focuses on complaints involving health, safety, and large-scale problems.

When businesses complain about their competitors' ads, they often resolve disputes out of court through the National Advertising Division of the Council of Better Business Bureaus. The NAD investigates allegations of deceptive advertising and provides advertisers the opportunity to resolve their disputes out of court. The Web address is listed in the appendix.

Web site designers and advertising agencies are sometimes also liable for their client's deceptive or untruthful ads. Be careful about the ads you help to promote. Depending upon the circumstances, you may also share liability when you post other people's ads on your site. Be selective.

Advertising in Europe

Countries around the world generally prohibit deceptive and unfair advertising. In most of Europe, advertising that compares your product or service with your competitor's is permissible as long as it's not misleading, does not discredit or harm the other company's trademarks or trade name, and does not take unfair advantage of the reputation of any distinguishing trademarks of the competitor. Although Germany prohibited comparative ads, consistent laws regarding unfair advertising and comparative advertising within the European Union were to be enacted by 2000. Consult an attorney for more specific information on advertising abroad.

In Europe, advertisements must not mislead regarding the characteristics of the goods or services, the price, the conditions governing the supply of the goods or the provision of services or the nature, qualities, and rights of the advertiser. Special rules also apply when comparing your goods or services with those of others.

Making the Advertising Deal

How much does it cost to advertise online? What should your deals include? Web sites charge certain ad rates for banner advertising. Often they post these rates, called rate cards, on their site.

Calculating the cost

Banner ad rates are usually based on a number of *impressions,* which is the term used to designate each time someone calls up a Web page on his browser. The rate is based on CPM, which stands for cost-per-thousand impressions. Technically, CPM means cost per mille. *Mille* is the French word for thousand.

For instance, a banner ad that costs $40 CPM means that you pay $40 for 1,000 impressions. Many sites offer ad rates that guarantee a minimum number of impressions during a month. For instance, the rate card may be $40 CPM per month for one month, or $35 CPM per month for two months (a lower per-month rate if you advertise for two months) for 100,000 impressions.

Here's how you calculate the price. If you pay to advertise for one month, the Web site operator will periodically place your ad on a Web page during that month. When a person calls up a Web page on his browser, that's one impression. The Web site tallies this up. Someone else calls it up. That's two. On and on. You pay for your ad to be called up 100,000 times during that month. Your cost for that one month: $4,000 ($40 per thousand, so $4,000 for 100,000).

If you pay to advertise for two months at the lower rate, the Web site will do the same thing each month. That is, you pay for your ad to be called up a certain number of times per month. Your cost for two months: $7,000 ($35 per thousand, so $3,500 for 100,000 per month; two months equal $7,000).

Just because the page that includes your ad tallies 100,000 impressions doesn't mean that your ad will actually be seen 100,000 times. It may be one of several ads on that particular Web page. The user may not see it if he turns off the graphics for the site and just reads the text. He may not see it if your ad is on the bottom of the page and he never scrolls down. Maybe he just clicks on the page for an instant before moving on. It also doesn't mean that 100,000 different people access that page. The same person may call up that page many times. Discuss these issues with your advertising or marketing specialist to make sure you're promoting yourself the best way for your particular e-business. Ads work for some businesses. The more prominent the site, the higher the ad rates.

Some sites offer *banner exchanges*. They put your banner ad on their sites if you put theirs on your site. Just don't overdo it. Too many ads and no one will see much else! The visitors may decide to go elsewhere.

A sample Online Joint Marketing Agreement for banner and link exchanges with explanations, and a copy without explanations, are on this book's CD.

Attending to details: Online advertising deals

When you're making an online advertising deal, getting promises in writing is always a good idea. Consider the following points:

- ✔ Are you giving anyone exclusive rights? Are you agreeing to advertise only with that company or site and no one else? Maybe you'll work with one company or site exclusively in one area but not another.

- ✔ Will you receive a special designation, such as official sponsor?

- ✔ Where will your ad appear? What size will it be relative to the text and graphics? Are there special requirements to ensure sufficient download speeds?

- ✔ How often will the page change? Will new text be added to attract new visitors, or will the same material appear for an entire month?

- ✔ Is the site up to speed and does it work with all the latest browsers as well as old browsers?

- ✔ How is the entire Web site promoted? Do people know about the site?

- ✔ Will the link be updated for any change?

- ✔ If using a trademark, make sure it appears properly and any registration designations (symbols) are used.

- ✔ Obtain information on who visits the site. Will figures be distorted due to hits to a *cached* version of the site? Caching is a storage mechanism. An Internet service provider's server may remember data on a popular Web page and save it for the next user. This capability speeds up access to the Web page for other users. Caching could affect the figures that a Web site operator provides to the advertiser.

- ✔ Will everyone comply with all privacy laws and policies?

Chapter 12

To Spam or Not to Spam?

. . . .

In This Chapter

▶ Knowing the problems with spam

▶ Focusing your online direct marketing

. . . .

To spam or not to spam? That is the question. Whether 'tis nobler in the mind to suffer the slings and arrows of outrageous fortune or to take arms against a sea of complaints, and by opposing end them? To delete?

Yes, Hamlet was a futurist. He foresaw a time when millions of e-mails would digitally appear in private In Boxes throughout every nation. A time when e-businesses searching for customers send messages to the masses in search of those precious few who will say, "Yes! I want that! Thank you for letting me know that I can buy it from you online!"

These people do exist in the world. Few, but some. Should you, as an e-business, promote your goods and services through direct e-mail marketing? It's a way to reach your potential customers directly rather than trying to get their attention through the media. But will you find new and loyal customers through bulk e-mail? Will this type of marketing result in sales, or will the recipients be angry that you're contacting them directly? This chapter gives you some hints.

Jamming with Spam

The spam on the Internet is not the canned ham-like meat product for sale. Duh. *Spam* is a word people use to describe unsolicited e-mail advertising — the ones people don't ask to receive. Why is it called spam? Reportedly someone began comparing all this e-mail to a scene from a Monty Python show. In the scene, the characters are in a restaurant where everything on the menu is spam — spam, spam, and more spam. The term stuck, and even government officials now refer to unsolicited bulk e-mail as spam!

When did it begin? As the Web began to develop, small Internet marketing companies sprang up and began gathering e-mail addresses from chat rooms, Usenets, and just about anywhere else they could grab them. Some software even sucks e-mail addresses into its database. Then, as if by magic, millions of e-mail advertisements are sent around the world to market directly to the masses.

Spam creates several problems. First, many of the e-mails are unsavory. They promote pornographic sites or questionable get-rich-quick schemes. Second, many senders use false names and secret routes, so recipients can't remove their names from the mailing list or track down the sender. Third, it costs recipients money in online time to download and get rid of them. Finally, spam jams computer servers and networks. In fact, many Internet service providers (ISPs) have been successful in suing spammers.

For instance, America Online and Compuserve won lawsuits against a company sending unsolicited e-mails to their subscribers. They were forced to handle high volumes of e-mail and extra demands on their facilities, lost goodwill among their subscribers, and suffered retaliatory attacks from angry recipients who tried to send thousands of e-mails to jam the spammers. The legal theory used most often to win a judgment against the spammers: breach of the user agreement and trespass. For more on user agreements, see Chapter 3.

You know what trespassing is, right? Remember those movies of the Old West in which cattlemen confronted sheepherders because the sheepherders wanted to put up fences on their land? The cattlemen wanted wide-open fields so they could herd their cattle to market. Sheepherders wanted fences to keep their sheep in place. When the cattlemen rode up to a house with rifles drawn, the sheepherders said, "Get off my land! You're trespassing!"

Well, ISPs say that spammers are trespassing on their property — their computer servers and networks. And they're winning in court.

In addition, about 14 states now have laws restricting spam. They refer to spam as UCE: unsolicited commercial (business) e-mail. Notice that it's commercial e-mail rather than petitions or jokes. Most of these laws prohibit anyone from sending UCE by using false headers (that falsely identify the sender) or fraudulent routing information (that does not accurately identify where they're sending it from). These laws give the ISPs a right to sue people who send these e-mails and to collect damages (money) from them.

A court limits the limits

In Washington, a direct mailer successfully challenged that state's anti-spam law, claiming that it violated due process and the commerce clause under the U.S. Constitution. His claim was that he couldn't tell from an e-mail address in which state a person is located. The person could access the e-mail from any state while traveling. How could he know whether he was violating a particular state's law? The court agreed with him and held that the Washington law is too restrictive. It could not be enforced. The case is on appeal as of this writing.

Spam on Capitol Hill

Several e-mail bills are pending in the U.S. Congress. These are just a few, and the summary does not include every part of the bill. The appendix provides Web site addresses where you can look up pending legislation.

The Unsolicited Electronic Mail Act of 1999 includes the following proposals:

- Requires senders to use a valid return address
- Requires senders to honor opt-out requests from recipients
- Prohibits senders from using false header information (which shows where the e-mail is coming from)
- Permits (but doesn't require) Internet service providers (ISPs) to post on their Web site, and to enforce in court, policies prohibiting (not allowing any) or regulating (allowing some under certain rules) the sending of spam to their users
- Allows ISPs to require companies that want to send unsolicited e-mail to their users to pay the ISP a fee for the privilege of sending the e-mail to their users as long as the ISP provides an opt-out mechanism for their users
- Allows ISPs to use spam filters (programs that block spam) without fear of liability (the law protects them from lawsuits by users) if those filters are not 100 percent effective
- Allows commercial e-mail if the sender and recipient have an existing business relationship
- Allows consumers to rescind permission (change their mind and take back their permission) to receive commercial e-mail

The Can Spam Act basically allows ISPs to protect their property (computer servers, equipment, and customers) by controlling spam any way they want as long as they post their policies on their Web sites or e-mail servers (the computers that handle e-mail). If spammers violate the policy, the ISP may sue them for $50 per message, up to a total of $25,000 per day. If the spammers try to disguise themselves by stealing someone else's domain name, they may be prosecuted as criminals.

The E-Mail User Protection Act prohibits e-mails with false sender information, a false return address, or other false header information. If a recipient opts out of future mailings, no one may send bulk e-mail to that recipient. If a sender still sends e-mail to an opt-out recipient, the sender may be imprisoned or fined. It also outlaws the sale or distribution of software designed to violate any part of this law, such as software that helps people provide false sender or header information.

The Inbox Privacy Act of 1999 also requires valid contact information in unsolicited commercial e-mails. It prohibits false information and requires senders to honor a recipient's opt-out preference. Owners of domain names could publish and enforce "no unsolicited commercial e-mails" notices. ISPs must maintain, and make available to others, lists of their users who request to receive UCE. The ISPs must also arrange to allow their users to opt out of the ISP programs that block UCE; in other words, ISPs that block all spam must allow some of their users to receive spam if they prefer it and at no additional charge. Domain owners and ISPs must register their preferences with the Federal Trade Commission.

Some laws require senders to use ADV, for advertisement, or ADV/ADLT, for adult advertisement, in the subject line of the e-mail when they're sending commercial e-mails. California law is very restrictive. One law defines unsolicited e-mail as any e-mail for the sale of goods or services that a person sends to anyone with whom he doesn't have an existing business or personal relationship unless the recipient requests it or expressly (written or verbally) consents to receive it.

California law also permits ISPs to post on their Web sites any restrictions regarding sending or receiving UCE. Under the law, when the restriction is posted, it's unlawful for anyone to send unsolicited commercial e-mail from or to a person signed up with that ISP.

There is software available that allows an Internet service provider's e-mail server (computer) to send a message in something called an SMTP Banner to provide notice of a "NO UCE HERE" message. This message is sent when the e-mail server is about to receive e-mail and greets the sending ISP e-mail server. However, the sender would then have to understand how to read that message and have access to it to understand that he's not supposed to be sending unsolicited e-mail to that ISP. This software gets pretty technical. Just be aware that software development is moving in that direction.

Federal bills are also pending in the U.S. House of Representatives and the U.S. Senate regarding spam. By the time you read this, they may have become law or other bills will be pending in Congress. See the sidebar "Spam on Capitol Hill" for a summary. Be sure to contact your representatives in Washington, D.C. to voice your opinion on this legislation.

For a list of Web sites to help keep you up-to-date on anti-spamming laws, check out the appendix.

Massive, unsolicited e-mails (that is, spam) may not be effective for you. Most people either delete spam without reading the messages or retaliate against spammers by sending thousands of e-mails in response to the messages. Effective marketing leads to success. If you're looking for repeat business, direct e-mail marketing can be effective if you target your audience. Therefore, perhaps the best way to market directly is to follow some professional guidelines. Serve up ham rather than spam.

Marketing Direct

Some legitimate direct marketers are very successful for their clients, and some people do want to buy from them. Targeted, direct marketing on the Internet is an effective way to go.

Who do these direct marketers send e-mail to? They send them to people who are clicking the "send me future promotions" or "you may contact me by e-mail" lines on Web sites. They're "opting in" to receive future promotions.

You don't have to wait for people to find your Web site and click on your line before you can begin direct marketing, however. Some companies want to partner with other e-businesses to share information, to sell their information, or to use their information and handle the promotions for you. In addition to marketing firms, list brokers, that is, people who buy and sell lists, can help you with your direct marketing efforts. They provide the contacts for you.

If you decide to market directly, follow these tips to attain your goal:

✔ Consider sending direct e-mail only to those who indicate they want to receive it.

✔ Place ADV (for *advertisement*) in the subject and use a catchy phrase to get your point across and to let the recipient know what you're offering them specifically.

✔ If your company name isn't your domain name, identify your company in the subject portion of the e-mail.

✔ Don't use false return addresses or headers.

✔ Provide an opt-out method that's easy and free to use for people who don't want to receive any e-mail.

✔ Delete those who opt out from your list.

✔ Don't send an e-mail with such rich content (with a lot of flash or animation) that it slows the download or causes an interruption for the recipient while she's downloading the messages.

Some e-businesses prefer to keep their customer lists and e-mail addresses highly confidential. They handle all the direct mail work on their own. Others prefer to *outsource* it — to hire someone else to do it for them. If you choose to work with others, think about the confidentiality of your own customer lists. Make sure that they keep your lists confidential and don't use them for other companies. Requiring the company to sign a nondisclosure agreement is a good idea.

A sample Nondisclosure Agreement (Independent Contractor) with explanations and a copy without explanations are on the CD that comes with this book.

Also, make sure that the company has a good reputation and won't harm your reputation. Remember, they'll have direct contact with your customers. Search the Better Business Bureau's Web site (www.bbb.org.) to determine whether a report on a company has been filed. Also see Chapter 25 for tips on checking on companies. Finally, make sure that your list and any list you buy is up-to-date.

Mining for data

For many years, direct-mail and catalog companies have been using personal information received from customers and survey participants to target their marketing efforts. Compiling this information and using it to determine how to target the right promotion for the right customer is called data mining.

Data-mining products are available to help you put the information you gather to work. You need a combination of products and personnel to do so effectively, such as databases, knowledge-discovery tools, customer-relationship management, and content management packages. The appendix lists Web site addresses for some of these products.

How is all this information processed? First, information is collected from your Web site visitors or customers who complete forms, fill out surveys, or use shopping carts on your site. This information is stored with other people's information inside a database. A database administrator reviews this information and decides which specific information should be sent to a data-analysis program (knowledge-discovery tool). This program searches for statistical information and patterns among the people. For example, it may discover that 15 percent of your visitors live in the desert region of the country where the weather is very hot in the summer, and that 25 percent of them live in the rainy region where it's very cool in the summer.

The information is then transferred to a customer relationship management product, where rules are created from patterns in the information. For instance, a rule may be: "In June, send advertisments for rain gear to those customers who live in the rainy region." A marketing specialist enters these rules into content-management software, which creates the advertisements and e-mails them in June to Web site visitors who live in rainy regions. The software may also display special banner ads for rain gear when the visitor returns to the site at that time.

You may not have enough visitors to your site to collect sufficient information at first. Therefore, you may want to purchase this information from other companies. In addition, you may not be ready to spend more than $50,000 to buy all the packages to conduct effective data mining yourself. In that case, form alliances with companies that offer complementary goods or services and share the work with them (see Chapter 8 for information on forming alliances).

Remember, your goal is to get and keep customers. Focus on your customers and their preferences rather than on the product you want to push. And don't collect data that isn't useful to you. Your customers may feel alienated if they believe you want too much personal information from them.

Chapter 13

Running Contests, Sweepstakes, and Lotteries

In This Chapter

▶ Understanding different games

▶ Keeping your contest legal

▶ Establishing the rules for your game

And the winner is . . . . Are you sitting on the edge of your seat? Maybe you're the winner! Wait a second, I need to check last night's lottery numbers.

People love to win stuff. They keep playing even if the prize for guessing the number of jellybeans in a jar is only a cake (it was chocolate, and there were 582). This is why Web sites run contests. Anything that attracts visitors to the site is a plus. There are even Internet guides to sites running contests! Do you want to run a sweepstakes or contest on your e-site? Then place your bets on how much you really know about running them. Odds are 100:1 that you could use some tips to set them up legally.

Hosting the Games

If you offer prizes that users can win on your site, you probably have two goals. The first goal is to attract zillions of visitors who will purchase your products or services or spend lots of time looking at advertisements on your site and purchase that stuff. The second goal is to abide by the law to avoid landing in jail, paying a hefty government fine, or defending yourself in court against a contestant's lawsuit.

To reach the first goal, be creative and check out Chapter 11 on how to promote your e-site. To reach the second goal, think about the kind of contest you want to run and how to keep it legal.

Each state and the federal government have laws regulating contests that award prizes and laws that prohibit certain kinds of gambling. A U.S. Senate bill prohibiting online gambling is inching its way toward becoming a federal law. Regulators want to make sure that people running contests treat contestants fairly and aren't conducting illegal games.

There are basically three types of games that involve prizes:

✔ **Gambling,** which includes lotteries, involves an entry fee or legal consideration (see the following section) for a *chance* to win a prize. Lotteries run by for-profit companies are illegal in all U.S. states. Sometimes nonprofit organizations may run lotteries with the government's permission. Even where gambling is legal, such as Nevada, lotteries are either illegal or are strictly regulated.

✔ **Sweepstakes** involve a *chance* to win a prize without requiring any consideration, payment, or purchase to enter. Sweepstakes are usually legal.

✔ **Contests** that require *skill* to win a prize are legal in most states. However, those that involve an entry fee or legal consideration are illegal in some states.

To keep it simple, I use the words *game* and *contest* in this chapter to refer to all three types of games — lotteries, sweepstakes, and contests. To set up a legal game on your site, you have three important concepts to think about: consideration, chance, and skill. Whether a game is legal or illegal depends on which of these three elements is part of the game. Understanding these concepts when setting up your official game rules reduces your risk of running afoul of the law.

These laws apply to games and contests that offer prizes. If you're just offering a game to play without a prize, you don't need to worry about these legal rules.

Playing with Legal Consideration

Illegal gambling is (1) a game of chance (2) for a prize (3) that involves consideration to participate. In a few states, *any* game that involves consideration to participate is illegal gambling — both games of chance and games of skill. Therefore, it's important to understand what consideration means.

Legal consideration is a concept that comes up in contract law. For a contract to be binding, there must be *consideration,* which in general means that each person to the agreement has some direct benefit and detriment from the deal. See Chapter 3 for more information about contracts.

For example, my agreement to write this book means that I give up my time to research and write it (a detriment) in exchange for money and potential *For Dummies* fame (a benefit). The publisher pays money (a detriment) in exchange for a book that it may sell and add to its catalog (a benefit).

Consideration in the gaming context often involves money — getting some or paying some. Requiring the contestant to pay an entry fee is an example. However, consideration may also be non-monetary benefits and detriments. Sometimes requiring the contestant to use substantial effort to compete is legal consideration. For instance, contests that require contestants to create complex computer software or write a book take substantial effort. Therefore, these types of games may be illegal in those states that prohibit any game involving consideration.

Allowing contestants to enter a contest only online may involve consideration; it requires people to pay for Internet access. Therefore, it's not free. At least one state (Florida) prohibits sweepstakes that contestants may only enter online. However, offering contestants an alternative way to enter for free by mail seems to get around this technicality. This option doesn't really make sense because people probably won't know about the sweepstakes unless they're already online, but regulations don't always make sense.

Taking the Chance or Using the Skill

When a contest requires consideration to enter, you must determine whether the contestant is taking a chance or using skill to win. Illegal gambling is a game of chance that involves consideration. In most states, contests of skill for consideration are lawful as long as you follow the state's laws.

A game of chance means that you select a winner at random. It's the luck of the draw. You're picking the winner out of a virtual hat. A contest of skill means that the contestant uses creative talents or acquired skills to win. Perhaps the contest involves writing a story about the person's experiences with Internet dating. Maybe the contestant creates something new, like computer software or an e-business slogan. Think science fairs and art fairs where participants win prizes for the best work. Think Oscars!

However, the law doesn't make it that easy to distinguish between a game of chance and a contest of skill in some cases. What may appear to be a contest of skill is, under the law, a game of chance. Parts of a contest that may turn it from one of skill into a game of chance are the contest's judging standards, the tasks that contestants must complete, and the rules for breaking ties for the prize.

Judging standards

When contestants who enter a contest of skill must use more guesswork than skill, the contest may become one of chance. For instance, contest rules that don't clearly communicate the precise criteria, or standards, for judging the entries require contestants to guess what kind of work to submit to win. They have no clear guidelines to follow to submit a potentially winning entry.

Chance or skill?

Do these contests require chance or skill? Test your ability to guess how courts decided cases involving these games.

1. Predict the outcome of football games during a week. Anyone who submits 20 correct predictions wins money. Chance or skill?

2. Compose a commercial jingle. You know, those little musical ditties you hear on radio and television commercials. They'll be judged on originality, neatness, etc. Chance or skill?

3. Look at 84 cartoons. Each one suggests or represents the name of a famous person, city, state, nation, book, song, or motion picture. The contestant who comes up with the most correct answers wins. Chance or skill?

Courts held all of these to be games of chance.

1. A court in Washington held that predicting results of football games is a game of chance. Although football fans may have more skill at predicting scores, predicting results of sporting events is dominantly one of chance.

2. The standards for judging the best jingle are unclear. What does "etc." include? Even worse, grocery store employees weeded out certain jingles before the judge ever listened to them. Therefore, it was chance whether the judge would hear a contestant's entry.

3. Each cartoon could have several interpretations, all technically correct. Therefore, providing answers that the company thought were the correct ones was a game of chance.

Therefore, the contest is not as much about skill as it is about how well the contestant guesses what the judges want.

Some contests have judges who aren't qualified to judge the entries according to the standards or criteria spelled out in the contest rules. For instance, a Russian figure skater may not be qualified to determine which contestant is the best football player. In other contests, the judges don't truly judge all the entries personally; other people who aren't qualified to be judges screen out certain entries before the judges see them all.

In these situations, the judges aren't using the contest's standards or criteria properly to select a winner. Therefore, the contestants' entries aren't being evaluated based on the contestants' skills. The game becomes one of chance.

Along the same line, some games seem to require a contestant's skill to interpret images. If there could be more than one interpretation, it's merely chance whether the contestant selects the "right" interpretation. As an extreme example, think about an inkblot. What does it look like to you? There's never a "right" answer. This inkblot contest is really a game of chance.

Tasks and ties

Contests that require people to perform a virtually impossible task may be games of chance. For example, skill doesn't make a slot machine stop at precisely the right moment, no matter how often you play. When you're running a contest of skill, any tiebreaker must also require skill. Breaking ties by chance may turn the entire contest into one of chance. Flipping a coin to break a tie doesn't truly award the prize to the one with the most skill.

In some states, a contest that leaves anything to chance is not a game of skill. In many states, however, games of skill may include some elements of chance. As long as skill is a material part of it — an important and major part — it is not a game of chance. Chance is fun, but skill may keep people on your e-site longer. See Chapter 11 for other ways to stick people to your site.

When you want to put together a contest of skill, keep these tips in mind:

- ✔ Make all your judging standards objective and clear to contestants.
- ✔ Select qualified judges who review all entries and select the winners according to the stated standards.
- ✔ Don't offer virtually impossible tasks to complete.
- ✔ Make your tiebreakers involve the skills on the same standards or other stated standards.

Playing by the Rules

Every game has rules. When you run an Internet contest, it's especially important to communicate the rules and to comply with state laws. To comply, you must make certain written *disclosures* to the public. The law requires you to communicate this information to the contestants.

Again, every state law is different. However, many of the laws require the same or similar disclosures. The following is a *general* list of disclosures. Check with a lawyer about your own contest.

Sample Sweepstakes Official Rules with explanations, plus a copy without explanations, are on this book's CD. This sample may provide you with ideas for your own sweepstakes or other contest rules. It also shows how important disclosures may be made to potential contestants.

Writing your own rules

Each contest has its own rules that must be spelled out to potential contestants. In addition, rules must include other information, such as who may enter the contest, how someone enters, the prizes to be awarded, the odds of winning the prizes, how someone may learn who wins, and the identity of the contest's sponsor. Including provisions limiting your liability and describing the circumstances in which you may disqualify a contestant is also a good idea.

Eligibility

Your rules must clearly state eligibility requirements. In other words, who may play to win? These requirements should include all your restrictions.

You may include restrictions based on geographical areas, age, and affiliation with you or any sponsor of the contest. You may, in some states, require contestants to consent to using their names or likenesses in promotional material if they win, to agree to sign affidavits of eligibility and compliance with the rules if they win, and to give an interview. However, requiring winners to give an interview is unlawful in some states.

You may want to limit your contest to residents of certain states or countries for legal or business reasons. If you don't want to comply with the laws of certain places, your rules should state that the contest is not open to residents of those states or is open only to residents of certain countries. Don't include this restriction in your rules simply to make it look like you're complying with state laws and then allow ineligible people to enter anyway. Make sure that your entry form requires the entrants to list their state of residence. Don't accept entries from people in prohibited states or countries. Otherwise, you open yourself up to liability everywhere for not following your own rules.

List any minimum age requirements because, under many circumstances, minors may void their contracts (ignore their responsibilities under them). Often, their parents must sign a contract to make it enforceable. If you're going to allow anyone under 18 or 19 years old to play, check on special restrictions for your particular type of contest throughout the states.

Contests restrict entrants to people other than the contest sponsors and people connected with them. Put this restriction under your eligibility section so the sponsor's employees are aware that they're not eligible to enter. If you want winners to promote your contest or company, include their agreement to participate in interviews and publicity photographs, as well as allowing you to use their name, photograph, and voice, if they win. These requirements may not be permissible in some places, so add a statement that the entrant agrees to these terms only where they're permitted by law.

Finally, make sure that the contestants agree that if they win, they will sign a legal affidavit stating that they meet the eligibility requirements and have complied with the rules.

Entry

Clearly state all of the ways that people may enter the contest. If they enter online, do they access (come to) your Web site? Must they accept cookies to track their movements? (See Chapters 11 and 15 for more about cookies.) Do they fill out a registration form? What information must they provide to you?

Perhaps you don't want entrants to bombard you with masses of electronic entries. In that case, you may want to limit anyone from using certain types of technology to enter the contest, such as robotic, automatic, macro, programmed, or other similar methods of entry.

Make sure that the information you're collecting and your use of cookies to track where users go on the Internet comply with privacy laws and policies. See Chapter 15 for more information.

If people may also enter by mail, must they use certain sizes of postcards? What should they write on it? Who should they address it to? Where should they mail it to? Through no fault of your own, you may not receive every entry sent to you. For mail-in entries, state that you will not be responsible for lost, late, incomplete, stolen, misdirected, illegible, or postage-due entries or mail.

For Internet entries, state that you're not responsible for any failures on the Internet such as cable, network, satellite, computer, telephone, electronic or Internet hardware or software failures, connections, malfunctions, or jumbled transmissions. State that you're also not responsible for problems with accessibility or availability, traffic congestion, or unauthorized human intervention (such as hackers) to the service provider, the Internet, or the Web site.

List the specific dates that the contest begins and ends. Be sure to state "No purchase is necessary" unless you're charging an entry fee. You may want to limit the number of times someone may enter per day or in total. You may also want to limit the number of winners per household.

Prizes and odds of winning

The law requires you to state the number and a description of the prizes you will award. Also list the approximate retail value of each prize. If contestants may substitute prizes for cash, state this fact. If the sponsor may make this substitution, state this as well.

Explain how and when winners will be selected. State how they will be notified. Also describe how and when winners may claim prizes.What will happen if there are any unclaimed prizes? Will they be awarded to someone else? How and when? Many states require you to disclose the odds of winning. If you limit the number of entries, you must state the exact odds. If you don't limit the entries, state that the odds of winning depend upon the number of entries received. Finally, explain that all taxes related to winning the prizes are the responsibility of the winner.

Winners list

Many states require you to provide a mailing address for people to request a list of prizewinners. You may require a stamped, self-addressed envelope. Posting the winners on the Web site should be sufficient for contestants who enter online. When you provide the list of winners, just provide the names unless specific state laws require differently. Remember the winners' privacy!

Name of sponsor and liability limitations

Only a few state require you to state the name and address of the contest sponsor — the company who's paying for the prizes. As a matter of good business policy, you should always do this anyway. Your rules are a contract. Like other contracts, you may want to limit your liability to disgruntled contestants who may want to take you to court. In most states, you may include a limitation of liability provision in your rules.

Sample Limitation of Liability Provisions with explanations are on the CD. Also see the sample Sweepstakes Official Rules.

Always state that the contest is "void where prohibited." This means you're trying not to break any laws. If you know for sure that you aren't complying with specific states' laws, this phrase really won't help you much. Be sure to also list specific states, as in "Void in Vermont." Let your contestants know that you have the right to stop or change the Internet contest if your site encounters computer viruses, bugs, or security risks.

Contestant disqualification

You may want to be able to disqualify individuals who tamper with the entry process, the operation of your contest, or your Web site. You may also want to disqualify anyone who violates the User Agreement (also called Terms of Service) on your Web site, violates the contest rules, or disrupts or intentionally annoys or harasses anyone using your Web site. Check out Chapter 3 for information about terms of a Web Site User Agreement and Chapter 24 for other Web site notices.

To find ideas for your rules, read the ones you receive in the mail. Also browse all the rules available on the Internet for Web site contests. Games run by huge, reputable corporations usually hire really good lawyers to write their rules. Although all these rules are a good starting point, consult an attorney with experience in gaming.

Registering your game

For certain contests of skill in Arizona, you must file a registration statement with a state agency before the contest begins. A few states (including Florida, New York, and Rhode Island) require anyone conducting a game of chance to file a registration statement before the contest begins. The statements include such information as your name and address, the rules for the game, the prizes you're offering, and who you're naming as your agent in that state in case a citizen of that state sues you. Check with the attorneys general's offices in these particular states to determine which agency handles these registrations.

To ensure that the prizes will be awarded, sometimes you must also file with the state agency a bond (a type of insurance) or establish a trust account (so

International games

Internet games cross international boundaries. If you accept entries from people in other countries, make sure that you comply with those countries' laws.

✔ Unlike the United States, Australia is embracing online gambling. Australian online gambling must follow its own country's regulations, of course. You shouldn't have legal problems running games of skill on the Internet that reach these contestants.

✔ If you comply with U.S. laws to run Internet contests of skill, you'll most likely comply with similar laws in Australia, Hong Kong, and Israel.

✔ In Germany, you can require an entry fee as long as it's truly a contest of skill and you don't also require purchase of the sponsor's product.

✔ As for games of chance, abide by the individual country's gambling laws.

✔ For all other countries, check with a local gaming expert and consult an attorney.

someone else has control of the money) for games of chance in these few states. You may need to file additional documents after the contest as well. As always, check with your lawyer before you begin your contest.

Part V

Information and Entertainment Sites

The 5th Wave
By Rich Tennant

@RICHTENNANT

"MISS LAMONT, WILL YOU GET ME TECHNICAL SUPPORT AT STRIPOC INTERACTIVE PLEASE?"

In this part . . .

*W*elcome to the major attractions on the Web: information and entertainment. In this part, you get some guidelines to providing content online — legally. Unlike news and magazine articles, information on the Net may not be edited or checked for accuracy unless the company providing the information online is a savvy publisher. E-companies do more than *provide* information; they also *collect* information from people on the Web. When you want to include things on your site that belong to someone else, such as stories, news articles, music, names, logos, technology, or photographs, you'll probably need the owner's permission. In this part, you'll learn the how to recognize rights in entertainment, such as music, film, and audiovisual works.

Chapter 14

Providing False Information

- -

- -

Think about the last few times you spent hanging out with business colleagues or acquaintances. Did you talk about other people or companies? Are you sure that the information you shared was accurate?

Most conversations and reports around the world don't really damage anyone's reputation or truly harm people. Much of the information people exchange every day is fairly accurate or is an expression of their opinions. Even obnoxious comments, name-calling, and obscene remarks are pretty much a part of life, unfortunately.

But what if a statement is not true? And instead of sharing it with a buddy over coffee, you've posted it on the Internet for thousands of people to read? And what if your statement actually harms someone's reputation? Well, that's the part of life that triggers the law of defamation.

Recognizing Defamation

Societies have a strong interest in protecting business and personal relationships. Therefore, lawmakers want to discourage wrongful disruption of these relationships and prevent attacks upon one's reputation. Lawmakers discourage these acts by making laws that hold people legally responsible to others for the harm they cause. One of these laws involves defamation.

Each state and every country have their own definition of defamation. In general, defamation is a false statement that seems to be a fact and that damages a person's reputation in the eyes of others or harms a person in her occupation. Does this make you think about lousy things people have said about you over the years? Well, don't get ready to sue that estranged cousin who's been bad-mouthing you just yet! It's really not as simple as it sounds.

Identifying the parties in a lawsuit

A lawsuit involves the plaintiff and the defendant. The *plaintiff* is the private citizen (an individual or a company) who files a lawsuit. The *defendant* is the person or company that is being sued. In a defamation lawsuit sometimes the person who made the statement and others that the law may hold responsible are sued. For example, if an employee makes the statement, the employee and her employer may be sued. If a reporter writes an article, the reporter and the publisher may be sued. Therefore, they are all defendants.

In a lawsuit, the plaintiff claims that something the defendant did, or did not do, harmed or injured the plaintiff by violating certain rights that the law protects. Generally, there can be more than one plaintiff and more than one defendant in a single lawsuit, as long as they're all involved in the event that prompted the lawsuit.

Defamation is the generic term that includes two kinds of legal wrongs: slander and libel. In general:

> ✔ **Slander** is defamation that is spoken (remember the *s* — slander, spoken).

> ✔ **Libel** is defamation expressed in written form or affixed in (made a part of) something tangible (something you can touch or read) like correspondence or newspapers.

Defamation is the noun (as in the law of defamation), *defamatory* is the adverb (the statement is defamatory), and *defame* is the verb (to defame someone). You can remember it as taking someone's fame away — defaming him.

Proving Defamation

Several critical elements are necessary to prove defamation. Before anyone can win a lawsuit against someone for defamation in most parts of the world, some questions must be asked. There must be *yes* answers to the following questions:

> ✔ Does the statement in question seem to be a fact rather than an expression of an opinion?

> ✔ Is the statement false?

> ✔ Is the false statement defamatory?

> ✔ Is the statement about the person who claims to be harmed by the statement (the plaintiff in a defamation lawsuit)?

> ✔ Was the statement made to someone other than the plaintiff?

> ✔ Did the communication of the statement to others harm the plaintiff's reputation, occupation, or business?
>
> ✔ Is the person being sued (the defendant) "at fault" for the harm?

The answer to the following question must be *no*:

> ✔ Is the person who made the statement protected from defamation lawsuits by some kind of legal privilege?

 Rarely will anyone agree with each other's answers in any particular situation, especially lawyers and judges. However, it's important to seek legal advice from a lawyer who handles defamation law in the appropriate jurisdiction (a certain state or country) when you need to know whether a statement could be defamatory.

Dissecting defamatory statements

Before a person may claim that she's been defamed, there must have been a statement. The statement must be false, appear to be a factual statement rather than an opinion, be defamatory, and be about the person claiming to be harmed by the statement.

A false statement

The law of defamation prohibits people from communicating *false* statements. You may have heard the expression, "Truth is a defense!" For defamation, the defendant can win a lawsuit if the statement is actually true. In fact, it doesn't even have to be the truth, the whole truth, and nothing but the truth. Slight and insignificant inaccuracies won't make a statement false under defamation law. However, just because a statement is true doesn't mean you can tell everyone about it. Check out Chapter 15 on privacy.

The disinformation age

We're used to reading books, magazines, and newspapers that editors check for accuracy, at least to some degree, before they ever reach our hands. That takes time, and many things never get published. The Internet is really great because there's so much more information available at a convenient location and whenever we want it. However, very little of it is checked by professionals for accuracy.

If you're reading information on the Internet, be aware that it might not be all that accurate. Read everything with a grain of salt, so to speak. If you're publishing information on the Internet, be a responsible publisher. When something doesn't seem quite right, check it out. Retractions usually don't get people off the hook for defamation.

England's Defamation Act of 1996

If your e-business includes activities in England, consult a lawyer in England about its defamation law. England's Defamation Act of 1996 defines three people who will be liable for defamatory content originated, edited, or published by them:

✔ **Author:** An originator of the statement that he or she intends to be published.

✔ **Editor:** A person having editorial or equivalent responsibility for the content of the statement or the decision to publish it.

✔ **Publisher:** A *commercial* publisher, that is, a person whose business is issuing material to the public, or a section of the public, and who issues material containing the statement in the course of that business. The term *issues* isn't defined. It could mean simply making it available.

Although there are other categories as well, an author, editor, or publisher *is not* any of the following:

✔ **Someone who operates or provides any equipment, system, or service** by means of which the statement is retrieved, copied, distributed, or made available in electronic form.

✔ **The broadcaster of a live program containing the statement** if the broadcaster has no effective control over the maker of the statement.

✔ **The operator or provider of access to a communications system** (like the Internet) by means of which the statement is transmitted, or made available, by a person over whom he/she has no effective control.

People who are not an author, an editor, or a publisher can still be sued for defamation. However, they have a defense (that is, will not have to pay) if they can show that they took reasonable care in relation to its publication and did not know, and had no reason to believe, that what they did caused or contributed to the publication of a defamatory statement.

A factual statement

The law also requires the statement to be one that appears to be a *fact*. It doesn't prohibit anyone from sharing opinions. After all, everyone is entitled to his or her own opinion. Right? Right. Well, almost. If it's an opinion, it must be *expressed* as an opinion.

One type of statement that's a clear "opinion" is a statement that *includes the facts upon which the opinion is based.* For example, "My neighbor told me he meets his friends at the lounge every night after work. I think he's an alcoholic." From this statement the listener can either agree or disagree with the opinion that the neighbor is an alcoholic because she heard the reason for the opinion.

The statement is also an "opinion" if the listener or reader is already aware of the facts upon which the opinion is based. Sometimes complete explanations just aren't necessary for someone to understand that a statement is really an opinion.

Bite your tongue (Until the funeral)

In some jurisdictions, the law presumes that a defamatory statement is false, and the defendant must come up with proof that the statement is true to avoid becoming legally responsible for any harm the plaintiff suffers. In other jurisdictions, it's the plaintiff's responsibility to come up with evidence that a statement is false before a defendant will be liable for defamation. In most places, the only person who can sue for defamation is the person or company whom the statement is about. Brothers, sisters, cousins, and uncles can't sue. Neither can dead people (or their heirs), which means that a dead person cannot be defamed.

When might an opinion get you into trouble? When you express an opinion in such a way that you're implying it's based upon facts that you know, but won't disclose (wink wink), and those "facts" are actually wrong. A court might view this as a speaker stating an opinion while simultaneously *implying* the existence of defamatory facts. If those undisclosed facts are false, Bingo! You might win a trip to court!

A defamatory statement

The false statement must also be *defamatory*. What's a defamatory statement? In most countries, it's one that tends to harm the reputation of the person in such a way that it lowers him or her in the esteem of the community or deters other people from associating or dealing with the person. The statement tends to diminish others' respect, goodwill, or confidence in the person. It might even create derogatory or unpleasant feelings or opinions about the person.

Publishing the statement

Before a false, defamatory statement can affect a person's reputation or harm his occupation, someone must communicate it to others. Communicating it to others is called *publishing* the statement (or publication of the statement).

How many people must hear or read the statement before it can harm a person? In the United States, most courts require that a large number of people know about the statement and that it leads an appreciable fraction of them to regard the plaintiff with contempt.

The fact that a single individual or very small group of people knows about the statement usually isn't enough for defamation law to protect the person *unless it's truly affecting the person's business or occupation*. And it can't just be any group of people (like a splinter wacko group who no longer believes the person is as wacko as them). The group must consist of "reasonable" people of a respectable size who lower their opinion of the person or stop doing business with him or her. As noted, however, communicating the statement to a single person could be unlawful if it truly affects one's business or occupation.

In other countries such as England, a court often considers the effect the communication would have in the eyes of society at large or in the eyes of a "reasonable person." In other words, the court ponders, "How would a reasonable person in a similar situation and under similar circumstances respond to this statement?"

Finding the fault

Before someone will be liable for defamation, she must be legally *at fault*. This means that the person (the defendant) did something that the law prohibits or did not do something that the law requires to be done. As a result, someone else (the plaintiff) suffered the harm. The harm must be somewhat substantial, however, The law doesn't force anyone to compensate for hurt feelings. Compensation is called *damages,* which usually take the form of money — as in paying big bucks to the plaintiff.

Figuring out the figures

When a person suffers harm as a result of a false, defamatory statement communicated about her, she may sue. However, there are different rules in the United States for public officials or public figures, private figures involved in a public controversy, and private figures not involved in a public controversy.

Public officials and public figures

Public officials include politicians and government officials. Public figures are generally people who seek the public arena, such as celebrities.

Someone writing a statement that defames a public official or a public figure is at fault only if the statement is written with actual malice. The plaintiff must prove *actual malice,* which means that the people writing, editing, or publishing the statement either knew, at the time of writing or publishing it, that the statement was false or that they acted with reckless disregard as to whether or not the statement was false.

Reckless disregard could include matters like hearing that a statement might not be true, learning that the source of the information isn't reliable, or hearing contradictory statements that cast serious doubt upon the truth of the statement. Despite all this, they write and publish the statement anyway.

STATE BY STATE

Defamation and the tangled Web we weave

Slander is a spoken communication of the false, defamatory statement. Libel is the printed, or other tangible, form of the statement. Those definitions seem simple enough, but what if you hear a defamatory statement during a video-conference, read it during a live Internet chat, or see it during a live Webcast? Is it spoken or written?

And what if someone's Web site has live video shots from a secret camera that appears to be taping someone famous doing something pretty nasty, but the person you see is really just an actor pretending to be that famous person? Body gestures are normally slander, but they're appearing on tape. So is it libel?

The distinction between slander and libel can be important in some jurisdictions. For example, a court could decide that something spoken during a videoconference is slander rather than libel. In some places, that decision means the plaintiff must prove actual financial loss — not just harm to the plaintiff's reputation or business relationship, or emotional distress — from the statement. Trying to prove actual financial loss is harder than proving harm to one's reputation.

The reason for this distinction may be due, in part, to the limited number of people who may "hear" slander. Spoken words last but a moment. Harm to one's reputation may be just as brief, so a person needs proof that the words actually caused financial loss.

On the other hand, a large number of people can read text that is libelous for a long time to come. Harm to one's reputation could continue for as long as the writing is available. Therefore, the person may have to prove only this harm without the extra requirement of showing financial loss.

In the jurisdictions that require the plaintiff to prove actual financial loss for slander, there's normally an exception if the slander is *slander per se*. This usually involves a statement that attributes a serious crime involving moral turpitude to the plaintiff; concerns a "loathsome" disease; attacks a plaintiff's competency in his or her business, trade, or profession; or claims that a woman is unchaste. (A crime involving moral turpitude is the type of crime involving immorality or one that is particularly hateful like theft or rape, rather than running a red light.)

A person isn't necessarily acting in reckless disregard of the truth by failing to investigate the facts, however. The writer and publisher have to be pretty sloppy and reckless before any false statement will result in liability for defamation.

Private figures

Celebrities aren't the only ones who can be public figures. Some private figures (private citizens) may be, under the law, public figures for a particular purpose. Courts call them "limited public figures." This often occurs when a private citizen ends up in the middle of a public controversy. This type of public figure must also prove actual malice before someone who publishes a defamatory statement about him will be liable for defamation.

Whether or not a private figure becomes a limited public figure depends on the situation. Usually, the following must occur:

De price of defame

Why are public figures treated differently when it comes to defamatory statements? Well, once upon a time the U.S. Supreme Court decided that people who seek public office or media attention must accept greater public scrutiny of what they do. Therefore, they must accept the possible exposure to defamation as a price for their fame. Public figures also enjoy greater access to various channels of communication, like the press, than do private figures. This access allows them the opportunity to contradict lies or correct errors and communicate that to the public. In other words, they can help themselves rather than resort to the courts.

Public figures aren't necessarily public figures for all purposes. There may be parts of their lives that should be private, and courts often protect that privacy.

✔ There must be a realistic expectation that the person's involvement will have a major impact on the controversy.

✔ The person must be more than a bystander or an observer.

✔ It should be foreseeable that the controversy, or its resolution, will have a substantial impact on people in addition to the actual participants in the controversy.

✔ Sometimes the person must voluntarily become part of the controversy before she will be a limited public figure.

For those private figures who become involved in public controversies but are not public figures, they may need to prove only that the defendant was merely negligent to win a lawsuit for defamation. Negligent means that the defendant needed to do a bit of investigating to make sure the statement was true before communicating it to others. In effect, the defendant may need to do more checking when the statement isn't about public figures.

As for private figures who are not involved in public controversies, often people who defame them don't even need to be negligent before they'll be liable for defamation. In fact, publishers who act conscientiously and merely publish someone else's defamatory statements about private figures who are not part of a public controversy may still be liable!

Who can be liable for defamation?

A person or a company can be sued for defamation even if someone else makes the false statement. Often, the person who is liable is not only the initial communicator, but may also be all those who publish or distribute the statement. The person being sued could even be someone who reprints or republishes a statement from another publisher.

Naturally, the author — the person who starts it all — is normally responsible. Others who might share the responsibility include editors who review and revise content. Publishers may also share the blame for providing the libelous statements to the public, their subscribers, or their group of readers.

Most courts permit publishers to rely upon professional third parties, such as news wire services and freelance writers, without being held at fault for republishing a defamatory statement.

Employers are often responsible for their employees' defamatory statements made while performing their job duties. Usually, essential interoffice e-mails and communications between management regarding termination or other employment decisions cannot be the subject of a defamation lawsuit. See Chapter 10 for more information about employee e-mail.

In contrast, false and defamatory e-mails or other information that managers or employees share with others might lead to liability. In addition, false and defamatory communications that are not essential to employment decisions might also result in the employer's liability.

In the United States, a federal law protects providers and users of interactive computer services for any information provided by another information content provider. In other words, an Internet Service Provider or online service is not normally held responsible for the content provided by someone else. There's a debate among legal professionals as to whether or not this law allows all online services off the hook. It may not if the service actually monitors the content.

The privileged few

In the United States, some people have legal privileges that prevent them from being sued. They cannot be held liable for any defamatory statements they make under certain circumstances. These people include the following:

When you leave the U.S., bring a suit

In England, defamation laws are similar to those in the United States except they don't distinguish between public figures and private figures. Writers and publishers might be liable for defamation even if they check out all the facts thoroughly! This is one reason that some famous celebrities flock to London to sue international magazines under England's laws. Winning a defamation lawsuit there is much easier to do than in the United States.

The defamation laws of Australia, Canada, France, Germany, Israel, and Singapore are similar to those of the United States except that most of these countries, like England, don't distinguish between public figures and private figures. Some of them, such as France and Germany, severely punish those who publish defamatory statements about their citizens.

✔ Anyone who makes a defamatory statement with a person's consent. In other words, the plaintiff allowed the defendant to make the defamatory statement. Think of a roast or some other comedic situation.

✔ Participants in judicial proceedings (judges, lawyers, witnesses, jurors) regarding statements made that were relevant to those proceedings. This may not include statements made during press conferences.

✔ Participants in legislative proceedings.

✔ Executive and administrative officials.

✔ Spouses in their communications with each other. (You and your spouse can tear into everyone and everything in confidence, if you like. Just don't share it with others.)

Avoiding Libel, Liability, and Slander Suits

When you spread false information about other people, the law of defamation may protect them. The purpose of the law is to protect reputations and relationships. The law also acts as a checks-and-balances of the media to make sure they don't stray too far from the truth.

Although the law for defamation on the Internet is evolving, the following situations show how you might trigger libel or slander laws if you provide information in your e-business:

✔ You like to keep in touch with customers and colleagues, so you e-mail a newsletter to people periodically. The newsletter includes reports on business activities that you hear about as well as interesting postings you find on the Web. You select the content, but you don't check the credibility of the authors or whether the content may be harmful to anyone.

✔ You read some stories written by other e-business entrepreneurs on the Internet that interest you. Potential customers who visit your site may find them interesting, too. You set up your Web site so that it links to those specific Web pages — the other site's content gets pulled into a frame on your site. Now it looks like it's part of your site. People can read all those articles and never leave your home page!

✔ You like to hear opinions from other people. Your site allows any user to post anything that's on his or her mind.

You may have good intentions. You don't mean to do anything wrong. But don't fool yourself into believing that your good faith will keep you out of hot water. "I didn't do it on *purpose!*" might be meaningless if you get sued. The laws in most countries state that certain people are legally responsible for defamation even if they don't intend to hurt anyone. In fact, in some countries, communicating false information is a crime punishable by imprisonment under certain circumstances!

The important point is to be responsible about the information and statements you share with others. Take the time to think before you post.

Chapter 15

Privacy in the Information Wonderland

*I*f you could step through Alice's looking glass and discover Wonderland, would you? Could you keep your experiences secret or would you share what you saw and heard with others? Maybe you could sell what you learned to others. After all, inside information has value!

Many Internet companies think they found Wonderland in the form of vast amounts of information about people and their habits. They're learning what people prefer in such areas as entertainment, food, cars, stockbrokers, news, and electronics. Their Wonderland is a place where e-companies can match generic information about buyers' likes and dislikes with real people around the world. Once they make this match, they hope to satisfy each individual's desire with the products or services they're promoting.

Navigating the Internet's Wonderland

How do e-companies get to Wonderland? By collecting information from people online — those surfing the Internet. One source of this information is online registration forms or purchase orders that visitors complete on the companies' Web sites.

Other sites have computer programs that track and gather information from Web site visitors, such as the type of computer and browser they're using. Still other Web site owners use cookies, a computer file that the Web site's computer stores on the visitor's personal computer hard drive. *Cookies* collect and retain information about the visitor's online activities and send it back to the site's computer. See Chapter 11 for more information.

However, you'll face a hurdle on the way to Wonderland. It's called privacy. When people who surf the Net realize that someone is tracking their every move, a lot of the people get angry. As a result, the 21st century is beginning with private individuals filing lawsuits against a handful of high-profile U.S. companies for invasion of privacy, among other things. Don't assume from these lawsuits that a law prohibits the gathering of information from the Internet. Unlike the European Union, privacy laws that clearly regulate the Internet in the United States are pretty scarce (but see the section "Collecting information from kids," later in this chapter). Governments have been trying to let Internet companies regulate themselves when it comes to privacy. Unfortunately, this system isn't working really well. Therefore, some e-companies are coming under attack and are trying to defend their practices of collecting and sharing personal information they obtain from people using the Internet.

Lawyers and lawmakers are now bellying up to the bar to make their preferences about privacy known. Until the law settles, try following general Internet privacy guidelines if you plan to collect or share information you gather at your e-site. Abide by general laws that may not specifically refer to the Internet and you may just find a safe harbor to wait out the storm.

Understanding the right to privacy

When does someone have a right to keep information private? There is no single privacy law in the U.S. that can answer this question as of this writing. A handful of federal laws require companies to keep some things private, like credit reports and tax returns. Also, most states have general privacy laws as well as laws concerning certain information like medical or financial information.

In addition, privacy under state common law has evolved from court decisions over the years (see Chapter 1 for more information on common law). Under common law, there are generally four ways you can invade a person's privacy:

- ✔ By disclosing a person's private information to the public in a highly objectionable manner
- ✔ By intruding upon a person's physical solitude or seclusion
- ✔ By using someone's name or likeness (photograph, drawing, and so on) for your own benefit
- ✔ By publicizing something about a person that places her in a false light in the public eye

None of these really fit precisely with Internet activities that involve collecting information. For instance, many Web site owners probably aren't providing the information they collect *to the public*; they're probably keeping it for their own use. It's questionable whether cookies or other tracking programs intrude on a person's *physical* space. Although some legal experts may argue that sending cookies to a person's computer may be a form of trespass on her property, others would argue that visitors can set their browsers to reject cookies from Web sites.

Collecting information doesn't usually involve using someone's name or likeness for the benefit of the Web site owner. It also rarely, if ever, involves publicity.

So is anyone successful in stopping a site from collecting information? Yes. The Federal Trade Commission forced some e-sites to change their collection activities when they weren't following their own privacy policies. In fact, an e-business that collects and shares information secretly, or sells it when the company goes bankrupt, could be conducting unfair and deceptive trade practices, which are unlawful.

The only federal law about Internet privacy in effect by April 2000 is the Children's Online Privacy Protection Act described in the section "Collecting information from kids." Several states are now considering privacy legislation to regulate the collection and sharing of information on the Net. This legislation could make it difficult for e-businesses to comply with all the different laws. Therefore, bills on this subject have also been introduced in the U.S. Congress. They will most likely require companies to do the following:

- Take some measure to make sure that the information collected is secure from people trying to access it without permission.

- Allow visitors to choose whether they want their information collected or used by anyone.

- Allow people access to their own information to correct or delete it.

- Provide clear privacy policies for visitors to read on the Web sites.

When it comes to the Internet, the European Union (the EU) is in the lead on regulating privacy (see Chapter 1 for more information on the EU). The countries that are members of the EU have passed laws or regulations to comply with a 1995 EU "Directive on Data Protection." As described in the section "Collecting information from adults," later in this chapter, it regulates the collection of personal information from people in these European countries.

To help your e-business stay in a safe harbor, think about what type of information you may collect, who you may share it with, and what to include in your privacy policy.

Collecting information from your visitors

It's amazing how much personal information people give to complete strangers simply because they ask. The situation is no different on the Web.

What's the big deal? Many people prefer to keep their affairs private, and their wishes should be honored. In addition, providing too much information could cause problems for them for years.

Some unscrupulous people steal identities to do all sorts of nasty things while they pretend to be someone else. With a complete name, residence address, birth date, and social security number, they can become anyone! News programs often report stories about imposters running up debts under someone else's identity. It might take years and cost thousands of dollars for the person to clean up the mess — if he ever can! Often creditors won't believe the debts were incurred by an imposter. Computer hackers may also commit crimes using someone else's online identity, and it may be difficult to prove innocence when the crimes were committed behind closed doors where no one could see what the hacker looked like.

Some people believe that collecting information from people secretly means that the information is more accurate. However, it's more important that people feel safe and secure at your e-site. After all, repeat business leads to success. Therefore, many e-business entrepreneurs are learning that it's more important to let visitors know what information is being collected and that the e-site exercises caution with any information collected and shared.

How much caution you should exercise depends on the type of information you collect. There are two types of information:

- **Generic information** doesn't identify any specific person. It may include likes and dislikes, range of income, job duties, profession, or other general information.

- **Personally identifiable information** is the kind that allows someone to actually identify a person, either by that information alone or when it's combined with other information. This type of information includes names, addresses, telephone numbers, e-mail addresses, birth dates, social security numbers, driver's license numbers, and mothers' maiden names.

Most Americans don't realize that social security numbers are protected by law — *they're private!* With only a few exceptions, individuals are not required to give them to anyone. However, companies may lawfully refuse to do business with someone who doesn't provide a social security number.

When any Web site asks for my social security number or my mother's maiden name, I leave. I'm sure that I'm not the only one who responds this way. Ask only for information you truly believe you need. If you ask for more, people may become suspicious about your activities.

Information that can identify someone personally and the secret collection of information are the main focus of regulators and privacy advocates. Therefore, pay special attention to the privacy rights of others when you set up your plan to gather information.

Collecting information from kids

Children using the Internet are very vulnerable to heavy-handed advertisers and, well, weirdoes lurking in chat rooms. Therefore, Congress passed the Children's Online Privacy Protection Act. It requires certain companies that collect information on the Internet to follow special regulations. For a checklist of important points your privacy policy should cover as it pertains to children, read the "Privacy policies just for children" section later in this chapter.

If your e-business operates a commercial Web site or an online service directed to children under the age of 13 and you collect or keep personal information about them, you must comply with the act. If your e-business operates a commercial Web site or an online service directed to a general audience, but you know that you're collecting or keeping personal information from children under the age of 13, you must comply with the act.

Do you collect *personal* information? This law regulates companies that collect or keep information that may help someone identify or contact a child. Such information includes a full name, home address, e-mail address, telephone number, or any other similar information. Personal information also includes generic information like interests, hobbies, or other facts collected through cookies or other tracking mechanisms that can identify the individual child when the generic information is tied to full names, addresses, or similar information.

If you aren't involved with collecting or keeping this kind of information, you don't need to be concerned with this particular law. If you are involved, you must do the following:

- ✔ Disclose what you're going to do with the information and provide certain statements and notices in your privacy policy.
- ✔ Get consent from a parent or guardian to use the personal information of kids.
- ✔ Allow parents to access the information you collect.
- ✔ Follow certain guidelines to protect the privacy and safety of the kids.

The Federal Trade Commission (FTC) makes the regulations also called *rules* that you must follow under this law. The FTC's Web site at www.ftc.gov has more information to help you figure out whether you need to comply with this law and how you can comply with the FTC's regulations.

Disclosing what you're going to do with the information

If you're collecting or keeping personally identifiable information about children, you need to let them and their parents know what you might do with it. In other words, you need to have a privacy notice for your site, and you must follow it. The specific requirements are in the section "Privacy policies just for children," later in this chapter.

Frequent slamming program

I visited a major airline's Web site in 1999 to sign up for its frequent flyer program online. The form asked for my name, residence address, birth date, and other information. Because it's a well-known company and it needed that information for the program, I listed everything except my birth date, which was optional on the form. I wouldn't mind giving them the year I was born, but I wouldn't provide my complete birth date.

One week later, I received a telephone call from my long-distance telephone company. "Did you change your long-distance service?" the woman asked. Of course not! But someone changed my long-distance carrier without my permission! I'd been slammed by another major long-distance carrier.

I began to investigate. The "new" long-distance carrier had a partnership with the airline for its frequent flyer program. Therefore, that Web site shared my information with the phone company, who hired independent telemarketers to try to get people to change services.

It seems that one of the independent telemarketers (who probably worked on commission)

used the information I provided to the site, pretended to be me, and changed my service. The only problem was that she needed my birth date to confirm it was me — and I hadn't provided my birth date on the site. I asked the "new" company what birth date the person used to verify she was me. I learned that the birth date the person used was not mine!

Someone used my information to try to make a commission by changing my long-distance service, but she had to make up a birth date. The airline's personnel helped me discover how it happened, but the telephone company denied even the possibility of the occurrence. I considered suing the telephone company, but other business obligations prevented me from filing suit. I will never again do business with that long-distance service.

No company can control all of its independent marketers. However, sites can be more careful about the information they share, who they share it with, and how it's used.

Getting consent you can verify

The law also requires you to provide notice directly to parents about your collection of personal information about children. Your notice must include the same information included on the Web site notice described in the section "Privacy policies just for children," later in this chapter. In addition, the notice must include the following information:

- ✔ A notice that you want to collect personal information from the child
- ✔ A statement that the parent's consent is required for the collection, use, and disclosure of the information
- ✔ An explanation of how the parent can provide consent to you

Your notice to parents must be written in a clear and understandable way. It may not contain any unrelated or confusing information. You may send the notice by e-mail, postal mail, or certain other methods. Sending a notice is not enough, however. You must also obtain a parent's consent under certain circumstances.

Before you may collect, use, or disclose personal information from a child, you must obtain parental consent and verify it. The ways to verify the consent vary depending on the way you want to use the information.

For instance, you may normally obtain consent by e-mail, a telephone call, or a letter if you use the personal information only for your own internal purposes, such as sending promotional updates about the site to a child. If you plan to let third parties or the public see any of the information, however, you must use a more reliable method to verify a parent's consent. This method may include the following:

- A mailed or faxed form with a parent's signature

- The acceptance and verification of a credit card number

- A call from a parent on a toll-free telephone line answered by trained personnel

- An e-mail accompanied by a digital signature (see Chapter 3 to find out about digital signatures)

- An e-mail accompanied by a PIN (personal identification number) or password obtained through one of the verification methods described in the preceding four checked points

Even if you already obtained a parent's consent, you may have to get the consent again! If you change anything about collecting, using, or disclosing the personal information, you need to provide a new notice and obtain a new consent if you make any material (important) changes. For instance, maybe you want to disclose the information to more companies in other lines of business. You need to get new consent from the parents of the kids in your data pool.

The Federal Trade Commission will begin to review these regulations in October 2001 to see whether they're working well. Stay tuned to its Web site for updates (www.ftc.gov). The rules for obtaining consent may change in April 2002.

Providing parents access to the information and other guidelines

When you collect personal information from a child, you must allow a parent to consent to collecting the information but to prohibit you from disclosing it to anyone else. You cannot require a parent to consent to both.

If a parent requests it, you must disclose the general *kinds* of personal information you collect from kids, such as "names, e-mail addresses, and hobbies." You must also tell them the specific information you collect from their children.

Directing your site to kids

What's a Web site *directed to children* under the age of 13? The Children's Online Privacy Protection Act has a pretty general definition for this kind of site. It's any *commercial* Web site or online service, or any portion of that site or service, that is targeted to children under the age of 13. Although the law doesn't define commercial, this word normally means that the site is a business site rather than an individual's site.

The law also states that a commercial Web site or online service is *not* one that is directed to children if the site or service simply uses information location tools (such as a directory, index, reference, pointer, or hypertext links) to refer or link people to a site or service directed to children.

Make sure that you're dealing with the child's parent or legal guardian before you provide access to the child's specific information that you collect. Some of the ways you can make sure you're dealing with the right person are the same as verifying consent to disclose information to a third party, as described in the section "Getting consent you can verify," earlier in this chapter.

You must allow a parent to revoke his or her consent at any time. Parents may refuse to allow you to continue using or collecting their child's personal information, and they may direct you to delete it. If so, you must comply with their request.

You may terminate any service you provide to a child when a parent will not allow you to collect or use the kid's personal information, *but only if* the information is reasonably necessary for the kid to participate in that activity. For example, perhaps you require children to provide their e-mail addresses to participate in a chat room so you can contact anyone misbehaving in the room. If a parent later revokes consent to use the e-mail address, which requires you to delete the e-mail address, you may refuse to allow the child to take part in the chat room. However, you can't refuse to allow the child to participate in other parts of the site that don't require an e-mail address.

Collecting information from adults

There are no laws in the U.S. regarding the collection of personal information from adults that are similar to the children's law. However, some bills on the topic are pending in some states and in Congress.

Unlike the U.S., European countries that are members of the European Union have begun regulating the collection and use of all personal information. They protect the processing of personal data.

Under these laws, personal data is any information relating to an identified or identifiable person, called a *data subject*. Who is an identifiable person? It's anyone who can be identified by an identification number. It's also anyone who can be identified by any specific factors relating to his or her physical, physiological, mental, economic, cultural, or social identity. In other words, if you can link information to a specific person, that information is probably personal data.

Generally, these laws regulate companies that collect, organize, store, adapt, alter, consult, use, or disclose personal data from Europeans. It's called *processing* the data. In other words, practically anything a company can do with information is considered processing.

When companies process this information, the European laws require (among other things) them to do the following:

✔ Process the data fairly and lawfully.

✔ Have, and explain, a legitimate purpose for collecting the data.

✔ Collect only information that is relevant to this purpose.

✔ Not collect more information than is needed for this purpose.

✔ Keep the information only as long as is necessary for this purpose.

You don't need parental consent if . . .

The Federal Trade Commission's regulations include several exceptions that may allow you to collect a kid's e-mail address without getting consent. You don't need to obtain consent when:

✔ You collect a child's or a parent's e-mail address in order to provide the parent with notice and to obtain consent.

✔ You collect an e-mail address to respond to a one-time request from a child, and you then delete it from your system.

✔ You collect an e-mail address to respond more than once, but only to a specific request such as a subscription to a newsletter. In this case, you must notify the parent that you're communicating regularly with

the child. You must give the parent the opportunity to stop the communication before you send or deliver a second communication to the child.

✔ You collect a child's name or online contact information to protect the safety of a child who is participating on the site. If you do this, you must notify the parent and give the parent the opportunity to prevent further use of the information.

✔ You collect a child's name or online contact information to protect the security or liability of the site or to respond to law enforcement, if necessary. You may not use it for any other purpose.

✔ Keep the information up-to-date and accurate.

✔ Provide adequate security to protect the information.

✔ Allow individuals to access their own information to correct any incorrect information.

✔ Allow individuals to object to their information being used for any direct marketing.

✔ Provide the person with the identity of the company that controls collection of the information, the purpose for collecting it, and the identity of any third parties who will receive the information.

✔ Explain whether the persona *must* or *may* (optional) provide the information and the consequences to the person if he does not provide the information.

✔ Process the information only with the person's specific, informed, and unambiguous consent. In other words, the person must receive sufficient information to consent to the specific use, and the consent must be very clear.

These laws also restrict any company from sharing this information with a company in any country outside the European Union that does not have laws similar to these laws. The United States does not have such laws, which means that European companies may be prohibited from sharing information with U.S. companies. The U.S. government is trying to help U.S. companies. At the time of this writing, it's trying to finalize a deal with the EU that may allow some individual companies that comply with these standards to share information from the EU.

Preparing Your Privacy Policy

A privacy policy explains how a Web site handles information obtained from Web site visitors that may be private. It may be called a privacy *notice* or *statement* or *policy*. Often the words mean the same thing. I call it a policy because it's more than what you state in a notice on a Web site; it should be the way you require everyone associated with your site to handle your visitors' information.

Privacy policies are a very important part of the Web. If people don't trust the Web, they won't become your e-business customers. Therefore, putting together your own privacy policy is a must.

Read through some privacy policies before you put your own one together. They will give you an idea of how to set up your own procedures. Take the time to plan your strategy to handle this information. Explain your policy in the statement on your site; the statement shouldn't be a mere form with no bearing on your actual activities. If you don't follow your policy as stated on your site, you could mislead your visitors.

Make your privacy policy a separate page on your site. Have a link to it on your home page as well as near every place where your visitors provide information to you. If you must comply with the Children's Online Privacy Protection Act, have a separate privacy policy for the children's stuff.

Privacy policies just for children

If you collect or keep information from children under the age of 13, you must have a privacy policy regarding this information, you must state this policy on your Web site, and you must follow this policy.

Your privacy policy and statement on the Web site must meet the following Federal Trade Commission regulations:

- ✔ You must have links to your Web page where you describe your collection practices and provide the privacy notice. The links must be on your home page and at each area where you collect personal information from children. If you have a site or online service for a general audience, the home page means the home page to the children's area.

- ✔ Visitors to your site must be able to see the links clearly. They must be able to distinguish these links from other links. Simply providing a small link at the bottom of a page or one that looks like other links isn't sufficient.

- ✔ Your privacy notice must be clearly written and understandable. Don't include any material that's unrelated or confusing.

- ✔ Your privacy notice must include the names of every company collecting or maintaining children's personal information from your Web site or online service. It must also list contact information (address, telephone number, and e-mail address) for at least one of these companies — the one that will respond to inquiries from parents.

- ✔ Your privacy notice must include a description of the kind of personal information you collect from children and how you collect it. For example, you might state that you collect their names, e-mail addresses, and hobbies directly from children on the site and through cookies.

- ✔ Your privacy notice must describe how you might use the personal information. For instance, will you use the e-mail address to send promotions back to the child? Will you use it to notify the children if they win a prize? Will you allow other people to see names in a chat room?

✔ If you might disclose the information to third parties or to anyone else, your privacy notice must state this. Your privacy notice must also state the following:

- A list of the kinds of businesses (for example, advertising companies) run by those third parties, what they might use the information for, and whether the third parties have agreed to maintain the confidentiality and security of the information.

- An option for the child's parent to agree to the collection and use of the child's information without consenting to the disclosure of the information to third parties.

✔ If you may require a child to provide personal information in order to participate in some activity on the site, you may not require any more information than is reasonably necessary to participate in it. Explain this in your privacy notice.

✔ You must allow the parent to review the child's personal information, ask to have it deleted, or refuse to allow any further collection or use of the child's information. You must state this in your privacy notice with an explanation of your procedures for the parent to follow to do these things.

The CD with this book includes samples of a Privacy Policy for Adults & Kids (Parental Consent) with explanations and a copy without explanations, and a sample Privacy Policy Provision (Kids under 13) (a copy with and a copy without explanations).

You may have to obtain consent *again* if you change your collection practices or policies after you obtain a parent's consent. Take the time to think about them before you gather your consents.

Privacy policies for everyone

Although there are no specific requirements for a privacy policy, the Internet industry has begun to put together suggestions and guidelines. Based on these suggestions and other e-companies' experiences, it's a good idea to set up a system to handle personal information by answering the following questions:

✔ What are your e-business goals? What information do you want from your Web site visitors to help achieve these goals? Will gathering this information be troublesome to your visitors?

✔ How will you make sure that the information is secure on your computers and remains private?

✔ How will you provide access to individuals to review, change, or delete their information? How can you do so affordably?

✔ How will you allow individuals to decide whether they want to provide information to you? How will they be able to let you know? Who will be responding to them for your e-company?

✔ How will you make sure the information is accurate and up-to-date?

✔ Will you share information with other e-companies? Will they keep the information safe? How will they use it? Will you sell it if you sell your e-business?

Once you answer these questions, you're on your way to developing your privacy policy. Your computer programmers need to make sure that your site works the way you want it to work to implement your privacy policy. Then you should prepare your privacy policy for your Web site.

Many e-companies believe that stating the following in your privacy policy is a good idea:

✔ The kind of personal information you will be gathering (such as name, address, e-mail address)

✔ Who will be collecting the information (you or some other company)

✔ How you will be collecting the information (online forms, cookies, or other technology)

✔ Why and how you or others will be using the information

✔ Who will be sharing the information (the types of companies, such as advertisers or content partners)

✔ The choices that visitors may make regarding the collection, use, or sharing of their information (most companies prefer allowing visitors to opt out of marketing promotions or other uses)

✔ Any restrictions for visitors who don't provide the information (such as limited access to certain parts or all of the Web site)

✔ The security procedures that you and others will use to protect the information from others misusing or altering it

✔ How visitors can update or correct any inaccurate information

A sample Privacy Policy with explanations and a copy without explanations are on the CD.

Selecting Privacy Seals of Approval

In addition to your privacy policy, you may want to add a privacy organization's "seal of approval." Some organizations offer privacy programs for Web sites. If you comply with their guidelines and pay a fee, you can include their logo on your site.

Two of these organizations are BBB Online (www.bbbonline.org), part of the Council of Better Business Bureaus, and TRUSTe (www.truste.org). They also monitor your privacy collection policies and practices. Whether these seals of approval are worth the money to you is an individual decision based on the customers you want to attract to your site. They may be more helpful for business-to-consumer e-businesses. Business-to-business e-companies tend to have more direct relationships with their visitors.

The success of your e-business Web site may depend upon trust. A thought-out privacy policy that you monitor and enforce will do a lot toward achieving success.

Chapter 16

Clearing Rights to Use Someone Else's Work

*N*o man is an island. I get by with a little help from my friends. And isn't it ironic, don't you think? We like to use stuff that others create.

I'm talking about stories and music and movies and pictures, logos and icons, and songs and text. On the Web, it's so easy to copy the stuff, to print or record, or even to morph. But much of the stuff isn't free for the taking. It's property with rights that belongs to another person. Don't think that this means *all* property is off limits. It just means that you need to ask for permission to use it.

Learning the Lingo and Preparing for the Process

Clearing rights is the phrase that intellectual property attorneys use to describe a process by which you seek permission to use something that belongs to someone else in your creative projects. *Clearances* are the written permissions, or licenses, that you receive from the owners.

You may want to use someone else's intellectual property, such as a copyrighted work, a trademark, or a patent. You may also want to use someone's name, likeness, or voice. Since copyrightable creations are called *works of authorship,* I refer to all intellectual property, names, likenesses, and voices as a *work* in this chapter to keep it simple.

When you discover work that you want to include on your Web site or in your creative projects, try the following procedure to get permission to use stuff that belongs to someone else:

1. **Look at the entire work that you want to use, and then separate it into parts. Determine whether you may need permission to use one or more works (see the section "Separating the Work into Parts," later in this chapter).**

2. **Determine whether the works you want to use may be protected by copyright, trademark, patent, or publicity and privacy laws (see the section "Determining Which Law Protects Which Work," later in this chapter).**

3. **Consider how you want to use the work, and then determine whether the way in which you want to use the work requires permission from the owner of the work (see the section "Figuring Out Which Rights You Need," in this chapter).**

4. **Determine who owns the rights you need (see the section "Finding the Owners," later in this chapter).**

    Search the Internet for contact information.

5. **Double-check with an experienced intellectual property lawyer to make sure that you're moving in the right direction.**

6. **Prepare a professional letter, requesting permission to use the work, to send to the owner of the work (see the section "Requesting Permission," later in this chapter).**

7. **Obtain written permission from the owner of the work you want to use or the owner's legal representative (see the section "Confirming Permission," in this chapter).**

Separating the Work into Parts

When you see photographs, hear music, watch a program, or read an article that you want to include on your Web site or in your creative work, look closely at the work as a whole. Are there parts to that work? A photograph depicts the photographer's vision of something or someone who appears in the photograph. A music CD includes a song (lyrics and melody) and sounds. A television program may include a script, music, people, products (like a cola bottle), and creative works by a director, set designer, set decorator, and others.

Whatever the work is that you want to use, it probably has several parts. Break it down. Separate the parts. Each part may involve different legal rights, and each part may belong to someone else. How do you know whether the work you want to use is protected by law? Maybe it doesn't belong to anyone. Maybe it's just property that no longer belongs to anyone.

Assume that someone owns rights to anything that seems creative, artistic, original, personal, or valuable before you use it without permission. The following are some examples:

- ✔ Stories (published and unpublished), magazine articles, and poems
- ✔ Computer programs in software and games
- ✔ Plays, teleplays, and screenplays (for the stage, television, and motion pictures, respectively)
- ✔ Song lyrics, music, pantomimes, and choreography
- ✔ Photographs, fine art, posters, comic strips, and some comic strip characters
- ✔ Two- and three-dimensional pictures, graphics, and sculptures
- ✔ Maps, globes, charts, diagrams, models, technical drawings, and architectural plans
- ✔ Motion pictures, audiovisual works, and multimedia productions
- ✔ Business names, product names, and service providers' names
- ✔ Personal names, voices, and likenesses including photographs or drawings of specific people
- ✔ Inventions, technology, and business processes

The law doesn't protect every story, song, map, and so on. Each creation must meet certain legal requirements before someone may prevent others from using it. Intellectual property law is extremely complex. Double-check with an intellectual property expert before you make a final decision to use, or not to use, a work.

Determining Which Law Protects Which Work

The works you want to use most likely fall into one of five legal areas: copyright, trademark, patent, publicity, or privacy. The following sections give you an idea of what kinds of things might be copyrighted, trademarked, patented, or protected by publicity or privacy rights.

What copyright protects

People associate a copyright with something artistic, and that's fairly accurate. It depends upon your definition of art. Copyright protects *works of authorship,* which include fine art as well as computer programs, music, and maps.

Copyright laws protect certain types of work that a person's mind creates (thus the name *intellectual* property). The work must be all of the following:

- ✔ Original
- ✔ A work of authorship as defined in copyright law
- ✔ Expressed and fixed (attached, stored, or made a part of) to a tangible medium that someone can perceive (feel, see, or hear), use to reproduce the work, or communicate the work in some other way

Originality

There's no precise definition of copyright originality. Generally, it means that someone creates a work independently instead of copying it entirely from someone else. The work must also have something else that makes it special, like a touch of the creator's personality.

Originality means that the work is more than something functional. For instance, clothing serves a functional purpose. Although a dress design on fabric may be copyrightable, a dress is not. A dress is functional; it covers the body. A creative computer source code is copyrightable, but portions of the computer program that are common or necessary to all computer programs are not copyrightable. The common or necessary parts are more functional than original.

Facts are not original creations. Therefore, such things as telephone number listings and history books that merely state facts are not copyrightable. Telephone number listings could, however, become a copyrightable compilation (see the sidebar "Works protected by U.S. copyright law"). To create a copyrightable history book, the author would need to express the historical facts in an original way. Copyright originality doesn't mean *unique.* In fact, two people could create exactly the same thing and each own copyrights to the work, as long as they come up with the idea and express it in the work independently.

Works of authorship

In the United States, copyright law protects only works of authorship that fall into one of the following 11 categories: Literary works; musical works; sound recordings; pictures, graphics, and sculptures; dramatic works; motion pictures and audiovisual works; pantomimes and choreography; architecture; collections; compilations; and derivative works.

When do copyright rights arise?

The owner of a copyrighted work doesn't need to register her work with the U.S. Copyright Office for copyright law to protect the work. In fact, the work doesn't even need to include a copyright symbol © for the work to be protected. Once an original work of authorship is expressed and fixed in a tangible medium, copyright law protects it. Instantly. For instance, sing your song as you record it on a tape recorder. You've just expresssed and fixed it in a tangible medium — the tape. Your song is protected by copyright. Type your story into a word processing program and save the file. Copyright law protects it.

Registration and copyright notice provide copyright owners with special benefits, but the law still protects the work without registration or notice. See Chapter 17 for more information on registering a copyrightable work.

The creator of any of these works is called an author. When I use this word, it means the creator. If the original work you'd like to use falls into one of these categories, it's probably a work that copyright law protects. Descriptions of these works are in the sidebar "Works protected by U.S. copyright law."

Ideas, titles, phrases, and names are not copyrightable (see the section, "What trademark laws protect" later in this chapter). They don't have enough substance to be a work of authorship. For example, many people write about the idea of a romance between people and the conflicts that arise. The writer must create an original expression — more than just the idea — to create a work of authorship. She needs to express the idea in something like a book or a play.

Fixed in a tangible medium of expression

How does that expression go? "He's a legend in his own mind." If so, he must have a whole story going on in his head. In that case, he won't hold a copyright to it because it's only in his head. Copyright protection automatically exists when the author *fixes* an original work of authorship in a tangible medium of expression. Fixes means that it's attached to something so it's going to last awhile. Someone must be able to perceive it, reproduce it, or communicate it in some other way to people.

In the United States, performing an impromptu sketch live on stage won't protect the work because it's not fixed on paper or on tape. Copyright won't protect an online story written in a chat room if no one saves it — the story isn't fixed in something that lasts for a while.

Do you think that the work you want to use, or any of its parts, is a copyrightable work? If an original work of authorship is fixed in a tangible medium of expression, you may need permission to use it.

Works protected by U.S. copyright law

In the United States, only works of authorship that fall into one of the following categories are protected by copyright law.

✔ **Literary works:** A literary work is a work expressed in words or numbers. Examples are stories, song lyrics, poems, speeches, magazine articles, and some portions of computer programs. The work must have enough substance or length to be original. A few sentences that fully describe a fictional character may provide enough substance despite its limited length. A few sentences describing historical facts are not original. An entire history book, however, may be copyrightable if original ideas are presented in the book in an original way.

✔ **Musical works:** A musical work is instrumental music or the combination of music and lyrics. A few notes aren't enough music to be original. Although there is no set number of notes that make the combination original, a musical work must usually include rhythm, harmony, and melody.

✔ **Sound recordings:** A sound recording results from fixing a series of musical, spoken, or other sounds onto a tape, compact disc (CD), digital audiotape (DAT), or other object. The combination of sounds that you hear is the work of authorship. It is not the physical CD or tape (which is the tangible medium). When you listen to a music CD, you may hear drums, guitars, vocals, and other sounds. These sounds mixed together and affixed to the CD are the sound recording. If the sounds are remixed in a studio and affixed to another CD so they sound differently, that's a different sound recording. The song that's recorded — the lyrics and musical notes — is the separate musical work. So a music CD is actually two copyrightable works — a musical work and a sound recording.

✔ **Pictures, graphics, and sculptures:** These works include two-dimensional and three-dimensional works of fine art, graphic art, applied art, photographs, prints, art reproductions, maps, globes, charts, diagrams, models, and technical drawings (including architectural plans). However, arranging material on a page, selecting graphic elements such as font or color, and selecting or creating familiar designs and symbols are not expressions that are original enough to become a copyrightable work. Photographs must be more than mere snapshots to be original works. The way the photographer uses lighting, positions the subject, and captures a mood are the original expressions that create a copyrightable work.

✔ **Dramatic works:** A dramatic work consists of some type of dialogue (verbal or nonverbal) and action that tells a *connected* story. A comic strip with pictures of characters and words of dialogue or a play with written dialogue and descriptions of movement may be dramatic works. A narration, which is someone telling a story, is a literary work rather than a dramatic work because it doesn't involve dialogue and action. Think of a dramatic work as a story that you're actually reading and seeing *in action* as it unfolds.

✔ **Motion pictures and audiovisual works:** An audiovisual work (audio plus visual) is a series of *related* images that the author intends for you to see with machines or devices such as projectors, viewers, or electronic equipment. Any sounds become part of the audiovisual work. A motion picture is a type of audiovisual work that gives an impression of motion when you see its parts in succession. Any sounds with the motion picture become part of this work. In other words, the owner of the motion picture usually owns the rights to the musical score.

- **Pantomimes and choreography:** Copyright protects original pantomimes (think Marcel Marceau) that involve more than just routine or minimal gestures. Ditto for original choreography that's more than mere social or simple dance steps.

- **Architecture:** Copyright protects architectural designs.

- **Collections:** A collection is a number of independent works that are individually works of authorship. The creator assembles these works into a *collective* whole. Examples are magazines (with individual copyrightable articles) and books of professional photographs. Although their creators may own the individual works, the one who creates the collective whole may own the collection.

- **Compilations:** A compilation is more than a collection. It may include only copyrightable

works like a collection, or it may also include items that are not works of authorship. For example, a telephone book containing only telephone numbers (not copyrightable) could become a copyrightable compilation if it becomes a directory put together in an original way. Dividing the directory into functional or commonly used sections isn't original, but there are some creative ways to organize one to make it subject to copyright protection.

- **Derivative works:** A derivative work is a transformation, an adaptation, or a recasting of another work of authorship. For instance, a novel is copyrightable. Making it into a motion picture creates a derivative work — a motion picture derived from the literary work. A German translation of an English novel that includes original interpretation may be a derivative work.

What trademark laws protect

Marks are words, names, phrases, and certain designs such as logos. They become trademarks or service marks protected by trademark laws when businesses use them to identify the source of the goods (trademarks) and services (service marks) and to distinguish them from the goods and services of others. People often use the word *trademark* to refer to both trademarks and service marks. For more information on trademarks, see Chapter 7.

When you see the ® designation next to a mark, it means the mark is registered with a trademark office. TM or SM after the mark means that someone is claiming these rights to the mark, but it's not completely registered. Some businesses use the ® even if they don't register the mark because they don't understand the distinction. Therefore, don't assume a mark is registered just because you see ®.

On the other hand, don't assume the mark is available to use simply because you don't see a trademark or service mark designation. If the work you want to use includes a name, word, phrase, or design that appears to identify some product (Coca-Cola, for example) or some service (Stompin' Good Catering Service, for example), you better check further into any rights that someone may own. For information on searching trademark registrations, see Chapter 7.

International copyright protection

International treaties make copyright law very similar around the world. Some countries list specific categories of work they protect, such as the U.S. designation of 11 categories in its copyright act. Other countries do not limit protection to any particular list. France simply protects "works of the mind," which includes many different creations from arguments in court to scientific sketches.

In certain countries, the phrase *artistic works* refers to pictures, graphic art, pantomimes, and similar works. Those laws simply lump many of the works into this one category.

Copyright in some countries may not protect certain works like sound recordings, photographs, and computer programs. However, laws other than copyright may protect them.

What patent law protects

Patents are for new and innovative processes, machines, or manufacture (an article that's made) or compositions of matter (like chemicals) that are useful. Think of fire extinguishers, safety pins, certain telecommunications equipment, and prescription drugs. There are many technical requirements for something to be patentable.

A patent exists only if the country's patent office registers it. In the U.S., it's the U.S. Patent and Trademark Office. Anyone who owns a patent may prevent everyone else in the country from using the process, machine, article, or chemical. The owner may also grant someone rights to use it. Patent law doesn't protect anything that is not new or unique. It doesn't protect methods of doing business or other commonly used processes.

However, software patent attorneys know a way to actually get patents in the U.S. for methods of doing business on the Internet. Because the Internet involves other technology, attorneys present a company's business method as a new and unique technology process even though the business method itself is not patentable. For instance, companies are receiving patents in the U.S. for the technology used to pay someone to read an advertisement on the Web, deliver advertisements for people to see on the Internet, offer users the opportunity to name their own price to buy something on a site, and other similar processes for marketing and selling things on the Web.

The U.S. Patent and Trademark Office has started an uproar in the Internet community by granting these and similar patents to e-businesses for technology that allows the sites to perform certain methods of doing business. At the time of this writing, most European countries don't grant patent rights for software. In addition, at least one patent application in the United Kingdom had been denied because the technology was believed to merely implement a method of doing business and, therefore, was not patentable.

People may file lawsuits to challenge these patents. Some courts may allow the patents, and other courts may not. In the meantime, you may think that you're simply doing business as usual on the Web when, in fact, you may be using someone else's patent without permission.

If you're developing technology to run your site, make sure you're not using patented technology that someone else owns. Working with patents requires very technical and specialized experience. To search for patented technology, it's best to work with a patent attorney who understands the Internet. See Chapter 23 for tips on finding a lawyer.

What publicity and privacy laws protect

The *right of publicity*, which exists in about half of the U.S. states, protects a person's right to prevent others from using his or her identity for commercial reasons. For instance, you may not use a person's name or likeness (what the person looks like) for product endorsements, advertisements, motion pictures, photographs or e-business Web sites without the person's permission.

When a state doesn't recognize a right of publicity, privacy law may step in to fill the void. Every state protects a person's privacy. Use of a person's name or likeness is sometimes an invasion of privacy.

Is any person's name or *persona* identifiable in the work you want to use? Can you see a person, read or hear a person's name, or hear a person's voice in a way that a significant number of people could identify the person? Most states that have a right of publicity protect *any* person's identity. The person doesn't have to be a celebrity to have these rights unless the identity that you want to use happens to be just a voice. Usually only people whose voices are very well known may prevent others from using or imitating their voices.

For example, an advertiser wanted people to believe that a famous singer was doing a commercial. The company employed someone to sing and imitate the voice of Bette Midler without her permission. A court held that this commercial use of a soundalike version of her voice violated Bette Midler's right of publicity.

The right of publicity belongs only to human beings, not to corporations or other business entities. However, some courts protect the names and likenesses of music groups.

Usually only living people have the right to prevent others from using their identities. In 11 states, however, the heirs of deceased persons may prevent any commercial use of the deceased's identity under certain circumstances: California, Florida, Indiana, Kentucky, Nebraska, Nevada, Oklahoma, Tennessee, Texas, Virginia, and Washington. Check with your lawyer for updates.

Figuring Out Which Rights You Need

Owning rights in intellectual property, such as a copyright, a trademark, or a patent, is a little like owning a car. It may be valuable, like a Mercedes with a great resale value, or it may be as worthless as a junker. The car could exist just for the owner's personal enjoyment, it could earn money through leases, or it could lead to fortune and fame if it were a formula racer. The owner may sue people who damage the car or press criminal charges against someone for stealing it.

Intellectual property may be very valuable with a great resale value, or it may be worthless. The owner may simply enjoy the work without earning money from it — or she may use it to earn fortune and fame, loan it for free, lease it for money, sell it for something valuable, protect it by going to court to sue people for using it without permission, or press criminal charges against someone for stealing it.

There are many different rights that belong to owners of intellectual property and to a person regarding her name, likeness, and voice. They may involve the right to copy, use, sell, sue, and so on. Therefore, you must understand which rights you need to obtain.

Rights of copyright owners

Copyright law entitles copyright owners and their heirs to certain economic rights throughout the world for a specific number of years. An *economic right* is a right to earn money from the work. Most countries also grant moral rights to the authors. Since authors may sell their rights in copyrights to others who then become the copyright owners, *moral rights* ensure recognition and special control over the work for authors. See the section "Finding the Owners," later in this chapter, for more information about ownership.

Moral rights

Moral rights give the author, regardless of who actually owns the copyright, the right to do the following:

- ✔ Prevent anyone from using the work without providing the author credit (listing his or her name) as the creator of the work.

- ✔ Control how and when the work will first be published (presented to the public).

- ✔ Prevent anyone from incorporating the work into another work.

- ✔ Prevent anyone from altering the work or from using only part of it.

The United States grants moral rights only to authors of certain fine art, and these rights are very limited. European laws fully protect author's moral rights. If you want to be the first to publish the work, incorporate the work into another work, alter the work in any way, or use just a part of it in a country other than the United States, you may need permission from the author as well as the copyright owner.

For more information on copyrights, visit the U.S. Copyright Office's Web site, at `lcweb.loc.gov/copyright/` (see Figure 16-1).

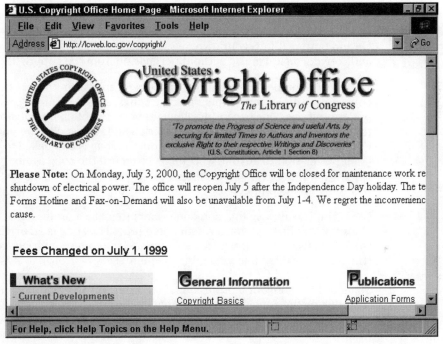

Figure 16-1:
Helpful information and forms for U.S. copyright protection are just a click away at the U.S. Copyright Office's Web site.

Economic rights

Every country grants copyright owners economic rights. The owner may sell (assign) or lease (license) all rights throughout the world to the work, certain rights throughout the world, all rights within a geographic region (territory), or some rights within a specific territory. He may also limit the permission to a certain time period, such as a right to use the work for five years.

These economic rights allow the copyright owner to prevent others from doing the following:

✔ Reproducing the work, which means making copies or phonorecords (the material objects on which sounds are fixed) of the original work

✔ Distributing copies of the work to the public

✔ Performing the work to the public

✔ Displaying the work to the public

✔ Making a derivative work from the original work

Making copies

Although you may usually make a copy of something for your own personal, *private* enjoyment, you may not make copies to give or sell to others. You may not make a copy to display the work on your Web site because that's a public place.

Web sites aren't private even though you're in the privacy of your own office when you're creating it. The law prohibits things like copying an online article and putting it into your own newsletter, downloading software onto disks, and copying digital music without permission from the copyright owner.

There are a number of exceptions to the right to prevent others from making copies of a work. A few of them involve songs, sound recordings, and computer programs. One exception allows anyone to obtain a *compulsory* license to record a song that was already recorded and released to the public in the United States. In other words, the owner of the song is compelled to — must — grant permission to anyone who wants to record the song again (which is copying, or reproducing, the song onto a sound recording) as long as the recording artist complies with certain procedures.

For example, suppose that someone wants to make a professional recording of a song that he heard on a rough demo tape. The song is an original musical work. Because the song was recorded on a demo tape, copyright protects it (the recording fixed it in a tangible medium of expression).

To record the song for a professional recording means that the person will be reproducing the song onto a tape. That is, the person is making a phonorecord of it. If a recording of the song has never been released to the public in the United States, the person must negotiate a license with the copyright owner of the song to reproduce it. The owner may legally refuse to give this permission.

Once a song is recorded and released to the public with permission of the copyright owner, anyone else may record her own version of the song as long as she complies with certain procedures and pays a royalty at a rate set by law (called the *statutory rate* because it's set by federal statute). A *royalty* is a percentage of money for every copy distributed to people. The copyright owner, by law, must grant her a license to reproduce the song, called a *mechanical license,* as long as she complies with some rules and pays for it. See Chapter 17 for more information on mechanical reproduction rights.

Another exception involves sound recordings. Copyright owners may only prevent others from reproducing actual sounds taken from the sound recordings. Copying sounds is called *sampling,* as in taking a sample from the recording. However, a person may *imitate* and re-record these sounds without the copyright owner's permission.

Don't forget that music CDs involve two works: musical works and sound recordings. Although you may imitate the sound recordings, it doesn't mean you may use the exact musical arrangement, chorus, or any other substantial part of the song without permission. For more information on music, see Chapter 17.

An exception also exists for computer programs. You may make a temporary copy of a computer program if it's necessary in order to use the program effectively with your computer or other machine. You may also make a copy to keep as backup. Otherwise, no copying of software for others to use unless you have permission!

Distributing copies

Copyright owners may prevent others from distributing copies of the work to the public. Distributing includes selling, lending, renting, and transferring any rights in it. For example, a photographer may prevent anyone from copying her photograph and selling the copies.

An exception to this right is called the *first sale doctrine*. If a person owns a copy of the work that was lawfully made (that is, with the owner's permission), that person may sell or get rid of *that individual copy*. This is how video stores rent movie videos. The stores buy movie videos, so they own those copies. They then rent them to the public. You buy a CD, so you own that copy. You may sell that one copy, and the buyer may sell that copy, and that buyer may sell that copy, and so on.

There's an exception to this exception — for music CDs and computer programs. Because most people rent movie videos simply to watch them, stores may rent the videos. However, U.S. copyright law does not permit anyone to rent or lend a music sound recording or a computer program for commercial reasons (wanting to make a profit by it). Lawmakers figure that people would rent music and computer programs to use over and over and over again, which wouldn't be fair to the copyright owners who are trying to sell them.

Performing and displaying to the public

Copyright owners also have the right to prevent anyone from *performing* or *displaying* a copyrighted work *to the public*. Works such as music, motion pictures, plays, and pantomimes are *performed*. Public performances include broadcasts (such as radio and television), Webcasts, and live performances. Pictures, photographs, graphic art, and stories are *displayed* for people to see. Web pages are places where these works, depending on their nature, are either performed (music) or displayed (graphic images).

Private performances and displays are cool to do without permission, but they must be truly private (not for an audience that you simply refer to as a private audience). For instance, displaying work online on your "private" Web page to subscribers from the general public wouldn't be private under copyright law because it's really available to members of the public who subscribe.

Owners of sound recording copyrights don't have a public performance right unless it's a digital performance of the recording. The law restricts the way people may play music over digital radio stations and the Internet. There are also several exceptions to this right for certain educational, non-profit, religious, and non-commercial performances and displays. Some of them are very technical, so check with a copyright attorney to discuss them and browse the Web site of the U.S. Copyright Office (listed in the appendix).

Making derivative works

Copyright owners may prevent others from making derivative works from their original works. If someone has permission to make a derivative work, the creator of this new work owns the copyright to the derivative (unless the agreement states differently).

Pretend that you want to make a short digital film from a story. You get permission to make this adaptation from the story author. You will own the copyright to the film, while the story author keeps the copyright to the story.

How long copyright protection lasts

Copyrights last only for a specified number of years. Once that time is up, the work becomes part of the public domain. Anyone may use public domain work for free without the copyright owner's permission.

Creation and publication dates

Copyright laws around the world have changed over the years. Therefore, the time periods for copyright protection have also changed. When you want to use a work, you need to figure out when it was created and when it was first *published* (a technical word basically meaning that copies of the work were distributed to the public). Often you can find one of these years next to the © symbol. Searching for credits and background information for the work on the Internet may also help you locate these dates.

For instance, check out book sites to find out when a book was first published if you want to use part of a story. Search music e-tailers (that's e-commerce retail stores) for information on music sound recordings. Find movie buff sites for information on old films. Get the picture?

Protection in the United States

Prior to 1989 when the Untied States became a signatory to a treaty, all works in the United States had to contain a copyright notice, or the work became part of the public domain. Major changes in U.S. copyright law also occurred in 1978 when the current Copyright Act became law. Therefore, it's wise to consult someone experienced in copyrights to investigate rights in any work created or published in the United States before 1989.

In general, copyright protection in the United States lasts for the following lengths of time:

- ✔ For works created on or after January 1, 1978, copyright protection begins when the work is fixed in a tangible medium of expression and lasts for the life of the author plus 70 years. This means that a copyright owner's rights in a work whose author is living will continue until 70 years after the author dies. For works made for hire (see Chapter 8), protection lasts for 95 years from publication or 120 years from creation, whichever is shorter. Generally, a work is published when copies of the work are distributed to the public; merely performing or displaying a work may not mean that the work is published.

- ✔ For works created and published before January 1, 1978, copyright protection began when the work was published with a copyright notice or when it was registered with the U.S. Copyright Office, whichever was earlier. Protection continued for 28 years, when protection for the work could then be renewed for another 28 years. If it wasn't renewed, then copyright protection was lost and the work became part of the public domain. For works still protected on January 1, 1978, the term of protection was extended from 28 years to 47 years. If it was still protected on October 27, 1998, the term was extended by an additional 20 years.

- ✔ For most works created before January 1, 1978, but not published or registered by that date, copyright protection lasts for the life of the author plus 70 years. In no case will works in this category expire before December 31, 2002. For works published on or before December 31, 2002, copyright protection will not expire before December 31, 2047.

Using copyrighted work internationally

When you want to use copyrighted material in the United States, you must comply with U.S. laws. When you reproduce (make the copies), distribute (sell or get copies into other people's hands), display or perform, or make a derivative work in other countries, you must comply with the copyright law of each of those countries. According to international copyright treaties, the law of the country where you are using each right usually applies. Therefore, you should comply with German copyright law if you're selling a copy of an American work in Germany, and you should comply with U.S. law if you're performing a French work in the United States. A work created in a country other than the country where the owner is trying to protect it is called a *foreign work*.

How long copyright lasts in other countries

The *term* or *duration* of a copyright means how long copyright protection lasts. Sometimes copyright protects certain works longer than other works; motion pictures (cinematographic works), sound recordings, and photographs often have different terms.

When you're trying to figure out whether a work is in the public domain so you may use it without permission, look at the law of the country where the work was created. This country is called the country of origin. Then look at the law of the countries where you're going to copy, distribute, display, or perform someone else's copyrighted work. Most countries protect a copyright for either the term of the country of origin or the term it provides in its own country, *whichever is shorter*.

Copyright laws in other countries also change in response to treaties and other international agreements. The terms for protection of works created or published before certain dates may be different than the terms listed below, so consult an expert for that country.

- **Australia:** For works created after May 1, 1968, copyright in literary, dramatic, and musical works lasts for the author's life plus 50 years, unless the work was not published or performed before the author died. In that case, copyright protects it until 50 years after it's published or performed. Check with a local expert. Copyright for artistic works (except photographs and engravings) lasts for the life of the author plus 50 years regardless of whether it's ever published. Copyright for photographs, sound recordings, and cinematographic films lasts for 50 years after they're first published, which means supplying copies to the public.

- **Brazil:** For works created after June 21, 1998, copyright generally lasts for the author's life plus 70 years. Copyright for photographs and audiovisual works lasts for 70 years from the first disclosure to the public. Computer programs fall under a different law, the 1998 Software Act. For computer programs created after February 20, 1998, protection lasts for 50 years after published or, if not published, after created. Moral rights to control the first showing to the public, to provide credit to the author, and to maintain the work as created appear to last forever; the government may enforce these rights once the work becomes part of the public domain. Experts disagree on whether Brazil will use its own term for copyright protection of foreign works or will use the term of the country of origin.

- **Canada:** For most works created after January 1, 1994, copyright lasts for the author's life plus 50 years. There are special rules for photographs, cinematographic works, and sound recordings. Moral rights last as long as the copyright in the same work. Canada's law regarding how long it protects foreign works is complex. Check with a local expert.

- **France:** For most works created after March 28, 1997, copyright lasts for the author's life plus 70 years. Moral rights last forever.

- **Germany:** Copyright in most works created after July 1, 1995, lasts for the author's life plus 70 years. There are special rules for sound recordings, audiovisual recordings, photographs, and database contents. Moral rights are a part of economic rights under German law and last as long as the copyright in the same work.

- **Israel:** Copyright protects most works for the author's life plus 70 years. It protects sound recordings for 50 years from the making of the master recording. It protects photographs for 50 years from the making of the negative. Protection for moral rights is unclear; it may last for the life of the author, or it may last for the author's life plus 70 years.

✔ **Japan:** For most works created after January 1, 1971, copyright lasts for the author's life plus 50 years. The law protects a cinematographic work for 50 years after it was first made public or, if not made public, for 50 years after created. There are special rules for photographs and sound recordings. Moral rights generally last forever.

✔ **United Kingdom:** For most works created after December 1, 1996, copyright protection lasts for the author's life plus 70 years. There are special rules for sound recordings and "computer-generated works." Moral rights last as long as the copyright, except that the right to prevent others from providing credit as an author to the wrong person lasts for the true author's life plus 20 years.

Laws change. The appendix includes Web site addresses for intellectual property organizations around the world if you need more information or an update.

Fair use exception

There's an exception to all of the copyright owners' rights. It's known as fair use, and people really get confused about this concept.

Fair use is easier to understand if you remember that the U.S. Constitution recognizes an author's right to control use of her creations. Granting this right encourages authors to create. Limiting this right to a certain number of years and creating exceptions to it keeps a balance between the author's right to control use of the work and the public's right to experience and enjoy the work.

There are two "unfortunates" about fair use. First, it's a defense. This means that you won't be able to claim it until you're sued, and you may not be able to prove it until you're in court. Defending yourself gets expensive. Second, figuring out whether fair use applies to a particular situation requires a legal analysis, and lawyers don't always agree. Neither will the courts. Determining whether something is a fair use is purely a matter of opinion based on certain legal guidelines.

These guidelines are based on a number of factors, or things to consider, when looking at the particular use of a copyrighted work. The answer to any one factor won't determine whether you may claim fair use. It's a balancing process. Here are four factors that courts would consider when deciding whether your use is fair use:

✔ **The purpose or the way you're using the work:** If you're using the work for criticism, comment, news reporting, teaching, scholarship or research, then it might be fair use. If you're using it to make a profit or for other commercial reasons, then it probably won't be fair use.

✔ **The nature of the original work:** If the work is extremely original or complex, then you might not be able to use it without permission. If the work isn't very creative, then it helps your claim of fair use.

- ✔ **The amount and quality of the original work that you use:** When you use an entire work, then it might not be fair use. You're trying to use the efforts of another for your own benefit without permission. Even a small portion can be too significant to use without permission. A short song chorus is a part people remember because it repeats during a song. Using a small part of the original work that's barely identifiable might help you in claiming fair use.

- ✔ **Whether the use will have an economic impact on the original work's potential market and value:** If your use of the work may interfere with, or take value away from, the original work, then you probably won't get the fair use defense. The copyright owner shouldn't have to let other people use her work to compete with her.

Rights of trademark owners

Trademark law prohibits anyone from using another person's trademark on goods or services under certain conditions. Essentially you can't use other people's trademarks to pretend that your goods or services come from them or are endorsed by them.

In addition, some courts do not allow using someone's trademark to draw business to your Web site. Be careful with famous trademarks as well. You may not use famous trademarks like Coca-Cola or Sony without permission. Often the owners of famous marks claim that you're diluting the value of their mark by using it.

Fair use examples

If you want to play 15 seconds of a famous song that people will recognize on your e-business Web site, it probably won't be a fair use. You're doing it to attract people to your for-profit site. Music is generally pretty original compared to other types of works. You're using a substantial part of the song if people can name that tune in 15 seconds or less. Even if you're not really interfering with the record company's right to sell the entire song, the other factors outweigh this single point in your favor. No fair use, dude.

A court case in California involves a search engine using a thumbnail-size copy of a photograph from a Web site to help people searching for photographs on the Web. The photographer claims that the search engine is copying the entire original work and displaying it to the public. It's not for any news or educational reason; it's part of the search engine's commercial business. The court held that it's fair use. The court seems to think that such a small size (poor quality for someone to try to copy) plus the importance of search engines to the Web outweigh the photographer's rights. As of the spring of 2000, the appeal is pending. Stay tuned to your intellectual property reports on the Web. (See the appendix for intellectual property Web site addresses.)

Therefore, if you want to use a trademark or service mark that belongs to someone else, get permission unless your use qualifies as a fair use. In other words, using the trademark without permission for an incidental purpose — such as commentary or fair and truthful comparisons — rather than for purposes of trade or unfair competition is probably okay. For more information about trademark rights and fair use, see Chapter 7.

Rights of patent holders

Patent law prohibits anyone from using the patent without permission. Patent owners normally charge a royalty for using their work. They probably won't permit competitors to use it unless there's some other reason that they want to do business with each other.

Rights in names, likenesses, and voices

The right of publicity allows people to control the commercial use of their names, likenesses, and sometimes voices. The right to privacy generally allows a person to prevent you from doing the following:

✔ Using the person's name for your own benefit

✔ Intruding upon the person's physical solitude or seclusion, like placing a camera in a private place to Webcast the people on the Internet

✔ Disclosing private information about a person in a highly objectionable manner

✔ Publicizing something that places a person in a false light so that even if the statement is true, the way in which it's presented allows people to make assumptions or conclusions about the person that aren't true

Canada, Japan, and Germany appear to have laws that effectively prevent people from using a person's identity in advertising or commercial promotion. Australia offers some protection. The United Kingdom offers little protection except for cases involving defamation and copyright.

There are certain ways to use a person's identity without invading their rights, however. News media may use names and likenesses for newsworthy events. Writers may use names and personalities in works of fiction because there's really no such thing as a completely fictional character. Writing a biography is usually all right. However, using names and identities for things like games or other merchandise requires permission. Whenever you want to use a person's identity, consider getting permission from the person.

Finding the Owners

Figuring out who owns what rights isn't always easy. People who create intellectual property may sell it all to other individuals or companies. Those companies may grant another company an exclusive right (such as the right to distribute copies of a work) for one territory (such as Europe) and grant yet another company an exclusive right (such as the right to perform a work) for another territory (such as North America). Even a person may grant a company the exclusive right to use her name in connection with records in one country and grant another company the exclusive right to use her name in connection with T-shirts in another country. The challenge is to find the people who have the right to grant you the rights you need. Read that sentence again slowly — you'll get it the second time around.

Copyright owners

Copyright owners are not always easy to find. When a work is first created, the author/creator owns the copyright. The author may sell all rights to someone else, grant someone all rights within certain countries, and authorize other companies to license rights and collect payments.

Finding anyone who holds any rights in the copyright of the work is your first step. Search the Internet for the work and look for a name by any copyright notice or © symbol. Try contacting the U.S. Copyright Office for the name on any registration. To help you get started searching for copyright owners, the appendix provides Web site addresses for organizations around the world.

Once you locate anyone with a connection to the work, ask the person or company whether the person or company owns all rights throughout the world. If so, you're in luck, and you don't need to look any further. If they don't, they can tell you who licensed rights to them. You then start connecting the dots to locate the company you need. To help you understand who might own a copyright, the following are some general rules about copyright owners.

Joint authors

If more than one person creates a work, they may be joint authors. People are only joint authors if they intend to create one work together. If the final work is merely two or more separate works put together from works that were previously prepared separately, then there won't be joint ownership in the final work.

For example, a Web page may include a written story with photographs. If the writer and photographer intend to share ownership of the final work, the story is written specifically for the Web page, and the photographs are taken specifically for the Web page, then the writer and photographer may be joint owners of the Web page. However, if the photographs were taken without the Web page in mind, the photographer would simply own her photographs, and the writer would own the text. Neither would own the entire work.

Any author may grant permission to use the work without the other author's permission unless the request is for an *exclusive* license. An exclusive license, which is giving a right to only one party to the exclusion of all others, and any sale of the work require consent of all authors. The exclusive license and sale (assignment) must also be in writing to be effective.

Work-for-hire authors

A copyright owner may also be an individual or company that hired someone to create the work. These owners are called *work-for-hire authors*. Under the work-made-for-hire provision of the U.S. Copyright Act, an employer is the author of a copyrightable work created by an employee under certain circumstances. In addition, a person or company that hires an independent contractor to create copyrightable work may be the owner of the copyright in that work if certain legal requirements are met. Therefore, investigate whether anyone hired the creator of the work to find the rightful owner. Work-for-hire arrangements are explained in more detail in Chapter 8.

Trademark and patent owners

Owners of trademarks and patents are much easier to find than copyright owners. For trademarks registered in the U.S., you may simply search the U.S. Patent and Trademark Office's database on the Internet or another country's registration (see the appendix for the Web site addresses). If you're aware of a trademark that isn't registered, you may hire a trademark search firm to track the owner down. The appendix lists Web site addresses for some search firms.

Because patents must be registered to secure these rights, you may request information from the U.S. Patent and Trademark Office or another countries patent office.

Publicity and privacy rights holders

Tracking down people who appear in a photograph, film, or other program or who sang on a record or in a commercial can be very difficult unless the person is a member of an entertainment industry union. Hopefully the original creators of the work obtained permission from these people. The creators should have releases or some other type of written permission from the people. If not, the authors might have contact numbers for the people, or you may contact the appropriate union for contact information. The appendix includes Web site addresses for some of the unions.

If you can't locate the people whose likenesses appear in a work, consider doing something to the work to blur their appearance. Of course, you need to get permission from the copyright owner to smudge the work!

Celebrities and other famous people often grant more than one company the rights to use their names or likenesses in connection with various products. For instance, a musician may grant an exclusive right to a record company to use her name and likeness in connection with the sale of records and music videos, an exclusive right to a merchandising company to use her name and likeness in connection with clothing and music memorabilia, and to a cosmetic company in connection with cosmetics. Therefore, make sure you ask the person whether she has given permission to anyone else who may restrict the way you use that person's name or likeness.

Requesting Permission

Owners of intellectual property and individuals don't have to let anyone use their stuff. Keep this in mind. If you sound like you're demanding anything, you won't get very far. If you contact them or bug them too often, they'll turn off to you as well.

Most people want to receive your request in writing. Include the following information:

- ✔ Your name, address, telephone and fax numbers, e-mail address, and Web address

- ✔ Some very brief background about yourself (or whoever is requesting permission to use the work)

- ✔ The name or other identifying characteristic of the work you want to use

- ✔ A description of precisely how you want to use the work (for example, including it in an advertisement or putting it on your Web site)

- ✔ All of the rights you're requesting (for example, allowing people to download it, buy it, view it, and so on)

- ✔ Where you want to use the work (on the Web and in which countries)

- ✔ Any deadline date by which you need permission

Normally, I don't offer any money to license the work in the initial request. The owners often let you know how much they want. You may either accept their offer or try to negotiate the amount. Sometimes negotiating by telephone is more successful and less time-consuming than negotiating by e-mail or fax.

After you send the written request, give the owner enough time to consider it, check things out, and reply. This process may take a week or ten days. Then try calling or e-mailing as a polite follow-up. If the recipient hasn't looked at your request, ask when you may call to follow up again. If you receive permission, the copyright owner either sends you her standard clearance form or asks you to send one to her.

A sample Permission Request Letter with explanations and a copy without explanations are on the CD.

Confirming Permission

Getting your rights in writing is a good idea. If you're asking for exclusive rights so that no one else may use the work in your territory, the permission must be in writing to be effective. This type of document is called a *license,* which is an agreement (a contract) that grants you the right to use something that belongs to someone else. If the party is actually selling you all his rights rather than merely giving you permission to use his work, then the agreement is called an *assignment.*

At a minimum, include the following information in your agreement:

- The date and how long you have the rights

- All the rights you're receiving

- The territories in which you may use these rights

- The fee, if any, and when it's due

- A statement that the owner represents he has the right to grant you the rights you're requesting

- If there are no other owners, a statement that the owner represents there are no other rights holders from whom you must get permission

The CD includes samples of an Assignment of Master Sound Recording (a copy with explanations and a copy without explanations); an Assignment of Musical Composition (copies with and without explanations); an Assignment of Photograph (copies with and without explanations); an Assignment of Video Footage (copies with and without explanations); a Master Sound Recording License for use on an Audiovisual Web Site (copies with and without explanations); a Permission to Use Name and Likeness Provisions with explanations; a Photograph License for Web Site (copies with and without explanations); a Talent Release (copies with and without explanations); and a Video Footage License (copies with and without explanations).

Life's lessons

Planning ahead is the critical part of clearing rights. Getting permission takes time. Once you locate the owners of the works you want to use and send a request for permission, they may not make you their highest priority. Their business obligations have their attention. They may have other obligations that take priority.

After waiting and waiting, they may even decide to deny your request. Give yourself plenty of time to accomplish work through this process. It could take weeks or months. Have a back-up work to use in case you can't get permission.

For one very special project, I was asked to clear rights for over 100 works created throughout the world from 1903 through 1999. The artist was creating a production about human interaction with matter throughout the 20th century. The production would be performed live before an audience of thousands. The production would include over 170 performers (musician, vocalists, and dancers), music performed live and prerecorded, and audiovisual clips showing text from poems, literature, speeches, and song lyrics. The clips would also embody sound recordings, photographs, translations, and derivative works from film and video of movies, news reports, and documentaries.

I had only three months to locate the owners, negotiate licenses in five different languages, and get the rights to perform the production (which embodied their works) live as well as record it for later video, DVD, CD, and television release — all at an affordable price. The Internet made this possible.

In my request for permission, it was important to convey to the copyright owners the creative nature of this phenomenal project and why their work should be a part of it. It was also important to let them know that there was a small budget to put this work together. I needed to make them want to be a part of this production.

One work had to be pulled out of the production when the owner didn't want to grant the right to have the work part of the event because it was being Webcast live over the Internet (she was afraid the work would be stolen). However, rights in all other works were granted — the last one from a company in France the morning of the premiere (someone was ready to pull that work from the production at the last minute if necessary). Persistence — not pushiness — paid off. And a magnificent production about the 20th century was born. Its name is *Life* by Ryuichi Sakamoto.

Chapter 17

Let Me Entertain You

● ●

In This Chapter

▶ Becoming acquainted with the entertainment industry

▶ Registering and watermarking your creations

▶ Getting the okay to use the music and audiovisual works of others

▶ Creating your own e-tainment model

● ●

*M*usicians, record companies, film studios, and organizations representing entertainment companies are scrambling to stop their work from being traded, performed, or displayed for free over the Internet. Lawsuits, court decisions, and settlement negotiations are taking center stage when it comes to digital entertainment and the Net. Why is so much legal maneuvering going on? Because people want to be entertained at a low cost, and many of those people are finding ways to share entertainment on the Web without paying the creators.

For an update on legal issues facing the entertainment industry and the Internet, visit some of the entertainment Web sites listed in the appendix, such as the ones for the Recording Industry Association of America (RIIA) and the Motion Picture Association of America. See Figure 17-1 for a view of RIIA's home page.

All of this activity shouldn't stop you from pursuing your entertainment dreams on the Web. If you're an e-business entrepreneur ready to start your own e-tainment site, then read on. All you need to do to stay out of the legal fray is to protect your copyrighted work and get permission to use the work of others. You may even find yourself building a new e-tainment business model to offer entertainment in the digital world.

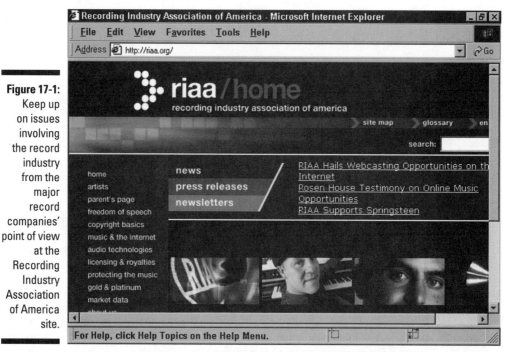

Courtesy of RIAA © 2000 Recording Industry Association of America, Inc. All rights reserved.

Understanding the Entertainment Industry

For most of the 20th century, the entertainment industry has been controlled by a handful of heavyweight players. They pretty much control the distribution channels — in other words, how entertainment gets to the public. Therefore, they wield a great deal of power in deciding what the public sees and hears.

There are also "independent" companies — those that the major companies do not own. However, they have difficulty getting their products to the public because of limited record store space, relatively few movie theaters, and only a handful of cable and television broadcast outlets. The independents, also called "indies," don't hold as much clout to get their entertainment products in those places.

The Internet could change all this as soon as technology and Internet connections get up to speed. It could happen in a big way as early as 2003. Although the entertainment industry will always have high-budget productions, the Web makes room for everyone else as well.

As in any open market where there is little oversight or editing, plenty of awful entertainment with no artistic value whatsoever will appear on the Web. But you will also find wonderful, creative entertainment. When entertainment products become readily available on the Internet, we'll probably locate the good work by reading critical reviews, press coverage, and entertainment guides on the Net.

Entertaining on the Internet

At the time of this writing, there are two general ways to make entertainment available on the Internet. You can stream data to watch videos or listen to audio on a computer. *Streaming* is a technique for transferring data in a steady and continuous stream so that moving pictures, such as video, can be viewed over the Internet. You can also create digital files for people to download onto their computer hard drives to listen to or view with compatible players. By the time you read this, even more ways to access entertainment may be available.

For users to be able to watch or hear entertainment from the Internet, they must have *players* that are compatible with the entertainment *files* offered by a Web site. For instance, you can't use a cassette tape player to listen to a CD, and you can't use a VCR to watch a DVD. The pieces just don't fit! Currently there are a variety of players and a variety of media files that aren't compatible with one another. Before entertainment can be purchased or enjoyed easily on the Internet by a mass audience, the technology on both ends (players and media files) must become compatible.

Although short films and video are on the Internet, this chapter focuses more on music because the Web is readily adaptable to this form of entertainment at the moment. I include a brief discussion about audiovisual rights with the expectation that these works will be a big part of the Net very soon.

So, whether you want to include music and video on your Web site to entertain your visitors or you want to create your own e-tainment site, get ready to enter a complicated maze of legal rights. After the details totally confuse you, I provide some tips for those adventurous souls who really want to rock the entertainment world.

This chapter refers only to music and videos that are still protected by copyright law. Figuring out the duration of copyright in the U.S. is tricky. Copyright law has undergone major changes a few times since the 1970s. Before assuming that something is in the *public domain* for you to use without an owner's permission, be sure to check with a copyright lawyer or the U.S. Copyright Office Web site and copyright books for details. I include some additional information in Chapter 16 and Web site addresses in the appendix.

Managing the legal maze

Legal rights in music, motion pictures, and other audiovisual works are often complex. In fact, a world-renowned copyright expert referred to one of the many U.S. copyright laws as "frightfully complex legislation." And he's an expert!

Part of the reason for this complexity is that lawyers must understand the entertainment business, not just the law, to advise clients properly regarding this industry. If a lawyer doesn't know the difference between a recording studio and a record label or between public performance of a song and repro-duction of a sound recording, he'll never figure out who owns rights in music and who is entitled to royalties.

Another reason is that the many nuances involved with the business, the entertainment products, the creators of the entertainment, and intellectual property laws must work together. Foreign laws and international treaties also come into play. Therefore, remember that you need one-on-one advice from an experienced entertainment lawyer who understands the Internet if you want to gain a competitive edge in online entertainment.

Protecting Your Creations on the Web

When it comes to protecting copyrightable work that you create, it's pretty simple. You can protect your creations in a couple ways. You can register your work with the U.S. Copyright Office. You can also watermark your work.

Registering your work

If your creation is the kind of work that copyright law protects, then your copyright begins as soon as you put it onto something tangible that is also somewhat permanent. For example, type lyrics into your word processing program and save the file, record your music onto a cassette tape or DAT (digital audio tape) with your guitar or your voice, draw your animation on a storyboard, or create your artwork and save it in a program file. To under-stand the kind of works that copyright law protects, see Chapter 16.

Registering your copyrighted work is a good idea. You don't *have* to register it to have legal protection, but you must do so before you ever sue in the United States for copyright infringement. You also receive certain legal bene-fits if you register it. To register a copyright in the United States, you com-plete a form to file with the U.S. Copyright Office, which is part of the Library of Congress. You pay a filing fee of $30 or more and follow a few other basic requirements explained on the forms.

Forms are available for *free* on the Copyright Office's Web site or by calling them, so don't pay companies who sell copyright registration packets! They're just trying to make money from something that the government gives away. The U.S. Copyright Office Web site has great information and forms (go to `http://lcweb.loc.gov/copyright`).

Copies of the U.S. Copyright Office applications for registration with instructions are also on the CD with this book.

Unlike trademarks, copyrights do not need to be registered in foreign countries in order to get legal protection. In fact, some countries don't register copyrights at all. See Chapter 16 for more information. Many books about copyrights are available, so check them out if you'd like more in-depth information.

Watermarking your work

Have you ever held up an expensive piece of stationery to the light? Try it. You'll probably see a symbol or some writing on it. That's a watermark, which identifies the maker of the stationery. Watermarks can be clearly visible, like the television network and cable logos you see on the corner of your television screen during their programs. They can be somewhat visible, like the ones on stationery. They can also be invisible to the human eye. Digital watermarks are important for entertainment products with new Internet technologies. These watermarks are embedded in the digital media, as described in the following sections.

Understanding digital media

Media doesn't refer only to the press or news agencies. It's also a word that describes the means by which something is communicated. Media includes such things as paper (newspaper publishers use paper to communicate news), broadcast transmissions (for example, transmissions for network television), cable transmissions (for cable programs), and cassette tapes (to hear things recorded on that tape).

Media are often divided into two categories: analog and digital. Compare the sound of an album on cassette tape (analog) to the sound of the same album on CD (digital). Watch a movie on videotape (analog) and then watch the same movie on DVD (digital). Depending upon how it was recorded initially, you should be able to hear or see a difference.

One type of digital media is an *MP3 file,* which is a compressed audio file that allows sound from a CD to be transferred across the Internet easily. Digital media, such as CDs, CD-ROMs, DATs, MP3 files, and other formats, are made up of a series of numbers — digits — that a machine reads. The machine, or player, then performs what it's programmed to do. For instance, a CD player reads numbers from the CD (compact disc) and, when plugged into speakers or headphones, lets the user hear what's on the CD. A player compatible with MP3 digital files reads the files and lets you hear them.

Embedding digital watermarks

Digital media is made up of data, which is a combination of digits (numbers) that a machine reads. For instance, each music CD has its own special combination of digits that the CD player reads and transforms into music you hear. Digital watermarking is *additional* data (an additional combination of digits) embedded in the other data. This additional data, like traditional watermarks, identifies the owner or origin of the digital media. That is, it identifies where the CD or file came from. So a music CD with a special watermark includes the original data for you to hear the music plus additional data that, with the right machine, uniquely identifies that particular CD.

Unlike television network logos that are the same in every one of their shows, digital watermarks don't have to be the same on every one of your files. There are unique watermarks called *fingerprints*. For entertainment products, each digital file downloaded probably has its own fingerprint — a slightly different watermark for each and every file or copy. If someone makes a bunch of copies from the downloaded file and sells them without permission, the copyright owner can figure out which authorized download was used to make the unauthorized copies. In other words, the copyright owner can track down the person who made the copies without permission. Watermarking is a way to prevent criminal piracy of copyrighted works (also known as stealing).

Different *schemes* — ways — are available to hide digital watermarks in digital files. Be aware that some digital watermark technologies are better than others. For example, sometimes the watermarks are easy for others to find, and therefore they're easy to remove so copies can't be traced. Other schemes make it more difficult to find and remove the watermarks.

Certain schemes unintentionally allow watermarks to be removed when various techniques are used to *compress* files (make them smaller) so they download more easily and more quickly. If the compression techniques end up removing certain data, they could be throwing away your watermark! Schemes that allow a watermark to be lost during compression or certain other techniques are called *fragile* schemes. The ones that can keep the watermark intact during compression are called *robust* schemes.

If you're going to sell entertainment as downloadable files, check out the available digital watermarking technology. It's changing all the time. The appendix lists some Web sites that offer digital watermarking technology. Before you select which technology to use, read reviews of technologies that have been tested by computer magazines such as *PC Magazine* and *PC World* as well as online reviews at ZDNet (the Web site addresses are in the appendix).

If you're a copyright owner, digital watermarking only helps you *identify* the *copy* where the additional, and unauthorized, copies came from. It's not perfect protection. Whether you can identify that *person* who made the additional copies depends upon how you require purchasers to identify themselves when they download your files. Make sure that your digital watermarks can be tracked with Web crawlers currently available to you on the Web. Digital Rights Management (DRM) companies may provide some help. If you can't find your work and identify the infringers, it's hard to stop the infringement. And don't forget — your works may not even be on the Web! They could be on someone's homemade CD.

Using the Music of Others

Maybe you want to use music that someone else created. Even if you don't charge people to listen to it or sell files or CDs to the public, you must still get permission from the copyright owners to use it.

When you listen to a music CD or MP3 file, you're listening to more than one element. A music CD includes a musical composition (song) made up of rhythm, musical arrangements, and melody. Also part of the CD is a sound recording made up of musical performances, vocal performances, sound mixes, and other technical sounds. If you want to use the music of others, obtain permission from the copyright owners, or their representatives, for each song and sound recording.

The CD with this book includes a sample Permission Request Letter with explanations and another copy without explanations. Please note that many entertainment companies insist on using their own form licenses if they grant permission to use their copyrightable work.

Owners of songs

A song — called a *musical composition* under copyright law — may have music and lyrics or just music. *Lyrics* are the words. *Music* usually consists of the rhythm, the musical arrangement of the instruments (the parts each instrument plays at certain times during the song), and the melody (normally the part you hear the lead vocalist sing). The melody is usually the part you find yourself humming long after the song stops playing on the radio. The rhythm is what makes you shake your booty.

Sometimes one person writes a song, and other times more than one person writes a song. Almost always the songwriters own the copyright in the song when they create it.

Often the songwriters enter into business deals for all or most of their songs with companies called music publishers or, more simply, publishers. These companies make money by exploiting songs. *Exploit* sometimes has a bad meaning. In this case, however, it simply means that they find ways to make money from the song. For example, they charge a fee to use the song in a movie or in a television commercial. The collection of all the songs a company handles is called its *catalog* of songs.

Sometimes songwriters start their own music publishing companies. The biggest publishing companies, however, are affiliated with the major record companies. Music publishing companies most often acquire rights to songs in one of three ways:

- ✔ The publishing company buys all copyright interest in the songs and pays the songwriters a *royalty* (a percentage of money received) every time the publisher receives money from exploiting the songs. It's called a publishing deal. See the section "Using songs" for an explanation on how songs earn money.

- ✔ The publishing company buys only part of the copyrights in the songs, handles all licensing of the songs (giving permissions to use the songs for a fee), collects all money earned for the songs, and pays the songwriters' publishing companies (or other publishing company) roughly half of the money the songs earn. It's called a *co-publishing deal*.

- ✔ The publishing company doesn't own any copyrights. It only has the right to license and exploit the songs and to collect all money earned for the songs. The company then pays the songwriters or other publishers the amount received less a percentage of that amount as a fee for its services. It's called an administration deal; the company is *administering* (handling all the business matters for) the copyrights of the songs.

There are variations on the deals, but these are the most common. Therefore, when you want to contact the owner of a song, look for the *music publisher* or, as described in the following section, one of its representative organizations.

Using songs

Whether you should contact the music publisher directly or some other organization for permission to use a song depends on how you want to use it. Here are some of the ways that you may want to use a song:

- ✔ You want to let people hear a recording of a song on your site.

- ✔ You want to make records (CDs, DATs, or other "phonorecords") from recordings of the song and distribute them (sell or give away) to people who order them online.

✔ You want to make recordings of the song available as a digital file that people can download from your site.

✔ You want to use the music with audiovisual works or other motion pictures.

✔ You want to make the lyrics or music available in typewritten form to people on the Internet.

These uses of a song fall into one of four categories of rights: public performance, mechanical reproduction, synchronization, or print (sheet) music.

Public performance rights

If you want to let people hear a recording of a song on your site, you're dealing with *public performance* rights. Public performance is when the public hears the song. It includes live performances (concert halls, nightclubs, and festivals) as well as transmissions over radio, television, cable, and the Internet (Webcasts). In many countries outside the United States, public performance includes hearing it in a movie. Copyright owners of songs can require payment for performing their songs to the public.

Because it would be extremely difficult for every radio and television station to contact each music publisher or songwriter to get permission for every song it plays, most songwriters and music publishers sign up with one of the performing rights societies in the United States (or the society in their country). These organizations *license* (permit others to perform) the songs of their members. They collect license fees and, according to some calculation that few human beings ever try to figure out, pay their member songwriters and publishers royalties. They also collect royalties for their members from overseas affiliates for foreign performances.

The owner of the *venue* — the place where the music is performed — is the one who obtains a public performance license. Musicians and singers who want to perform the songs live don't need to get the license. On the Internet, the Web site is the venue. Therefore, the site owner should obtain the license.

The main performing rights societies in the United States are The American Society of Composers, Authors and Publishers (ASCAP) and Broadcast Music Inc. (BMI). A small, third such society is called SESAC, Inc. They are competitors, so members belong to only one society at a time (they may switch from time to time). ASCAP and BMI cover most of the songs by U.S. songwriters. They also collect for U.S. performances of songs by members of their foreign "sister societies."

The license fee covers use of all the songs in the entire catalog of the performing rights society — songs by the society's member songwriters and music publishers. If you're a Webcaster (an Internet radio e-business), you probably have to obtain licenses from both ASCAP and BMI.

If you're using only a few songs on your Web site, however, you may seek a license either from the copyright owner directly (the music publisher) or from ASCAP or BMI. You can search the online databases by song title and songwriter to find out the names of music publishers on the societies' Web sites. The appendix lists Web site addresses for performing rights societies around the world, including ASCAP, BMI, and SESAC.

Mechanical reproduction

If you want to manufacture records (called *phonorecords* under copyright law) or create digital files of recordings of songs and distribute them to people, you're dealing with mechanical rights. The U.S. Copyright Act defines phonorecords as material objects in which sounds are fixed, and from which the sounds can be perceived, reproduced, or otherwise communicated either directly or with the aid of a machine or device.

Did I lose you with that last sentence? Well, "phonorecords" includes tapes (cassettes and DATs), discs (CDs and CD-ROMs), digital files, and other types of objects that communicate sound. Most people in the music industry refer to them all simply as *records* and *digital downloads*.

Copyright owners have certain rights when it involves someone recording their songs. They can prevent people from recording their songs and selling records without their permission. There's an exception, however, for songs previously recorded *as phonorecords* and released to the public in the United States.

Once a song is recorded as a record (as opposed to being a part of a movie, for example) and released to the public in the United States with the owner's permission, anyone can record that song again as long as he pays a certain royalty to the song's copyright owner and complies with the payment requirements described in the Copyright Act.

Music publishers, as owners of songs, may charge a fee for each record that is manufactured and distributed (not only sold, but given away for free) and which includes a recording of the song. The fee is called a *mechanical royalty*. The record company that sells the records normally pays the mechanical royalties.

Although the amount of the royalty can be negotiated, copyright regulations set a maximum rate that copyright owners may charge to people who want to record a song that's already been released to the public as described above. The rate, called the *statutory rate* because it's described in the copyright statute (law), usually increases every two years. As of January 2000, the statutory mechanical royalty rate is 7.55 cents per song or 1.45 cents per minute, whichever is greater. The music business breaks things down to hundredths of a cent.

For example, a song that's 3 minutes long costs 7.55 cents for every download or record distributed. A song that's 6 minutes long costs 8.7 cents for every download or record (1.45 cents per minute is greater than 7.55 cents, so it's 1.45 cents × 6 minutes). If one album contains ten 6-minute songs, then the mechanical royalty for the entire album download is 87 cents per album downloaded or sold (10 songs × 8.7 cents per 6-minute song).

Although mechanical licenses can be given directly by music publishers to people requesting them, most music publishers in the United States don't deal directly with the public on these matters. They have The Harry Fox Agency in New York handle mechanical licenses for them. The Harry Fox Agency has a Web site with relevant information posted. It also has a searchable database where you can find information about songs, songwriters, and publishers.

The mechanical royalty rate for digital downloads is being re-examined by the Powers That Be. For updated information, check out the Web site for The Harry Fox Agency at `www.nmpa.org/hfa.html`.

In other countries, laws require record companies to pay mechanical royalties only to certain organizations rather than directly to music publishers. If you plan to sell records or to let people download recordings of songs that belong to someone else, you need to obtain that mechanical license in advance.

Synchronization and print rights

If you want to get permission to include a song with some visual image, such as a motion picture, video, or other type of audiovisual work, you must normally obtain a synchronization license directly from the music publisher. This is the right related to *synchronizing* the song with a visual image. It's called a *synch* (pronounced like "sink") *license* for short.

A few music publishers delegate synch licensing to other agencies such as The Harry Fox Agency, but most music publishers do it themselves. They charge a synchronization fee that can be a few hundred dollars or hundreds of thousands of dollars, depending on the way the song will be used and the popularity of the song.

In addition to synchronization rights, there are print rights. No one may make a copy of a music composition without the copyright owner's permission. If you want to display or sell printed versions of lyrics or music, you must obtain permission from the music publisher. If a publisher grants you permission, it normally requires a *royalty* (a specific number of cents or a percentage of the price) for each copy printed or sold.

Owners of sound recordings

If you like the way someone recorded the song, you also have to *license* (get permission to use) the sound recording. For instance, Smashing Pumpkins may record a song, and Will Smith may record his version of the same song. The sound recording (referred to as the *master recording* in the music industry) is either the Smashing Pumpkins version or the Will Smith version. You need permission not only from the music publisher for the song but also from the copyright owner of the specific master recording that you want to use.

Record companies (Record labels)

If you want permission to use a sound recording, then the first company to contact is the record company. Record companies often pay for the recording of records as well as other promotional and sales efforts. These companies are also called *record labels,* a term that comes from an old reference to the identifying label or imprint that appeared on vinyl albums. Some people simply refer to the record company as "the label." *Recording studios* are places where recordings are made. *Record distributors* are companies that get the records to retail outlets or other places of sale. Recording studios and record distributors don't own copyrights in master recordings.

Currently, five companies own most of the record labels and, therefore, most of the records sold throughout the world. The record labels that they own are called "major labels." These companies normally insist upon owning all copyright to the master recordings they sell. Other independent record companies that are not owned by these major companies either own the master recordings or license the right to sell them exclusively within certain territories around the world. They're also called "indie labels."

Other owners

If the record company doesn't own the copyrights in the master recordings, then the record company gets permission to manufacture and sell the records from the original copyright owners. The original copyright owners could be a number of different people, depending on the particular business deals made for the recording, such as record producers, recording engineers, or featured musical performers.

Under copyright law, those who make *substantial original contributions* to the final version of the master recording own the copyright in it. The people who make substantial contributions could include a record producer who directs everyone during the recording session. The record producer is to a record what a film director is to a movie.

Substantial original contributions may also be from the following people:

- A recording engineer who actually works the machines to make musical instruments, voices, and computer programs sound a certain way.
- A mixing engineer who mixes all the sounds to make the final sound you hear.
- Musicians, programmers, or rap DJs who create the musical sounds.
- Musicians who are either sidemen or featured performers. Sidemen are those who normally perform for a set fee, while featured performers usually share in royalties (a percentage of sales) for records sold.
- Vocalists who are background singers or lead singers.

Although many people may make substantial contributions to a sound recording, custom and practice in the entertainment industry normally recognize copyright owners as the producer and featured performers. Sometimes the recording or mixing engineers may also share the copyright, depending upon their contribution. Normally everyone except the featured performers (featured musicians and lead singers) and the record producer give up their copyright in return for a fee for their services. However, even the featured artists and producers must give up their copyrights to major labels. It's part of the deal that the major record labels insist upon.

Therefore, when you're trying to find the owner of a master recording, first try the record company. The name is normally listed next to the copyright symbol on a CD or on the Web site that sells the CDs. If the record company doesn't own the rights you need, it should be able to direct you to the copyright owner.

Using master (sound) recordings

Owners of sound recordings may prevent others in the United States from making copies of the recordings to sell to others and from renting them to others. For instance, you need a license — usually called a *Master Use License* — to use a sound recording with a movie, commercial, video, or other audiovisual work.

You may want to make a recording available on your site "on demand." In other words, you want people to be able to hear the recording by clicking on the name of a song on your site. To do this, you must get permission from the sound recording owner. Keep in mind that the copyright owner doesn't have to grant you permission.

Unlike the owners of songs, the owners of sound recordings don't have a public performance right in most cases. In other words, radio stations and other broadcasters don't have to pay license fees to the owners of master recordings; they have to pay license fees only to the owners of songs. However, the Digital Performance in Sound Recordings Act changed this with respect to certain *digital* performances. It gave certain public performance rights to owners of sound recordings so that they could prevent others from transmitting the recordings in certain digital forms. The specific digital performances and rights are too extensive to explain in this book. Check with a copyright attorney for more specific information.

The Digital Millennium Copyright Act expanded this right to include the Internet. If you're a Webcaster, the sound recording owners must now grant you permission to perform the recordings as long as you comply with certain guidelines and pay a license fee.

If the master recording is subject to certain union rules, you may have to pay master re-use fees (to re-use it). In general, master recordings made for one purpose, such as records, and then used for another purpose, such as background music for a film, may require additional fees to be paid to the union. This requirement is a way to make sure that musicians are paid for all uses of the master recordings. If you see something in an agreement about being responsible for payment of any union or master re-use fees, check things out with a lawyer, or you may have to pay lots of additional money.

A sample Master Sound Recording License with explanations and a copy without explanations are on the CD with this book. Often record companies insist on using their own license forms.

Using the Audiovisual Works of Others

Audiovisual works are those creative works that combine audio with visual images. The Copyright Act defines an *audiovisual work* as a series of related images that are intended to be shown by the use of machines or devices such as projectors, viewers, or electronic equipment, together with accompanying sounds. A slide show is an audiovisual work. When it also gives the impression of motion as the images are shown in succession, the audiovisual work is called a *motion picture*. Motion pictures include movies, short films, and music videos.

Movies are normally owned by motion picture studios, movie production companies, or movie producers. Movie producers are often the people who raise money for the film as well as put the whole project together. Directors are more hands-on in the creative process. The types of movies you may use for your e-business site will most likely be short films or videos. The smaller companies or individuals who create these works rarely have their paperwork in order. Therefore, be sure that they obtain for you all the rights you need to use the work.

Owners of audiovisual works

Those who make substantial, creative contributions to audiovisual works share copyright ownership, just as they do in sound recordings, unless they're working under a work-for-hire arrangement. See Chapter 8 for more information on work-for-hire agreements.

The creation of audiovisual works often includes people who write a script or story, compose the music, and direct the work. Set designers or cinematographers may also be involved, depending upon the type of work and their contributions.

To obtain rights for audiovisual works, check first with the producer or director to find out who made creative contributions. Then obtain permission from all those who made substantial contributions to the work unless they previously signed written agreements assigning all copyright ownership to the producer or director. If they signed such agreements, obtain copies of the agreements.

In 1999, a director wanted to license part (a *clip*) of a documentary film about a man who was deceased. The clip was an interview with the man when he was alive. A company in the business of licensing video clips represented the documentary filmmaker to license his work. The company offered to license the clip of the interview to the director for a lot of money; however, the license included a statement that they (the company and filmmaker) were not representing that they held all rights to the video clip. Because the film-maker made the documentary after the man in the video clip died, he certainly was not the creator of that live interview. As it turned out, the filmmaker got it from a television network that actually owned that clip. The company (and filmmaker) had no right whatsoever to license that clip to someone else. But they tried to, and for a lot of money. Be warned! Just because a company is charging a fee doesn't mean that it actually owns rights to a work. Double-check and get people who license work to you to represent in writing that they have the right to license it to you and to grant you the rights you're requesting!

Using audiovisual works

Copyright owners have the right to prevent others from copying, selling, or distributing their work. They may also prevent others from displaying or performing their work to the public. Therefore, you may not use audiovisual works created by someone else on your site without their permission.

You must usually obtain rights for audiovisual works directly from the copyright owners rather than organizations, unlike the process for songs and master recordings. Normally, music that's part of the audiovisual work is not a separate musical work. Therefore, obtaining rights for the entire audiovisual work normally includes rights to the music as used in that work. It doesn't, however, include the right to make records or sound recordings of just the music. In other words, you can't offer downloads of the music just because you obtain rights to the audiovisual work.

It's doubtful that any audiovisual works you use will be made under rules of unions such as SAG (Screen Actors Guild) or DGA (Directors Guild of America). However, if you get into that realm, you absolutely need an experienced entertainment lawyer to help you wade through those rules and regulations.

A sample Video Footage License with explanations and a copy without explanations are on the CD with this book.

Take a second look!

Obtaining rights to use music and audiovisual works doesn't necessarily mean you have the right to use the performers' names, voices, or likenesses (including photographs). Often the copyright owners of the works obtained these rights, but you need to make sure that you may use them, too. See Chapter 16 for more information on publicity rights and obtaining permission from performers.

Building Your Own e-Tainment Model

The complex legal maze governing rights in entertainment exists because people want to use, and make money from, entertainment created by other people. The major companies want to make lots of money. Retail outlets, concert promoters, movie theaters, television stations, radio stations, and now e-businesses want to make money from it, too. Even most performers want the money and the fame. Therefore, these laws developed to protect the creators. In reality, however, they protect those who own the work — often the powerful entertainment companies.

Most of these laws restrict how creations of others may be used. However, you need not worry too much about all these complicated laws if you create your own work and make your own business deals with new, creative artists. Over the Internet, you won't even need to sell as much as traditional artists in order to make the same money!

Chapter 18

Linking to Other Sites

....

....

A university student in Germany awoke to police knocking on her door early one morning. They had a search warrant. Her Web site linked to a left-wing newspaper site that violated German criminal laws. The court previously ordered that access to the site be blocked. The student faced criminal charges. Eventually, the court let her off, reportedly finding that the link did not violate the criminal law. However, she was still dragged through the criminal process.

Across the pond, mega-ticket seller Ticketmaster sued mega-software maker Microsoft for linking deep into Ticketmaster's site, bypassing its home page and advertisements. The two parties settled the lawsuit without going to trial, and the terms of the settlement are secret.

These incidents are just a couple legal actions involving Web site links around the world. Links weave the Web together. By clicking on hypertext links on a Web site, you can get more information on relevant topics or find additional things you need very quickly. Links can lead to other parts of the same Web site, the home page of another Web site, or a page deep within another Web site. When you're visiting a site with frames, a link may even bring stuff from another site into that frame. For a definition of frames, see the section "Bringing other content into your frame," later in this chapter.

As with most things new and beneficial, there are a few bad apples in the bunch. The sites that misuse links create controversy. The controversy mainly concerns advertising, fair competition, and *intellectual property*, meaning copyrights, trademarks, and trade secrets. So people are asking, "Is it okay to link to a site without permission?" The law isn't settled regarding links. Some lawyers advise their clients to always obtain permission to link to another site. But face it. There are *millions* of links out there! Who has the time to respond to all these requests for permission?

And guess what? I don't think that the law regarding links will *ever* be settled. If a state or a country passes a law involving links, someone will inevitably challenge it in court. The state of Georgia passed one, but the courts held it was unconstitutional. Whenever one court makes a decision in a case involving links, it doesn't legally apply to everyone. Other people will continue challenging any law or any court decision that severely restricts linking because linking is so integral to the Web.

Don't forget that lawyers aren't the final decision makers. Just because a lawyer writes a cease-and-desist letter that states you can't link to certain sites doesn't mean you can't link to those sites. Lawyers fight for their clients. Judges make final decisions.

Because lawsuits will continue, maybe the best approach is to figure out ways to go about your business without making people angry enough to sue you. The people who get into trouble for linking will be those who do it for the wrong *reason* or in the wrong *way*. First take a look at some of the reasons people link to other Web sites, and then consider the best way to do it.

Thinking of Linking

There are many reasons — good and bad — that e-businesses link to other Web sites. Your e-site can promote business relationships with other e-companies by referring visitors to other sites through links. You'll enhance your relationship with your Web site visitors by offering links to information that they may find helpful. You may also support your relationship with your clients or customers by providing links to their Web sites on your site.

Links may, however, harm relationships as well. Those who strive too hard for a competitive edge may use links to well-known companies to falsely imply some business relationship with that company. Some sites also use links with famous trademarks to get listed in search engine results to divert people to the sites. Still other sites try to benefit from the content in other sites by linking to those sites and pulling their content into a frame.

Whatever your reason, think before you link to achieve the best results for your e-business.

Referring business

Small business owners usually appreciate referrals of new customers and clients. You might link to complementary e-business sites hoping that they will provide links back to your site. Because you want to develop a reciprocal relationship with the other sites, you contact them for permission to include links. As a result, you shouldn't have any trouble.

A sample Linking and Joint Marketing Agreement with explanations and a copy without explanations are on the CD that comes with this book.

However, don't be surprised if some companies don't want to participate in a link exchange. Many e-businesses have a target market they're after, so too many inquiries from users whom they don't service could clog up their plans.

For instance, many professional service providers practice very specific types of work. A computer consultant may work only with Java technology. A lawyer may practice only family law. A freelance journalist may write only about political issues. If these professionals begin receiving e-mails from hundreds of people inquiring about services in completely different areas, then they're forced to take time away from their real work to dig through all these inquiries. Therefore, having links from all sorts of sites does them more harm than good.

See Chapter 8 for more information on forming business alliances.

Providing information

Linking to other sites to provide helpful information to your visitors is probably the most common reason to link. Perhaps you don't have the resources — money or people — to provide as much information as you would like to offer. So you link. People often express their appreciation for all this information by doing business with you.

Providing information is a positive reason to link. If it's done in the right way, you shouldn't have a problem. When the information is controversial or perhaps obtained illegally, however, some problems could arise.

In Utah, a court stopped, at least temporarily, one Web site from linking to a site that included alleged copyrighted material taken from a church and posted without permission. In California, a San Francisco professor sued creators of a Web site that posted student critiques of professors *and* also sued a student group whose site merely linked to the site. The lawsuit claimed that the posted statements and critiques were defamatory, among other things.

Promoting relationships

Promoting business relationships is also a positive reason to link. Businesses often expand by association. For instance, you may want to link to your clients' or customers' sites if they don't mind. Links to their sites act as a promotional tool for your products and services.

Striving for a competitive edge

One reason for linking that usually gets people into trouble involves the desire to *imply* an association with someone else that doesn't exist. The link is like name-dropping, and a well-known or famous trademark is often used for the link. The company hopes that potential customers will assume that a relationship exists between the companies, leading to more business and more revenue.

Trying to create an implied association through a link may cause that some-one else (the business you're linking to) to look closely at the *way* the site is linking to her site. If the way the site is linking to her site misleads the public or her customers in some way, then she may have legal grounds to stop the other site from linking to her site.

Some companies use links to try skirting the law. In Germany a company got into trouble for this. A Japanese company had subsidiary companies in America and Germany. The American company's Web site compared its soft-ware product with a competitor's product. Doing so is legal in the United States In Germany, however, comparative advertising is not permitted under its unfair competition law. The German company's Web site linked to the American site. A court in Frankfurt ruled that the German company was liable for unfair commercial practices and breach of the national competition law. The German company had to remove the link and pay damages.

Still another troublesome reason to link is to benefit from using the name of a reputable or famous company (or product) to attract all types of visitors to a site. For example, assume that you're a graphic designer who creates Web sites for individuals and businesses. Anyone could be a potential customer, so you want to attract as many people as possible to your site. You link to sites for Disneyland, online bookstores, online CD stores, and airlines. After all, millions of people search for those sites. Your link (using those names) may show up in a search. This approach draws people to your site, but it may backfire on you. People are often annoyed when they're led to a site that doesn't provide the information they want.

Using trademarks and famous marks can land you in hot water. See Chapter 7 for more information about trademark infringement and trademark dilution.

Linking and Framing

Companies usually don't have the time to go after other Web site owners for linking to their sites unless they believe that their intellectual property or their revenue (or customer base) is at risk. Therefore, the *way* that links divert revenue or use the content — the intellectual property — of others is the spark that lights the ire of Web site owners.

Some sites simply provide links that lead people to other sites. Many sites include frames, and their links pull into the frame the content from other sites. Often sites link to a page deep within another site, rather than to the home page. Linking in any of these ways may raise legal issues.

Links that use words and designs

A link uses a word, a phrase, or a design (icon or logo) to move a person from one site to another. Trademark law often comes into play where links are involved.

Using trademarks

A *trademark* is a word, a phrase, or a drawing intended to identify the source of certain goods. A service mark is a word, a phrase, or a drawing intended to identify the source of certain services. As the mark becomes known within a certain market, that mark also begins to stand for a certain quality of goods or services. For more information on trademarks, see Chapter 7.

Companies have a good reason for reacting so strongly when someone uses their marks without their permission. The purchasing public may confuse the other goods or services and believe the goods or services of both companies are connected in some way. The infringing company (the one using the trademark without permission) could benefit by the consumers' mistakes as to the true source of the goods or services. Therefore, the infringing company is making money off the hard work, expense, and reputation of the true owner of the mark. The law won't permit this.

Using famous trademarks

It doesn't always matter to the owner of a famous mark whether anyone confuses the two companies or sites. Mere use of a famous mark by someone else may dilute the value of the mark. Trademark infringement can also detrimentally affect the reputation of the original company. Owners of famous marks can prevent everyone else from using them whether their goods and services are similar or not.

Famous marks are those that really acquire distinct meanings. For instance, if you're going to see a children's movie, the mark Disney means something. It means the movie has something to do with the company that owns the rights to the mark Disney. That name also means that any product or service that may include that mark has a certain level of excellence. When consumers see the mark Disney, they associate a certain standard with that mark and everything used with it. Because it's a famous mark, the Walt Disney Company can prevent others from using it at all — except when using it for certain legally permissible reasons (like news reporting).

Using trademarks fairly

You will probably be safe in most situations when you use trademarks in links in such a way that you're not diverting customers from the trademark owner's company and your Web site visitors aren't deceived.

Bringing other content into your frame

Frames are sections of a Web page that allow one part of the page to stay the same while another part changes. If your link brings the content of another site into your site through a frame, proceed with caution. Not only may trademark laws be involved, but copyright laws as well.

In general terms, copyright is a group of rights that are owned by creators of original works such as stories, music, computer programs, choreography, drawings, and movies. Owners of copyrighted works have the exclusive right to prevent others from copying the work, distributing it to others, displaying or performing it to the public, or making new works from that original work. For more information on copyright, see Chapters 16 and 17.

Suppose that you have links to various news agencies. When a visitor clicks on a link, a story from *The New York Times* appears on your site in your frame. That story belongs to the copyright owner. You may have just copied it and displayed it to the public without the owner's permission. Although the law is not settled, this is probably copyright infringement.

In fact, imagine that your advertising banners surround their content. No one sees the other site's advertising. The visitors probably don't even see the other site's Web address unless they know how to do some technical stuff. It looks like the story is your story. Such deceptive actions make copyright owners very angry, and a process server could be handing you a summons requiring you to defend yourself in a copyright infringement lawsuit!

Think about it. If it's your creative work, do you want other sites making your work look like it's their work? When you use links and frames, use them respectfully.

The deeper you go

Deep linking is linking to a page on a site other than the home page. Some companies don't mind if you link to their sites — or even use their trademarks. But they do mind if you deep link into their site. Why?

Those companies that insist on links only to their home pages have a valid reason. Most home pages are the places where the most expensive banner advertisements appear. And let's face it: Right now, the major revenue for

Internet sites is advertising dollars. So if people bypass a home page, they may not see the advertisements. Both the e-site and the advertisers that pay higher prices for this exposure lose out.

The people who promote the right to deep link have a very good point, too. Most users won't remember, or won't be able to follow, directions written on one site that direct a user how to locate specific information within another site. Users may not even click a link that requires them to follow directions. In my opinion, sites should be able to link directly to information on a page deep within another site. A link that leads the user directly to the desired destination and information accomplishes this goal.

I hope that courts consider the reasons people provide deep links before they make anyone stop linking. People providing deep links for good reasons shouldn't be prevented from doing it.

Playing It Safe

If you want to really play it safe when creating links, here are a few tips for you:

✔ Search the federal trademark database on the Internet to check on registered and pending trademarks so you can avoid using a registered trademark. Keep in mind that trademark rights may arise even without registration. The appendix includes the Web site address for the U.S. Patent and Trademark Office's searchable database. If you decide to use a trademark in a link, then use it fairly and without deceiving the users regarding your association with the owner of that mark.

✔ Think about why you're linking to the other sites, and link only for honorable reasons. That is, don't take advantage of other companies' hard work or famous status.

✔ Never, ever use a famous logo, cartoon character, photograph, likeness, or person's name unless you have permission or unless you seek legal advice about the use. Although an attorney may advise you to go ahead and use it, at least seek that specific advice before taking on the risk of a lawsuit.

✔ Ask (never demand) permission from the other sites to link to their sites and get their permission in writing.

Protecting Against Copyright Infringement Claims

The Web scares many copyright owners because they can't keep track of all the sites posting copyrighted work. Yes, posting the copyrighted work of others without permission is a copyright infringement, and the owners may sue the infringers. But who are the infringers? What does it take to violate copyright law?

What if you operate a portal site and you link or *point* (refer people without a link) to other Web sites that are infringing on someone's copyright? What if you operate a search engine and some of the sites you offer to users include material that infringes someone's copyright? What if you provide Web site hosting services and one of the sites you host is infringing on someone's copyright? Can you be liable for that copyright infringement, too?

In the United States, it depends on whether you qualify as a service provider under the Digital Millennium Copyright Act of 1998 (DMCA) and you comply with its requirements.

The DMCA provisions are very technical, so check with a copyright lawyer for specifics in your situation.

The Digital Millennium Copyright Act

Generally, the DMCA provides that online service providers will not be liable for copyright infringement if they fall into any of the following categories:

- ✔ Anyone who transmits, routes, or provides connections for digital online communications, referred to as *transitory communications,* such as Internet service providers (ISPs)

- ✔ Anyone who provides (or operates) online services or network access and uses information location tools, such as links, online directories, and search engines

- ✔ Anyone who provides (or operates) online services or network access and who stores information on systems or networks at the direction of users, such as Web site hosts

- ✔ Anyone who provides (or operates) online services or network access and who utilizes *system caching,* or very temporary data storage.

If you're a service provider and you don't meet the requirements in this section, you're not necessarily liable for copyright infringement. The copyright owner must still prove a case against you. This law simply provides additional protection for service providers.

The Digital Millennium Copyright Act (DMCA) prohibits anyone from circumventing technological measures used by copyright owners to protect their work. It also prohibits anyone from tampering with any of the owners' copyright management information, such as watermarks (see Chapter 17). DMCA was adopted to comply with World Intellectual Property Organization (WIPO) treaties, which means that all countries that signed the WIPO Copyright

Treaty have — or will have — this portion of the law as part of their law. These countries include Canada, France, Germany, Israel, the United Kingdom, the United States, and the European Union (see the European Union in Chapter 1). See the appendix for the WIPO Web site address.

Linking, directing, and searching: Information location tools

Information location tools include links, online directories, search engines, and other similar tools used to locate information. When a site contains material that infringes someone's copyright, anyone who uses information location tools to direct users to that site will *not* be liable for copyright infringement if all the following conditions are met:

- The provider does not have actual knowledge of the infringement and is not aware of facts or circumstances that make it apparent that the activity on the other site is infringing.

- Even if the provider is unaware of the infringement, the provider may still be liable for infringement if the provider has the right — or the ability — to control the infringing activity on the other site and receives a financial benefit directly attributable to the infringing activity.

- As soon as the provider becomes aware of the infringing material or receives notice that someone is claiming that the material is infringing someone's copyright, the provider expeditiously takes down or blocks access to the material (see the section "Providing proper notice for the millennium," later in this chapter).

Although there is no specific or final court decision at the time of this writing, the following is an example of how a provider that uses information tools could (arguably — not definitely) be receiving a financial benefit from infringing activity. Assume that the provider receives fees through an affiliate program or under a contract with a company to refer users to the company's site. The provider receives money every time a user downloads music from the company's site. If the company's site offers music without the copyright owners' permission, the provider could be receiving a financial benefit directly attributable to the infringing activity — downloading music without the copyright owners' permission.

Transmitting transitory communications

To understand *transitory communications*, think of a communication in transit — the copyrighted material in digital form is being sent from one point on a network to another point. The material is kept by a company only briefly; thus it's transitory (of brief duration). For instance, the provider may be transmitting e-mail from one point to another point or transmitting Web site files from a personal computer to a Web server that hosts a Web site. The transitory communications referred to in this law are those that contain copyrighted material when the copyright owner hasn't given anyone permission to transmit it.

Generally, a service provider that transmits, routes, or provides connections for digital online communications won't be liable for copyright infringement of the material being transmitted if all the following conditions are met:

- ✔ Someone other than the service provider sends the communication.
- ✔ The provider isn't involved in selecting which material will be transmitted because the material is automatically sent through a technical computer process.
- ✔ The user, not the provider, specifies who will receive the material.
- ✔ The provider doesn't retain the material any longer than reasonably necessary to transmit the material and doesn't ordinarily allow anyone else access to the material (such as other users) other than the recipient of the material.
- ✔ The provider transmits the material without modifying or changing its content.

Storing material

Service providers that host Web sites or store other information on their systems or networks will *not* be liable for the material on those sites if all the following conditions are met:

- ✔ The provider does not have actual knowledge of the infringement and is not aware of facts or circumstances that make it apparent that the activity on the other site is infringing.
- ✔ As soon as the provider becomes aware of the infringing material or receives notice that someone is claiming that the material is infringing someone's copyright, the provider expeditiously takes down or blocks access to the material. See the section "Providing proper notice for the millennium," later in this chapter.
- ✔ Even if the provider is unaware of the infringement, the provider may still be liable for infringement if the provider has the right — or the ability — to control the infringing activity on the other site and receives a financial benefit directly attributable to the infringing activity (see the section "Linking, directing, and searching: Information location tools," earlier in this chapter, for an example).
- ✔ The provider filed (*filed* in the past tense) with the U.S. Copyright Office (see the appendix for its Web site address) a form designating (naming) an agent (a person) to receive notification of any claimed infringement. The copyright office's Web site includes forms and a list of agents. See the section "Providing proper notice for the millennium," later in this chapter.

Caching the material

Caching (pronounced *cashing*) is the verb for the noun cache (pronounced *cash*). *Cache* is a special mechanism used to store data. Most computer programs (including Web browsers) access the same data or information over and over. Caching stores this information in memory. In other words, it's a process of retaining copies of the material. When a program needs to access the data again, such as a Web page, the data is available to the user more quickly.

Service providers will not be liable for caching (retaining copies of) copyrighted material without the copyright owners' permission if all the following conditions are met:

- The content of the retained material is not modified.

- The provider complies with industry standards ("generally accepted industry standard data communication protocol") about *refreshing* material, that is, replacing retained copies of material with material from the original location (fresh copies of the material).

- The provider does not interfere with technology that returns hit information to the person who posted the material as long as the person's technology meets certain technical requirements. *Hit information* is the number of times data is found in the copy, like the number of times a search engine returns that page to someone searching for specific information. Hit information is important to Web site owners for many reasons, such as learning how many people visit their site or see their advertisements (see Chapter 11).

- The provider follows any conditions limiting access to users (like only allowing those with passwords to access the material) that are imposed by the person who posted the material.

- The provider removes or blocks promptly any material posted without the copyright owners' permission once the provider has been notified that the material has been removed, blocked, or ordered to be removed or blocked (such as a court order or a proper notice) at the originating site. See the section "Providing proper notice for the millennium," later in this chapter.

Providing proper notice for the millennium

A copyright owner must follow certain rules and procedures when notifying a service provider about infringement. It's called a *notice and takedown procedure*. If the service provider receives a notice that doesn't comply with these requirements, then the provider hasn't received proper notice under the law. Therefore, a court will consider that the provider did *not* have knowledge of the copyright infringement as a result of a notice.

The copyright owner's notice must be made under penalty of perjury (swearing that the statements in the notice are true). The notice must include a list of specified elements spelled out in the law. This issue gets very technical, so check with a copyright lawyer if this situation arises for you. The notice must be sent to the service provider's designated agent, which is a person legally authorized to accept legal notices for the company or is listed as the company's agent on the U.S. Copyright Office Web site (see the section "Storing material," earlier in this chapter).

If, upon receiving a proper notification, the provider promptly removes or blocks access to the material identified in the notice, the provider will not be liable for money damages to the copyright owner; however, the provider may still have to comply with a court order that doesn't involve payment of money. What a court may order a provider to do depends on the infringement involved.

If the provider wants to be protected from any liability to any person who posted the material just in case the person claiming the infringement isn't right, the provider must promptly notify the person (the subscriber) that the provider has removed or disabled access to the material. The person may follow some legal technicalities and *serve* (a legal word that involves various ways to properly send notice) a counternotice that complies with the law's requirements, including a statement under penalty of perjury that the material was removed or disabled through mistake or misidentification. After receiving this notice, the provider must put the material back up within 10 to 14 business days (not counting weekends and legal holidays) after receiving the counternotice *unless* the copyright owner files a court action against the person (the subscriber).

Accommodating copyright owners

The DMCA lists a couple more requirements for service providers that want to limit their liability for copyright infringement. The service providers must adopt and implement a policy of terminating, in appropriate circumstances, the accounts of subscribers who are repeat infringers.

In addition, the providers must accommodate, and not interfere with, technical measures that copyright owners use to identify or protect copyrighted works *if* the technical measures meet the following conditions:

- ✔ The technical measures have been developed pursuant to a broad consensus of copyright owners and service providers in an open, fair, and voluntary multi-industry process.

- ✔ The technical measures are available to anyone to use on reasonable nondiscriminatory terms (meaning the owners of the technology cannot demand unreasonable fees or discriminate with respect to which companies they will license to).

- ✔ The technical measures do not impose costs or burdens on service providers.

Part VI
Making Money from Your Site

The 5th Wave   By Rich Tennant

"I like getting complaint letters by e-mail.
It's easier to delete than to shred."

In this part . . .

Money makes the world go 'round. It keeps your
e-site online, too.

Selling goods and information on your e-site is one way to
generate cash from your Web site. In this part, you'll get
help navigating through the tangled mess of sales contracts, logistical problems, and questions about processing
payments online. You'll also learn about a proposed law
governing computer information that's making its way to a
state legislature near you. Do you want to protect the
money you make? If so, you'll probably need to hire a
lawyer. In this part, you'll learn the best way to do so.

Chapter 19

Selling Goods and Information

· ·

In This Chapter

▶ Getting the goods to your customers

▶ Making sales in Europe

▶ Setting up sales and auction sites

▶ Processing payments

▶ Dealing with information

· ·

Do I have a bid? Will you give me two? Give me 2,000? There's two in the back. Do I hear three? Three? Where's three? No three? Going once. Going twice. Sold for $2,000 to the lady in the back row.

Shopping. Bidding. Ordering. We gotta have it. And where better to buy it than the World Wide Web? But is the Net catching the buyers unaware? Is the old Latin phrase *Caveat emptor* still true on the Web? Buyer beware?

The Internet won't reach its full commercial potential until customers feel safe to buy on its sites. Online shopping is similar to offline shopping; consumers want companies to deal with them fairly and truthfully. You can make a difference online if you know some of the rules of fair play.

Read Chapter 3 with this chapter for a more complete understanding about sales contracts. Chapter 3 includes some basics about contracts as well as information about point-and-click agreements on the Web, which companies often use for their mass-market contracts discussed in this chapter.

Delivering the Goods: Federal Regulations

Maybe you got the goods, baby, but can you deliver? And I mean deliver on time? As far as the Federal Trade Commission is concerned, you better be able to put up or pay back when it comes to delivering the goods.

A federal regulation, sometimes called the prompt delivery rule, governs sales of merchandise by mail or telephone order. The Federal Trade Commission (FTC), whose Web site appears in Figure 19-1, says this rule applies to online orders as well. If you're taking orders online for merchandise, you have to follow the rule. Basically, you must make sure that people get what they want when they want it. Here's how it goes.

- When you offer merchandise for sale on your Web site, you must either list a shipping date clearly and prominently, or you must ship the merchandise within 30 days after the order. If your delivery guys get backed up or your stock gets low so you can't meet this deadline, you must notify your customer by e-mail, letter, or fax. You must notify her within a reasonable time after you first learn that you won't be able to meet the deadline.

- In your notice, advise your customer of the delay, provide a new and definite shipping date, and state that she may either consent to the delay or request a full and prompt refund. You must state this right to a refund clearly and prominently in the notice. If you don't have a new, definite shipping date, tell your customer that you don't and explain the reason for the delay.

- When you provide your customer with a new, definite shipping date for a delay of up to 30 days, you may consider your customer's silence in response to the notice as agreeing to the delay. For longer or indefinite delays (as well as second or subsequent delays), you must get your customer's consent to the delay. If you don't, you must promptly refund all the money he paid to you even if he doesn't ask for a refund.

Here are a few additional pieces of information to put in your notice, depending on how long your delay will be:

- If your revised shipping date is more than 30 days, but less than 61 days, after the order, you must also state that the buyer will be deemed to have consented to the delay unless you receive a response rejecting the delay and canceling the order before you ship the product or prior to the revised shipping date, whichever is later.

- If your revised shipping date is more than 60 days after the order or you cannot provide a revised shipping date (and you explain the reason for the delay), you must also state in your notice that you will automatically cancel the order unless: (1) you ship within 60 days after the order and do not receive a cancellation from your customer prior to shipment, or (2) you receive, within 30 days, a response from your customer specifically consenting to the shipping delay.

- If you're unable to provide a definite shipping date and the buyer consents to an indefinite delay, your notice must state that the buyer has a continuing right to cancel the order at any time after the initial 30 days by notifying you prior to actual shipment.

You don't need to send any delay notices if you change your shipping date on your site before the customer places the order.

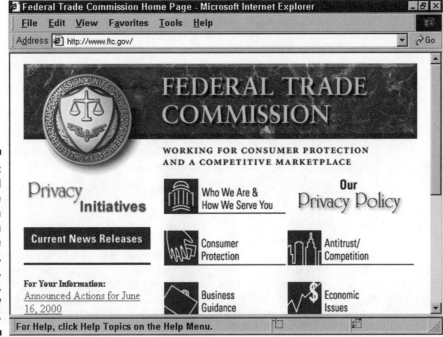

Figure 19-1:
The Federal Trade Commission keeps you up-to-date on sales, advertising, warranty, and privacy regulations.

The prompt delivery rule makes your conduct an "unfair or deceptive business practice" if you don't comply with it. When you provide a shipping date to a customer, you must have some valid reason to believe you can meet that deadline. Don't provide dates based on hope, faith, or desire. Doing so won't cut it with the feds.

Selling in Europe: Distance Selling

When you sell over the Internet to consumers in Europe, you must usually comply with laws in those countries (see Chapter 2 for more information about jurisdiction and contracts with consumers). The European Union (EU) approved a directive regarding *distance selling* (not face-to-face) to consumers (not business-to-business). This directive applies to the sale of goods as well as the sale of services. Each European country that is a member of the EU will adopt (or already has adopted) laws to follow this directive. They may also adopt laws that more strictly protect consumers.

Under the law, suppliers of goods or services must provide certain information to consumers before they make their purchase. Among other things, you must provide consumers with the following:

- ✔ Your name and address
- ✔ A description of the main features of the goods or services
- ✔ The price for the goods and services, including all taxes and delivery costs
- ✔ Information regarding payment and delivery
- ✔ A description of anything that the sales contract requires you or the consumer to do to comply with the contract
- ✔ A notice stating whether the consumer has a right to withdraw from the contract
- ✔ How long the terms of the contract will last (the duration of the contract)

In addition, you must confirm the above information to the consumer by using some "durable medium" that the consumer can access. In other words, you must use something that you can save and see or hear at another time, such as paper or a saved digital file. The consumer also has the right to get out of the deal for at least seven working days after placing the order.

If you're shipping goods across national borders, customs, duties, and taxes (such as VAT — see Chapter 22) may apply. Include these amounts in your price. You must also comply with import/export laws that may apply. Check with a lawyer who handles international sales transactions.

Contracting to Sell Goods: Uniform Commercial Code

The *freedom of contract* is an important part of a democratic society. This freedom grants individuals and businesses the right to set their own contract terms without a whole lot of interference by the law. Businesses entering contracts with other businesses have much leeway to set the terms of their deals. They usually have equal bargaining power to negotiate, so courts often enforce the exact terms of the agreement — even if the parties accidentally make a really bad deal.

When it comes to contracts with consumers, however, the law provides more protection to consumers. They don't have equal bargaining power with businesses. The law regulates certain terms in consumer contracts because they're often take-it-or-leave-it deals.

The Uniform Commercial Code (UCC) is a law in all 50 states. One article (section) of it governs transactions in the sale of goods (this article was not adopted in Louisiana). Goods are tangible (something you can touch or see), moveable property, such as merchandise.

The UCC primarily focuses on commercial contracts (business-to-business), although it also includes some provisions for sales to consumers. Remember, even a simple purchase involves a sales contract (see Chapter 3). When a contract doesn't cover a certain point that later results in a controversy, the UCC comes into play. It guides parties and the courts to resolve those points.

For example, a contract may not state what happens if the goods delivered aren't precisely what the company ordered. May the company reject and return them? The parties may argue over this point. The UCC then becomes important. It permits a buyer to reject any goods that do not conform precisely to the contract; however, the law permits the seller to correct the problem under certain circumstances. The law steps in when the contract is silent about certain issues.

The UCC includes many provisions, and each state's law may vary from other states' laws a bit. A group is currently revising parts of this law; when it's completed, the group will take the revision to all the state legislatures and urge them to adopt the updated version. (The UCC is too complex to describe in detail in this book.)

However, the UCC covers certain general categories or issues that I can discuss here. You may want to consider these topics when you put your sales contracts together so that all parties to the agreement know what the deal is about. They involve the following:

- A description of the quantity and quality of the goods being sold. If one party will be selecting certain goods from a lot, how will she go about selecting them?

- How and when will the title (ownership) to the goods transfer from one party to the other? Will the title pass when the contract is signed, when payment is made, or when the goods are delivered?

- Which warranties is the party making regarding the goods? Is there a warranty of good title (is she warranting that she really owns the goods or has the legal right to transfer them) or a warranty regarding the quality of the goods? Are there any warranties the party wants to disclaim? In other words, does the party want to state that there is no warranty regarding something? Do these contract provisions comply with the UCC warranty requirements? For more information about warranties, see Chapter 20.

✔ Will the party limit her liability (in order to reduce her financial risk) in the event she breaches any warranty? Does this contract provision comply with the UCC requirements?

✔ Who will bear the risk of loss in case the goods don't arrive in good condition? Will either party obtain insurance to cover this risk?

✔ When, where, and how will the seller deliver the goods? If the goods aren't precisely as ordered, does the seller have the right to correct the mistake? How long will she have to correct it?

✔ May the buyer return the goods for any reason? If so, what procedure should he follow? Is there a time limit as to when he may return them? Who pays for the shipping costs?

✔ Will the buyer have the right to inspect the goods before accepting delivery of them? May he reject the goods if he doesn't like them? If he may reject them, what's the procedure he should follow? Must he explain why he's rejecting them? Must he take care of them while they're in his possession?

✔ If the buyer discovers that the seller breached the agreement, must he notify the seller so they can try to resolve it out of court?

✔ When must the buyer pay for the goods? How and when will he pay? Must he pay before he has the right to inspect them?

✔ How long will the contract last (its duration or term)?

✔ If either party wants to end (terminate) the contract, under what conditions may they terminate it? How will they go about notifying each other, and what happens to the goods after termination?

✔ If one party becomes insolvent (runs out of money or files bankruptcy) during the contract, should the other party have the right to terminate the agreement?

✔ If there is an earthquake, flood, fire, or other act of God (called a *force majeure* event) and one party cannot perform the agreement, may the other party terminate the agreement?

✔ May one of the parties change the terms of the contract if the party wants to add or change something? If so, must it be in writing and signed by both parties?

✔ May the parties delegate their obligations to someone else to perform their obligations under the contract?

✔ May either party assign (sell) their rights under the contract to another company?

✔ If a dispute arises between the parties, should the party in possession of the goods preserve them until they resolve the dispute?

✔ Do the parties want to agree to a "liquidated damages" clause, which means that they agree that any breach of contract will not result in any payment to the other party for more than a specific amount of money stated in the agreement?

✔ Which law do the parties want to govern the terms of their contract, and which forum do they want to use to resolve any dispute (for example, a court in the County of Los Angeles, State of California)? Would they prefer to arbitrate (an informal legal proceeding) any dispute to save money and time? If they agree to arbitrate, will they agree to abide by the arbitrator's decision, or may they appeal the decision to a court?

As you can see, your sales contract may be simple, moderately complex (involving all the issues in the preceding list), or very complex (the issues in the preceding list plus lots more). The complexity of your contract depends upon the amount of money involved in the deal, what your lawyer advises you to do, and the relationship you have with the other party to the contract.

Everybody loves an auction

Auctions are hot on the Net. Big and small auctions are popping up on the Web, and people can buy just about anything from guitars to car parts. Sellers are connected to potential buyers through the sites, the items go up for sale, the bidders make offers, and the lucky bidder hooks up with the seller to finalize the payment and delivery terms. Anyone anywhere in the world may buy and sell items.

Usually an auction is defined as a public sale of property to the highest bidder. It's all about competitive bidding among potential buyers. State and local governments may regulate auction sales, auctioneers, and people who conduct an auction business. Some states require auctioneers and auction companies to obtain a license to run a public auction, while other states require them to post a bond with a state agency to make sure that money is available for people who may get hurt by the auctions. Those states that require a license often make it a criminal misdemeanor for anyone to act as an auctioneer or an auction company without a license.

Each state may define an auctioneer a little bit differently. Sometimes it's a person who, for a commission or some other compensation, conducts an auction to sell property that belongs to someone else. Other times, it's anyone who calls for, and accepts offers for, the purchase of goods at an auction. An auction company is often anyone who arranges, sponsors, advertises, or carries out an auction at some location.

Does this mean that every e-business and person who runs an auction on a Web site needs to obtain a license or post a bond for several thousands of dollars in the state where they are set up? Do they have to obtain licenses or post bonds in every state where buyers interact with their site? Unfortunately, there's no answer to this question currently, but I spoke to some state agencies and conducted a bit of research so you can at least have some information to keep in mind.

A government source who asked me not to identify him (sounds mysterious, doesn't it?) in a

(continued)

state that requires auctioneers to post a $20,000 bond says the state has no official policy regarding Internet auctions, and lawyers for auction sites should simply read the law and make their own interpretations for their clients. So far that state agency has a hands-off policy regarding auction sites. In other words, it's not going after them to post a bond and doesn't really consider them to be running a public auction.

Companies running auction sites seem to promote this legal position, too. Even though they often commission part of the price and the sale is on their auction site, they claim to be offering a listing service rather than acting as an auction company. In most Internet auctions, the transactions go on directly between the seller and the buyer. In other words, the seller usually hangs on to the property and works out delivery details directly with the buyer. The money normally flows directly between the buyer and seller, and the seller pays some portion to the auction site operator according to their agreement. In this way, the auction site may truly be a service that lists items for sale, allows sellers and buyers to use their technology, and allows buyers and sellers to handle their own transactions.

Germany also has licensing requirements for those who run auctions. In France, Web site auctions may need to have a French auctioneer involved with the site — at least one French court required this in a case. However, a French Internet attorney informs me that he believes French law will change soon so that this is not required. Also in France, new goods cannot be sold by auction, and items that violate French law may not appear on Web auction sites that are accessible by French citizens. A French court ordered Yahoo! to pay damages to an organization and to restrict access by French citizens to its U.S. auction site because neo-Nazi items appeared on the site, which violated a French law prohibiting the sale or display of any items that incite racism (the case is still pending as of this writing). The United Kingdom doesn't appear to have restrictions for auctions yet. Consult a lawyer in the countries where you plan to run auction sites.

If you're thinking about running an auction site, become familiar with the various auctioneer licensing laws. You may even want to stay away from handling the money or the property that moves back and forth between buyers and sellers. Be sure to check with your lawyer.

Processing Payments and Disclosing Details

Crucial questions that owners of all e-commerce sites should ask are: "How will we process payments securely?" and "How will we handle returns?" E-commerce entrepreneurs must think carefully about the answers to these questions. Here are a few tips to help you find your answers.

Processing the payments

Several companies, big and small, offer e-commerce solutions for small e-businesses. They offer solutions to get you started on the Internet and to process payments online. Some companies offer consulting services; they advise you about which combination of software packages work together to meet your goals. Other companies sell software packages that they developed or that they sell to e-businesses. Web site addresses for a few of these companies are in the appendix.

Whichever payment mechanism you choose, it should

✔ Be easy for the customer to use.

✔ Be safe so that the information won't be stolen.

✔ Work well internationally.

✔ Result in immediate settlement of payment obligations, without delay, so that the seller doesn't wait long for payment.

When you want to accept payment for goods or services by credit card, you set up a merchant account with a company to process the transactions and get the money to you. Some companies that offer merchant accounts offer free software to make the transactions safe and secure. According to technology experts I asked, this software is normally very secure — it includes the type of encryption that the U.S. government won't allow the companies to export to other countries. For more information on setting up secure payment mechanisms for your site, check out some of the Web sites listed in the appendix regarding e-commerce solutions, payment processing, and merchant accounts. It may cost you only $50 per month to hire a company to set up a payment processing system for you and to keep it running.

Don't skimp on the technology for this portion of your Web site. Remember, security and privacy are the biggest concerns of people doing business on the Net. Explore all your options before making a final decision on which technology to use for your site.

Disclosing prices, policies, and procedures

When a Web site sells goods rather than simply providing information, some state laws require more information to be disclosed on the sites. Therefore, you might include the following information for your customers:

✔ Your complete business name, business address (some laws require a physical office location) including the country, and e-mail address or telephone number for customers to contact you

✔ A detailed description of the products you're selling

✔ All costs, including the price, any taxes, shipping charges, and delivery fees

✔ Any restrictions or limitations on the sale

✔ Any warranties or guarantees (see Chapter 20)

✔ An estimate when you will ship the goods (see the delivery rules in the section "Delivering the Goods: Federal Regulations," earlier in this chapter, if you don't want to include a shipping date)

✔ Details about the payment options, such as credit cards transactions on the site or by telephone, C.O.D., and so on

✔ Your return policy and how buyers may return the items, get a refund or credit, or make an exchange

✔ Where customers should call, write, or e-mail you with complaints or problems

✔ How you will confirm customers' orders

The Information Exchange: Uniform Computer Information Transactions Act

The Uniform Commercial Code governs only transactions involving the sale of goods. What about things that aren't technically goods? For instance, hiring someone to create a computer program is really contracting for that person's creative services and, as such, falls outside the UCC. Over the Internet, people are selling information, such as digital newsletters and other Web site content. Does any contract law help with these sales or licensing agreements when there's a problem between the contracting parties?

In 1999, a proposed law was finally completed. It's called the Uniform Computer Information Transactions Act (UCITA). The group who drafted UCITA is taking it to every state legislature in the United States for adoption. In 2000, Virginia and Maryland became the first states to adopt it as law. There's a good chance that a majority of the states will adopt it eventually. Therefore, it's important to understand some of its provisions. See the Web site www.nccus/.org/uniformact-factsheets/uniformacts-fs-ucita.htm to keep up on which states adopt UCITA.

When UCITA applies to a contract

Like the UCC, the provisions of UCITA apply only when the contract is silent on certain points. In other words, it governs only when the parties do not choose a different result. The parties may state in their contract that they elect (are choosing) to have their agreement interpreted according to UCITA if they don't want to cover each and every possible issue in their agreement; however, UCITA applies only to certain types of contracts.

UCITA applies only to contracts to create, modify (change), transfer, or license (granting the right to use) "computer information." Computer information is information in a form that's directly capable of being processed in, or received from, a computer. It includes contracts relating to software, computer programs, computer games, multimedia products, and the distribution of information on the Internet (such as Internet news sites, multimedia encyclopedias, and other information sites).

Computer information also includes online access to databases. These databases have information that a visitor retrieves from a site. For example, a visitor may go to a Web site and search for information on movies or alternative healing methods. This information is part of the site's searchable database. Contracts relating to these databases may involve an agreement between a Web site user and the site owner regarding the terms of use for the site, or they may involve an agreement between a Web site owner and the person who provides the information to the site.

UCITA applies to contracts between businesses as well as some contracts between a business and consumers. It doesn't trump consumer protection laws. In other words, you can't include a provision in the contract forcing a consumer to waive her rights under any consumer protection laws, and your contracts with consumers must still comply with those laws.

UCITA rules and guidelines

UCITA provides rules (guidelines) for interpreting the rights of parties who are making deals involving computer information. In effect, it helps the parties to an agreement and courts determine who has what rights in certain situations when the provisions in contracts aren't clear enough to define these rights. The following are some of these rules.

Warranties: UCITA includes a number of warranty provisions for contracts. It recognizes *express warranties,* which are written or verbal commitments. It also recognizes a number of *implied warranties,* which are warranties that the law automatically includes in the contracts unless the parties state in their agreements that they do not apply (and the parties comply with legal requirements on how to do this). See Chapter 20 for more information.

Published information content: The proposed law also refers to "published information content," which refers to information that people read, hear, or communicate over the Internet, such as newsletters and online databases as explained in the section "When UCITA applies to a contract," earlier in this chapter. This type of information content is the First Amendment kind of stuff — you know, freedom of speech to report the news, to express an opinion, and all that.

To ensure that these information providers, like newspaper publishers in the offline world, don't take too much risk for sharing their information, UCITA adopts the rule that members of the public may not sue these providers simply because the information is incorrect. For instance, if a newspaper could be sued by anyone for publishing incorrect information, the constant risk of being sued for any inaccurate piece of information really would have a chilling effect on the freedom of speech — writers and publishers would be afraid to share their opinions and information, so everyone could be deprived of news and the exchange of ideas. Under UCITA, providers of published information content won't be liable for inaccurate information unless they have a special relationship with an individual who relies on information, like a writer providing content to a publisher.

UCITA implies a warranty in this special relationship. The person who provides information is making a warranty that there are no errors caused by his failure to use reasonable care. In other words, he needs to make sure that he's not acting irresponsibly. There are, however, no warranties to anyone who does not have a special relationship with the provider. In other words, the provider won't be liable to readers under UCITA for inaccurate information (but see Chapter 14 for other laws, such as libel).

Breach of contract

Under the UCC for the sale of goods, the buyer may reject goods if they don't precisely comply with the description in the contract. The seller has breached the contract, and the buyer may cancel (terminate) the contract. There are, of course, some exceptions, but this is the general rule.

Under UCITA, this rule applies only in mass-market deals (explained later in this section). Otherwise, UCITA follows the common law of contracts and international contract law, which provides that a party may not cancel the contract unless there is a material breach of contract rather than a minor breach of contract. You see, the people who drafted this law realize that software products are so complex that these products will have some imperfections. Technology is such that creating perfect software simply isn't attainable right now. Therefore, minor imperfections shouldn't permit someone to cancel a contract.

For example, an e-company may hire a Web technology company to develop the program to run the e-commerce site. This Web developer may develop the technology to run with certain types of Web site browsers that visitors may use, as well as other software applications that run with the browsers to listen to music (like a RealAudio player) or read special text files (such as Acrobat Reader). The e-company may want its site to work with every single program the visitor may use to interact with the site.

The developer spends thousands of hours over several months to develop the technology. However, some software that the visitors use may have bugs (things that make the software not work perfectly). That software may make the browser do weird things, too. The developer turns in the finished program, but on rare occasions the program doesn't work perfectly for some visitors because the software they're using has flaws. The developer would have to fix another company's software to resolve it, which he cannot do (it's not his job and he doesn't have access to the protected source code of the other software).

Under the UCC, this minor failure to conform with the contract to provide technology to run an e-commerce site might allow the e-company to cancel the contract (claiming the developer breached the agreement) and not pay the developer. Canceling these contracts would be grossly unfair because computer programs are inherently (by their very complex nature) imperfect.

Under UCITA, the e-company could cancel the contract and refuse to pay only if the developer materially breached the contract. This language generally means that the party either did, or did not do, something that substantially deprived (or was likely to substantially deprive) the other party of a significant benefit that it reasonably expected under the contract. In other words, not complying with a provision in the contract (called a breach) must involve a really important and major point in the contract for the breach to be a material breach. There's an exception, however. If the party who materially breaches the contract substantially performs all of her other obligations under the contract, the other party cannot simply cancel the contract and refuse to pay the entire amount due under the contract. The party who suffers damages may be able to recover something from the breaching party, but he can't cancel the entire contract and walk away from it.

Mass-market contracts

UCITA has special rules for mass-market licenses. These are standard form contracts that companies often use in retail transactions with the general public. Although companies use these contracts with consumers most often, UCITA also covers mass-market contracts involving business-to-business deals. Therefore, UCITA covers your standard form contracts even if your customers are all businesses making retail purchases rather than consumers. Web sites often use a point-and-click agreement for mass-market licenses on the Internet. See Chapter 3 for information about these agreements.

For you to be able to enforce these contracts under UCITA, the contracts must conform with the following rules:

✔ The other party must "manifest assent" to the terms of the agreement, such as doing something to show that he is agreeing to the provisions of the contract (see Chapter 3 regarding contract basics and point-and-click agreements).

✔ The other party must have an opportunity to review the contract terms before purchase. This provision of the agreement doesn't necessarily mean that she has to actually read them. In other words, she can't get out of the contract just because she says she clicked "I Agree," but didn't actually read the contract. She must simply have the opportunity to read it before purchase.

✔ The terms cannot be unconscionable (see Chapter 3 for an explanation of unconscionable terms, such as a contract provision limiting a company's liability in the event a consumer is physically injured by the company's product).

✔ The terms of the contract may not violate fundamental public policy of the state or country (like violating extremely important rights of citizens regarding such things as health, safety, and the pursuit of happiness).

✔ The terms may not conflict with any actual one-on-one agreement between the parties. For example, you may not use your form to change your one-on-one deal already agreed upon.

Choosing the law to govern the contract

UCITA also recognizes the parties' right to agree which state's law will govern the terms of the contract. They may state their choice in their contract. If the contract is with a consumer, however, the contract may not change any legal requirements under any consumer protection law that applies.

If the parties do not include their choice of law in the contract, UCITA jumps in with the following rules:

✔ To determine which state's law will govern deals involving Internet transactions, ask the question: "Where is the principal place of business for the company that is providing the information?" This is the state whose law governs the deals.

✔ To determine which state's law will govern transactions involving the delivery of tangible products to consumers, ask the question: "Where will the consumer receive the tangible product?" This is the state whose law governs the transaction.

✔ In all other cases, the law of the state with the most significant relationship to the transaction applies. Check out Chapter 2 on jurisdiction for more information.

Chapter 20

Providing Warranties

- -

- -

*E*very second of every day products are en route from manufacturers to distributors to sellers to buyers to users. Money spent to purchase these products flows back to sellers to distributors to manufacturers to workers to families. And the flow goes on.

All types of warranties are floating in this stream of commerce. You probably know something about warranties. Don't you wonder whether or not something you're buying comes with a warranty? Most of us have come to expect them.

Warranty law came about when the Powers That Be thought that certain warranties, or promises about quality and performance, should come with the goods we buy. If the products don't meet these promises, then the buyers should have some recourse or remedy against the makers or sellers.

In today's world, most people don't pay much attention to the specific terms in warranties until a product breaks down. Then they want someone else to fix it or to replace it for free. At this point the maker, the seller, and the buyer all begin to pay lots of attention to the warranty.

Warranties aren't merely slips of paper you find in a box when you buy some product. Warranties are contracts in some instances and parts of contracts in others. They're especially important to you as an e-business entrepreneur when you're using technology, providing software, or gathering certain types of information for Internet sites.

Warranties affect every e-business. Whether you're making, buying, selling, or leasing, you either need to stand behind the quality and performance of your products or you want to make sure that other people stand behind theirs.

Defining Warranties

A *warranty* is simply a type of promise or a statement of fact about the quality or performance of some *thing*. Before the Internet, warranties normally covered products or goods. Laws are now changing to make room for other things that people are providing over the Internet, like digital information. This includes material that you can download from the Web.

There are two general kinds of warranties:

- **Express warranties** are certain promises or facts actually expressed to someone by writing them, saying them, or acting in a certain way that expresses them. The law does not require anyone to provide an express warranty. It's a choice. Companies provide them as a sales incentive.

  To be an express warranty, the promises or facts must usually be a *basis of the bargain*. This means that the promises or statements about quality, performance, repairs, or refunds affect whether a person will buy the product for a certain price. The precise statement doesn't have to actually enter the individual buyer's mind at the time of sale, but that type of statement has to be something that people generally consider when making a purchasing decision.

- **Implied warranties** are obligations that the law imposes upon manufacturers and certain sellers. These warranties apply to certain sales whether or not anyone wants to provide the warranty.

The precise definition of a warranty varies between federal and state laws. In addition, some of these laws apply only to sales to consumers (consumer law), while others regulate only sales to other businesses (commercial law).

Consumers usually can't negotiate with a company when they're buying something. When one business buys from another business, however, there's usually room for negotiating the deal. Businesses often have equal bargaining power when dealing with each other. Therefore, laws protect consumers more vigorously by providing more rules and regulations for businesses to follow when their sales are to consumers, and fewer regulations when their sales are to other businesses.

Complying with Federal Warranty Law

If you don't distribute or sell consumer goods, usually state law applies to your warranties. The federal law, called the Magnuson-Moss Warranty Act, covers only consumer goods. The Federal Trade Commission (FTC) makes regulations to carry out the intent of this act. The regulations and other valuable warranty information are on the FTC's Web site (www.ftc.gov).

Your e-business must comply with this federal law if *all* of the following apply to you:

- ✔ You distribute consumer products.
- ✔ You distribute consumer products in commerce across state lines.
- ✔ You choose to provide a written warranty to buyers, or the law obligates you to comply with an implied warranty.

Are you a B2B e-company (a business selling to other businesses) that believes you don't sell consumer goods? Before you ignore this part, make sure that you understand how federal law *defines* consumer goods.

Distributing consumer goods

The federal warranty law controls only warranties for *consumer goods* that you distribute. A consumer good is tangible personal property that is *normally* used for personal, family, or household purposes. To determine whether something is a consumer good, it doesn't matter how the product is *actually* being used. The question is how it's normally, or commonly, used.

Answering this question gets tricky when consumers and businesses use the same products, like personal computers, cars, and cell phones. If it's a close call on how something is *normally* used — it could be for business reasons or for personal reasons — courts often call the product a consumer good and require warranties to comply with this law.

Distributing in commerce

In general, *distributing in commerce* means that you're in the business of manufacturing, selling, or distributing goods. You're putting your products into the stream of commerce.

The distribution must also be across state lines for this federal law to govern your activities. Only a few federal laws can actually regulate the activities you perform entirely within a single state. This isn't one of those laws.

Providing written and implied warranties

An *express* warranty is a warranty that someone makes in writing or orally. No law or regulation requires a company to make an express warranty. On the other hand, an *implied* warranty is a warranty that state laws create. It exists whether you like it or not.

Familiarize yourself with a couple important implied warranties. The *implied warranty of merchantability* requires merchants to provide products that do what those types of products are supposed to do. A car should operate like a car is supposed to operate. A computer monitor should have a screen that lights up and displays your programs. The *implied warranty of fitness for a particular purpose* requires anyone who recommends a product to an individual buyer in response to the buyer's explanation of needs to make sure it fits that purpose. More information about these warranties is in the section "Following State Warranty Laws," later in this chapter.

Federal law refers only to implied warranties under state law and to written (not oral) warranties. It does not use the term *express*.

You must comply with the Magnuson-Moss Warranty Act and the Federal Trade Commission's regulations if you distribute consumer goods in commerce across state lines and you offer a written warranty and/or you are required under state law to comply with that state's implied warranty.

A written warranty is a written factual statement *or* a written promise that states one or more of the following: the product's material or workmanship is free of defects; the product will perform at a specified level of performance for a specified time; the person or company making the statement or promise will refund, repair, replace, or take other action to remedy the product if it fails to meet the promised specifications.

The written statement or promise doesn't have to include the words *warranty* or *guarantee* for it to be a warranty. However, the statement or promise must be part of the reason a person wants to buy the product or pay a certain price for it. It's a basis of the bargain. If the statement or promise isn't a basis for the bargain, then it's not a written warranty. Therefore, the statement doesn't have to comply with this federal warranty law.

Obviously, some statements and promises are not warranties. For example, the following are not warranties:

- ✔ Statements about the seller, because they don't refer to the product

- ✔ General statements about the quality or value of the product

- ✔ Product information or descriptions that the product meets certain standards without specifically stating that it's free of defects or will meet specific levels of performance within specific times

- ✔ Conditions of sale such as a free trial period or the company's trade-in policy

If the statement or promise you provide is a written warranty, under federal law you must do the following:

- ✔ Write the warranty in simple language that can be readily understood without minute garbled print.

- ✔ Label the written warranty as a *full* or a *limited* warranty.

- ✔ Make the written warranty available to consumers to read before the sale (if it isn't, then any limitations or exclusions may not be valid).

- ✔ Describe what types of things the warranty covers (like damage not caused by the user).

- ✔ State how long the warranty lasts and who can enforce the warranty.

- ✔ State what you, as the person who is making the warranty, will do.

- ✔ State what the consumer must do to comply with the terms of the warranty (like keeping the shipping box or contacting you within a certain number of days).

- ✔ State any informal dispute alternatives that are available for the consumer (as an alternative to going to court) if a dispute arises between the consumer and you regarding the warranty or the product.

- ✔ State any limitations you're making regarding implied warranties.

- ✔ State any limitations you're making regarding any recourse or remedies the consumer will have, to make the company comply with the warranty.

- ✔ Provide notice of the consumer's rights under state warranty laws.

- ✔ State any requirement you may have regarding the return of registration cards.

The CD with this book includes sample Express Limited Warranty Provisions for Products with explanations and a copy without explanations.

In addition, you may not disclaim (refuse to honor) or modify (change the protections provided by) the implied warranty of merchantability or the implied warranty of fitness for a particular purpose that state laws provide. You may not require the buyers to use other specific products or services (such as certain suppliers or repair facilities) in order for you to honor the warranty unless those products or services are provided without charge to the buyer. This practice is called a *tying arrangement,* which federal warranty law prohibits.

About half the states in the United States either prohibit or restrict the ability of a company to disclaim (refuse to honor), in their written warranties, the states' implied warranties. For more information on disclaimers, see the section "Disclaimers" later in this chapter.

Enforcing warranties

The federal warranty law provides certain rights to consumers. It not only permits the actual buyer to seek recourse for any problems concerning the warranties, but also grants rights to the following people:

- ✔ The buyer of any consumer product as long as she is not buying it to resell to others

- ✔ Any person who receives the product from the original buyer (by purchase, gift, or other type of transfer) while the written or implied warranty is in effect

- ✔ Anyone else who the written warranty or any law allows to enforce the warranty

These people may enforce warranties through certain informal dispute proceedings set up by independent agencies. They may file a lawsuit in court. They may also lodge complaints with the Federal Trade Commission and attorneys general's offices in individual states. Although the FTC and the attorneys general do not represent individual people, they may impose fines and other sanctions on companies that do not comply with the law.

The federal warranty law and the FTC regulations are much more specific than the general statements in this chapter. Be sure to consult an expert before assuming that you're complying with all the federal requirements in your warranties.

Following State Warranty Laws

Every state and foreign country has its own consumer protection laws. Some of these laws include warranty requirements. Covering all these laws would fill another *For Dummies* book, so they're not spelled out in this book. The main warranty laws are pretty much the same throughout the United States thanks to a group of legal experts known as the National Conference of Commissioners on Uniform State Laws (NCCUSL). The NCCUSL members work together to write proposed laws for various legal issues. They hope to make the laws in all the states more uniform with each other and, therefore, predictable for people doing business in more than one state. Once the NCCUSL puts together the proposed laws, the members take them to each state legislature to try to get them enacted as law.

Two important acts regarding warranties are the Uniform Commercial Code and the Uniform Computer Information Transactions Act (a new, *proposed* law making its way into state legislatures).

Uniform Commercial Code (UCC)

The Uniform Commercial Code governs many aspects of commercial dealings. Every state adopted the UCC, but not every state's version is exactly the same. UCC Article 2 governs sales transactions in goods, provides basic commercial (business-to-business) warranty law, and governs some consumer warranty law. Louisiana didn't adopt this part of the code.

In 1995, the NCCUSL began revising parts of the UCC to keep up with changes in society and the law. As of this writing, the revised Article 2 is still in the drafting stage. When it becomes effective, some changes concerning warranties may take place.

The UCC warranty provisions apply to sales transaction in goods. Although federal law includes information that written warranties must include, the UCC deals more with how you create express warranties, how you may limit the buyers' rights, how people may enforce warranties, and who may enforce them. It also creates implied warranties.

Sales transactions in goods

Every sale involves a contract. When you buy a shirt, the store offers the shirt for sale at a price, you pay the price, and you walk out of the store with it. Sometimes these sales transactions are very simple. Other times sales transactions involve more conditions. Often these conditions are on the back of a sales invoice or receipt. The terms of sale, especially when it comes to warranties, vary depending upon what people buy. The conditions for returning the product and warranties are very different for shirts, personal computers, and Ferraris.

A written contract often names a state whose laws govern everything related to the contract. This means that the warranty law of that state will probably apply to a sales contract when the parties to the contract want to enforce it or have a dispute with each other about the contract. Under the UCC, warranties apply to sales transactions in goods — any *thing* that's movable when someone decides to buy it. In all but a few states, these warranties apply to new and used goods. Goods can also be referred to as *products*.

Express warranties

The UCC defines three different types of express warranties. You could be making an express warranty without intending to make one, so pay attention to what you do (your conduct), what you say, and what you write. You may have to back it up!

Express warranties are one or more of the following:

- A statement of fact or promise that the goods will conform to the statement or promise and that's made by a seller to a buyer, relates to goods, and becomes part of the basis of the bargain.

- A description of the goods that can reasonably be considered to have any role in the overall bargain between the seller and buyer.

- A sample or model of the goods that implies the actual product purchased will conform to the sample or model shown to the buyer or displayed at a store. No verbal description is necessary, and no particular representation is necessary. However, the implication that the product purchased will conform to the sample or model must be part of the basis of the bargain.

These definitions mean that the following can become express warranties that the person must back up if they involve the preceding types of statements, promises, descriptions, samples, or models, even if the person doesn't *intend* to make a "warranty":

- Advertising, invoices, bills of sale, and labels

- Voluntary (not forced) statements made by the one making the warranty

> ✓ Responses to questions by the one making the warranty
>
> ✓ Statements made by the seller after a sale if it's still a basis for the bargain

Statements of opinions rather than of fact and descriptions that merely illustrate the market appeal of the goods aren't warranties.

Implied warranties

Two important warranties under the UCC are the implied warranty of merchantability and the implied warranty of fitness for a particular purpose.

The *implied warranty of merchantability* only obligates *merchants* to comply with the warranty. In general, merchants are those people who deal in the particular goods or claim to have special knowledge or skill regarding the goods involved in the transaction. They're not the average Joe Schmoe who sells a variety of things out of his garage without any special knowledge or skill regarding the merchandise.

The law implies that every sales transaction by a merchant includes the warranty that the goods are merchantable. To be merchantable, the goods must pass six requirements spelled out in the UCC. Basically, the goods must do what they are ordinarily supposed to do when someone uses them. They also must be able to do an ordinary job with reasonable safety, efficiency, and comfort.

For instance, your personal computer should run software programs designed for you to use on that PC. Your MP3 player should play MP3 files. If they don't, the merchant must remedy the situation.

The *implied warranty of fitness for a particular purpose* places obligations on all sellers, not just on merchants. However, it doesn't apply to every sales transaction. It applies only when the following occurs:

> ✓ The buyer is purchasing the product for some particular purpose.
>
> ✓ The buyer relies upon the seller to provide the right product to satisfy this purpose.
>
> ✓ The seller has reason to know the buyer's purpose because of something the buyer says or something that's obvious to the seller.
>
> ✓ The seller has reason to know that the buyer is relying upon the seller to provide the right product.

If the product doesn't fulfill this purpose, then the buyer has recourse even if the product isn't technically defective. A possible exception to enforcing this warranty occurs when a basic inspection of the product would reveal that the product really isn't suitable for the special purpose and the buyer doesn't inspect it.

Disclaimers

Some sales contracts are written on receipts or invoices. Often these written documents disclaim warranties, which means that the seller is not responsible for the condition of the goods. Under the UCC, a statement in a sales contract that says the seller excludes "all warranties, express or implied" will not be enforced by courts if, considering the circumstances of the sale, it is unreasonable or unfair to the buyer to enforce it. Disclaimers that are unconscionable, such as statements that are lies or intentional concealments of important information, won't be enforced. Even sales with the statement that the goods are sold *as is* may not be enforced if the seller's *conduct* is contrary to that statement.

The laws in about half of the states prohibit or restrict manufacturers and sellers from disclaiming implied warranties. In those states that permit disclaimers, the statements must usually be in writing, specific about what is being disclaimed, conspicuous so that people will notice them, and include certain words. For instance, to exclude or modify the implied warranty of merchantability, the statement must use the word *merchantability*.

Sample Warranty Disclaimer Provisions with explanations are on the CD with this book.

Remedies

The UCC provides various remedies for commercial buyers and consumers. They include self-help remedies like the right to cancel the contract of sale and get money returned and the right to deduct damages from any outstanding balance due to the seller. Naturally, the parties may also sue in court.

Uniform Computer Information Transactions Act (UCITA)

In 1999, the NCCUSL completed a proposed law called the Uniform Computer Information Transactions Act (UCITA). Virginia and Maryland were the first states to adopt it, and many experts believe most states will adopt it.

UCITA provides legal guidelines for contracts involving "computer information." Essentially, computer information is information in electronic form that's obtained by using a computer or that can be processed by a computer — basically, digital information. UCITA covers contracts for software, multimedia products, computer games, online access to databases (like Web sites that charge a subscription fee to access information on the site), and other information such as Web site content.

The contracts may involve sales or licenses (permission to use) for this information. However, UCITA refers to licensors and licensees rather than sellers and buyers. For more information on UCITA contracts, see Chapter 19. UCITA is very similar to the UCC, and includes warranty provisions for both commercial and consumer contracts.

UCITA also provides rules for warranties relating to computer information contracts.

Express warranties

You can create express warranties under UCITA without actually using the words *warranty* or *guarantee*. An express warranty is any of the following:

- ✔ A statement of fact or promise (not an opinion) that the computer information will conform to that statement or promise made; the statement or promise is made by a licensor to a licensee; it concerns the computer information (rather than company policies or other matters); and becomes part of the basis of the bargain

- ✔ A description of the information that becomes part of the bargain between the licensor and the licensee

- ✔ A sample, model, or demonstration of the *final* product that implies the performance of the information you're providing reasonably conforms to the sample, model, or demo

If what you say, what you write, what you show, or how you act is described by the preceding three bulleted points, you're giving your licensee an express warranty. Your information must live up to the expectations you've created or the licensee has legal recourse against you.

Implied warranties

UCITA includes a number of implied warranties. The following are a few of them:

- ✔ Although it's not called an implied warranty, there is a warranty with which merchants must comply that concerns "noninterference and non-infringment." The proposed law regarding this warranty is long, but the gist of it is this: If you're a merchant and you license information to someone, you're promising that you have the right to license that particular information. No one else will interfere with the contract by claiming that they own those rights. For instance, if the information is protected by a patent, the licensor/merchant warrants that he has the right to license it.

✔ Merchants that license computer programs must comply with an *implied warranty of merchantability of computer program.* It requires merchants to promise the following:

- To end users, a promise that the computer program will do what it's basically supposed to do. In other words, a word processing program will process words, an accounting program will perform certain accounting processes, and so on.

- To distributors, a promise that the program is packaged and labeled as agreed and will do what the label claims it will do, and that each copy of it will be basically the same.

- Merchants that work with licensees who rely upon their expertise must promise to be reasonably careful in providing accurate informational content to them. This is the *implied warranty of informational content.* For this warranty, merchants aren't only those who supply content to Web sites; the term includes other businesses as well.

Remember that UCITA involves contracts, and licensors and licensees are free to change the terms of their contracts. These implied warranties normally only apply when the parties *do not* disclaim them in the contract. Not every licensee (such as consumers) has the bargaining power to affect a contract, so many times these implied warranties are disclaimed by the licensor without the licensee having the ability to do anything about it (see "Disclaimers").

Disclaimers

UCITA permits licensors to disclaim or modify the warranties. However, they must comply with certain requirements. Normally they must use specific words and make them conspicuous so that licensees (businesses and consumers) will notice the change.

If you are the information provider, you might want to disclaim all of the implied warranties. General disclaimers don't usually do the job unless you disclaim each implied warranty. Alternatively, you may put the following statement, or something very similar to it, in a conspicuous place: "Except for express warranties stated in this contract, if any, this [insert either *information* or *computer program,* whichever applies] is provided with all faults, as is, and the entire risk as to satisfactory quality, performance, accuracy, and effort is with the user."

Sample Warranty Disclaimer Provisions with explanations are on the CD.

Chapter 21

Professional Services: Healing Arts, Law, and Public Accounting

In This Chapter

▶ Discovering how professionals use the Internet

▶ Figuring out what's allowed on health, legal, and accounting Web sites

*O*nly two things in life are certain: death and taxes. A close third is the fact that there will always be a lawyer offering services to deal with the technicalities. It makes sense, then, that the Internet is filled with Web sites about staying healthy, making money, and locating a lawyer.

Often the people providing this kind of information aren't licensed professionals, however. Doctors, lawyers, and public accountants must have licenses to practice their professions. On the Net, health advice isn't always from doctors and nurses. Legal sites include hints from students, clerks, and paralegals. Tax advice might come from part-time tax preparers rather than licensed public accountants.

Even if doctors, lawyers, and public accountants run the sites, these professionals aren't supposed to practice in states where they are not licensed (with some exceptions, of course). Because the Internet has no boundaries, it's not surprising that a debate is going on behind the scenes about how to regulate online activity.

Sorting out all the legal and ethical issues may take a while. In the meantime, who can offer what services over the Net? How can these people offer these services without getting into trouble? Read on, professional dot-commers, for some tips from behind the scenes.

Using the Internet: How Professionals Do It

Doctors, lawyers, and public accountants have many opportunities to use the Internet to enhance their professions. Now and in the near future, doctors will most likely use Web sites to provide general medical information about diseases and treatments; answer medical questions that the public submits on a Web site or by e-mail; prescribe medicine in response to a Web site or e-mail request; provide answers or prescribe medicine to patients who also visit the doctor's office; and access a patient's medical records stored in a different location.

Lawyers might use Web sites to provide general legal information; answer legal questions that a site visitor submits on a Web site or via e-mail; and answer legal questions from current or new clients through a Web site or by e-mail.

Currently, few public accountants and certified public accountants have Web sites. However, they could use the Web to provide tax or accounting tips; offer an interactive site that allows users to calculate their own taxes; and set up networks to access out-of-town clients' records stored on the clients' computers.

These professionals may set up their own Web sites. They may also become part of a *portal* — a central Web site that includes Web pages by other people and companies. For example, a doctor may become part of a health portal. This health-related Web site links its visitors to Web pages of the various doctors. The same situation could be true for law and tax portals.

All these uses of the Net raise important issues for licensed professionals. Three primary questions involve the legal effect of practicing the profession in a state where they are not licensed, disclaiming liability, and advertising.

Figuring out what requires a license

States or territories within a country license and regulate people who want to practice medicine, law, and public accounting. Why? Public safety. Those who are educated, tested, and experienced in these fields are more likely to provide proper care and advice to the public than those who don't have the education, knowledge, and experience.

Licensing laws often require persons to have certain educational degrees, hands-on experience, or examination results to obtain a license. They usually require payment of license fees. Some states also require certain professionals to continue taking educational courses over the years and to comply with rules of ethics.

Professional services on the Web

These sites offer helpful information for professionals, including tips on conducting business on the Internet:

- www.abanet.org/adrules. The American Bar Association map with links to the advertising rules in each state

- www.ama-assn.org/about/guidelines.htm. The American Medical Association's Guidelines for

Medical and Health Information Sites on the Internet

- www.hon.ch. Health on the Net Foundation

- www.fsmb.org. Federation of State Medical Boards

- www.aicpa.org. The American Institute of Certified Public Accountants

Laws in each state of the United States also prohibit anyone from practicing medicine, law, or public accounting without a license from that state. In fact, most states make it a crime under certain circumstances to practice medicine or law in their states without a license.

Do these state laws mean that licensed professionals cannot provide information about medical issues, the law, or taxes to people outside their state? Do these laws mean that other people cannot share information? If they do, then the impact of such laws would be unfair to everyone because it means that those professionals who are experts in their field couldn't share their knowledge and experience beyond a designated border. Such an interpretation of the law would also inhibit the free exchange of information.

Fortunately, professionals may provide information. However, a very fine line exists between breaking the law and abiding by the law when providing professional services in these fields. Unfortunately, there are no consistent, clear guidelines.

Providing general information

We all watch television shows that have doctors, lawyers, and tax experts giving the viewers information on a topic of interest. Are these people licensed in every state where the show is broadcast? No. And they don't need to be.

Nothing is wrong with providing general information about the healing arts, law, or taxes. It doesn't matter whether it appears on television, in a magazine, or on a Web site. If the person provides more than general information, however, he needs to be careful about crossing the line and *practicing* a regulated profession.

Practicing a Healing Art

Due to the high cost of health care in the United States and the unavailability of certain specialists in areas outside major cities, people are searching the Internet for medical help. In the 21st century, all sorts of healing arts exist, from herbology to aromatherapy, from acupuncture to orthopedics.

State laws require persons to be either licensed or registered with a medical board or state agency to practice certain types of healing arts. For example, physicians, surgeons, chiropractors, podiatrists, dentists, optometrists, physical therapists, and nurses must normally obtain a license to practice in their field or go through a registration process in their state.

Because each state prohibits the unauthorized (unlicensed) practice of medicine, what does it mean to practice medicine? The specific laws defining the practice of medicine in each state differ.

Usually, however, a person is practicing medicine unlawfully when he or she *is not licensed in the state* and does, or offers to do, any of the following for a particular person:

- ✔ Prevents, diagnoses, corrects, or treats any disease, illness, pain, wound, fracture, infirmity, defect, or abnormal physical or mental condition of a person

- ✔ Prescribes, orders, gives, or administers any drug or medicine for a person or performs any surgical operation

- ✔ Provides a written or documented medical opinion concerning the diagnosis or treatment of a person

- ✔ Determines whether proposed treatment for a person is medically necessary or appropriate

- ✔ Uses the designation of Doctor, Doctor of Medicine, Doctor of Osteopathy, Physician, Surgeon, Dr., M.D., or D.O. in connection with work that involves the prevention, diagnosis, or treatment of human diseases or conditions

- ✔ Advertises or represents to the public that she is authorized to practice medicine in the state

The preceding list explains actions that people cannot do (or offer to do) unless they are licensed. Exceptions to these guidelines exist so that, under certain circumstances, performing these activities is not the unauthorized practice of medicine; however, the exceptions wouldn't change the guidelines in the preceding list for those who provide medical services over the Internet.

A doctor's bill

A registration program is taking shape at the California Medical Board at the time of this writing. Instead of requiring physicians in other states to become licensed to practice medicine in California, this program may allow physicians located and licensed in other states to work with patients in California over the Internet under certain conditions if they comply with the registration requirements.

In addition, the Federation of State Medical Boards, an organization to which individual state medical boards belong, put together a proposed Model Act to Regulate the Practice of Medicine Across State Lines. Because it's a Model Act, it's merely a recommendation for state legislatures to consider when, and if, they draft their own laws.

Normally, a one-on-one relationship must be established between the person providing the services and the one receiving the services (like a physician-patient relationship) before someone is considered to be practicing medicine. How does one form this relationship? Charging a fee for the service often creates it.

Crossing state lines

Physicians would find it extremely expensive and difficult to take written examinations and become licensed in every single state in order to provide services over the Internet. Some medical professionals and organizations are encouraging licensing boards and lawmakers to enact laws and rules to allow physicians to practice across state lines. See the sidebar "A doctor's bill."

Prescribing and diagnosing

According to various medical boards and organizations around the world, concern over medical Web sites focuses primarily on two areas: prescribing medicine and diagnosing medical conditions over the Internet without a physical examination of the patient.

Although most laws require a physician to physically examine a patient before prescribing medication, the debate continues regarding the importance of this examination. Many physicians and medical organizations firmly believe that prescribing based on a patient's answers to an online questionnaire could be malpractice. Others believe that examinations are not necessary in many cases.

According to executives at medical boards and medical associations, valid points are being presented regarding the physical examination requirement. An emergency room physician claims that ER physicians routinely diagnose and write prescriptions for patients after extremely brief or minimal examinations in the emergency room. Other physicians claim that they obtain more information from patients by asking questions over the telephone or the Internet than they would in a short office visit. Therefore, physical examinations may not be essential.

Practicing Law

Lawyers are finding the Internet a good place to provide information to potential clients. Some sites even offer visitors the opportunity to submit legal questions that various lawyers answer on the site. Lawyers must be careful, however, to ensure that they are not practicing law in states where they're not licensed. Doing so could result in penalties for the unauthorized practice of law.

With few exceptions, state laws prohibit anyone from practicing law in a state without a license. Some states permit lawyers to obtain licenses if they continually practice in another state for a number of years and meet certain other requirements. Other states don't permit out-of-state lawyers to practice in the state without passing a written examination.

Defining the practice of law

Laws defining the practice of law vary in each state and are written in general terms. In addition to appearing in court to represent a client, practicing law normally includes the following:

- ✔ Giving legal advice to someone
- ✔ Rendering a service that requires the use of legal skill or knowledge
- ✔ Preparing or revising contracts or other documents that secure legal rights

Lawyers could get into trouble for the unauthorized practice of law with their Web sites in a couple ways. One is by providing forms and instructions for people without recommending one-on-one advice. Another is by providing individual advice, either by e-mail or on an interactive site, regarding laws in a state where the lawyer isn't licensed.

Usually the lawyer must create a one-on-one relationship with a person before the advice or conduct will be the practice of law. In fact, some courts have held that selling books and forms with specific information on how a non-lawyer may achieve a legal result without consulting an attorney isn't the unauthorized practice of law because there is no one-on-one, attorney-client relationship.

However, courts in other states don't require an attorney-client relationship before they crack down on people. These courts have held that kits including fill-in-the-blank forms, instructions on how to file the forms with courts, and advice about the forms are the unauthorized practice of law. In other words, these kits really encourage people to complete the forms on their own and use them in court proceedings.

The bottom line seems to be that it's not cool for a lawyer to encourage people to handle their own legal work without getting legal advice and to show them how to complete forms to file in court. Also, it's probably not okay to provide legal advice to clients in other states about specific laws in their state unless licensed in that state.

Web sites as advertisements

Advertisements for all businesses, as well as professional service providers, must not be false, deceptive, or misleading. (Chapter 11 goes into more detail about all advertisements.) Licensed professionals must abide by additional, special restrictions. Legal advertisements seem to have more restrictions than the other professions.

Each state has its own legal advertising restrictions. The state licensing organizations regulate these ads, and most of them consider Web sites to be advertisements for services.

The state of the profession

Becoming licensed as a lawyer in several states can be extremely expensive and time-consuming. Very few lawyers are licensed in more than two or three states. Some lawyers and professional organizations are exploring the possibility of a uniform admission to practice law in all the states, which is especially important to attorneys who work for national and international companies.

The American Bar Association appointed a Commission on Multijurisdictional Practice in July 2000 to recommend legal ethics and bar admission policies to govern the practice of law in multiple jurisdictions. Its recommendations will be submitted to the ABA House of Delegates in August 2001

Some rules are very lengthy, while others are brief. Lawyers with Web sites should refer to the advertising rules in each state where

- ✔ They practice law.
- ✔ They have an office.
- ✔ Any lawyer with their firm is licensed to practice law.
- ✔ Their clients are located or do business.

Although not all advertising rules currently refer to Web sites, lawyers should insert the phrase *the site* as they read the rules. Depending upon the state, some advertising requirements include the following:

- ✔ The ad (the site) must not include factual statements that cannot be substantiated.
- ✔ The ad (the site) should not create an unjustified expectation about results the lawyer can achieve.
- ✔ The ad (the site) must disclose the cities, towns, or counties in which (or a description of where) the lawyers who will actually perform the services maintain an office or principally practice law.
- ✔ The ad (the site) must state the name of at least one lawyer or the lawyer referral service responsible for the content of the ad (the site).
- ✔ The lawyer must keep a copy of the ad (probably the Web pages) for some period of time, often one to three years.

The State Bar of California is recommending that Web sites include a statement that the attorney does not seek to represent anyone based solely on a visit to the attorney's Web site. (This recommendation may eventually become a rule.) Texas has special requirements for the state bar to review copies of the advertisements. Florida has a special rule for computer-accessed communications, which include Web sites.

The American Bar Association's Web site includes a map of the United States with links to the advertising rules in each state. Check out www.abanet.org/adrules.

Furnishing Accounting Services

Not every bookkeeper or accountant is a public accountant. Generally, public accountants are those who furnish accounting or auditing services for a fee for more than one employer.

Public accounting generally requires knowledge of tax laws, trade practices, securities laws, regulations, governmental agency report requirements, and financial statements. Therefore, states regulate who may be a public accountant and how they operate within their states.

Certified public accountants (CPAs) are public accountants who meet certain higher standards of knowledge and must pass examinations to be licensed in a state.

As with other professionals who work with clients over the Internet, an important question is whether a public accountant is practicing in the state where the accountant works or where the client resides or does business. Generally accepted accounting principles don't change from state to state; however, an accountant's client may be regulated in a different state. Therefore, a determination about whether a public accountant is practicing in a state without a license may be based on which state's laws must be complied with to perform these services.

Disclosing Disclaimers

How can doctors on national radio respond to callers asking medical questions? What if they're not licensed in the state where the caller lives? I asked a number of professionals these questions. They all came up with the same answer: disclaimers.

A *disclaimer* is a statement or contract that basically tries to get a person to agree not to hold anyone responsible if he receives bad advice. You've seen this type of notice on the back of parking garage receipts and on sporting event tickets. It states that the owners aren't responsible for stolen or damaged property (in garages) or harm (like getting hit by a hockey puck).

Throughout this book, I tip, warn, and remind you to get the advice of an attorney for specific, one-on-one advice. By doing so, I'm letting you know that this book provides general information, and you need more specific information or advice to make a decision on your own legal matter. These statements are disclaimers.

Disclaimers are often effective. In one court case, a person owned a health school. He specifically stated that it was not a medical institution; that no medicine, drugs, serums, vaccines or surgery were used; and that the school existed for the purpose of building health through corrective exercises and other efforts. A court held that the owner was not engaged in the practice of medicine.

Disclaimers that attempt to limit someone's responsibility for death or physical injury to a person are unconscionable. This means they won't be enforced. In addition, courts look very closely at disclaimers involving health or safety; if they're not in the public interest, they will not be enforced. See Chapter 3 for more information about disclaimers and limitations of liability.

People providing disclaimers need to keep two goals in mind:

- ✓ The disclaimer must protect the person receiving information, making sure the person understands that decisions shouldn't be made with only general information, and that he must be careful.

- ✓ The disclaimer must limit the chances of the person giving the information being sued by anyone who doesn't get one-on-one advice and gets angry.

Disclaimers don't meet these goals if they're nothing more than lip service, however. In other words, a person can't always *do* one thing and try to disclaim responsibility for it. The person must also act responsibly.

A sample Disclaimer for Health or Medical Web Site, Disclaimer for Attorney Web Site, and Disclaimer for Certified Public Accountant Web Site are on the CD that comes with this book.

Honoring the code of Web site conduct

Web sites contain content — those pages of information, products, and graphics. Whether or not this content is of high quality, accurate, and timely depends upon the source.

In the fields of medicine, law, and accounting, accurate and timely information is especially important. Therefore, Web site visitors should be given answers to the following questions:

- ✓ Who writes the content? Is the person qualified?

- ✓ Where are the writers obtaining their information? What's their source?

- ✓ Who is paying for the site to exist? Do they have some motive to promote certain goods and services over others?

- ✓ How current is the information?

Various organizations around the world are compiling guidelines for Web site owners to follow when providing this information. Some of them offer an icon to place on sites to let visitors know

that the sites follow certain codes of conduct. As with all important notices, your visitors should be able to find information easily on your site. Web site addresses for organizations that have written guidelines are in this book's appendix.

These icons are only as good as the organizations handing them out. The organizations should make sure that site owners comply with the requirements. If sites don't comply, the governing organizations should force the sites to remove the icons. This can be done by a contract or by trademarking the icon.

For licensed professionals, the absence of boundaries shouldn't keep you from expanding or shifting your practice to the Web. Simply check out your licensing organization's Web site from time to time to keep up on changes in the rules. As with any other e-business carving its own niche, there's always a market for good Web content. So go ahead and strut your stuff!

Chapter 22

Will Taxes Today Keep e-Commerce at Bay?

In This Chapter

▶ Explaining the Internet Tax Freedom Act

▶ Differentiating between sales and use taxes

▶ Looking at the Internet tax debate

▶ Conducting business with other countries

Thirty thousand. Three followed by four zeros. 30,000. That's about how many different local, state, and federal taxing authorities there are in the United States. Think about it! Towns, cities, counties, states, and the federal government all with separate tax authorities that tax things from income to alcohol to tobacco to self-employment to shoes! Different places, different things, different rates.

Then along comes the Internet with people doing business everywhere. A single Web site may appear in every town, city, county, state, and country where a person may access the Internet. Must e-businesses pay taxes to every taxing authority? If not, must they comply with some regulations in certain places? Which ones? E-businesses want to be able to anticipate legal regulations and costs. How can they when they might have to comply with hundreds or thousands of different regulations? Talk about red tape!

The feds made a move to promote e-commerce and to help companies doing business on the Internet by enacting the Internet Tax Freedom Act. Tax freedom sure sounds cool! This law prohibits all tax authorities from imposing any new taxes on Internet access through October 2001. Lawmakers need time to figure out whether anything related to the Internet should be taxed and, if so, who should tax which goods or services at what rate, and who should pay the taxes. Does this law mean that e-companies don't have to pay taxes? The law prohibits new taxes. Read my lips. "No *new* taxes." So what about old taxes such as sales taxes and use taxes? Do they apply to e-commerce? Yup.

Understanding the Internet Tax Freedom Act

The Web is a prime target for tax authorities from several states and localities to try taxing a single transaction. For instance, suppose an e-company located in San Francisco has its Web site hosted by a company located in Washington. The e-company hires a company in Chicago to process orders. When a New York resident places an order, the e-company has the order fulfilled (packaged and sent) from Connecticut. All the communication between the companies is over the Internet, connected by telephone line. If tax authorities could create taxes that apply specifically to the Internet, the e-company could have to pay a lot of different taxes to several different local, state, and federal tax authorities. That e-company couldn't stay in business.

The Internet Tax Freedom Act protects e-companies like this one in a few different ways:

- First, tax authorities may not impose taxes that would make buyers or sellers conducting e-commerce subject to taxes in multiple states.

- Second, if the transaction is already taxable (see the section "Sales and Use Taxes," later in this chapter), the tax authority must treat the out-of-state company the same as it does in-state companies when it sets the tax rate and other requirements. In other words, the law prohibits discriminating against out-of-state businesses, such as imposing greater taxes on their activities.

- Third, the law protects goods and services sold exclusively over the Internet from taxes when no comparable offline taxes are charged for those goods or services.

A commission established by the law to study electronic commerce tax issues reported back to Congress in April 2000. The commission recommended that the moratorium holding off any new taxes continue for another five years, which currently expires in October 2001.

As of the date of this writing, the issues are still not resolved. The House of Representatives passed a bill to extend the moratorium for another five years to 2006, but Washington observers aren't sure whether the Senate or the President will go along with this bill. The debate continues over Internet taxes (see the section "Debating Internet Tax Issues," later in this chapter).

Sales and Use Taxes

To understand the Internet tax debate over new taxes, it's helpful to understand some things about old taxes. All but a few U.S. states charge sales tax and use tax.

Sales tax you know about, right? It's the tax charged on the sale of things. Companies charge customers sales tax when the companies are required to pay sales tax to the tax authorities within their city and state. Normally, companies must pay sales tax for sales made to people in the state where the company is located. Companies do not pay sales tax for sales outside the company's state, so they don't charge sales tax to their out-of-state customers for out-of-state purchases.

This is where use tax comes into play. It normally involves mail-order companies that sell to customers in other states. Use taxes are assessed in the purchaser's state on purchases from companies that do not operate in, or have a *nexus* (a strong connection) with, the purchaser's state. Because the company does not pay sales taxes for sales outside the state, the purchaser's state charges a tax for the use of the goods in its own state.

Now here's the glitch. The U.S. Supreme Court held that state and local governments cannot force companies to collect and pay these use taxes unless the companies have a nexus with the purchaser's state. For example, they must have a store or offices or maybe even a sales force working in the purchaser's state. Simply mailing catalogs and shipping orders isn't enough. Unlike sales taxes collected from in-state companies, states can't always collect use tax from out-of-state businesses.

Suppose that you own a bricks-and-mortar store in San Francisco. You sell only to people who physically come into your store. When customers come into your shop, you sell them products. For these sales, you charge customers the sales tax. You then pay part of the sales tax to the city government and part of it to the state government.

Do you ask your customers where they live and adjust the tax accordingly? Is the sales tax for California residents different than other states' residents who are merely visiting California? Of course not. The sales tax is based on the location of the store.

What if you sell products by mail order to people in other states? Do you collect California sales tax from everyone who orders by mail?

Normally, mail order companies collect sales taxes only from customers in their own states. Your California mail order company would collect sales taxes only for shipments made to California residents. People in other states do not pay the California tax. Take a look at the next mail order catalog you receive, and check out the place where you tally up the sales taxes.

The order form in a catalog I just received in the mail states: "Please add state and local taxes. Orders shipped to AL, AZ, CA, CO, FL, GA, HI, IL, MA, MD, MI, NJ, NY, OR, PA, RI, TX, VA, WA: Please add all applicable sales taxes." In another part of the catalog, the company lists locations of its stores. Because the company has stores in these 19 states, it collects and pays sales taxes in those states.

For the sales in all other states, purchasers are technically supposed to pay a use tax (to "use" the stuff they buy — the use tax). However, most states don't try to collect it from them. How would the states know who the buyers are? Because the purchaser's state can't force out-of-state companies to collect or pay the taxes, the companies certainly wouldn't cooperate with the purchaser's state tax authority and provide the names of buyers to them! States want to collect from the sellers because they can find them. But the U.S. Supreme Court said no.

According to the National Governors Association Web site, most governors propose that states be permitted to enforce the use tax for all Internet sales even though they can't enforce this tax for mail orders. The governors seem to want to get around the U.S. Supreme Court decision and collect from companies even if the companies don't have a location or nexus with a state; shipping to the residents in these states would be grounds to tax the transaction.

The debate about Internet taxes often centers on sales and use taxes. It's a controversial issue that has politicians from both political parties taking strong positions that aren't necessarily along party lines. Some Democrats are teaming up with Republicans and vice versa!

Debating Internet Tax Issues

If e-companies are supposed to pay sales tax for sales in their states, and they're treated the same as mail-order companies, why is there a problem? First, many e-companies are not paying sales taxes. Second, state and local governments are concerned that they will lose substantial revenue from sales tax that they use for education and emergency services as more people begin buying online from out-of-state companies. At the very least, they want to force out-of-state companies to pay the use tax.

The main problem many anti-Internet tax groups and politicians have about sales taxes is their inconsistency. While one state may tax a can of cola, another state does not. Even within a single state, figuring out which items are subject to sales tax and which items are not can be very complicated. Therefore, these groups do not want Internet sales taxed until the rates and the items taxed are made more consistent throughout the country.

Taxing the sale of goods or services

If tax authorities begin to tax sales over the Internet, will they be taxing the sale of goods *and* services? Most states don't tax the sale of services. If they tax only the sale of goods, figuring out whether certain sales involve goods can be complicated, because the Internet blurs the distinction between goods and services.

When a company sells software to download over the Internet, is it a product or a service? Software programs are often categorized as products unless someone custom-builds the software, and then building the software is a service. Is a musician who offers music to download as an MP3 file but not as a CD providing a product or a service? Is an online publisher offering a magazine (product) or information (service)? What is a story that you can download? Is it a book? Should both be taxed?

 States may decide that they want to tax these types of services sold over the Internet because purchasers may buy the tax-free service rather than the taxable goods. In other words, a purchaser may not buy a CD if he can download an MP3 file from the Web. If the states begin taxing Internet services but not offline services, the Internet companies are being discriminated against (paying more taxes). It's a complicated issue, this Internet tax.

Passing state or federal Internet tax laws

Many state government representatives do not want the federal government regulating or restricting how states may tax Internet companies. They urge that each state, as a sovereign entity, should have the right to decide how to tax the Internet in its state. Others argue that states should not tax Internet companies until they can create a uniform system of taxing within their states so that the regulations will be predictable.

Still others point out that the federal government regulates interstate commerce. Because complying with different laws in every state severely restricts anyone wanting to do business throughout the country, one federal law regulating Internet taxation should be enacted. Small e-businesses may not have the manpower or money to learn about the law in each state or to handle all the paperwork involved. Inconsistent and multiple taxes would severely inhibit their ability to become a success.

Shopping online or offline?

Polls indicate that online shopping continues to increase. Local and state governments seem to believe that more people will be shopping online than offline in the future. News headlines claim that states are losing billions of dollars in sales taxes for sales over the Internet. But is this true? They may not be receiving sales tax from all Internet sales, but are the states *losing* money?

Referring to these amounts as lost taxes must mean that people who buy online would, without the Internet, buy offline. However, how much of the online shopping is impulse buying? In other words, is anyone sure that those who shop on the Net would still purchase the products if they had to look for a bricks-and-mortar store and then look for a product within the store? Perhaps they wouldn't buy that item at all.

Some polls also report that people claim they wouldn't shop online if they had to pay sales taxes *and* delivery charges. Other polls indicate that sales taxes aren't an important consideration to a majority of online purchasers. Nothing is crystal clear when it comes to the Internet or taxes!

One question is asked consistently: Is it fair to require only bricks-and-mortar companies to pay sales taxes? What if a company has both online and offline stores (called clicks-and-mortar stores)? Many of these clicks-and-mortar companies are paying sales taxes only in the states where their Web sites are hosted on computer servers and where they have traditional stores (and warehouses or a similar physical presence).

You can see why such a controversy is brewing. There are many complex tax issues involving the Internet.

Defining the Value Added Tax

World leaders generally have two goals in mind when it comes to taxes and e-commerce. They want to protect their tax revenue that supports their governments and ensure that e-commerce development is not hindered by discriminatory taxes. For the most part, they want taxes that e-businesses can determine with legal certainty and without surprises, taxes that are simple to calculate, and taxes that are neutral (they treat similar things alike).

In addition to sales tax, European countries have another tax called the value added tax, or VAT. Businesses in these countries charge VAT to people purchasing certain goods and services, which are referred to as supplies. The categories and rate structures for VAT are very complex.

Some categories of these supplies, such as certain types of financial services, are exempt from the tax. Other supplies, such as international services, are outside the scope of the tax so that there is no charge. Therefore, determining whether digital files downloaded over the Internet are goods or services becomes important. Depending on the country, computer software is considered either goods or services, creating an inconsistency within the EU. The European Commission (EC) is considering this issue so that the laws can be made more uniform throughout the EU.

Taxable supplies have various rates, and some supplies, such as books, the export of goods outside the European Union (EU), and the export of goods to another EU country, have a zero rate. Therefore, no VAT is charged for these supplies.

Although each European country has its own way of calculating and collecting VAT, the rates and collection processes should eventually be consistent throughout all member countries of the EU when the EU addresses these issues. Until that time, each country has its laws and special rules for cross-border transactions. Normally, American companies conducting international transactions don't charge VAT unless they set up shop in these European countries.

Generally, the EC has been working under certain guidelines and principles to figure out the Internet tax situation. One such principle is that countries should not adopt new or additional taxes at this stage for e-commerce.

Instead, the EC is focusing its efforts on adapting existing taxes, such as VAT, to deal with e-commerce developments. The EC guidelines recommend that digital products (those that are delivered through the computer) should be treated as a supply of services rather than goods for VAT. In addition, services supplied for consumption within the EU should be taxed within the EU, and those supplied for consumption outside the EU should not be subject to VAT. The commission wants to make sure that VAT collection for goods and services is the same regardless of how they are transported to someone (whether computer or truck) or whether they are delivered online or offline.

Help with a taxing issue

Finding a tax accountant with knowledge about international transactions is difficult. Traditionally, there are very few of them. They often work with one of the major public accounting firms. Hopefully the Internet will encourage public accountants to become familiar with international tax issues. In the meantime, check with your own tax accountant and do your best to comply with tax regulations.

And don't forget! When you ship goods overseas, customs duties may be payable upon import goods at the point of entry. Most countries have agreed not to charge duties on electronic transmissions over the Internet, but goods actually shipped overseas are charged.

Chapter 23

Working with a Lawyer

Contrary to popular belief, not all lawyers are the same. Some are smart, and some are idiots. There are nice ones, mean ones, geniuses, and jerks. A few are dishonest and steal from their clients, but more are ethical, honest, and fair.

Somewhere out there is the right lawyer for you. In fact, you may even decide to work with a few different lawyers to meet the special legal needs of your e-business. For instance, you may discover that you prefer one lawyer for employment issues, another one for contracts, and a third one for litigation.

Most people have little experience in working with business lawyers on an ongoing basis. They may have very high and unrealistic expectations. If so, they may find themselves disappointed in their lawyers. Building a relationship with a lawyer is like developing any other kind of business relationship. Take your time to make a wise selection and communicate your expectations. The following are a few extra clues to help you understand the attorney-client relationship.

Understanding Legal Expertise

If you've just broken your leg, do you hop to a psychiatrist to fix it? Orthopedic surgeons and psychiatrists attended medical school. They're doctors. But is a psychiatrist the best kind of doctor for what you need? Of course not. You'll get much better advice and service from an orthopedic surgeon for your broken leg.

Often people believe that almost any kind of lawyer can handle their legal matters. It's true that lawyers may practice any kind of law under certain conditions. But that's a technicality. Lawyers should handle only those matters for which they have the proper education, skill *and* experience.

Authority to practice law

In the United States, lawyers are graduates of law schools. The degree is a doctorate degree in jurisprudence, referred to as a J.D. Often you see "attorney at law" or "Esq." after their names. Esq. is short for Esquire, an old British word relating to lawyers.

American lawyers are licensed by the individual states and must follow state rules and regulations. Generally, they may practice law only in the states in which they're currently licensed. This license means they may also appear before courts in those states. To appear in federal courts, the attorneys must go through a special admission process for each federal court. You can normally assume that an attorney with a law firm is licensed. If someone simply offers consulting or other legal assistance, make sure that they're licensed to advise you on the law.

People rarely ask lawyers how long they've been practicing law. I think it's important to ask. You may also ask the lawyer in which states she is licensed to practice law and when she was admitted to practice law in each of those states. If you contact state licensing boards or bar associations, they will normally provide basic information about individual attorneys licensed in their states, such as the college attended, the law school attended, and the year admitted to practice law in that state. Some of them, like the California Bar Association, have databases on their Web sites to search for this information.

Areas of practice

Lawyers usually select the areas of law in which they practice by focusing on particular personal rights, commercial industries, or very specialized areas of law. For example, personal rights include family law (marital relations and children) and personal injury (car accidents, slip-and-fall accidents, and so on). Commercial industries include fields such as high-tech (computer software and hardware), real estate, product manufacturing, and entertainment (film, television, theatre, and music). Some highly specialized areas of law, such as tax law and patent law, require special expertise and knowledge.

Many states prohibit lawyers from referring to themselves as specialists unless they pass additional tests. These tests may be given only in certain areas of law (such as family law or workers' compensation). Lawyers who pass the additional test are often called *certified specialists.* Many lawyers' business cards, stationery, and advertisements include the phrase "we specialize in." This wording usually means that the law practice focuses on those types of legal issues. However, it doesn't necessarily mean that anyone met specialized requirements or that they're truly experts in that field.

In addition to the area of practice, lawyers choose whether they want to represent people in lawsuits or to handle other matters. *Litigation lawyers* are those who appear in court and handle lawsuits. They're supposed to be knowledgeable about the hundreds of court rules pertaining to court procedure and the presentation of evidence. They must also be well versed in the statutes and case law that apply to any given situation. It is extremely important to hire an experienced litigator for any lawsuit.

Transactional lawyers are those who negotiate and write contracts as well as deal in other out-of-court matters. In other words, they handle issues relating to transactions. Some transactional lawyers also litigate.

Many lawyers are beginning to practice law relating to the Internet. They're coming from all types of background: technology, entertainment, general business, employment, and personal injury. Hire a lawyer who works in the area of law that you need and has experience in your industry.

You can get some idea of the lawyer's experience by asking him the type of clients he works with (for example, distributors, retailers, software developers, and content providers), the types of transactions he's been involved with in the past (such as copyright licenses, trademark litigation, and Internet content licenses), and how often he handles the types of transactions that you may need.

Choosing Big Firms or Small Offices

Big law firms, small firms, and sole practitioners each have their advantages and disadvantages. Think about your needs and choose the type of firm that best suits you. The following are some factors to consider:

- ✔ The number of different types of legal matters you may encounter
- ✔ How quickly you need a response to your legal requests
- ✔ The legal fees and expenses you're able to pay
- ✔ Any additional business contacts you may need for your business

Big law firms offer a variety of legal services. They usually have lawyers in different departments who handle separate legal matters. For instance, a large firm may have departments for tax, intellectual property, employment, bankruptcy, litigation, and real estate. It's a one-stop shop.

Unless you're a very important company that pays lots of money in legal fees, however, you may not receive prompt attention at a big firm. Often the newer, less experienced lawyers in the big firm actually do the work for smaller and newer clients. Even if you talk to the more experienced lawyers, usually they delegate the work to lawyers or legal assistants who may not have any contact with you at all. This practice isn't necessarily a bad thing, but it does mean that you should be aware of who is handling your legal matters.

Big firms tend to be very strict in their billing and expense reimbursement policies. Often they bill for two or more of their lawyers confering with each other about your legal issues. As a result, your bill may show three lawyers' time at each of their hourly rates for the same hour. In addition, the rates they charge for faxes and photocopies can often add up to more than the price of the latest photocopy machine!

Large firms often carry clout when push comes to shove. If you want to push or shove, make sure that you can afford them if shoving doesn't resolve the dispute and they commence a lengthy battle for you. Big firms may also have business contacts to help you build alliances and partners. However, don't assume that simply because they have these contacts that they'll use them for all their clients. You have to have some clout, too.

Be cautious of conflicts of interest in any firm, big or small. A conflict of interest means that a lawyer or a lawyer's client has interests that may conflict with yours. The conflict may involve business, financial, personal, or legal interests that could cause the lawyer to have difficulty being objective and keeping your interests the priority. However, a conflict of interest isn't necessarily illegal. Lawyers must simply explain the bad things that could happen to each of the parties due to the conflict, make sure that their clients understand it, and then obtain a signed waiver of the conflict by the people involved. Some law firms will not risk representing clients when there is a conflict of interest between their clients, but others will continue to represent them after a waiver is signed.

Small firms and sole practitioners often offer more personalized supervision and attention. Sometimes they're more flexible in their billing so you're not charged for every second they spend with you or for every photocopy they make for you. The smaller size means that they usually focus on more limited areas of practice.

Firms with eight or ten lawyers often call themselves a *boutique law firm*. They compare themselves to a specialty shop as opposed to a department store. They could have a number of business contacts that may help your e-business as well. Sometimes response time to your legal needs increases with a smaller firm or a sole practitioner. However, the response time always depends upon how busy the firm is and how many clients it represents.

Asking Questions

When you're going to be working with a lawyer for a while, find someone who's compatible with you. You must feel comfortable enough to ask your lawyer *anything you want to ask*. Don't be afraid to ask questions, because there's no such thing as a dumb question about the law. It's not *your* job to know the legal issues. That's why you're hiring a professional in that field. It's the lawyer's job to help you understand.

Like any other working relationship, the attorney-client relationship should be one of open communication and attention. Communication is expressed in different ways. Some people actually feel like they're not getting the right kind of service if their lawyers aren't arguing with them all the time and trying to convince them to follow their advice. They like this interplay. Others want to avoid the lectures. A few people want to be involved in every single detail of the legal process. Many executives, on the other hand, prefer to let their lawyers know what they want and to leave the rest up to the lawyers to do the best they can to reach that goal.

Your lawyer may find it difficult to respond to several separate calls from clients who say they only have "a quick question." Even though the question may take only a minute to ask, the lawyer must stop focusing on the current project, focus on the other client, listen to the question and respond, and then try to focus back on the original project. The one-minute question can actually end up taking 15 minutes or more of the lawyer's time before he can focus on the other project again. Most importantly, your lawyer may not have been paying really close attention to your question since he was focusing on another project, and the response may not be the best response your lawyer could give you.

Instead, try this approach: Gather your questions for a while and then set up a time to ask them all at once. You'll probably get more effective answers when your lawyer can get ready for your call and focus her attention on you. However, don't misinterpret this advice to mean that you should delay asking time-sensitive questions. Ultimately, it's up to you and your lawyer to figure out the best way to work effectively together.

Anticipating Fees and Expenses

Technically, fees are negotiable between clients and attorneys. As with other businesses, however, nearly all attorneys have basic rates already established. Most business lawyers charge an hourly fee. Depending upon the city and the area of law, fees range from $100 per hour to $350 or $400 per hour.

Axe the fax charge

Sometimes firms don't charge for faxes, while others may charge $1.50 or more *per page*. If they're faxing you often, these charges can add up. I saw one bill from a firm that totaled over $3,000 in fax charges! The client would have saved over $2,000 had the lawyer's secretary photocopied and mailed the documents to the client. None of the faxes needed immediate response, but the firm's lawyer simply preferred faxing everything.

I've known lawyers with their own practice and only a few years of experience charging the same hourly rate as lawyers who have been practicing three times as long! These young lawyers believe they're simply charging market rate. If the less experienced lawyers are charging the same as the more experienced, by all means go with the more experienced ones!

The hourly rate is normally broken down into portions of an hour. Some firms charge by quarters of an hour, and others charge by $\frac{1}{10}$ (0.1) of an hour. These are minimum times so that anything they do is billed for at least this amount of time. Breaking it down to exact minutes is a real accounting and billing hassle, so I don't know anyone who will do that.

How the hourly rate is broken down is important. For instance, suppose that a lawyer makes ten 5-minute calls, all on different days. If the lawyer bills at $\frac{1}{10}$ of an hour, your bill will show one hour of billable time (.10 hour = 6 minutes, so ten 5-minute calls would be $10 \times .10$ hour = 1.0 hour). If the lawyer bills at $\frac{1}{4}$ hour, your bill will show 2½ hours (10 calls at the minimum .25 hours per call would be $10 \times .25$ hour = 2.5 hours). If the hourly rate is $250 per hour, one bill would be $250 while the other would be $625. Quite a difference!

If your lawyer isn't working on your matter, then he could be working on another's client's matter and earning money. Therefore, nearly every lawyer charges for all time spent on a client's matter, including telephone time and travel time to meetings or court. Keep this in mind if you ask your lawyer to stop by your office.

Some lawyers don't make sure that the time they spend asking you about your kids and making other small talk is kept out of their billing time. I think that such careless accounting is tacky. Watch your bill when part of your lunch or your call with your lawyer is advice and part is friendly chitchat. If you get charged for chatting, talk it over with your lawyer to be sure that you're not overcharged.

Most firms require reimbursement for certain expenses. This can add up, so understand these charges up front. They may include photocopy, fax, and long-distance telephone charges. Some lawyers don't charge for minimal photocopies, some charge a basic small rate of 8 or 10 cents per copy, and others use these fees as a way to compensate their staff and charge 35 cents or more per copy. If you're in litigation or have lengthy contracts requiring lots of copies, photocopy charges can get expensive.

When you put your budget together for your e-business, be sure to anticipate potential legal fees and expenses. Keep in mind that these fees and expenses are considered a business expense on your tax returns. They're usually tax deductible.

Keeping costs down

Here are some ways to help keep your legal costs to a minimum:

✔ Be organized and complete when you provide information to your lawyer.

✔ Remember that whatever you provide to your lawyer will need to be reviewed and billed by your lawyer. Be complete, but brief.

✔ Think about what you hope to accomplish and let your lawyer know about it.

✔ Try to ask your questions all at once instead of piece by piece to prevent the minimum billing time from adding up.

✔ Ask whether you can do some things — gather information, summarize figures, or outline documents in a table of contents, for example — to save the lawyer time in reviewing lengthy documents.

Just looking it over

People often believe that they can keep legal costs down by using a contract they put together. They get to a certain point and then ask a lawyer, "Can you just take a quick look at this?"

Once a lawyer agrees to advise a client, the two parties create an attorney-client relationship that carries certain legal responsibilities for the lawyer. Therefore, many lawyers prefer not to simply "look over" a contract written by someone who is not a lawyer. Fixing your do-it-yourself contract may actually take longer than drafting a new one for you.

Each lawyer has her own particular style and preferences for contracts. Don't spend too much time on your own contract before showing it to a lawyer. If you've found a form you'd like to use, simply show it to your lawyer and ask whether it's okay to use. Don't insist on using it by forcing your lawyer to merely edit that agreement. If the form contract is pretty good, your lawyer will tell you so. If her particular style and preferences are different, however, let her do her own thing. That's what she's trained to do.

Completing the work

When you get your lawyer on the telephone or send an e-mail, expecting your legal matter to be handled that day or the following day may seem reasonable to you. But only rarely can your lawyer respond that quickly.

When you call to have things like a contract reviewed or negotiated, it's put in line. Lawyers have other clients — sometimes a couple dozen and other times hundreds — waiting for answers, too. Every day lawyers receive calls, letters, faxes, e-mails, and in-person visits. Successful lawyers may work non-stop, hour after hour. Some projects and contracts take dozens of hours to complete. So when your work comes in, lawyers normally have plenty of work that came in before yours.

Like every other effective business executive, lawyers must give priority to certain work. They often give priority to the following matters:

- ✔ Work for clients who have been working with the lawyer for a very long time

- ✔ Work for clients who use the lawyer's services the most or often (major sources of revenue)

- ✔ Matters that have court deadlines because missing one of these deadlines can be financially devastating to businesses and lawyers

- ✔ Business deals that involve a lot of money for the clients

- ✔ Any other matter that could have serious business or legal consequences if not completed by a certain date

In order to provide the best service to all clients, an effective lawyer learns how to give priority to the most important matters in order to represent everyone to the best of his ability. If the only reason you need a contract completed in one day is because you're excited about your new business deal, don't be surprised if the lawyer can't make it the highest priority.

To assure your work is completed within your time deadlines, try the following:

- ✔ Give your lawyer as much advance notice as possible.

- ✔ Be clear about any deadlines you have and why it's important to have the work completed by then.

- ✔ Ask for a time estimate from the lawyer, but remember it's only an estimate. Between the time your work comes in and the deadline date, your lawyer may need to handle other emergencies or urgent matters that take priority over your matter.

Delegating the work

You may believe that you're working effectively if you handle many of your contract negotiations or business deals on your own. However, often your time could be better spent.

Whether or not you charge by the hour in your e-business, your time has value. You could spend your time raising money, earning money, or meeting with potential customers. Therefore, delegating the contract stuff to your lawyer may

be a better idea. In the long run, the money you earn should far exceed the legal fees. You will also have less strain on your mind at night. Don't try to do everything yourself. For your international deals, however, business executives in other countries may not want to negotiate with an American lawyer early in the deal (see Chapter 8 for more information.)

Locating a Lawyer

The first place to look for a lawyer to represent you is in the state or country where you're doing business, where you're suing someone, or where you're being sued.

The terms lawyer and attorney (or attorney at law) are used interchangeably in the United States. An *attorney-in-fact* is not a lawyer; it's a person who's given certain legal rights to do something for someone, like the right to sign legal documents. E-businesses searching the Internet for a lawyer to handle contracts in other countries may search for an avocat in France and Quebec, a rechtsanwalt in Germany, an attorney or lawyer in Japan, and a solicitor (also listed as lawyers on the Web) in Australia, Canada, and the United Kingdom.

For specialized work, finding experienced lawyers in your city or state is sometimes difficult. For certain industries, experienced lawyers tend to be in a few major hubs where the industry is based.

When you're looking for the right lawyer for your e-business, try the following:

- ✔ Ask other executives in your industry (as long as you don't do business with them) the names of their lawyers and whether they're happy with them.

- ✔ Ask any lawyers in other fields of law whom you know personally for a referral.

- ✔ Ask other business colleagues for recommendations based on their experiences.

✔ Contact the bar association in your county and state.

✔ Look in public libraries for specialized industry directories.

✔ Search the Internet for legal directories and individual Web sites.

✔ Contact your industry's professional associations or organizations for the names of lawyers who specialize in your industry.

Finding the right lawyer takes time. It's a trial-and-error process to some extent. You have a good chance of finding the right match if your expectations are reasonable. With a little luck, you'll find a loyal ally to help your e-business grow and prosper.

Searching for a Lawyer

Online directories of lawyers and law firms can help you locate a lawyer who works in specific areas of law and within certain states and countries. These sites can help you locate lawyers in the U.S., Canada, and Japan:

✔ www.lawoffice.com: Law office directory for the United States

✔ www.martindale.com/locator/home.html: Martindale-Hubbell Law Directory for United States and Canada

✔ www.dntba.ab.psiweb.com: Daini Tokyo Bar Association for Japan

Part VII
The Part of Tens

The 5th Wave   By Rich Tennant

"...and that's not the worst of it, your Honor. It appears the good doctor is not even <u>licensed</u> to practice re-animation of the dead in this village!"

In this part . . .

*W*hy is this a part of ten instead of a dozen? So you'll remember a tip for each finger! (And the publisher made me write a part of tens.) So hold up your fingers and start the final countdown to blast off into . . . dare I use that overused word, *Cyberspace!* Double check before you double-click to be sure you've covered the details in Chapter 24 to keep your e-site running in uptime rather than downtime. Then assess your assets to make sure they're fully covered in Chapter 25. Appendix A is stuffed with sites to make your online venture sing, dance, and make money. Appendix B gives you the rundown on the samples and software on the CD.

Chapter 24

Ten Ways to Dot the i and Cross the t

. . . .

In This Chapter

▶ Posting your Web site notices

▶ Testing your site

▶ Organizing your e-business

. . . .

*W*hat does it mean to cross the *t* and dot the *i*? It means taking care of all the final details to make sure that you get the result you want. Cover your bases. Double-check everything.

When you have your Web site ready for the public to see, take some time to do a final check. Sit back, open up your home page, and begin reviewing your site. Follow these steps to make sure you've covered all the bases.

Identifying Yourself

Visitors to your site should be able to learn about your e-business. Do you list your company name somewhere on the home page? To make sure people get to know who you are, it's important for them to see your name as soon as they arrive at your site.

Often sites offer a link entitled "About the Company" to a separate Web page where visitors can learn information about your company. You may want to provide a narrative giving background on the company, its founders, and its executives. Are you a sole proprietorship — a business of one? Let people know about your background and your mission. It's a way to personalize your business to your visitors to let them know there are real people behind the site. This company page should also include information on how to contact you.

While laws in some states require certain types of e-businesses to provide an address, remember that someday millions of people may be seeing this information. Therefore, you may want to keep private telephone numbers or home addresses private by not posting them on your site. Many companies rent a mailbox at a post office or at a for-profit mail center for this reason. If you do rent a box, make sure you don't refer to the box number as a "suite." It's now unlawful to do so in the United States because it's not accurate and may mislead the public.

Providing Your Privacy Policy

By now you know that visitors want to be assured you'll respect their privacy. Is your privacy policy on the site? Although you should make the policy prominent enough so that every visitor will see it, remember that your home page must interest your visitors and encourage them to browse your entire site. Placing policies and agreements on the home page may not be very interesting to your visitors. Therefore, many sites place a link to the privacy policy page at the bottom center of the home page.

If you collect information from children under the age of 13, the link to your privacy policy must be prominent and distinct from other links. If your site, or any part of it, is directed to kids of this age, make sure you comply with federal laws. See Chapter 15 for more information.

Click through your site to every place on every page where you collect information from your visitors. Is there a link to the privacy policy? Make sure to remind your visitors about the policy and give them an opportunity to read it wherever you ask them for information.

Using a User Agreement

Unless you're simply providing information to visitors, you'll probably need a User Agreement (also called Terms of Use) for your e-business site. When you want this agreement to be enforceable, you must make your visitors aware that they are agreeing to these terms when they use your site. Like the privacy policy link, most sites provide a prominent link to the page containing the agreement at the bottom center of the home page.

Have your users *do* something to confirm that they agree to the terms. You may provide a button where the user can click "I Agree" and a button that states "I Don't Agree." If the user clicks "I Don't Agree," the technology on your site must be set up so that the user may not use your site. See Chapter 3 for more about user agreements.

Informing Users about Intellectual Property

Most Web sites include intellectual property, such as copyrighted work and trademarks. There are symbols that provide notice to the public that someone claims ownership rights in intellectual property. For copyrights, the international symbol is © or, for sound recordings,℗. See Chapter 16 for information on copyrights. For trademarks and service marks that are not registered, the symbols are TM and SM, respectively. For trademarks and service marks that are registered, the symbol is ®. For more information, see Chapter 7. These symbols usually appear on Web sites.

In addition to the symbols, most sites include a statement (a notice to the public) on a separate Web page about the intellectual property that appears on the site. A link to the intellectual property notices page normally appears at the bottom center of the home page. The link often states, "Legal Notices" or "Intellectual Property Notices."

Copyright notices

A copyright notice includes the copyright symbol followed by the year the work was created, published (distributed to the public), or registered, and then the name of the copyright owner. Several years may be listed, such as *1989, 1990, 1991,* or *1998–2000,* which means that there are copyrightable contributions to the work that were created during each of those years. For instance, the Web site content may have been created in 1998, additional copyrighted work added to it in 1999, and more copyrighted work added in 2000. The work that you see, therefore, includes work from each of those years.

Sometimes people add the word *copyright* to the notice, but the symbol is an international symbol (not everyone uses the English word) and should always be included with your notice. Many people also add a phrase after the copyright notice stating that all rights are reserved, which lets the person who sees the notice know that the copyright owner isn't letting everyone use her work simply because it appears on a particular Web site or other work. Here are some examples of copyright notices:

Copyright © 2000 IDG Books Worldwide, Inc. All Rights Reserved.

Copyright © 1998–2000 Susan P. Butler. All Rights Reserved. No part of this Web site may be reproduced or transmitted in any form or by any means without prior, written permission.

Providing copyright notice is not required in order to protect your work under copyright law. However, anyone who infringes your rights could not claim it was done unintentionally — that he didn't know it was a copyrighted work — if you provide notice. Copyright law permits additional damages to the copyright owner if an infringement was intentional.

You may claim copyright ownership to your entire Web site if it qualifies as a compilation or collective work (see Chapter 16 for a description of these types of copyrightable works). If it qualifies, you may want to provide a copyright notice for the entire site by placing it at the bottom center of the home page — the location where many sites place a notice of copyright for the site.

You may also claim copyright ownership, or other contributors to your site may claim copyright ownership, to certain portions of the content on your site. You may provide a copyright notice at the beginning (near the title or author's name) of each work or at the end of each work; however, most people simply provide notice for all of the individual contributions on the intellectual property notice page on the site.

Trademark notices

You may include trademarks or service marks that belong to you or to someone else on your site. Trademark symbols appear as a superscript (like an exponential number, small and raised to the top of a letter) after the word, phrase or logo that's trademarked. You can superscript the TM or SM in your word processing program by formatting it as a superscript.

Unlike copyright notice, the owner's name and year of registration aren't included by the trademark symbol. However, a statement that the marks are trademarks or service marks (or registered trademarks) of the owner (listed by name) is normally included somewhere in the material that includes the trademark (such as an advertisement) or on the intellectual property notice Web page.

Web sites also include notices about others' trademarks. For instance, a separate intellectual property notice page may include a list of the owners of all marks or may simply provide a statement such as, "All company names, brand names, product names, and service names used on this site are trade names, service marks, trademarks, or registered trademarks of their respective owners." This notice includes a reference to trade names (company names) as well as trademarks. See Chapter 7 for an explanation of the difference between the two.

Remember, trademarks are valid only where you use them (in common law countries) and where you register them (in civil law countries). Another company could be using the same mark in other countries. Because the Internet makes your site accessible to people around the world, you don't want the other company suing you for trademark infringement in its country! If you place a statement on your site that the trademark for the goods or services offered at your site does not belong to you in all countries, or you list the specific countries in which you claim rights, you may be able to avoid being sued for trademark infringement by someone who owns the same mark in another country.

Trademark infringement occurs when the public or the trademark owner's market (customers or potential customers) are confused or misled regarding the source of the goods or services associated with the mark when someone else is using the mark. Your notice should prevent the public or the other company's market from confusing your goods or services with the other company's goods or services if you don't list that country as one in which you claim rights. This notice will not work for a famous mark, however, since the owner of a famous mark does not need to prove confusion to recover for dilution of the famous mark. For more information on infringement, see Chapter 7.

Patent notices

Those Web site owners who claim ownership to patents list them on their site in order to provide notice to the public. For instance, some sites provide notice that one or more patents cover the site. They list the patents by their official patent number provided by the patent office. Other sites list the patent numbers as well as a description of the patents. On the U.S. Patent and Trademark Office's Web site (www.uspto.gov), users may search for patent descriptions and other patent information.

Putting Your Order Forms in Order

Before launching your site, review and test any order forms you provide for customers ordering products or services on your site. Try typing information into the order forms to see how mistakes are handled by your technology. For example, do you ask for a telephone number? If so, may the customer use (415) 555-5555 or 415-555-5555 or 4155555555 for the form to process properly? If not, place instructions near the space on the order form showing the user how to type the numbers in the space.

Does your form provide two lines for a street address? There are many different combinations for a street address that includes an apartment number, suite number, or post office box number. Will the form accept all variations and still work? For instance, people may type *apt, #, suite, po, P.O., room,* and other designations. Will these all work?

What happens if the user doesn't type in the information properly? Does a screen pop up explaining the problem and then return the user to the order form? If so, what information is lost on this return? Play with your order forms. Have some friends play with your order forms. Make sure they work easily. If helpful, provide an example for users.

In addition, make your notices regarding your return policies or any other conditions concerning the sale easily accessible from your order form. Provide a link to the terms of sale or write the terms near the order form. Since you're collecting information from customers, you should also provide a link to your privacy policy near this form. You may also wish to explain the security for your site near the form to make customers feel safe submitting information to you.

Navigating Your Site

Make sure your site works well for the users. Try navigating throughout your site using different computers, different Web browsers, and different versions of browsers (older versions and the latest versions). If your site requires visitors to use plug-ins or other applications to use your site, make sure these work well with your site, too. Don't forget to make sure that anything you offer to be downloaded will actually download!

How can you try using your site with different computers if you only own one computer? Call your friends, family, and business colleagues. Ask them to browse your site as if they were your potential customers or users. Make sure to ask experienced Web surfers as well as newbies to the Web. Everyone should be able to navigate your site. If you run into technology problems, do your best to get them fixed. If you put off fixing them and the problems frustrate visitors to your site, those visitors may never come back again.

Assigning Tasks to Your Personnel

Once your site goes live so that anyone surfing the Net can access your site, you must be ready to monitor and maintain your site and interact with users. Remember, building good customer relationships is important to staying in business for the long term. Assign various responsibilities to your personnel, such as the following:

- Testing links on your site to make sure they still lead your visitors to the right places. In other words, all links should be active links.

- Periodically testing your site to make sure everything is working properly.

- Reviewing the reports from your Web site host regarding information about your users and where they go on your site.

✔ Reviewing and analyzing any information you gather from your users that you plan to use for marketing purposes (see Chapter 11).

✔ Supervising all activities within your company concerning the collection and use of information to ensure you're complying with your privacy policy (see Chapter 15).

✔ Responding to users' inquiries or complaints.

✔ Periodically searching the Internet to make sure that no one is using your trademarks without permission (search the Web by using your trademark as a keyword).

If your company personnel consists of one person — you — keep the preceding list nearby to ensure that you follow up with these activities. As an e-business entrepreneur, you'll have many matters on your mind concerning your business. Keeping a written checklist of things to check will leave room in your mind for all the other things!

Lining Up Your Promoters and Protectors

Preparing for the launch of your site includes getting your *promoters* and *protectors* in line to be ready when you need them. Your promoters may include marketing firms and publicists. If, however, you're not ready to foot the bill for these independent promoters, then be sure you're prepared to handle the promotion on your own for your e-business and your Web site. See Chapter 11 for promotion information. At the very least, spread the word to all your friends, family and business colleagues so they can spread the word about your site to everyone they know, who can tell everyone they know, and so on. Word-of-mouth promotion can be effective!

If you haven't done so already, line up your protectors as well. They're accountants, lawyers, and insurance agents. Ask them to help you anticipate problems, prepare for them, and stay within your budget. Some people are financially able to hire protectors right away, while others need some time to get the money together. At the very least put together a list of "potentials" for your team so you won't waste time searching for them when you need them.

Scheduling Domain Name Follow-Up

Your right to a domain name doesn't automatically last forever. Domain name registrations expire at some point — when it expires depends upon your agreement with the registrar. Although some registrars claim they will notify domain name owners when it's time to renew, notices can slip through the virtual crack (especially if the companies change owners at any point during that time). You may also change addresses and forget to notify them.

Place in your calendar a reminder of when you must renew your registration. Did you say you don't have a three-year calendar on hand? Try doing what I do. I have a list of renewal or due dates on my calendar for December 31. The list has future renewal dates. When I start using a calendar the following year, I roll over those dates to December 31 of that year, and so on.

For instance, in the year 2000 I know that I must renew my domain name registration before August 18, 2002. On my 2000 calendar for December 31, I list the following: *domain name renewal due 8/18/02.* When I begin my 2001 calendar, I look at the last day in the prior year's calendar and then list on December 31, 2001: *domain name renewal due 8/18/02.* When I begin my 2002 calendar, I look on my 2001 calendar to see what's listed for the last day of that year, and then list on August 18, 2002: *last day to renew domain name.*

If you're using a calendar on your computer, be sure to update any new calendar you begin to use on a new computer!

Looking One Last Time Before Showtime

Do you have your site ready now? Are you stressing a bit? Worried about not crossing every *t* and dotting every *i*? Relax. It's only a goal. Getting it all totally together takes some time. You can update your Web pages — they're not set in stone.

Just take one last look at your site. Does everything seem to be in order? Are your notices and agreements in place? Is your site working well? Are you assigning tasks and putting together your team of promoters and protectors? If you've gotten all these things together, then you're ready! Isn't it exciting? I can't wait to see your Web site!

Before you pop that champagne bottle open, I have one last tip for you. Be fair, be truthful, and be respectful of your users' personal and property rights. Do your best, but remember that perfection is not necessary. In fact, it can be boring. So don't worry if you haven't crossed every *t* and dotted every *i*. Sometimes it's the misses (crossing the occasional *i* and dotting an odd *t*) that make the journey worthwhile.

Chapter 25

Ten Tips to Cover Your Assets

Assets. We all want them. Computers, houses, money, cars, electronic toys, stock, money, furniture, clothes, money. Most of us work pretty hard to acquire them, too. After all that effort, you'd think people would be more careful about keeping their assets. Maybe they just don't know about the risks or how to protect them.

We can lose our assets in many ways. People steal them, trash them, destroy them, and repossess them. The government taxes and levies them. Sometimes people file lawsuits and take our assets away.

As a successful e-business entrepreneur, you want to acquire assets and you want to protect them. Cover them. Keep them out of harm's way. Here are a few tips on how to cover your assets.

Learning about Your Allies

When you want to protect your assets — including your reputation and good will — it's imperative that you know about the people and the companies with whom you'll be working. *It's imperative.* So many entrepreneurs mourn over the business deals and money they've lost because of bad relationships.

Be familiar with their ethics

Know the character and business ethics of the people with whom you work. If the way you manage a business is drastically different from one another, hassles and business interruptions may result. Fighting over management decisions destroys many alliances.

Know how they conduct business

The way your business partner or ally conducts business is very important. For instance, general partners normally share all responsibility. Therefore, one partner may incur debt. What if she's lousy with money, leaves the partnership, and can't pay her share of debt? You could be responsible for paying the entire amount.

Maybe your strategic ally or business colleague is representing both of your interests to another company. What if he makes false representations about your products or services? If these representations harm someone else's business, you both may be liable for any damages those representations caused.

Make sure they're in good standing

You could also discover — too late — that your contracts won't hold up if your ally is a corporation or limited liability company that isn't "in good standing." Corporations and limited liability companies usually have to pay certain taxes and fees to the state in which they incorporate or organize. If they aren't paid every year, the legal rights of the business entity may be suspended in some states. The company would not be in good standing.

In some places, business entities that are not in good standing may not enter contracts or defend themselves in court. If that company signs a contract with another company on behalf of you both, some courts could void that contract. This could really blow some of your business deals.

How do you check out your potential ally or consulting company? You must strike a fine balance between checking them out and invading their privacy. If you go too far, you'll anger them and perhaps end up with a bad reputation in your industry.

To find out whether a corporation or limited liability company is in good standing, you need to know in which state the company is incorporated or organized. This information should always be listed in a contract anyway, so it's not a big deal to ask the question. You can always say that your lawyer includes that information in contracts.

You may then contact that state's department of corporations, which is normally part of the state's secretary of state's office. Different divisions or departments may handle issues related to limited liability companies, depending on the state. Inquire about the corporate status or limited liability company's status. The secretary of state's office often provides you with the company's principal address, the name of the authorized agent for service of process, and whether the company is in good standing. If the company is not in good standing, the state agency may tell you the grounds for suspending the company.

Sometimes a company is still a good company even though it's not in good standing when you check it out. If you like the people running the company, let them know that they're listed as not in good standing. Perhaps they merely need to get some paperwork filed or they didn't realize anything happened. However, note that the company isn't watching their paperwork carefully just in case this bears on the work they'll be doing with you. If you really like them, give them a chance to clean up their act.

Ask about their credits

You can discover more about a company's experience by looking at its client list or prior work description. Some companies list names of their former and current clients. Claiming high-profile companies as clients may make the company look very cool. However, sometimes the clients are past clients, and they aren't even on good terms any longer. At other times, the work they performed was trivial.

Ask your potential ally about the type of work it did for any companies that impress you. Question whether the company performed the work on its own or with other companies. Also ask whether they still work with those companies. Remember, there's no right or wrong answer to these questions. They're simply meant to provide you with information that may be valuable in forming your potential alliance.

Clearing Rights

Being sued is no fun. Aside from the legal fees, you face the risk of a judgment against your e-business. To collect a judgment, the creditor may take your assets away from you.

The money is just part of the problem. A lawsuit causes stress. Thoughts of it will creep into your mind quite often, sometimes even interfering with your personal relationships.

You're at risk of being sued when you use property, including intellectual property, that belongs to someone else without his permission. Part V of this book goes into more detail about these rights and how to obtain permission.

At the very least, ask yourself the following questions. If you answer yes to any of them, watch those assets.

✔ Is it your responsibility to make sure that the information or content you provide to others doesn't defame anyone?

✔ Are you using trademarks that belong to someone else on your site or in your site's metatags? See Chapter 7 for information on metatags.

✔ Are you using any literary, musical, or other artistic works whose copyrights may belong to someone else?

✔ Are you using a process or method that someone may have patented?

✔ Are you using anyone's name, likeness, or voice that may require their permission?

✔ Are you linking to information from your site without a disclaimer on your site?

✔ Are you setting up your site so that links pull the content from other sites into your frames?

Did you answer *yes*? Then go back and read Part V of this book, do not pass go, and do the right thing so you can keep a couple hundred bucks in your pocket.

Collecting Information Properly

Collecting information from visitors to your Web site can be like walking over hot coals. If you know how to do it properly, you'll be cool. If you don't, you'll get burned.

Review the following checklist of questions. These things apply to you only if you're collecting information from people who visit your Web site, either by asking them to provide information, by using cookies (see Chapter 15 to find out about cookies), or by using any other method. If you answer *no* to any question, start looking for a bucket of cold water 'cause you're gonna get burned.

✔ Are your collection practices in line with privacy laws?

✔ If your site attracts children under the age of 13, are you complying with the special privacy laws for children?

✔ Do the privacy statement and other notices on your site truly reflect your policy and practices of collecting information?

✔ Are you complying with that policy?

✔ Do your business deals (contracts) with any advertisers or other companies require you to do something contrary to your collection policy?

✔ Are you adequately monitoring your employees to make sure that they enforce your policy and collection practices?

Issues involving privacy and advertising practices, as well as disclaimers and other notices on your Web site, are the subject of lawsuits and high-level government debates. You don't want to be on the wrong end of the stick if anyone starts making noises about your privacy policies. Lawsuits in this area can get very expensive.

Chapters 10, 11, and 15 explain some of the privacy issues. Check with your own legal counsel on these important concerns.

Selling the Right Way

Selling goods to businesses involves commercial law. Selling products to consumers is — you guessed it — consumer law. Did you read the part in Chapter 2 about how governments want to protect consumers? Because consumers usually don't have bargaining power equal to businesses, consumer laws place more restrictions regarding sales by companies to consumers.

Consumer laws can vary quite a bit from one state or country to the next. Commercial laws vary in some ways, but they're usually more consistent around the world. Therefore, being aware of the consumer or commercial law in the places where you'll be selling your products is important.

In addition, follow these tips if your e-business sells products:

✔ Make the proper disclosures about who you are and any other information that various laws may require you to post on your site.

✔ Understand the warranties that may go along with the products you sell.

✔ Be prepared to back up any warranties that you make.

✔ Have your products available to ship.

✔ Comply with the laws that require you to notify customers if their orders won't be on time.

✔ Have your invoicing and billing procedures in place and secure.

✔ Check out any import/export or tax regulations that may apply to your sales.

When you're selling services over the Internet, be sure to do the following:

- ✔ Plan for the best way to invoice and collect payment for your services.

- ✔ If your services require a professional license, remember to provide services only where you're licensed to do so.

- ✔ Make all necessary legal disclosures on your site.

- ✔ Be prepared to meet the expectations of your clients when the e-mail starts flooding in.

Identifying and Protecting Your Assets

Whether your e-business provides information, entertainment, products, or services, you most likely include valuable assets on your Web site that others can see. These assets may be your trademarks, logos, and copyrighted works. Don't forget to protect your own works!

After you figure out everything of value on your site, consider the following tips:

- ✔ If you own intellectual property and you're in a country that has a registration system for it, register it.

- ✔ Provide the correct symbols as notice next to your trademarks, service marks, and copyrighted works to show that you own them, such as TM, SM, ® or ©.

- ✔ If you're offering digital works to download from your site, consider digital watermarking (see Chapter 17). It's the next best thing to handing your work to your Web site visitors with your fingerprints all over them.

- ✔ Keep periodic copies of your Web pages as you change them. This way, you'll always know what you displayed at any given time. These copies may come in handy if you ever have to sue someone for using your work without permission.

- ✔ Make sure that your Internet Service Provider or Web site host has proper firewalls in place to protect your information.

- ✔ Communicate with your employees so that they all understand the importance of confidentiality and discretion concerning your business information.

Budgeting and Insuring

Preparation gives you an edge above your competitors. Plan ahead and budget for overhead, technology, consultants, legal expenses, and insurance.

Not only will you have an economic advantage, but you'll have added confidence knowing that you're ready for anything.

Spend plenty of time working on your e-business budget. Do your best to stick with it. You don't want to have to pull money from one thing to cover something else. Your energy can be spent in better ways.

To make sure the roof stays over your head, check out available liability insurance for your business dealings and property insurance for your assets. When you have some loss, the protection far exceeds any cost in premiums. Consider insurance a safety net for the Net. (See Chapter 2.)

Lining Up Your Professional Team

Many people put off looking for the right accountant, lawyer, or other professional until the need arises. Sometimes you can get into trouble by waiting so long. Remember that professionals have other clients, so they may not be willing or able to drop everything to give you attention at the last minute.

On the other hand, many professionals don't have the time to meet with someone who doesn't have business for them to handle right away. Talking or meeting with these professionals simply because you may have a need for their services someday is often a waste of time.

Therefore, I recommend that you compile a list of several possible candidates to be your accountants and attorneys. When you need one, you'll have some options. You'll be able to find out who can help you when you need it.

When you do need an accountant or attorney, don't wait until the last minute. When it looks extremely likely that you'll need someone's services, begin making the calls. Even when you find the person, she'll need some time to work you into her schedule.

Avoiding the Cut-and-Paste Jobs

When most people put together their own contracts, they start looking for contract forms. Often they cut and paste paragraphs, clauses, and provisions that they like from several different documents. Pretty soon, they have a very impressive-looking document upon which they rely in doing business.

What's wrong with this approach? Well, when you put all the pieces together, the result could spell disaster. You may have built a monster that is more harmful than helpful to you personally and professionally. Or worse, the document may make no legal sense at all and get tossed out of court.

There are *at least* four reasons a cut-and-paste contract could be a disaster:

- ✔ Your contract is probably missing some very important elements.
- ✔ Your contract could be violating the laws of your state or country.
- ✔ Your contract may not reflect your true intentions.
- ✔ Your contract could make little or no sense to a judge if a dispute ever arises.

Experienced lawyers draft (write) contracts like an author writes a novel. Each paragraph or section should work in connection with the other parts to outline and guide the parties to the contract as they proceed with their business deal. When you try to rewrite it with a bunch of forms, you'll probably end up with a mess. No one can make you hire a lawyer. However, doing so is a wise move if you want to protect your assets.

Preparing Your Recourse Source List

You already know this, but it's time to remind you: You'll run over some bumps in the road to building your e-business. Therefore, be prepared to act quickly when you encounter them.

Think about putting together a help list of organizations or people to whom you can turn when you stumble upon various problems. Your help list may include governmental agencies, professional organizations, and business organizations.

Visit the U.S. government's various Web sites to find out about governmental agencies. One important agency for Internet issues is the Federal Trade Commission. Spend a little bit of time looking over the agencies' sites to understand when, and how, they may be able to help you when you run into trouble. Add them to your Favorites list in your Web browser or in your personal digital assistant. Explore some of your industry's specialized organizations. They may offer assistance in times of need. Often they have referral services for a quick response.

Other business organizations include the Better Business Bureau, chambers of commerce, privacy organizations such as TRUSTe, and intellectual property organizations like the World Intellectual Property Organization, the World Trade Organization, and their affiliates that offer dispute resolution services.

The more sources you have at your fingertips to solve your disputes or problems, the more quickly you can respond. A prompt response ensures that you can minimize both your business interruption and your stress. The appendix includes Web site addresses for many sources of information.

Appendix A

Very Cool Web Sites

• •

*I*nformation, information, and more information. That's what the World Wide Web has waiting for you! Unfortunately, e-business entrepreneurs don't have all day and all night to surf and browse. To save you some time, I searched the Net for you to find some sites that can help you build your e-business.

Defining Words

As you venture into the e-business world, you need to know the language. `www.zdwebopedia.com` is a great resource for computer terms, and `www.wwlia.org/diction.htm` covers legal terms.

Doing Digital Deals

Companies are set up to help keep your messages and signatures secure. The following sites offer a variety of security services and technology: Entrust Technologies at `www.entrust.com`; Digital Signature Trust at `www.digsigtrust.com`; VeriSign at `www.verisign.com`; Symantec at `www.symantec.com`; and Network Associates at `www.networkassociates.com`.

Designing, Hosting, and Connecting Your e-Site

Designing and developing your Web site is fun, but you can probably use a little help. At the very least, check on the Web for additional information. If you want to work with someone, you can find contacts online, too.

✔ `dreamink.com`: A brief Web design guide

✔ `www.zdnet.com/zdhelp/stories/main/0,5594,2340346,00.html`: Information on building your own Web site

- ✔ www.graphics-design.com: Free graphics, buttons, and backgrounds
- ✔ www.website-designs.com: Free graphics, buttons, and backgrounds

Locating a Web site designer

Maybe you're trying to find someone to design your site. You have a lot of companies to choose from! One effective way to locate a Web designer is to type **web design** into any of the major search engines such as Yahoo, AltaVista, Google, Northernlight, Excite, HotBot, or Lycos. One site in particular is a good resource: designlist.internet.com. Once your site is up and running, visit websitegarage.netscape.com to give your site a tune-up.

Internet service provider information and directories

Whether you want to learn about business and legal issue facing Internet service providers (ISPs) or you just want to connect with one, take a look at the following sites:

- ✔ www.ispc.org: The Internet Service Providers' Consortium is a trade organization. Its site provides updates on legislation and other information relating to ISP service.
- ✔ www.findisps.com: Find an Internet service provider in your area.
- ✔ boardwatch.internet.com/isp/ac/index.html: Search a directory of ISPs.
- ✔ www.verio.com: Verio offers a variety of services.
- ✔ www.earthlink.net: EarthLink, an ISP.

- ✔ thelist.internet.com: International directory for ISPs.
- ✔ www.topology.org/isp.html: Australia.
- ✔ thelist.com/countrycode/55: Brazil.
- ✔ boardwatch.internet.com/isp/ac/index.html: Canada.
- ✔ www.europeonline.com: Europe.
- ✔ hareshima.com/Israel/Business/internet.asp: Israel.
- ✔ www.cjmag.co.jp/resources/providers/isptbla.html: Japan.
- ✔ thelist.com/countrycode/65: Singapore.
- ✔ thelist.com/countrycode.html: Europe.

Getting Domains and Wrestling for Names

Where do you register domain names and resolve disputes over who owns the name without going to court? These sites can answer your questions:

- ✔ `www.icann.org/registrars/accredited-list.html`: List of accredited registrars for the .com, .org, and .net domains

- ✔ `www.icann.org/udrp/udrp.htm`: Domain-name dispute resolution information

- ✔ `www.icann.org/udrp/approved-providers.htm`: Organizations that resolve domain-name disputes

- ✔ `www.iana.org/domain-names.htm`: Locate who provides domain names that end with country codes

Protecting Copyrights, Trademarks, and Patents

Protecting your intellectual property may involve registration and watermarking. You can learn more about these topics on the Internet.

- ✔ `www.uspto.gov`: U.S. Patent and Trademark Office

- ✔ `www.loc.gov/copyright`: U.S. Copyright Office

- ✔ `www.ipaustralia.gov.au`: Australian patents and trademarks

- ✔ `www.inpi.gov.br/ingles.htm`: Brazilian patents and trademarks

- ✔ `strategis.ic.gc.ca/sc_mrksv/cipo/welcome/welcom-e.html`: Canadian patents, trademarks, and copyrights

- ✔ `www.european-patent-office.org`: European patents

- ✔ `oami.eu.int/en/default.htm`: European Union community trademarks

- ✔ `www.inpi.fr/inpi/accueil.htm`: French patents

- ✔ `www.dpma.de`: German patents and trademarks

- ✔ `www.jpo-miti.go.jp`: Japanese patents and trademarks

- ✔ `www.patent.gov.uk`: United Kingdom patents, trademarks, and copyrights

- ✔ `www.wipo.org`: World Intellectual Property Organization

Search firms

Sometimes it's best to hire an experienced search firm to conduct a thorough trademark search for you. Many of the firms also search records for patents and copyrights. Consider Compu-Mark at www.compu-mark.com; Thomson & Thomson at www.thomson-thomson.com; Corsearch at www.corsearch.com; and MicroPatent at www.micropat.com.

Digital watermarking information

Companies that create digital watermarking technology also offer valuable information about the process on their sites. Check out Digimarc at www.digimarc.com; Liquid Audio at www.liquidaudio.com; Signum Technologies at www.signumtech.com; and Blue Spike at www.bluespike.com.

Forming Strategic Alliances

To form alliances, you need to meet people and get to know the types of businesses that might complement your e-business. This section includes some sites to get you out there.

- ✔ www.sba.gov: Small Business Administration
- ✔ www.uschamber.com: United States Chamber of Commerce
- ✔ www.bbb.com: Better Business Bureau
- ✔ www.iccwbo.org: International Chamber of Commerce
- ✔ www.shop.org: An Internet retailing trade association
- ✔ www.siia.net: Software & Information Industry Association (formerly the Software Publisher's Association)
- ✔ www.association.org: Association of Internet Professionals

Application service providers

Application service providers make it affordable to be a small yet full-service e-business. You can hire ASPs to do your work — that is, you can outsource your work to them. Some of them offer a variety of services, while others offer specialized work. Here is a selection of ASPs:

- ✔ www.everdream.com: Everdream (computing solutions)
- ✔ www.concur.com: Concur (workplace solutions)

- `www.eality.com`: eAlity (small- to medium-sized business solutions)
- `www.smartonline.com`: SmartOnline.com (smart business applications)
- `www.bigstep.com`: BigStep.com (site hosting)
- `www.centerbeam.com`: CenterBeam (whole office solutions)
- `www.digitalwork.com`: DigitalWork (general office solutions)
- `www.office.com`: Office.com (hosting, support, and application solutions)
- `www.employease.com`: Employease (human resources)
- `www.headlight.com`: Headlight.com (online training)
- `www.salesforce.com`: Salesforce.com (sales and customer relationships services)
- `www.upshot.com`: UpShot.com (sales force automation)
- `www.timebills.com`: TimeBills.com (expense tracking services)
- `www.hotbiz.com`: Hotbiz.com (online store administration)
- `www.hotoffice.com`: HotOffice.com (office services)

Affiliate programs

Affiliate programs, also called associate programs, that offer referral fees on the Web are growing rapidly. When you want to find programs that complement your e-site, try searching for them in the following directories that list sites offering affiliate programs. Check out AssociatePrograms at `www.associateprograms.com` and Refer-It.com at `www.refer-it.com`.

B2Bs

Business-to-business sites get businesses together. There are a variety of B2B sites. A few of the many B2B sites, to give you an idea of what it means to be a B2B, include Ubarter.com at `www.ubarter.com`, VerticalNet at `verticalnet.com`, Printbid.com at `www.printbid.com`, and Arbinet at `www.arbinet.com`.

Searching for company information

If you're trying to find out about a company you'd like to do business with, a few states have their public records online. Check out California companies at `www.ss.ca.gov/business/business.htm`; Georgia companies at `www.sos.state.ga.us/corporations/corpsearch.htm`; and New York companies at `www.dos.state.ny.us`.

Implementing Employer E-Mail and Internet Use Policies

If you're looking for the technology to monitor, report, and filter Internet use from your office, take a look at the technology offered at LittleBrother Software, www.littlebrother.com, and Websense at www.websense.com.

Advertising, Marketing, and Spamming

Advertising tips are close at hand. Many sites offer guidelines and legal information. Check out the International Chamber of Commerce at www.iccwbo.org/home/menu_advert_marketing.asp for guidelines on advertising and marketing on the Internet. The Better Business Bureau, www.bbb.org/advertising/index.asp, provides advertising guidelines, and the United States Federal Trade Commission, www.ftc.gov, provides guidance on Federal electronic advertising.

Many companies develop advertisements, offer product promotion services, and provide business and media strategies for e-businesses. Check out WinWin.com at www.winwin.com; Hook Media at www.hookmedia.com; Beenz.com at www.beenz.com; Engage at www.engage.com; AllAdvantage at www.alladvantage.com; MyPoints at www.mypoints.com; and Affinia at www.affinia.com.

Also check out www.bbb.org/advertising/index.asp, the Better Business Bureau's National Advertising Division (NAD), which helps companies resolve advertising disputes outside of court.

A number of companies conduct research, analyze trends, and provide information to businesses and journalists. Some of their sites provide free information. If you want more in-depth analysis, the companies offer various services at different rates.

- www.247media.com: 24/7 Media
- www.jupitercommunications.com: Jupiter Communications
- www.forrester.com: Forrester Research

Data mining solutions

You may need a number of products (solutions) to gather and analyze information, prepare your marketing and ad promotions, and then get the right message to the right people at the right time. They include databases, content management software, knowledge discovery tools, and customer relationship management solutions. Here are some companies that offer these solutions. Many sites also include information about data mining.

- www.broadvision.com: BroadVision
- www.vignette.com: Vignette
- www.sas.com: SAS Institute
- www.spss.com: SPSS
- www.broadbase.com: Broadbase
- www.epiphany.com: E.piphany
- www.personify.com: Personify
- www.remedy.com: Remedy
- www.ibm.com: IBM
- www.microsoft.com: Microsoft
- www.microstrategy.com: MicroStrategy
- www.oracle.com: Oracle

Marketing associations around the world

Direct marketing associations offer tips on their sites and help companies around the world keep up on the latest trends. Keep up on state and national information at these sites.

- www.the-dma.org: The Direct Marketing Association
- www.ifdma.org: International Federation of Direct Marketing Associations
- www.jadma.org/e_page/index_e.shtml: Japan Direct Marketing Association
- www.cdma.org: Canadian Marketing Association
- www.adma.com.au: Australian Direct Marketing Association
- www.dma.org.uk: United Kingdom Direct Marketing Association
- www.ddv.de: German Direct Marketing Association

Direct e-mail marketing services

Many companies offer their services to prepare direct marketing e-mail for online and offline businesses. Many offer permissive e-mail marketing — that is, not spam!

✔ www.yesmail.com: Yesmail.com

✔ www.radicalmail.com: RadicalMail.com

✔ www.digitalimpact.com: Digital Impact

✔ www.delivere.com: DeliverE

Spammers beware! You can find updates on spam laws and regulations, as well as tips on how to avoid spam. Check out the U.S. and European sites for the Coalition Against Unsolicited Commercial Email (CAUCE) at www.cauce.org/legislation/index.shtml and www.euro.cauce.org/en/index.html. Also visit Junkbusters at www.junkbusters.com.

Keeping Up with Internet Industry News

I prefer to read a few high-quality trade magazines and reports to keep up with the industry. After all, no one has time to read all day long. The following are some of my favorite sources for up-to-date and accurate Internet industry news:

✔ www.thestandard.com: *The Industry Standard,* a weekly magazine that also provides online newsletters

✔ www.zdnet.com: ZDNet, an online source for Internet and computer information, learning, small business tips, and more

✔ www.nytimes.com: *The New York Times* Web site provides CyberTimes as part of its Technology news coverage online and includes news about legal skirmishes

✔ www.smartbusinessmag.com: Ziff Davis Smart Business for the New Economy (formerly *PC Computing*), a monthly magazine that also provides online information

✔ www.wsj.com: The Wall Street Journal Interactive

Keeping It Private

Privacy is a major issue for e-businesses. The following sites keep people up-to-date on the changes in the law. Some companies also offer privacy seals of approval and help you write your Web site privacy policy. Check out the Electronic Privacy Information Center at www.epic.org; the Center for Democracy and Technology at www.cdt.org; The Federal Trade Commission at www.ftc.gov; TRUSTe at www.truste.org; and the Better Business Bureau Online at bbbonline.org.

Clearing Intellectual Property Rights and Finding Owners

Finding owners of property is a real challenge when you want to use it for a Web site or production. The help of sites like these makes it possible for small businesses to accomplish this task. Some of these sites also provide valuable information about legal issues facing the entertainment industry and the Internet.

- ✔ www.dga.org/dga_links_page.htm: United States — Directors Guild of America. Links to sites for film studios, television networks, entertainment industry unions, entertainment organizations, and entertainment publications.

- ✔ www.ascap.com: United States — American Society of Composers, Authors, and Publishers (ASCAP), a performing rights society, to obtain information about songs and to obtain licenses for public performance of songs from their members.

- ✔ www.bmi.com: United States — Broadcast Music Inc. (BMI), a performing rights society.

- ✔ www.sesac.com: United States — Society of Songwriters, Authors, and Composers (SESAC), a performing rights society.

- ✔ nmpa.org/hfa.html: United States — The Harry Fox Agency (National Music Publishers Association), a mechanical (copyright reproduction) rights society for songs.

- ✔ www.riaa.org: United States — The Recording Industry Association of America (RIAA) represents record companies and offers information about the music industry on its site.

- ✔ www.mpaa.org: United States — The Motion Picture Association of America (MPAA) promotes the interest of film makers and offers information about the movie industry on its site.

- ✔ www.apra.com.au: Australia — Australasian Performing Right Association Limited (APRA), a performing rights society.

- ✔ www.amcos.com.au: Australia — Australasian Mechanical Copyright Owners Society (AMCOS), a mechanical (reproduction) rights society.

- ✔ www.socan.ca: Canada — Society of Composers, Authors and Music Publishers of Canada (SOCAN), a performing rights society.

- ✔ www.cmrra.ca: Canada — The Canadian Musical Reproduction Rights Agency Ltd. (CMRRA), a mechanical (reproduction) rights society.

- ✔ www.sacem.org: France — Société des Auteurs, Compositeurs et Editeurs de Musique (SACEM) (Society of Authors, Composers and Publishers of Music), a performing rights society, and Société pour l'administration du Droit de Reproduction Mécanique des Auteurs, Compositeurs et Editeurs (SDRM) (Society for the Administration of Mechanical Reproduction Rights for Authors, Composers and Publishers), a mechanical rights society.

✔ www.sesam.org: France — SESAM, a society licensing copyrighted work for interactive multimedia products and online services.

✔ www.gema.de: Germany — Gesellschaft für Musikalische Aufführungs (GEMA), the German copyright society for performing rights and mechanical rights.

✔ www.jasrac.or.jp/ejhp: Japan — JASRAC, the performing rights and mechanical rights society.

✔ www.prs.co.uk: United Kingdom — Performing Rights Society (PRS), a performing rights society.

✔ www.mcps.co.uk: United Kingdom — Mechanical Copyright Protection Society (MCPS), a mechanical rights society.

Selling Goods and Information, and UCITA

Setting up an e-site and selling goods over the Internet is easier than you might think. These companies offer help to those ready to venture into e-commerce:

✔ www.ibm.com: IBM offers small business services and products to get you started.

✔ www.dell.com: Dell Computer Corporation's Dell E Com offers help for small businesses.

✔ www.merchantworkz.com: Merchantworkz.com provides articles about merchant accounts for credit card purchases.

✔ www.verisign.com: VeriSign helps secure your e-site.

✔ www.cybercash.com: CyberCash provides assistance to secure your e-site.

✔ www.goemerchant.com: GoEmerchant.com.

The Uniform Computer Information Transactions Act (UCITA) has been passed by a limited number of states. This act, however, could be a harbinger of legislation to come. Visit www.nccusl.org/uniformact_factsheets/uniformacts-fs-ucita.htm to keep up with the latest information on states that pass this law.

Appendix B

About the CD

•••

*H*ere's some of what you can find on the *eBusiness Legal Kit For Dummies* CD-ROM:

- ✔ MindSpring, a popular Internet service
- ✔ HotDog Professional, a useful Web page creation tool
- ✔ Acrobat Reader, a popular PDF document viewer
- ✔ FrontPage, a useful Web page creation program
- ✔ Stuffit Lite 3.6, a decompression utility for the Mac

System Requirements

Make sure your computer meets the minimum system requirements listed below. If your computer doesn't match up to most of these specifications, you may have problems in using the contents of the CD.

- ✔ A PC with a 486 or faster processor, or a Mac OS computer with a 68040 or faster processor.
- ✔ Microsoft Windows 95 or later, or Mac OS system software 7.55 or later.
- ✔ At least 16MB of total RAM installed on your computer. For best performance, we recommend at least 32MB of RAM installed.
- ✔ At least 250MB of hard drive space available to install all the software from this CD. (You'll need less space if you don't install every program.)
- ✔ A CD-ROM drive — double-speed (2x) or faster.
- ✔ A sound card for PCs. (Mac OS computers have built-in sound support.)
- ✔ A monitor capable of displaying at least 256 colors or grayscale.
- ✔ A modem with a speed of at least 14,400 bps.

If you need more information on the basics, check out *PCs For Dummies,* 7th Edition, by Dan Gookin; *Macs For Dummies,* 6th Edition, by David Pogue; *iMacs For Dummies,* by David Pogue; *Windows 95 For Dummies,* 2nd Edition, by Andy Rathbone, or *Windows 98 For Dummies*, by Andy Rathbone (all published by IDG Books Worldwide, Inc.).

Using the CD with Microsoft Windows

1. **Insert the CD into your computer's CD-ROM drive.**

2. **Open your browser.**

   If you do not have a browser, we have included Microsoft Internet Explorer as well as Netscape Communicator. They can be found in the Programs folders at the root of the CD.

3. **Click Start⇨Run.**

4. **Type D:\START.HTM in the dialogue box that appears.**

   Replace *D* with the proper drive letter if your CD-ROM drive uses a different letter. (If you don't know the letter, see how your CD-ROM drive is listed under My Computer.)

5. **Read through the license agreement, nod your head, and then click the Accept button if you want to use the CD — after you click Accept, you'll jump to the Main Menu.**

   This action will display the file that will walk you through the content of the CD.

6. **To navigate within the interface, simply click on any topic of interest to take you to an explanation of the files on the CD and how to use or install them.**

7. **To install the software from the CD, simply click on the software name.**

   You'll see two options — the option to run or open the file from the current location or the option to save the file to your hard drive. Choose to run or open the file from its current location and the installation procedure will continue. After you are done with the interface, simply close your browser as usual.

To run some of the programs, you may need to keep the CD inside your CD-ROM drive. This is a good thing. Otherwise, the installed program will require you to install a very large chunk of the program on your hard drive, which will keep you from installing other software.

Using the CD with Mac OS

To install the items from the CD to your hard drive, follow these steps.

1. **Insert the CD into your computer's CD-ROM drive.**

   In a moment, an icon representing the CD you just inserted appears on your Mac desktop. Chances are, the icon looks like a CD-ROM.

2. **Double-click the CD icon to show the CD's contents.**

3. **Double-click the Read Me First icon.**

   This text file contains information about the CD's programs and any last-minute instructions you need to know about installing the programs on the CD that we don't cover in this appendix.

4. **Open your browser.** If you don't have a browser, we have included the two most popular ones for your convenience — Microsoft Internet Explorer and Netscape Communicator.

5. **Click on File⇨Open and select the CD entitled eBiz Legal Kit FD. Click on the Links.htm file to see an explanation of all files and folders included on the CD.**

6. **Some programs come with installer programs — with those you simply open the program's folder on the CD, and double click the icon with the words Install or Installer.**

   Once you have installed the programs that you want, you can eject the CD. Carefully place it back in the plastic jacket of the book for safekeeping.

What You'll Find

Here are some terms you may need to know to understand the descriptions of the goodies that are on the CD:

Author Files is where you'll find 100 sample document files from the author separated into seven folders. Be sure to click your menu to view "All" types of files to find them in the folders. Use Acrobat Reader (on this CD or your own version) to read or print the government forms and documents that include the author's comments and explanations. They're saved as pdf files. Use Word or a word processing program that converts rtf files (Rich Text Format) to read or print the author's documents that do not include comments. They're saved as rtf files.

Shareware programs are fully functional, free, trial versions of copyrighted programs. If you like particular programs, register with their authors for a nominal fee and receive licenses, enhanced versions, and technical support. *Freeware* programs are free, copyrighted games, applications, and utilities. You can copy them to as many PCs as you like — free — but they have no technical support. *GNU* software is governed by its own license, which is included inside the folder of the GNU software. There are no restrictions on distribution of this software. See the GNU license for more details. Trial, demo, or evaluation versions are usually limited either by time or functionality (such as being unable to save projects).

Here's a summary of the software on the CD:

Comercial Product. Netscape Communicator 4.7

Netscape Communicator, from Netscape Communications, is one of the best-known Web browsers available. The CD-ROM installs Netscape Communicator Version 4.7. You also have the option of installing Real Player G2 (to play streaming audio and video files) and Winamp (to play MPEG3 files). You can find information about Netscape Navigator from its Help menu or at its Web site, home.netscape.com.

Shareware Version. Stuffit Lite 3.6

Stuffit Lite 3.6, from Aladdin Systems, Inc., is an invaluable file-decompression shareware utility for the Macintosh. Many files you find on the Internet are compressed, or shrunken in size, via some fancy programming tricks, both to save storage space and to cut down on the amount of time they require for downloading. You may also occasionally receive compressed files as e-mail attachments. After you have a compressed file on your hard disk, you should use Stuffit Lite to decompress it and make it usable again.

Evaluation Version. WinZip 7

WinZip 7, from Nico Mak Computing, is an invaluable file compression and decompression utility. Many files you find on the Internet are compressed, or shrunken in size, via special programming tricks, both to save storage space and to cut down on the amount of time they require for downloading. You may occasionally receive compressed files (ZIP files) as e-mail attachments. After you have a compressed file on your hard disk, you can use WinZip to decompress it and make it usable again.

For information about using WinZip, choose Help⇨Contents from its menu or double-click the program's Online Manual icon in its folder. To learn more about WinZip, visit the program's Web site at www.winzip.com.

Commercial Product. Internet Explorer 5.0

Internet Explorer 5.0, from Microsoft, is one of the best-known Web browsers available. In addition to the browser, this package includes other Internet tools from Microsoft: Outlook Express 5, a mail and news reading program; Windows Media Player, a program that can display or play many types of audio and video files; and NetMeeting 3, a video conferencing program.

If you have a version of Windows 98, 2000, or NT that already includes Internet Explorer 5.0, don't install the CD-ROM version. Instead, go to Microsoft's Web site at www.microsoft.com/windows/ie/download/ windows.htm and see what updates are available to fix errors and security problems in the version you have. You can find information about Internet Explorer and other Microsoft Internet programs at Microsoft's Web site, www.microsoft.com/windows/ie or www.microsoft.com/mac/ie.

Trial Version. HotDog Professional

HotDog Professional 5.5, from Sausage Software, is a powerful but easy-to-use Windows shareware program that helps you create Web pages. Our CD-ROM contains a 30-day free trial version of the program.

To run HotDog, choose Start⇨Programs⇨Sausage Software⇨HotDog Professional 5. When the program starts, it gives you several ways to get help, including tutorials. For more information about HotDog, visit the program's web site at www.sausage.com/hotdog5.

Evaluation Version. Acrobat Reader

Acrobat Reader 4.0, from Adobe Systems, is a program that lets you view and print Portable Document Format, or PDF, files. The PDF format is used by many programs you find on the Internet for storing documentation, because it supports the use of such stylish elements as assorted fonts and colorful graphics (as opposed to plain text, or ASCII, which doesn't allow for any special effects in a document).

Once Acrobat Reader is running, you can view PDF files on this CD. To learn more about using Acrobat Reader, choose Reader Online Guide from the Help menu, or view the Acrobat.pdf file that was installed in the Help/ENU subfolder of the folder where the program was installed. You can also get more information by visiting the Adobe Systems Web site at www.adobe.com.

45-Day Trial Version. Microsoft FrontPage 2000

The Microsoft FrontPage 2000 Web site creation and management program gives you everything you need to create and manage your Web site. This 45-day trial will enable you to create an attractive Web site even if you are a novice to the Internet. You can find information about FrontPage 2000 and other Microsoft Internet programs at its Web site at www.microsoft.com/ frontpage/default.htm.

If You've Got Problems (Of the CD Kind)

I tried my best to compile programs that work on most computers with the minimum system requirements. Alas, your computer may differ, and some programs may not work properly for some reason.

The two likeliest problems are that you don't have enough memory (RAM) for the programs you want to use, or you have other programs running that are affecting installation or running of a program. If you get error messages like "Not enough memory" or "Setup cannot continue," try one or more of these methods and then try using the software again:

- Turn off any antivirus software that you have on your computer. Installers sometimes mimic virus activity and may make your computer incorrectly believe that it is being infected by a virus.

- Close all running programs. The more programs you're running, the less memory is available to other programs. Installers also typically update files and programs. So if you keep other programs running, installation may not work properly.

- Have your local computer store add more RAM to your computer. This is, admittedly, a drastic and somewhat expensive step. However, if you have a Windows 95 PC or a Mac OS computer with a PowerPC chip, adding more memory can really help the speed of your computer and allow more programs to run at the same time. This may include closing the CD interface and running a product's installation program from Windows Explorer.

If you still have trouble with installing the items from the CD, please call the IDG Books Worldwide Customer Service phone number: 800-762-2974 (outside the United States: 317-572-3342).

Index

• C •

• Z •